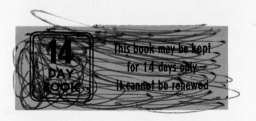

1919: Red Mirage

by the same author

WOMEN ON THE WARPATH

THE FIGHTING PANKHURSTS

1919

RED MIRAGE

DAVID MITCHELL

The Macmillan Company

The Macmillan Company
866 Third Avenue, New York, N.Y. 10022

Library of Congress Catalog Card Number: 70-83063

First American Edition 1970

1919: Red Mirage was first published in Great Britain in 1970 by Jonathan Cape Ltd., London

Printed in the United States of America

Contents

I: WARS WITHIN THE WAR

  1 Armistice and the Abyss   13
  2 Unholy Russia   20
  3 The Dream of Workers' Control   26
  4 The Workers' Republic   35
  5 Crowns are Tumbling   45
  6 Red Dawn or Dark Age?   66
  7 Bulwarks of Civilization   77

II: THE FOUR MAD MONTHS

  1 The Rape of Riga   87
  2 The Soil of Despair   92
  3 The Crop of Revolt   101
  4 Direct Action   122
  5 Capitals of the World: Paris   138
  6 Capitals of the World: Petrograd and Moscow   150
  7 A Spectre is Haunting Europe   167

III: MAY DAYS

  1 Don't Count Your Soviets   189
  2 Novelty Samples, Red Winnipeg   203
  3 And Then There Were Two   211

IV: BOLSHEVISM AT BAY

  1 The Circle Closes   215
  2 The Throttling of the Hungarian Revolution   219
  3 The Ninth Wave, the Russian Sieve   232
  4 Lenin's Greatest Ally   239
  5 Red Panic, Whiteslide   246

V: THE GREAT OUTSIDERS

  1 Nestor Makhno   263
  2 Il Comandante   274

VI: LAST RECKONINGS

　1 The Strange Calvary of Woodrow Wilson　285
　2 Judge Gary's Triumph　294
　3 A Man for All Classes　307

VII: WHERE DID IT ALL GO?

　1 The Romantic Amateurs　315
　2 The Professionals　322
　3 The Frozen Fountain　334

　BIBLIOGRAPHY　347
　INDEX　379

List of Illustrations

(Illustrations following page 192.)

Plate 1. Moscow, the Kremlin, March 2nd, 1919. Eberlein (Germany), Lenin and Fritz Platten (Switzerland) during one of the sessions which resulted in the launching of the Communist Third International. (James Klugmann Collection)

Plate 2. Makhno and his entourage foreshadowed, sartorially and ideologically, the hippie-style freedom-fighters of the 1960s.

Plate 3. Liberated proletarian giant smashes 'capitalist' chains on a globe of the world – the cover of the first issue of the *Communist International*, published in Petrograd in several languages, May 1919. (Communist Party of Great Britain Photo Library)

Plate 4. Budapest, May Day 1919. Michael Biró's famous Worker Giant poster. (James Klugmann Collection)

Plate 5. Overloaded trains in Petrograd railway station, September 1919. (Mansell Collection)

Plate 6. Fiume, October 1919. Gabriele d'Annunzio, the 'Dictator' of Fiume, harangues his legionaries. (Mansell Collection)

Plate 7. Bolshevik leaders in Hungary. Joseph Pogany, Sigismund Kunfi and Bela Kun. (*Radio Times* Hulton Picture Library)

Plate 8. Cartoon which appeared in the San Francisco *Examiner* at the height of the 1919 Red scare.

Plate 9. Napoleonic Churchill. A cartoon by Will Dyson in the *Daily Herald*, September 1919, at the time of the English rail strike. (Syndication International)

Plate 10. President Wilson arrives in Paris, December 1918 (*Radio Times* Hulton Picture Library)

Plate 11. Berlin, November 1918. A statue of Kaiser Wilhelm I overturned by revolutionary mobs in the early stages of the German revolution. (Mansell Collection)

Plate 12. Karl Liebknecht, son of a founder of the German Social Democratic Party. He became a leader of the Spartacus movement, and was murdered in Berlin in January 1919. (James Klugmann Collection)

Plate 13. Rosa Luxemburg, leader of the Spartacus movement which formed the nucleus of the German Communist Party (K.P.D.). She was murdered in Berlin in January 1919. (James Klugmann Collection)

Plate 14. Berlin riots, November 1918. Red flag carried through the streets. (*Radio Times* Hulton Picture Library)

Plate 15. October 1919. A snatched press shot of the exiled ex-Kaiser exercising in the grounds of Amerongen Castle, Holland. (Mansell Collection)

Plate 16. Berlin, March 1919. Troops escort prisoners during the second Spartacist revolt. (Mansell Collection)

Plate 17. Belfast, January 1919. The car of the Lord Mayor menaced by demonstrators during the general strike. (Mansell Collection)

Plate 18. Glasgow, January 31st, 1919. Strike leader William Gallacher and others being arrested and given first aid by the police. (Mansell Collection)

Plate 19. London, October 1919. Class war in Britain: gentlemen volunteers attacked by workers during the great rail strike. (Mansell Collection)

Plate 20. Mrs Fannie Sellins, Trade Union Organizer, killed by Steel Trust gunmen in West Natrona, Pennsylvania, on August 26th, 1919.

Acknowledgments

I am much indebted to Mr James Klugmann for allowing me to use his excellent library and for sparing the time to acquaint me with it; to Mr John Goodchild for valuable research assistance; to John Osborne Jr of Rutgers University, New Jersey, for suggesting several fruitful lines of research; to my wife for reading the typescript; and to my publishers for sustaining me while I wrote it.

My warm thanks are due to the staffs of the London Library, the Libraries of the London School of Economics and the Royal Institute of International Affairs, and the Public Record Office.

I am grateful to the Controller of Her Majesty's Stationery Office for permission to quote from the War Cabinet and other papers (in the Public Record Office) listed in the bibliography; to Mr Nigel Nicolson for permission to quote from the late Sir Harold Nicolson's *Peacemaking 1919*; to Allen & Unwin for permission to quote from the late Bertrand Russell's *Roads to Freedom* and *Autobiography*; to the late Leonard Woolf, Esq. for permission to quote from Virginia Woolf's *A Writer's Notebook;* to her executors for permission to quote from Beatrice Webb's *Diaries;* to MacGibbon & Kee for permission to quote from Volume II of Ilya Ehrenburg's autobiography, *Men, Years, Life,* and from C. E. Montague's *Disenchantment;* to the Executors of the Estate of H. G. Wells for permission to quote from his *Russia in the Shadows;* to Penguin Books for permission to quote from the translation of the poetry of Osip Mandelstam which appears in the *Penguin Book of Russian Verse;* and to Mr Jack Lindsay and the Bodley Head for permission to quote from a translation of the verse of Demyan Byedny which appears in Mr Lindsay's *Russian Poetry, 1917–55.*

October 1969   DAVID MITCHELL

(i) We are standing on the threshold of a new age. We are entering into the period of the emancipation of labour from the thraldom of wage slavery. It is the time of which poets have dreamed, the time for which in every country men and women have striven, have gone to prison, have sacrificed their lives. Thrones are tumbling like skittles. Revolution like a cleansing gale sweeps through Europe. Say! British and American soldiers, what are you? Are you just dull clods? Are you not stirred by the throb of new life that pulses through the veins of your fellow-workers?

(Bolshevik leaflet distributed among Allied troops in Russia, 1919)

(ii) The flames of civil war are blazing throughout Europe. The victory of communism in Germany is wholly inevitable. There may be a few isolated defeats, but it is to the Red that the victory will finally fall—and that in the next few months, perhaps weeks. The revolution is advancing so fast that one can say with certainty that in a year's time we will already begin to forget that there was a struggle for communism in Europe ...

(Zinoviev in the *Communist International*, April 1919)

(iii) Nineteen-nineteen. How ever did.they manage, poor dears?
   The children of the new age will read of the battles,
   Learn the names of the leaders and orators,
   The number of the dead and the dates.
   They will never know how sweet the roses smelt on the
      field of battle,
   How blackbirds sang amid the voices of the guns,
   How beautiful life was at that time.

(Ilya Ehrenburg in a poem written in Kiev, 1919)

(iv) In the fight between you and the world, back the world.

(Franz Kafka in a sequence of aphorisms written in 1919)

I

WARS WITHIN THE WAR

1. *Armistice and the Abyss*

'On most parts of the front,' reported the London *Annual Register*, 'fighting continued during the six hours' interval between the signing of the armistice and the moment when it came into operation ... It was said that the last shots of the war were fired by a troop of King Edward's Horse, who were proceeding to capture a field gun a few minutes before eleven o'clock. They shot two of the crew and were about to rush the gun when the officer in charge, watch in hand, stopped the operation.'

At 10.55 a.m. David Lloyd George, who presumed, with characteristic ebullience, to present himself as the Man Who Won the War, appeared on the steps of 10 Downing Street, arms waving, white hair ruffling in the breeze. Excitedly, repeatedly, with a flashing smile of proprietorial triumph, he shouted: 'At eleven o'clock this morning the war will be over!' As the crowd surged towards him, flattening the police cordon against the railings, he vanished indoors, dashed through the garden, and reappeared at the entrance to Horse Guards' Parade. People tried to seize his hands, to pat him on the back. Again he retreated, and stood laughing and joking with two of the squad of personal secretaries upon whom he relied in his tradition-slashing bid for personal rule.

That night the Prime Minister dined with a man who matched his own resilient individualism, a rogue patrician as contemptuous as himself of bureaucratic obstruction, as unabashed in the enjoyment of the marvellous game of politics. Even as a subaltern Winston Churchill had been free with hints to generals. As a Tory turned Liberal left-winger he was regarded in true-blue circles as a class traitor. Beneath the portraits of Charles James Fox and William Pitt, of Lord Nelson and the Duke of Wellington, the English aristocrat and the Welsh schoolteacher's son (in a convivial conjunction which symbolized the galloping democratization of politics) talked, in the first magnanimous flush of victory, of the superb fight Germany had made against tremendous odds, of the impossibility of rebuilding Europe without German co-operation, of the urgent need to rush food ships to Hamburg.

Outside, in primitive jamboree, the masses roared and cheered and drank and copulated in corners.

In Paris crowds dragged German guns from the Place de la Concorde. In the Chamber of Deputies the aged Premier, Georges Clemenceau (the Frenchman Who had Won the War), read out the armistice terms, then called for gratitude to the *poilus*. 'Thanks to them France, yesterday the soldier of God, today the soldier of humanity, will be for ever the soldier of the ideal.'

By a strange coincidence it happened that on armistice night, in New York, the Vieux Colombier company staged the American première of Clemenceau's one-act play *La Voile du Bonheur*. Its sentiments were in sharp contrast to his victory rhetoric. A blind Chinese poet, at peace with the world he cannot see, suddenly recovers his sight and is cruelly disabused. He finds that a cherished colleague has pirated his verses, that his dutiful wife is sleeping with his best friend, that his son makes mocking grimaces as he utters phrases of filial piety. Yearning for the darkness which has protected him from the knowledge of evil, the poet blinds himself. Yet Clemenceau's parliamentary patriotism was as sincere as his theatrical cynicism. Taken together they illustrated the accuracy of John Maynard Keynes's epigrammatic summary: 'He has one illusion — France: and one disillusion — mankind.'

That same night Clemenceau, as was his frequent custom, visited his old friend, the painter Claude Monet. Monet was undazzled by the victory of the Allies and the triumph of France. To Clemenceau it meant the chance to weaken the enemy and create a system of alliances that would give France security — not for ever, for Clemenceau was too worldly-wise to believe in fairy tales, but at least for a few decades, before the next lunge of the Huns. To Monet it had only one significance. 'Now,' he said, 'we can get on with the monument to Cézanne.'

For President Woodrow Wilson, too, the end of the war into which, tardily but bombastically, he had led the United States, signified the opportunity to put into practice a cherished project: that of redeeming the world, in the name of God and America, from the corruption into which it had been plunged by unscrupulous politicians contemptuous of the welfare of their peoples.

Despite the well-known fact that the exigencies of war had forced a series of hard-bargaining secret treaties—promising, for instance, to Italy lands inhabited by Greeks, Slavs, Albanians and Germans, to Rumania a large slice of Hungary, to Japan the Chinese province of Shantung—the Archangel Wilson (as H. L. Mencken called him) had laid down, as the most vital of his Fourteen Points, the doctrine of self-determination, whereby no populations should, against their will, be subjected to foreign rule.

Immense as was his capacity for self-insulation, it must have been known to him that the French and British had, as early as December 1917, signed an agreement which contemplated the not entirely unassisted fall of the Bolshevik regime in Russia. Yet his Sixth Point stipulated that all Russian territory should be cleared of foreign troops and Russia given every opportunity for self-development.

By the beginning of November 1918 Britain had objected to Point Two, which required absolute freedom of navigation in peace and war outside territorial waters; Belgium had protested against Point Three—the removal as far as possible of all economic barriers; and Italy had rejected Point Nine—the readjustment of Italian frontiers along lines of nationality. The Fourteen Points ('God', jeered Clemenceau, 'needed only Ten') had been supplemented by Four Principles and Five Particulars and finally by a diplomatic modulation contrived by Colonel House, President Wilson's confidential adviser and personal representative in Europe.

Despite all this, and despite the fact that the November elections had resulted in a Republican majority in both Houses of Congress, Wilson acted as though his breeze of destiny had positively freshened. Clearly the voters had wished to criticize not him but those Democratic politicians who had proved unworthy of his leadership.

In an exquisitely proportioned room in a Georgian house in Richmond Leonard and Virginia Woolf sat ruminating upon the consequences of the war. Ten million killed, 36 million casualties; millions of people in Central and Eastern Europe and Russia in a brutal limbo between life and death, capable of little more than an animal rummaging for food; idiot prating about the achievements of the war machine (the boast, for instance, that on September 20th, 1918, when it broke the Hindenburg Line, the British Army had fired 943,837 shells, costing £3,800,000 and weighing 40,000 tons – more than had been fired during the whole of the Boer War); cheap slogans about sacred union, the holiness of sacrifice, homes for heroes. How utterly nauseating it all was. The war, they decided, had destroyed the bases of European civilization. All was insecurity, vulgarity and darkness.

A nostalgia for vanished pre-war points of reference, a horror at the triumph of demagogy, was common to cultured progressives and resentful 'natural rulers'. The masses, whether they were to be improved or kept at bay, must stay in their place. Once let them get in on the act and anything might happen. Sophisticated reformers like Sidney and Beatrice Webb preferred to deal with enlightened Liberals or Tories rather than intellectually backward Labour types. All over Europe 'natural rulers' had hoped that the war – assuming that it was brought to a quick, victorious conclusion by the 'natural' leaders of the various officer corps – would compel a retreat from impudent industrial militancy to a position of healthy patriotism, based on gratitude to one's betters and a firm sense of the fixity of one's station in life. Their blissful ignorance about the masses (Alfonso XIII of Spain referred to them as 'that canaille') was epitomized by Lord Curzon's astonishment when he saw some Tommies stripped for a swim. 'Why', he complained, 'did no one tell me that the lower orders had such white bodies?'

When the 'People of the Abyss', as Jack London called them, went to war it was discovered that many were mentally and physically below the unexacting standards of the Army – into which, before 1914, the pick of the urban and rural slums had escaped from a morass of poverty and degradation. During the war millions of men found a soldier's pay and even a soldier's working conditions an improvement on civvy street. In London alone (and things were no better in Dublin, Paris or Budapest) nearly half a million people were dying miserably at the bottom of the social pit. They were sometimes incapable of telling their right hand from their left or of recognizing the number of their hovels. An accident at work, an illness, plunged a whole family into destitution. Over all loomed the shadow of the workhouse, where on a diet of skilly and dry bread inmates earned their keep by picking oakum or emptying germ-laden waste from sick wards, and slept on strips of canvas two feet wide and six inches apart.

Millions on the verge of the abyss lived in constant terror of the final slide. Sixty per cent of all agricultural labourers were, like the slaves of the cities, receiving wages below the subsistence line. Half a million men, women and children in Great Britain died annually of preventable disease. Old people perished and rotted in their beds in obscure tenements. Infant mortality in the filthy, soot-laden atmo-sphere of industrial areas was higher than that among the most primitive subjects of the colonial empire. Half the area of the United Kingdom was owned by 10,000 persons out of a total population of 45 millions.

The armies of 1914–18 were full of the victims of pirate capitalism fighting the battles of natural rulers for the ultimate benefit of profiteers. Yet at first some of them had believed in a classless equality of sacrifice. The first big agent of disillusion had been the 'natural' leaders of the regular armies – officers who regarded work as bad form, cleverness as anathema, polo as more important than a knowledge of military history. Then came the slow, stupid slaughter, the feeling of being trapped in a grinding futility, above all the knowledge of the great divide between leaders and led, between the men in the trenches or in stinking billets and the little gods luxuriating over their maps and fine wines in châteaux far from the front. The red tabs of staff officers became known as 'the Red Badge of Funk'. The peacetime social structure was being erected all over again. But this time the abyss was a genuine demo-cracy of the trench-slums, where all pretensions were scrapped and a tough comradeship of survival laughed at cant in Parliament, editorial offices, pulpits or generals' speeches.

War propaganda in which God was a rabid nationalist and the enemy were devils incarnate failed to take root in the ooze of the Somme and Passchendaele, the huge graveyard of Verdun. A new International of weary, wary cannon-fodder seemed rather to be sprouting there. George Lansbury foresaw that this brotherhood-in-arms would, when the war ended, be the basis for a great surge of militant revolt. In America the liberal *Nation* calculated that it might cleanse and revitalize democracy. Such possibilities were not over-looked by the more enlightened of Britain's natural rulers. A. J. ('Fanny') Balfour, former Tory Prime Minister, Foreign Secretary under Lloyd George, and a nephew of Lord Salisbury (that diehard defender of patrician rule), had prophesied such a development. In November 1917 the fifth Marquess of Lansdowne, for ten years leader of the Conservatives in the House of Lords, appealed for a negotiated peace. It was by no means certain that the war had smashed the myth of proletarian solidarity: but it had begun glaringly to expose the incompetence, selfishness and plain bewilderment of the *ancien régime*. The longer it continued, the greater seemed the likelihood of complete exposure and disastrous retaliation.

After the peasant armies of Russia had at last refused to fight, the trench-worms of Europe had begun to turn. In May 1917, following yet another ineffective attack, this time on the Aisne, this time led by Nivelle, one of the interchangeably lethal French generals, the secret mutterings of the overstrained French army had burst into open mutiny. Fifty-four divisions refused to obey orders. Russian units on the western front joined them. Over 100,000 *poilus* were court-martialled, 23,000 found guilty, 423 sentenced to death, 55 actually shot (according to official figures). Many others were shot without trial or pounded to death by artillery fire. A few months later the sailors of the German Grand Fleet at Kiel mutinied.

Trotsky's hectic appeals to the workers of Europe during the long-drawn-out peace negotiations with the Central Powers at Brest-Litovsk and the Bolsheviks' publication of the texts of the secret treaties (made behind the backs of 'the people') combined with increasing hunger and poverty to produce a crop of industrial strikes in 1918. In January hundreds of thousands of workers downed tools in Vienna, Budapest, Berlin and Munich, and talked of forming soviets. In February the Austro-Hungarian fleet, commanded by Admiral Nicholas Horthy, mutinied at Cattaro. In March French workers staged a series of big strikes. Everywhere the gap widened between official, 'collaborationist' trade unionism and the growing militancy of the rank-and-file. In Britain the King and Queen spent almost as much time making gracious personal appearances in restless industrial areas as visiting military hospitals or reviewing troops. By autumn 1918 German troops on the eastern front and in the Baltic States were infected by Bolshevik propaganda which told them that their place was on the side of the workers' revolution.

It seemed possible, even probable, that Lenin's furious demand, first heard in 1914 and thereafter relentlessly repeated, to turn the imperialist war into an international civil war might be heeded on a vast scale, that the war might have a terrific revolutionary post-script as the People of the Abyss rose in judgment on their exploiters.

Liberals and progressives, solid in their approval of the 'demo-cratic' revolution of March 1917 in Russia, had been alarmed by the implications of the Bolshevik coup. After analysing the doctrines of syndicalism, anarchism and socialism, Bertrand Russell, in *Roads to Freedom*, plumped for guild socialism, a careful culling of the 'best' in all three, as the likeliest nosegay to give the masses a whiff of revolution sufficient to overcome the alluring odour of brute Bolshevism. The Fourteen Points were Wilson's answer to the Bolshevik 'peace offensive'. On November 4th, 1918, Beatrice Webb, in her diary, shuddered at the possibility of a chain reaction of Soviet madness. 'The Bolsheviks grin at us from ruined Russia, and their creed, like the plague of influenza, seems to be spreading westwards ... Will western civilization flare up in the flames of anarchic revolution?'

The doors of power swung loose. Iconoclastic bourgeois renegades were rising from slimy depths. It was all most unhealthy, and it was all, somehow, connected with the Bolsheviks.

The stop-watches of the Allied officers on the Western Front could not arrest the spread of a spirit of revolutionary discontent. The monument to Cézanne would have to wait.

2. *Unholy Russia*

The cataclysm, the crash of an epoch, had come. The peasant soldiers of Russia had, in Lenin's phrase, voted with their feet despite frantic efforts, backed by Allied threats of blockade, to keep them in the war. The Liberal gentlemen of the February revolution – Prince Lvov, Milyukov, Kerensky – had been swept aside by the Bolsheviks, who early in 1918 cut short the newly-elected Constituent Assembly with insults and jeers.

'We shall not', warned Trotsky, 'enter into the kingdom of socialism in white gloves and on a polished floor.' Generals, high-ranking bureaucrats and lawyers, now jobless and on third-class rations, were reduced to begging in the streets – or forced, with their womenfolk, to sweep them. They were also together with other 'social parasites' (industrialists, stockbrokers, priests and monks) sent to dig trenches and empty latrines. Bourgeois professors were sacked from universities. Captain Cromie, acting head of the British Embassy in Petrograd, was killed on the grand staircase in a gun-fight with Bolshevik security police.

At Westminster the fact that the embassy had been a notorious centre of sabotage against the only semblance of government in Russia was forgotten or counted as a virtue. Sir Samuel Hoare, former chief of British Intelligence in Russia, described Cromie's action as heroic defiance of 'Bolshevik ruffians'. His 'martyrdom' was used in the House of Commons and in the press as another reason for using every means to end the 'criminal rule' of the Bolsheviks. American newspapers alleged that in Petrograd the Bolsheviks had set up an electrically-operated guillotine that lopped off five hundred heads an hour. Cartoonists symbolized Bolshevik rule as a smoking gun, a bomb, and a hangman's noose. Russians, thundered editorials, were un-American, and no more of them should be allowed to enter the country. The *New York Times* referred to the Bolsheviks as 'human scum'. Congressmen called them 'damnable beasts'.

There were frequent reports that Lenin and Trotsky had quarrelled, fled, committed suicide, or been shot. In England the *Morning Post* saw the Bolshevik regime as a farce in which 'unpractical visionaries, emancipated criminals, wild idealists, Jewish Internationalists, all the cranks and most of the crooks, have joined hands in an orgy of passion and unreason'. The *Nation*, quivering with that horror of violence characteristic of high-minded liberals in a tolerant, well-policed state, solemnly asked if Bolshevism could really be considered as 'the embodied protest of mankind against the order which has condemned humanity to four years of hell'.

One of the few influential voices to give an unqualified welcome to the Bolsheviks was that of George Bernard Shaw, who agreed with Engels and Lenin that 'a revolution is the most authoritarian thing imaginable', and gloried in the terrific sweep of the new broom. In the *Daily Chronicle* he outlined the Diplomats' Dilemma with fiendish glee. Patriots, he said, were in full cry against a separate peace by Russia. What they would dread if they had any sense was a separate war by Russia — 'a fight to a finish not only with the German throne but with *all* thrones; a war that will go on when the rest of the belligerents want to stop; a war that may develop into a blaze of civil wars in England, France and Italy, with the Foreign Offices and Courts and Capitalists fighting to restore the Tsar, and the proletarians of all lands fighting to reproduce the Russian Revolution in their own countries.'

At the end of 1917 'L'Accord Français-Anglais Définissant les Zones d'Action Françaises et Anglaises', negotiated in Paris, had apportioned spheres of influence in Russia. The British zone was to include the Caucasus, Armenia, Georgia and Kurdistan: the French Bessarabia, the Ukraine and the Crimea. It was dictated by economic interests: British investment was heaviest in the Caucasian oil fields, French in the coal and iron mines of the Ukraine. Until the last German offensive on the western front had been broken, the Paris Agreement remained a paper project. But Bolshevik appeals for military help against Germany, made while the Brest-Litovsk discussions were still going on, were studiously ignored, and orders for the transport of the Czechoslovak Legion, some forty thousand strong, to France were countermanded. The Legion, raised from prisoners of war, was, in the chaotic state of the Red

Army, the most disciplined and formidable military organization in Russia. Resisting feeble attempts to disarm it, it rapidly established a stranglehold on the Trans-Siberian Railway and, as the 'pilot' vanguard of Allied intervention, advanced swiftly from the Volga region towards Moscow.

Between June and September 1918 the Legion came incredibly close to complete victory. Its achievement not only made certain that Czechoslovak claims for national independence were given top priority, but confirmed the Allies' impression of the shakiness of the Soviet regime. When the Red Army, after frantic improvisation by Trotsky, halted the Legion's advance its continued presence in Russia provided a useful second-string excuse for intervention – to 'protect' the Legion against the vengeance of the Bolsheviks.

They, in any case, were rated as tools of the German High Command, and as such their overthrow was trumpeted as a legitimate war aim. Russian 'treachery' at Brest-Litovsk was alleged to have released a million troops for service on the western front. By mid-1918 a *New York Herald* cartoon, typical of many, showed a broken-hearted Russian bear led weeping between Judas-Trotsky (carrying a bag labelled '30 Pieces of Silver') and the Kaiser. Journalist Edgar Sisson, head of the American Public Relations Committee in Petrograd, gathered, from dubious sources, documentary proof that the Bolshevik coup had been planned and financed from Berlin. There was some truth in this. But it was part of the Bolshevik ethos not to refuse money or help wherever they came from. For Lenin, bourgeois inhibitions were a luxury unforgivable in a revolutionary out to get results. He had always said that money had no smell. This attitude was counted as another instance of godless Bolshevik nihilism. Churchill, writing ten years later, summed up the horror of the traditionalists. Russia had changed her very identity. 'An apparition with countenance different from any yet seen on earth stood in the place of the old Ally ... a state without a nation, an army without a country, a religion without a God.'

In the last eight months of 1918 a swarm of Allied expeditionary forces began to surround the maimed Red Beast (it was fashionable to identify the Bolshevik regime with the 'Nameless Beast' mentioned in the medieval Russian Old Believers' Apocalypse). Britons, Americans, Italians and Serbs went to the White Sea ports of Murmansk and Archangel (originally to safeguard war stores against a possible German snatch). Japanese, British and American troops landed in Vladivostock. The Czechs consolidated their hold on the Trans-Siberian Railway. After the defeat of the Central Powers in November munitions and military missions began to flow to the headquarters of the White (counter-revolutionary) armies in the Ukraine and Siberia. Japanese troops were supplied with pocket Russian dictionaries in which the word 'Bolshevik' was equated with 'barsuk' (badger or wild beast), followed by the comment: 'to be exterminated.'

In June 1918 Balfour blandly informed the House of Commons that 'Russia is going through a time of prolonged trial. Everybody sympathizes with the difficulties in which that vast population finds itself ... I do not despair of being able even now to do something material to restore the political unity and nationality of that great country. That is a question that rests in the future ... I can do no more than say that our good wishes for Russia, her freedom, her prosperity, her integrity, remain quite undiminished by recent events.'

Two months later British troops occupied the Caucasian oil centre of Baku.

French, British and Belgian stockholders, who before 1914 had invested mightily and at a heavy rate of interest in Russia's belated industrialization, were beginning to agitate for full-blast intervention. Japanese and American businessmen and industrialists were becoming restless. The *Japan Salesman* spoke of Russia 'with her 180 millions of people, with her fertile soil stretching from Central Europe across Asia to the shores of the Pacific, from the Arctic down to the Persian Gulf and the Black Sea. Here are market possibilities such as even the most optimistic dared not dream of—Russia, potentially the granary, the fishery, the lumber-yard, the coal, gold, silver and platinum mine of the world.' Eastern Siberia, said *Dun's Review*, a New York trade journal, was 'advantageously placed as regards labour. There is an almost unlimited supply of Chinese and Korean workmen.' The Federation of British Industries' *Bulletin* referred to the rich, under-exploited plains of western Siberia as 'the most gigantic prize offered to the civilized world since the discovery of the Americas.'

The *Petroleum World* reported Mr Herbert Allen, a director of five

Anglo-Russian oil companies, as saying that 'in the Caucasus, from Batum in the Black Sea eastwards to Baku on the Caspian, from Vladivkas southward to Tiflis; in Asia Minor, Mesopotamia and Persia, British forces have made their appearance and have been welcomed by nearly every race and creed who look to us to free them, some from Turkish rule and some from that of Bolshevism.' The only snag was 'the usual weak-kneed attitude of our own government who, cowed by the Little England attitude of the masses, have lost no time in announcing that the entry of our troops into these regions implies no intention of permanent occupation.'

The dim class-consciousness of the Labour movement was a drag on the chariot wheels of commerce. But there were other impediments. In November 1918 Central and Eastern Europe were shaken by a complex explosion of nationalist and socialist revolution. Fear of the westward spread of Bolshevism brought second thoughts about the fight to a finish with Germany. The triumphal March to Berlin was cancelled. Field-Marshal Sir Henry Wilson, Chief of the Imperial General Staff, recorded in his diary on November 9th: 'Cabinet meeting tonight ... Lloyd George read two telegrams from the Tiger [Clemenceau] in which he described Foch's interview with the Germans. The Tiger is afraid that Germany may collapse and Bolshevism gain control. Lloyd George asked me if I wanted that to happen or if I did not prefer an armistice. Without hesitation I replied "Armistice". The whole Cabinet agreed with me.' One clause of the armistice terms required German army units in southern Russia and the Baltic States to stay there, under Allied control, until such time as their services were no longer needed. Foch put forward plans for a swift knock-out to be delivered by American, French and German troops commanded by French officers.

But the politicians put a spoke in this plan too. Woodrow Wilson's disapproval was to be expected. But Clemenceau was also cautious. Why, he argued, bother with a full-scale military campaign when economic encirclement – the cutting off of Bolshevik central Russia from its raw materials in the south and east – was almost complete? On December 21st, 1918, in a telegram to General Franchet d'Esperey, commanding the French expeditionary force in Odessa, Clemenceau explained: 'The plan of action is to realise simultaneously the economic encirclement of the Bolsheviks and the organization of order by loyal Russian elements.'

In what he called 'an Armistice Dream' Winston Churchill sketched his notion of what might have been the ideal sequence of events. He imagined Germany being invited to play her 'full part' with the Allies in the 'liberation' of Russia and the 'reconstruction' of Eastern Europe. What a splendid opportunity this would have been for Germany to 'avoid all humiliation in defeat' and to 'slide by almost unconscious transition from cruel strife to natural co-operation with all of us.'

3. *The Dream of Workers' Control*

There were other dreams, factory workers' dreams, proletarian visions of a just society. Crudely millennial, deeply suspicious of condescending Marxist intellectuals, they had shaken the Establishment, whereas the manifestoes of the Second International and the meek reformism of official Labour movements had barely ruffled the surface of its complacency. Syndicalism—the idea of workers' control, of a radical industrial democracy—had originated in France in the 1890s. The *Confédération Générale du Travail* (C.G.T.) was its exponent, Georges Sorel its theorist, the power of the general strike its central dogma, professional politicians its main aversion. It had deeply influenced militant unionism throughout Europe and took its most spectacularly belligerent form in America, where capitalism was youngest and toughest.

Only a small minority of skilled workers, the 'aristocrats' of Labour, were organized into unions grouped within the American Federation of Labour (A.F.L.). Millions of unskilled workers, recruited in the city and village slums of Southern and Eastern Europe, found themselves plunged into an American Abyss. By the 1890s the mad competitive free-for-all of the old buccaneers—the Astors, the Vanderbilts, the Goulds—had given way to an era of enormous monopolies, euphemistically called trusts. The new giants, typified by John D. Rockefeller and J. P. Morgan, controlled banks and railroads as well as oil and steel and coal. They also manipulated politicians and judges and, apart from their own private armies of gunmen, could count on the support of federal and state troops to crush any sign of restlessness among their employees.

It was to fight such industrial slavery by organizing unskilled and itinerant workers that the Industrial Workers of the World (I.W.W.) had been founded in Chicago in 1905. Among its best-known leaders were Bill Haywood and Mother Jones. Eugene Debs, present at the founding conference, remained a strong supporter. Haywood, born in Salt Lake City, had earned his living since the age of ten as farmboy, cowboy, homesteader and miner. Debs, a railway-

men's leader who had become the outstanding personality of the
Socialist Party of America (and its candidate for the Presidency), had
been born in Indiana of parents who had immigrated from Alsace.
Mother Jones, born in Ireland in 1830, had been a labour agitator for
nearly fifty years. A fine-looking old woman with white hair and a
pink complexion, she was tough as teak and famed for her courage —
wading rivers to slip through military patrols during strikes,
leading mobs of broom-wielding miners' wives against troops and
company guards.

The I.W.W., whose members were known as the Wobblies, had a
simple vision. The struggle with monopoly capitalism could only, it
argued, be carried on effectively by a mass union: not just an alliance
of industrial unions including skilled and unskilled workers, but One
Big Union, divided into thirteen occupational sections. It declared
war not only on bosses and time-serving politicians but on the 'boss-
toadying' A.F.L. and its chief, Samuel Gompers. The Wobblies did not
aim to infiltrate existing unions. Theirs was to be a head-on assault.
Their manifesto claimed that 'the working class and the employing
class have nothing in common. There can be no peace so long as
hunger and want are found among millions of working people and
the few, who make up the employing class, have all the good things
of life ... It is the historic mission of the working class to do away
with capitalism. The army of production must be organized not only
for the everyday struggle with the capitalists but also to carry on
production when capitalism shall have been overthrown. By
organizing industrially we are forming the structure of the new
society within the shell of the old.'

Though the I.W.W.'s solid core of membership was never more
than about a hundred thousand, its genius for publicity soon gained
it a notoriety out of all proportion to its size. 'The I.W.W.', wrote
Debs, 'is organized not to conciliate but to fight the capitalist class ...
the capitalists own the tools they do not use, the workers use the
tools they do not own.' Sabotage, declared Haywood, 'means to push
back, pull out, or break off the fangs of capitalism'. There was to be
no bargaining with the bosses. Strikes were mere incidents in a
perpetual class war, 'periodic drills in which the workers prepare for
concerted action'. The final objective was a total strike in all sections
of the One Big Union (O.B.U.) to force employer capitulation. When
that point had been reached the workers could bring the capitalist
system to a standstill by simply folding their arms.

The I.W.W. was a miniature International. Its literature went out in Swedish, Finnish, Hungarian, Lithuanian, Russian, Flemish, Yiddish, Italian and Spanish as well as English. I.W.W. cartoons, speeches and articles, sometimes inciting to or boasting of violent sabotage — burning crops, slashed orchards, wrecked machinery — contained more rhetoric than fact. They appealed mainly to the itinerant workers of the west, an army of about a million hoboes who, in their poverty, walked the railroad tracks and jumped freight cars (or 'rode the rails' beneath them) to cover the vast distances between Californian fruit farms and canning factories, the mid-west harvest belt, and the lumber camps of the north-west. In four years four thousand of them were killed on the railroads, twenty-five thousand injured. Brakemen threw them off the trains, railroad police batoned and jailed them, Citizens' Associations beat them up and ran them out of Town. These hoboes, with their rolled blankets on their backs, were the travelling evangelists of the I.W.W. The lyrics in their *Little Red Songbook* — 'Paint 'Er Red', for instance, sung to the tune of 'Marching through Georgia' — put their message forcefully:

Slaves they call us, working plugs, inferior by birth,
But when we hit their pocket book we'll spoil their smiles of
    mirth,
We'll stop their dirty dividends and drive them from the earth —
With One Big Industrial Union!

We hate their rotten system more than any mortals do,
Our aim is not to patch it up but build it all anew,
And what we'll have for government when finally we're
    through,
Is One Big Industrial Union!

Hurrah! hurrah! We're going to paint 'er red!
Hurrah! hurrah! The way is clear ahead,
We're gaining shop democracy and liberty and bread
With One Big Industrial Union.

The I.W.W. sparked strikes — occasionally successful — among loggers, miners, steel-workers, window-washers, papermakers, textile workers and streetcar operators. But its most characteristic and sustained effort went into the long free-speech campaign fought in the west against frequent attempts to deny Wobblies the right to express their views in public. Hundreds, sometimes thousands of them would converge on a town, speaking one after another (often only the first words of the Declaration of Independence), being arrested, cramming the jails, singing their songs, raising unignorable and entertaining hell, and, when they were set free, singing again — 'Hallelujah, I'm a bum'. The campaign ended in violence at Everett, Washington, in November 1916. As a ferry-boat from Seattle carrying 250 freedom fighters neared the dock, the sheriff and a squad of vigilantes opened fire. The Wobblies fired back. Seven people were killed, nearly fifty wounded. Through the shooting the rebels continued to sing:

> Hold the fort for we are coming,
> Union men be strong,
> Side by side we battle onward,
> Victory will come.

But victory was denied to these reckless, swarming visionaries. The patriotic inquisitors of war-time found in them a prime target. DON'T BE A SOLDIER, BE A MAN was a favourite I.W.W. sticker. Workers were exhorted not to fight the battles of Rockefeller, Morgan and other capitalist pirates. By mid-1918 Theodore Roosevelt, once celebrated for his denunciations of 'malefactors of great wealth', was ranting about 'the homicidal march of the I.W.W.' Newspapers encouraged their readers to exterminate Wobblies — 'kill them,' said the *Tulsa Daily World*, 'as you would any other kind of snake.' I.W.W. halls were raided and wrecked, members beaten, kicked, whipped, tarred and feathered. Frank Little, an I.W.W. organizer, was lynched during a miners' strike at Butte, Montana. Federal troops occupied the town.

During the autumn of 1917 nearly 250 leading Wobblies were arrested and jailed. In April 1918 a final sifting of 101 of them, including Haywood, appeared in the white marble federal court in Chicago charged with sabotage and conspiracy to obstruct the war effort. The trial — the longest criminal trial in American history — went on for five months. Reporting it for the *Liberator*, John Reed, just back from an assignment in Soviet Russia (and soon to begin writing *Ten Days That Shook the World*), found it an extraordinary experience. The prisoners sat or lounged on rows of benches, often in their shirtsleeves, smoking, reading, dozing, using the spittoons freely. 'I doubt if ever in history there has been a sight like them,' wrote Reed. 'A hundred men better fitted to stand up for the social revolution could not have been collected from all America. Lumber-jacks, harvest hands, miners, editors ... who believe that the wealth of the world belongs to those who create it ... the outdoor men, hardrock blasters, tree-fellers, wheat-binders, longshoremen, the boys who do the strong work of the world ... The scene was strangely familiar—it looked like a meeting of the Central Executive Committee of the All-Russian Soviets in Petrograd!'

Defending counsel pleaded that when two per cent of Americans owned sixty per cent of the national wealth and two-thirds of the people owned less than five per cent, when boss violence was ever present, when the defence of property was considered more important than human values, then a revolutionary situation existed. But the mountain of ugly facts which built up day by day did not influence the jury. It was more impressed by prosecuting counsel's dramatic reading of 'Paint 'Er Red', and accepted his assertion that the American Constitution was divinely inspired and that Karl Marx was 'the foul swamp out of which the roots of the I.W.W. drew their sap.' All the prisoners were found guilty. Haywood and fourteen others got twenty years in jail, sixty-eight received sentences ranging from five to ten years. The fines imposed totalled more than 2½ million dollars.

The assault on militant radicalism was completed when in September 1918 Eugene Debs was sentenced to ten years' imprison-ment, hailing Lenin and Trotsky as 'the foremost statesmen of the age' and railing at the Supreme Court as 'a collection of begowned, bewhiskered old fossils.' When the Mayor of Toledo, Ohio, tried to keep socialists out of the hall where Debs gave a farewell address, they stormed the building, smashing doors and windows. Debs's cell in Atlanta Penitentiary, Georgia, became the virtual head-quarters of radicalism in America and, like Fort Leavenworth, Texas (where many Wobblies were imprisoned), a holy place to all those with a will to resist the juggernaut advance of monopoly capitalism.

The Wobbly message had spread far beyond the boundaries of the United States. It influenced the workers of western Canada (among whom were many Polish, Ukrainian, German and Hungarian immigrants), producing a series of determined strikes during 1918

and culminating in an anti-capitalist rally in Winnipeg, where
Bolshevism — direct action — was advocated and plans laid for the
launching of a One-Big-Union campaign. I.W.W. seamen had taken
the gospel of revolt to Australia and helped to syndicalize the
individualist anarchism that already flourished in South America. In
Mexico, Uruguay, Bolivia, Chile and Argentina its impact was
reflected in growing militancy and mass organization. By late 1918
this was threatening to paralyse the factories and waterfront of
Buenos Aires. In South Africa sea-borne I.W.W. propaganda played
a big part in the great Rand strikes of 1914 and in focusing resentment against wartime profiteering. When Martin Tranmael, a
socialist agitator who brought back a vision of industrial democracy
from a visit to I.W.W. centres in America, became Secretary of the
Norwegian Labour Party in 1918, it seemed that Norway was on the
verge of a violent revolution. In Ireland James Connolly, founder of
the socialist Labour Party, combined nationalism with militant
industrial unionism. Executed in 1916 for his part in the Easter
Rising in Dublin, Connolly had also had his first taste of the theory
and practice of workers' control with the I.W.W. in America.

In Britain I.W.W. tactics were followed with intense interest. But
the most effective champions of syndicalism, though insisting on the
need for direct industrial action, shied away from 'dual unionism' and
concentrated on reorganizing the old unions. Leaders such as Tom
Mann of the engineers and A. J. Cook of the miners condemned the
splitting up of some $2\frac{1}{2}$ million workers into 1,168 unions when
fourteen would have been ample. The reorganization of numerous
competing transport workers' unions into a Transport Workers'
Federation brought swift success in a succession of dock strikes in
Manchester, Liverpool and London. The formation of the National
Union of Railwaymen (N.U.R.) broke down most of the fifty-odd
pigeon-holes in the railway industry. By 1914 union membership
had reached four million and the N.U.R., the Transport Workers'
Federation and the Miners' Federation had agreed to form a Triple
Alliance with the object of delivering a massive 'straight left' to
capitalism's 'Chin of Fat.'

The war intervened to prevent this. But there remained a busy
underswell of syndicalist resentment, spreading south from the
great engineering centre of the Clyde. In France and Germany
equivalents of the Clyde shop-stewards' movement, defying official
union leadership, had come into being. In Spain nationalism —

Catalan nationalism—was explosively mixed with a revolutionary movement for workers' control. The anarcho-syndicalists of Barcelona, the toughest and most wildly millennial in the world, were out to end capitalism as well as rule from Madrid. Their aim was a Catalan Workers' Republic. In August 1917 a mass strike in Barcelona organized by the syndicalist Confederation of Labour (C.N.T.) and the socialist General Union of Labour (U.G.T.) had been machine-gunned into submission, leaving seventy dead, hundreds of wounded, and two thousand prisoners. During 1918 the C.N.T. gathered its forces for another trial of strength. Syndicalists and employers recruited professional gunmen—*pistoleros*. With both sides in a trigger-happy mood it looked as though Barcelona, notorious as the most turbulent city in Europe, was on the brink of a classic confrontation of Capital and Labour.

The London *Call* did not seem to be indulging in sheer fantasy when it claimed that 'in every land ravaged by capitalist war the labourer rears his head, stands erect, clothed in dignity as the creator of wealth, challenging the dissolving reign of the oppressors … from the red ruin of war the workers rise and claim their own.' At a *Herald* rally in the Albert Hall, London, in December 1918, Robert Williams, General Secretary of the Transport Workers' Federation, urged 'preparedness' for revolution. 'The sun of international socialism', he said, 'is melting capitalism throughout Europe. It will now exercise its thawing influence on the capitalists of Great Britain.'

It seemed, suddenly, as if the Great War had only dammed the force of workers' control, that it would leap forth with renewed and devastating power. In America, too, confrontation was in the air. The military call-up and the cutting-off of immigration had put labour in a stronger position than ever before. For every strike initiated by the I.W.W. a hundred or more were called by A.F.L. unions. For the time being the A.F.L. escaped the full wrath of the employers, largely because it confined itself to bargaining and did not speak of class war and industrial democracy. Yet many A.F.L. members were restless. There was a feeling that now was the time to make more radical demands.

Glutted with wartime profits, employers could easily afford to pay higher wages. Some even began to concede that shorter hours brought higher productivity. But there were exceptions—notably

J. P. Morgan's United States Steel Corporation, which controlled sixty per cent of America's basic steel industry. Morgan ruled his empire like a state within the state, and it was widely regarded as the last bastion of 'pure' capitalism. It had broken the steel unions. It forced employees to join company unions. It owned whole towns, complete with newspapers, pulpits and local authorities.

Morgan, busy with his banking operations (which made millions of dollars arranging loans to the Allied Powers), left his steel interests in the hands of Judge Elbert H. Gary, Chairman of the Corporation's Executive Committee. Grave in manner, giving the impression of a statesman rather than a businessman, Gary was a moralist, a Methodist and a total abstainer (H. L. Mencken called him 'the Christian hired man'). Under his supervision steel-men's wages were severely slashed. During the war the pay of unskilled workers was doubled, and still barely reached subsistence level. This gesture had been forced by the federal government's wartime intervention in industry. In August 1918 a huddle of steel executives met to consider 'the threat from Washington'. In September Gary was ordered to apply the eight-hour day and overtime rates in Corporation plants. He protested that time-and-a-half after eight hours was 'a sham, a method of obtaining a wage increase under false pretences'. But, threatened with an investigation by the new federal bureaucracy, he gave way—verbally. The Iron and Steel Institute hurriedly announced the adoption of a 'basic' eight-hour day.

Meantime rank-and-file rebels within the A.F.L. were demanding a determined effort to storm the steel industry's fortress of industrila reaction. Even Gompers, though passionately anti-extremist, had to come to terms with this demand. He agreed to act as chairman of a National Committee for Organizing Iron and Steel Workers on which twenty-four unions, speaking for some two million members, were represented. Its secretary-treasurer was William Zebulon Foster. Formerly a prominent I.W.W. organizer, he had left the Wobblies to concentrate on leavening the lump of the A.F.L.—a policy technically known as 'boring from within.' He now pressed for an early start to the steel drive, before the government dismantled its wartime controls and let big business off the leash. But the campaign did not really get started until after the armistice. In January 1919 Judge Gary masked his fire by a well-reported homily to his officers: 'It has', he said, 'always been our policy to keep out of trouble ... Be

sure we are liberal in the protection of our workmen and their
families ... Don't let them go hungry or cold ... Give them play-
grounds and schools and churches and every opportunity to keep
clean.' Charles Schwab, chief of the Bethlehem Steel Company, was
more straightforward. Any conferences with employee representatives were, he emphasized, simply discussions. He would not permit
himself to be in a position of 'having labour dictate to management'.

The steel crisis was watched with peculiar concern by socialists
and progressives, as well as syndicalists, in other countries. If
America, the last and hugest of the industrial giants, the Paymaster of
the West, could not match its technological revolution with a
revolution in human values, could not be swung into the search for
democracy in depth, what hope was there of a viable alternative to
the crudities and excesses of Bolshevism?

4. The Workers' Republic

The syndicalists of North and South America, Spain, France, Germany and Britain had been thrilled by the mighty attempt of the Russian masses to control their own destiny. But many had their doubts about the dictatorship of the proletariat. Of the fifteen members of the first Soviet government eleven were middle and upper class intellectuals, only four of working-class origin.

When soviets had first appeared during the Russian workers' revolt of 1905, Lenin had been angered by a tendency, even among his disciples, to see in them a spontaneous force which might supersede the necessity for control by a Marxist élite – the Party. The history of syndicalism, of 'pure' workers' control, was, in Lenin's opinion, the history of a romantic fallacy. He believed that in a revolution intelligent, scientific leadership was all-important, that the masses had to be shown the way, delivered from the agony of thought.

Only Lenin's Bolsheviks had had the will, the courage, and even the inkling of a plan to impose order upon a buzzing chaos of land-hungry peasants, war-hating soldiers, discipline-defying factory committees, and intoxicated bourgeois idealists. Splendid decrees had been issued – mostly, it seemed, for the historical record – by commissars almost as certain as the New York Times that their days were numbered.

In March 1918 the Germans had imposed on the Workers' Republic a 'peace' which tore away a huge territory containing 56 million inhabitants, a third of Russia's railway mileage, seventy-nine per cent of her iron and eighty-nine per cent of her coal production. When the Germans left, Russian counter-revolutionaries, helped by the Allies, took over. Stocks of raw material were almost completely exhausted. Turkestan, the only source of raw cotton; the Baltic States, a main source of flax; the oil of the Caucasus and Baku; the oil and coal of the Ukraine – all were cut off. Fuel and food were rationed to vanishing point. Hundreds of thousands of workers left Moscow and Petrograd to return to their native villages. Factories came to a standstill. Such locomotives and rolling stock as were serviceable (and could be fuelled) crawled along the tracks in case they burst into flames for lack of lubricants. Allied secret agents blew up strategic bridges—and were decorated for their exploits. The Red Army took priority in all factory production and had first call on food and transport. Schools, though in desperately short supply, were commandeered as barracks.

Always in the background was the fear of a German attack on Petrograd, which the scratch, mutinous Red Army could have done little to resist. In March 1918 the Bolshevik government moved to Moscow, and Lenin talked of moving even further east if necessary. The area of tenuous Bolshevik control had shrunk to the size of the Grand Duchy of Muscovy in the fifteenth century. Lenin and his colleagues, scarcely adjusted to the sudden, traumatic change from conspiratorial obscurity, faced a complex of problems that would have taxed the most subtle, forceful and experienced administration —and was not calculated to encourage tolerance. Lenin himself had stripped for action. For nearly thirty years he had lived with and for the revolution. Bolshevism was his own personal creation, fashioned in the teeth of constant opposition and Byzantine intrigue. He had been passionately addicted to chess, but gave it up because it was too time-consuming. He did not drink or smoke (at meetings in the Kremlin, commissars for whom smoking was a necessity had to take turns to use a special vent-hole). He liked to listen to Beethoven's violin sonatas, but rationed this indulgence for fear that the beauty of the music would make him too sentimental to cope with harsh reality.

There were many dreams in revolutionary Russia, and most of them had to be trodden upon. There was the liberated slave's dream of loot, rape, lynch and liquor; the democratized soldier's dream of rankers' control; the dream of workers' control in the factories; the orthodox Marxist dream of the Mensheviks—a long interlude of bourgeois democracy during which Capital and Labour would become so convinced of their 'historic' roles, so civilized, that there would be no need for nastiness, hardly a jolt when the takeover happened. The Menshevik programme was too absurd to merit serious attention. So, given the circumstances, was Prince Kropotkin's anarcho-communist vision of a society of interlocking co-operatives, a four-hour day, and a universal leisure enriched with cultural activity. 'Pure' anarchism was too hamstrung by distrust of authority and organization in any form to be more than a perpetual, impotent opposition.

The Social Revolutionaries (S.R.s) offered the only serious competition. They were the heirs of the *narodniki* (gentlemanly idealists who in the 1870s had tried to spread socialist ideas among the peasants) and of the terrorist *Narodnaya Volya* (People's Will). The tight, fanatical camaraderie of a tiny underground of S.R. terrorists had been influenced by the teaching of Michael Bakunin, the great Russian anarchist, and of his ruthless disciple Sergei Nechayev. Bakunin and Nechayev had insisted on the need for a highly-disciplined élite of revolutionaries. But whereas they wanted their 'professionals' to go to any lengths of deceit, to use any weapon, however conventionally vile, in a totally cynical fight with the bourgeoisie, the S.R.s were determined to remain ethically untarnished. Assassinations were postponed if it seemed that innocent bystanders were likely to get hurt. Martyrdom was regarded as a moral duty. He who took another's life must be willing to forfeit his own.

While the S.R. Organization for Combat, led by Boris Savinkov, borrowed from Bakunin, the S.R. programme stayed close to that of the *narodniki*, who had seen the peasant commune, the *mir*, as the starting point for a Russian revolution. Since Russia was so overwhelmingly a land of peasants, they had reasoned, it was logical to begin with socialization of the land. The S.R.s inherited a tradition of Tolstoyan contempt for the cities. Marx's exaltation of the industrial proletariat (a pitiful collection of degraded peasants to the S.R. way of thinking) seemed to them a reversal of sound values. Marxist plans to industrialize agriculture and proletarianize the peasants were regarded as a conspiracy to spread the disease of the cities.

When in 1917 the prisons and Siberian settlements were opened, a stream of eager, out-of-touch S.R. idealists headed for Petrograd. Dismayed by the flabby indecision of the existing party, they formed the Left Social Revolutionary Party (L.S.R.) and entered into uneasy coalition with the Bolsheviks. Three of them became People's Commissars and others filled minor government posts. But the soul and inspiration of the L.S.R.s was Maria Spiridonova. In 1905, disguised as a schoolgirl with long plaits, she had assassinated General Luzhenovsky, the commander of a brutal punitive expedition against the peasants of her native Tambov province. She had been beaten, raped and tortured by Luzhenovsky's Cossacks, then exiled to Siberia. She burned with an understandably psychopathic hatred for dictatorship and with a determination to protect 'her' peasants from the evil designs of political tricksters. 'It is', she told her colleagues, 'the duty of us Left Social Revolutionaries in this time of embittered struggle to cleanse the moral atmosphere ... Large masses stand behind the Bolsheviks today, but that is only temporary. Bolshevism has no inner inspiration. Everything in it is founded on hatred.' Now thirty-two Spiridonova, her hair still in plaits and her dark blue dress buttoned to the throat, remained curiously girlish, even conventual, in appearance – and (in Lenin's opinion) in mentality.

The Bolsheviks and L.S.R.s soon split over the issue of a 'coward's' peace with Germany. The L.S.R.s wanted to lead the peasants of the Ukraine in a guerrilla campaign against the imperialist invaders. Better, they insisted, to fail with honour than to survive with dishonour. When Lenin carried the Soviets in favour of the Brest-Litovsk treaty, the L.S.R.s resigned from the government and declared war on the Bolsheviks and their German 'allies'. Count Mirbach, the German ambassador, General Eichhorn, the commander of the German Army in the Ukraine, and Uritsky, head of the Petrograd Cheka, were assassinated in July 1918. An attempt was made on Lenin's life in September. The assassins were Left Socialist Revolutionaries, and Spiridonova proudly took responsibility for their deeds. But the fact was that the 'purity' of her party had been tarnished. The L.S.R. revolt in Moscow and Petrograd, coming at the crisis of the Czechoslovak Legion's offensive, was part of a promiscuous anti-Bolshevik mêlée in which Allied and German agents, open reactionaries, liberals, anarchists, Mensheviks, S.R.s and L.S.R.s whirled about clutching at any straw of support.

The 'White' counter-revolution, at first represented by a few refugee generals and a few thousand volunteers in the Crimea and the Ukraine, had, by mid-1918, turned into a real threat. To its head-quarters flocked fugitive socialist politicians – Menshevik and S.R. They hoped that the reactionary, restorationist sympathies of the White leaders would be restrained by the Allies and by the demo-cratically-minded Czechs. For a time – at Archangel in the north and at Samara, Omsk and Tomsk in the east, they were allowed to form puppet Social Democratic governments. But these, constantly bickering among themselves, were soon regarded as more trouble than they were worth, even as propaganda façades. General Denikin in the Ukraine, Admiral Kolchak in Siberia, and (under British supervision) Russian generals in the Archangel-Murmansk area, planning to join forces in a three-pronged assault on Moscow, set up military dictatorships. They kept some tame socialists and liberals in their teams of political advisers and issued vaguely enlightened proclamations, but were unable to control the prejudices of their officers or the open vengefulness and greed of the dispossessed landlords, industrialists and businessmen who swarmed in their wake.

One of the first assignments of the Cheka (the Extraordinary Commission for Combating Counter-revolution and Sabotage) was to smash the liberated slave's dream of saturnalia by a 'drink pogrom'. The industrial proletariat was told that any idea of workers' control would have to be abandoned, at least until the enemies of the Workers' Republic had been defeated. One-man management, by carefully-watched bourgeois experts, was restored. 'Democratic centralism', which meant control by the Bolshevik Central Committee, was applied to the soviet system. The peasant dream of being left alone to redistribute the land was shattered by the march and counter-march of Red and White armies. Both requisitioned food for their troops and the starving towns. Neither could offer payment. Money was worthless, there were no manufactured goods. Peasant conscripts were sent to the fronts in sealed trains and forced into battle with machine-guns behind them.

The political activity and the press of Mensheviks, S.R.s, L.S.R.s and anarchists were suppressed, and many of their leaders jailed. Spiridonova was imprisoned first in the Kremlin, then in a sanatorium—'to recover mental health'. Prosh Proshyan, a left Social Revolutionary ex-commissar, was sentenced to three years' hard labour *in absentia*. After months on the run he died of cold and hunger in a Moscow hospital. Lenin, in a tribute published in *Pravda*, praised him as 'almost a Bolshevik'. Trotsky jeered at 'that old fool Kropotkin' (the anarchist prince, now in his late seventies, returning to Russia after a long exile, had expressed horror at the violence of the revolution). Stalin defended Lenin against the criticisms of Maxim Gorky with the venom of an underground specialist in whom the word 'culture' roused a desire to reach for his gun or make a phone call to the Cheka. 'The revolution', wrote

Stalin, 'does not bow to great names ... it is incapable of either regretting or of burying its dead.'

Different from, but as implacable as, Stalin was Felix Dzherzhinsky, the head of the Cheka. The son of a rich Polish landowner, he had spent most of his life in jails or in Siberian exile. Ascetic, incorruptible, possessed of a power of intellectual abstraction remarkable even among the Bolsheviks, he was the perfect choice for the Grand Inquisitor of the revolution. Happiest when evolving bleak theorems of social justice in his cell-like office, he dreamed of hastening the establishment of a model communist society by 'altering the correlation of political and social forces' through 'the subjection or extermination of some classes of society.' It was estimated that the Red Terror liquidated a mere six thousand or so people in the last four months of 1918. But a word from Lenin and Dzherzhinsky would have tested the viability of his calculus on a more ambitious scale.

It was Lenin's remarkable achievement not only to understand, steal and shatter the dreams of his political rivals, but to hold together a group of scintillating and wayward colleagues. He could count on the loyalty of Stalin and Dzherzhinsky, and of Zinoviev and Kamenev (keen to atone for their opposition to the Bolshevik coup of October 1917). Other leading Bolsheviks were less predictable. Trotsky was a big problem. Until recently he had been by far the best-known Russian revolutionary figure. His reputation as theoretician, journalist and political strategist, and above all as the dashing President of the Petrograd Soviet in 1905, was immense. Right up to October 1917 he had remained a freelance, ridiculing the petty sectarianism of both Mensheviks and Bolsheviks. He had deplored Lenin's scepticism about the revolutionary potential of the masses. Lenin had called him a hollow bell and a facile phrasemonger. He had called Lenin (who had studied law at St Petersburg University) a 'slovenly attorney', 'malicious and morally repulsive', and 'a professional exploiter of the backwardness of the Russian Labour movement.' He had also criticized Lenin's encouragement of such uncultured gangsters as Stalin. The latter, who had found an alias, a talent for intrigue, and a revolver more useful than booklearning, had always regarded the polemics of the exiled intellectuals as a luxury which the cause could ill afford. To him Trotsky was 'a disrupter of unity in the name of unity' and 'a common noisy champion with fake muscles.' Lenin's protection alone, perhaps, preserved Trotsky from the murderous envy of the Bolshevik Old Guard: and the revolt of the 'Left' communists on the Central Committee drew the two men closer together. During the debates on Brest-Litovsk this group—which included Bukharin, Radek, Preobrazhensky, Pyatakov, Uritsky and Yaroslavsky—joined the L.S.R.s in demanding a continuation of the war with Germany and denounced a separate peace as an opportunist betrayal which would minimize the chances of revolution in Europe. It also backed Stalin in his clash with Trotsky over the use of Tsarist officers in the Red Army. Even after a journalistic gruelling from Lenin (in an article entitled 'Left Infantilism and the Petty-Bourgeois Spirit') it continued its 'purist' campaign.

But though heated argument up to the very moment of decision was acceptable, the decision—thanks to Lenin's unique authority—was final. The attempt on his life was a big factor in rallying waverers to the defence of the revolution, and of the Bolsheviks with whom it was now inseparably associated. It also inspired the beginnings of a personality cult. In a lyrical open letter to Lenin, written after news of the shooting had been released, Finnish communists in Russia, refugees from the White Terror of General Mannerheim, wrote: 'We have seen germinating and sprouting a nobler crop than we had imagined. We have seen grand and suffering Russia bring forth in reality the beautiful ideal of which the workers of the world have been dreaming for many thousands of years ... Comrade Lenin, you are sorely needed. Soon again you will take into your strong hands the rudder of the Socialist Soviet Republic and the international revolutionary movement ... '

The disintegration of the Tsarist Army had been so complete that the only battleworthy unit left was a division of Latvian riflemen led by Colonel Vatzetis. Faced with the challenge of the Czechoslovak Legion the Bolsheviks could no longer rely on inspired amateurs and peasant partisans. Trotsky, who had headed the Military Revolutionary Committee in the October days, was switched from the Commissariat of Foreign Affairs, re-emerging as Commissar for War and President of the Supreme War Council.

He was full of enthusiasm for his new job. The Red Army could, he saw, not only save the revolution but act as a school of basic communism for benighted peasants—and for the ex-Imperial Army officers who, for lack of communist alternatives, and under the close surveillance of political commissars, were now re-employed as 'military specialists'. Trotsky's melodramatic Red Army oath 'Before the working classes of Russia and of the whole world ... I swear that in the struggle for the Russian Soviet Republic and for the cause of the brotherhood of the peoples I shall spare neither my own strength nor my own life') stressed his view that the civil war was only the first stage of an international socialist revolution. To the officers he preached the moral grandeur of the revolution and tried to explain and justify the psychology of the masses. 'When the soldier, the slave of yesterday,' he said in a speech at the Military Academy in Moscow, 'all of a sudden found himself in a first-class railway carriage and ripped off the velvet upholstery to make puttees, even in such a destructive act there showed the awakening of personality ... Our task is to adjust this personality to the community, to make it feel not a slave, not merely an Ivanov or a Petrov, but Ivanov the Personality.'

In July 1918 Trotsky set out for the front at Kazan to organize the defence of Moscow against the Czechoslovak Legion—the first of many sorties made in the armoured train which was to be his head-quarters for the next two-and-a-half years. So heavy that two loco-motives were needed to pull it, the train contained a library, a printing press, an electricity generator, a radio and telegraph station, and a garage for the cars in which the War Commissar and his staff drove across the steppes. In the news-sheet *En Route* published on the train Trotsky provided a brilliant running commentary on all phases of the fight for survival and the progress of the international socialist revolution. In it, too, he castigated the slovenly-heroic spirit which was ready to die for the cause but refused to keep boots and rifles clean, and defended his officers from the sneers of armchair demagogues (especially Zinoviev) in Moscow.

The arrival of Trotsky and his fanatically devoted entourage averted, not for the last time, demoralizing rout. At the end of September he returned in triumph to reorganize the Supreme War Council into the Revolutionary War Council of the Republic.

In Moscow feverish attempts were being made to guide—and stimulate—the longed-for 'relief' revolution in Europe. During 1918 a Federation of Foreign Groups of the Russian Communist Party was formed (mainly from prisoner-of-war converts), with German,

Hungarian, Austrian and Yugoslav contingents. Under Bolshevik supervision, leaders worked on men of their own nationality, recruiting some for the Red Army, training others as agitators to work behind the enemy lines or go as missionaries to their native lands. So were laid the foundations of a Communist International — 'the International of Deeds.' Bela Kun, the leader of the Hungarian group, addressing a mass meeting of prisoners-of-war, exhorted them to 'sweep from the path all obstacles to the liberation of the enslaved, turn into ashes all castles, all palaces into which your wealth flows and from which poverty and hunger are spread all over the country ... Turn your weapons against your officers ... Let every one of you be a teacher of revolution in his regiment.' An All-Russian Congress of Internationalist Prisoners-of War, attended by four hundred delegates, adopted the slogan 'Long Live the Third International.'

Crack propagandists were smuggled into Scandinavia, Holland and Switzerland. Theirs, they were told, was a peculiarly important and difficult mission — the overthrow of the bourgeois-socialist set-up in these neutral states which were the strongest supporters of (and, in their smug prosperity, the best advertisement for) the anti-revolutionary 'gradualism' of the Second International. In August 1918, when Bolshevik chances of survival appeared most slender, Lenin, in a 'Letter to the Workers of America', pleaded for their support: 'For every hundred mistakes of ours there are ten thousand great and heroic acts. But if the situation were reversed, if there were ten thousand mistakes to every hundred fine acts, all the same our revolution would be and will be great and unconquerable, because for the first time not a minority, not only the rich, not only the educated, but the real mass of workers themselves begin to build up a new life.' In a desperate appeal to the proletarian conscience, forty Bolshevik workers in Petrograd staged a marathon hunger strike (from the effects of which ten of them died) in the hope that 'the workers of all countries,' hearing of their fate, would 'rise against their capitalist oppressors'. Foreign Commissar Chicherin, replying to a protest about the Red Terror from the Swiss ambassador in Moscow, indignantly asked: 'Have the representatives of the neutral powers not heard of the White Terror in Finland ... of the mass executions of peasants and workers in the Ukraine ... the mass shootings of working men by the brave Czechoslovaks, those hirelings of Anglo-French capital? ... We advise them not to threaten us with the indignation of a civilized world that is dripping from head to foot with the blood of the workers, but themselves to tremble before the wrath of the peoples ... who will rise against a "civilization" which has plunged the whole human race into the unspeakable misery of a butchery without end.'

At the end of September 1918, when news came of the collapse of the Bulgarian front, *Izvestia* flaunted banner headlines proclaiming the death-throes of imperialism and the imminence of social revolution. Lenin offered the support of a million soldiers and all the (barely existing) resources of the Workers' Republic, including consignments of grain, to the long-awaited German workers' revolution. Excitement and illusion were delirious. When, at a meeting of the Central Soviet Executive, L. B. Kamenev read a telegram from Berlin announcing the appointment of Prince Max von Baden as Imperial Chancellor with the object of 'liberalizing' the German constitution and making peace on the basis of the Fourteen Points, the announcement was greeted with howls of derision. 'He won't stay in long! The German workers will see to that!' Towards the end of October, fortified by news of the collapse of the German Army on the western front and by reports of pro-Bolshevik demonstrations in Berlin, Paris, Rome and Glasgow, even Lenin abandoned all caution. 'Bolshevism', he said, 'has become the world-wide theory and tactics of the international proletariat! Never have we been so near to world revolution ... Never has it been so evident that millions and tens of millions of workers will follow us!'

At the beginning of November, with Berlin, Vienna and Budapest in turmoil, the Red Army launched an attempt to reconquer the Ukraine and make contact with the European revolution. Lenin renewed his fantastic offer to the German people. It seemed as if Trotsky's poignant S.O.S. of a few months earlier had been answered: 'We vow to you, workers of other countries, that we shall stand our ground ... But you, brothers, do not exhaust our strength, our patience, too much. Hurry up, stop the slaughter, overthrow the bourgeoisie, take power into your own hands, and then we shall turn the whole globe into a workers' Republic ... The land which nature gave us we shall cultivate together and turn into one blossoming garden where our children, grandchildren and great-grandchildren will live as in paradise.'

5. Crowns are Tumbling

'Peace! Thrones are everywhere crashing and the men of property everywhere secretly trembling,' wrote Beatrice Webb in her diary on November 11th, 1918. 'How soon will the tide of revolution catch up with the tide of victory? That is the question which is exercising Whitehall and Buckingham Palace and causing anxiety even among the more thoughtful democrats.'

Within a few weeks the Habsburg, Hohenzollern and Ottoman Empires had joined the Romanovs in oblivion: so had some two dozen German princelings and the Wittelsbach dynasty in Bavaria. The political and social structure of half Europe was swaying, creaking and groaning. In Austria-Hungary nationalism jostled with dreams of a Danubian federation. The German Reich was threatened by a burst of separatism. From the eastern front and the Baltic hundreds of thousands of troops straggled back, demoralized, plundering, across Europe. From Moscow missionaries of revolution made their way to their allotted sectors, intent on whipping up a determined onslaught upon the failed socialists of the Second International — who were busy weaving, from odds and ends of electoral and constitutional reform, a decent, sober, conservative republicanism to please the eyes of President Wilson and the Allies.

In Germany the home front had been shaken by industrial strikes and hunger demonstrations since 1916. But the first saturnalian sparks did not fly until the beginning of November 1918. They came from the well-fed sailors of the Grand Fleet at Kiel. After years of inaction and barrack discipline (broken only by a brief baptism of fire at the Battle of Jutland) they were bored and restless. Now, an order to make ready for a suicidal duel of honour with the British Grand Fleet, issued by equally bored officers, brought a growl of anger from thirty thousand ratings who had no mind to be sacrificed on a Valhallan altar of duty.

Stokers drew and doused the fires in the engine rooms. Warships drifted in the great artificial lagoon of the Jade Basin belching clouds of white steam into the night sky. Hurriedly formed sailors' soviets demanded the abdication of the House of Hohenzollern, an end to martial law, the liberation of all military and political prisoners, universal suffrage with a secret ballot. A deputation went ashore to warn Admiral Souchon that any attempt to call in the army would be answered by the guns of the fleet. Red flags were run up. Three officers were killed. Others were arrested and threatened with drowning. Orators urged that the fleet should steam out of Kiel all right—to join the Red Navy at Kronstadt; or shouted, above blaring bugles and rolling drums, that the best plan rould be to seize all the big Hamburg-America liners, take them to Russia, and come back with a Red Army. Groups of rebels left Kiel on a hell-raising spree.

In Hamburg they saw red flags flying on ships, locomotives, trams and cars. Joining forces with other sailors, they seized Trade Union Hall 'for the revolution,' helped to storm the army barracks, and with a mob of red-armbanded workers, smashed open the heavy oak doors of the council chamber in the city hall. The burgomaster, his fat face beaded with sweat, rose to pray silence for an important announcement. 'The Senate', he said, 'is prepared to support the new order ... It desires that all the sturdy democratic forces latent in this our ancient and free community should join in what we believe will prove a great and lasting communal effort. But that will be possible only if we all stand solidly together, mindful of our duty to see that public peace and order are preserved under all circumstances ...' Hooting and jeering, the sailor-worker mob hurried away to hoist a red flag over the employment bureau of the Hamburg-America Line and to take possession, in the name of the sailors' and workers' councils, of its general offices. Hearing of their action Albert Ballin, the Jewish chief of this powerful organization (and a close confidant of the Kaiser), committed suicide with an overdose of veronal.

In Brunswick, while a socialist orator harangued an apathetic crowd about the evils of imperialism, a group of drunken sailors led a deputation to the castle to demand the Duke's abdication. Twenty elderly soldiers in archaic parade uniform, drawn up on the gravel of the courtyard, offered no resistance. The delegates helped themselves to cigars and brandy while the Duke conferred with his family and advisers. After a while he emerged with a six-line typescript dated November 8th, 1918: 'I, Ernst August, Duke of Brunswick, and Luneburg, hereby declare that I renounce the throne for myself and my heirs and put the government into the hands of the Soldiers' and Workers' Council.'

In Frankfurt crowds attacked army officers, tearing off their shoulder straps, forcing them off the pavements. Soldiers' councillors, installed in the elegant Frankfurter Hof Hotel, became so confused that they called on local socialist politicians for guidance. When a general arrived to put himself at the service of the 'new order', there was a shuffling of feet and embarrassed giggling. Four men were sent to arrest the Commissioner of Police. He was succeeded, reluctantly, by Dr Hugo Sinzheimer, Professor of Social Science at the university.

In Munich the revolution, so surprising in ultra-conservative, Catholic Bavaria, was largely a symptom of hatred for Protestant Prussia. It might never have happened but for a large-scale wartime building of munition factories and the consequent influx of tens of thousands of industrial workers. It was led by Kurt Eisner, a Jewish socialist intellectual and journalist from Berlin. A gentle, unworldly man of great charm but no following save a group of café disciples, he had twice been imprisoned for anti-militarist agitation. During his second imprisonment he had written a drama in which the sensitive hero, rejected by the uncomprehending masses, refuses to abandon his mission crying:

> I leapt upwards,
> Inflamed by a hitherto unfelt power,
> And ran through the streets exulting:
> 'The world is rich! The world is great and bright!
> Dare, brothers, just to live! Dare to think,
> To live in spirit and create through spirit!'
> They stared blankly, they smirked, sneered, reviled ...
> All the more passionately I loved,
> Somewhere in the far reaches, Humanity —
> And saw not one human on earth!

Released in October 1918, his white beard long and unkempt, Eisner stepped, a picturesque prophet, into an atmosphere of resentment and nervous tension in which he was able, incredibly, to act out the drama he had just composed. In a series of beer-hall tirades, he demanded the establishment of a Bavarian Socialist Republic. For the first time in his life Eisner found that people, a lot of people, in fact most of the people, were actually listening to him. So it happened that on the pleasantly warm afternoon of November 7th, while King Ludwig III was taking his customary stroll in the English Garden of the palace, Eisner put himself at the head of a procession of workers, soldiers and miscellaneous spectators, many of whom had never even heard of him. The demonstrators entered the barracks without opposition, proclaimed a revolution, and helped themselves to rifles and ammunition. The Landtag, after a leisurely debate on the potato shortage, adjourned at 6 p.m. and refused to believe the news of Eisner's coup. Two hours later King Ludwig and his family fled, certain that the fantasy would soon fade, that they would soon be back.

In the Mathäserbräu, Munich's largest beer-hall, Eisner was elected Chairman of the Council of Workers and Soldiers – the first elective office he had ever held. At 10.30 p.m., surrounded by an armed guard, he burst into the deserted Landtag building. Mounting the presidential podium, Eisner, hair dishevelled, shirt open at the collar, spectacles slipping to the tip of his nose, proclaimed the end of the Wittelsbach dynasty and the inauguration of the Bavarian Republic. Before stretching out to sleep on a sofa, he dashed off a manifesto: 'Fellow citizens! In order to rebuild after long years of destruction, the people have overthrown the power of the civil and military authorities and have taken the regime in hand ...'

Truckloads of armed workers hurtled festively through the streets. A few days later, at a celebration in the National (formerly Royal) Theatre, Bruno Walter conducted the orchestra in Beethoven's Leonora Overture, after which the curtain rose to reveal Kurt Eisner, frock-coated, his hair and beard carefully trimmed, lyrically praising the Bavarian revolution as 'the first in history to unite idea, ideal, and reality'. This was followed by a reading from Goethe, a rendering of the Egmont Overture, an aria from Handel's *Messiah*, and the finale as the audience rose to sing the last verse of Eisner's own *Hymn of the Peoples*.

In Berlin the situation was more confused. Potsdam, the metronome of Prussian militarism, was not far away. The parties of the Right and Centre lay low, avoiding provocation. There was a virtual contest between them and the leaders of the Right (Majority)

Socialists to avoid taking power—and negotiating the terms of a national humiliation. Some workers were content to follow the orthodox trade union leaders, others followed the syndicalist Revolutionary Shop Stewards' Organization headed by Richard Müller.

To the leaders of the Social Democratic Party (S.P.D.)—men like Fritz Ebert, Philip Scheidemann and Gustav Noske—the war had been a righteous crusade against barbaric Russia, a chance to spread the blessings of German *Kultur* all over Europe. The Kaiser claimed that he was the prisoner of the High Command. They were its willing allies. Their loyalty had its reward when, at the bidding of the all-powerful Ludendorff, Ebert and Scheidemann became the Reich's first Socialist Ministers, in a trumped-up 'democratic' caretaker government presided over by Prince Max von Baden. They were willing, indeed anxious, to leave the apparatus of government and the structure of capitalism intact. Now that the S.P.D. had broken, or rather been hauled across, the power-barrier, all that remained was to draw up a new constitution, hold new elections, and settle comfortably into the routine of parliamentary democracy.

For them, this *was* the revolution. Noske, the party's military expert, was sent post-haste to Kiel to calm the rebels. His appeal for restraint was successful. Arrested naval officers were released and a Marine corps formed to keep order in the city. On November 9th Kaiser Wilhelm abdicated. Prince Max handed over the Chancellorship to the fat, frightened ex-saddler Ebert, who assured him: 'I hate revolution like mortal sin.' Wilhelm Gröner, who had succeeded Ludendorff as Quartermaster-General, promised Ebert that the Army would support his efforts to resist extremism.

The Socialist opposition was far from united. Goaded at last into action by the spectacle of a leadership which continued to back the High Command in its attack on a 'democratic' Russia, those who favoured a negotiated peace had broken away to form the Independent Socialist Party (U.S.P.D.). Led by Hugo Haase, a lawyer, and clogged by the heavy dialectics of Karl Kautsky, the dean of Marxology, the U.S.P.D. was essentially Fabian. But embedded within it was a small but brilliant cluster of revolutionists—the Spartacus group (called after the leader of the Roman slave revolt)—led by Rosa Luxemburg and Karl Liebknecht.

Liebknecht, trained as a lawyer, had begun to denounce militarism

—the doing of the capitalists' dirty work—while performing his national service in a Guards regiment at Potsdam. In the Reichstag, to which he was elected while serving a two-year jail sentence for political agitation, he had clashed fiercely with Noske, whose speeches, he declared, contained 'not a whisper of the international solidarity of the working class'. In 1914, ordered to join a labour battalion on the western front, he had persisted in spreading his anti-militarist sentiments by word of mouth and pamphlet, and was howled down by his S.P.D. colleagues on his few appearances in the Reichstag. Formally expelled from the S.P.D. in 1916 (the fact that his wife was Russian did not help him), his trial and four-year sentence caused mass demonstrations of workers all over Germany. His open feud with the S.P.D. leaders was regarded as doubly reprehensible in the son of the revered Wilhelm Liebknecht (a close friend of Karl Marx and a founder of the S.P.D.), who had stressed the need for unity at almost any cost. At the end of October 1918 Liebknecht was released from prison. Damned as a mentally unstable, publicity-seeking sensationalist by Ebert and Scheidemann, he was given a hero's reception on his return to Berlin.

Rosa Luxemburg was a much more complicated personality. An intellectual of intellectuals, she had been one of the chief adornments of the Second International, more than able to hold her own in debate or literary controversy with Lenin, Jaurès, Trotsky or Kautsky. Born into a middle-class Jewish family in south-east Poland, she had joined an anti-Tsarist underground movement while still a schoolgirl in Warsaw. Her lover, Leo Jogiches, a wealthy Lithuanian socialist, not only helped to finance her studies at Zürich University but backed her in the formation of the Social Democratic Party of the Kingdom of Poland and Lithuania, which opposed the romantic nationalism of Josef Pilsudski's Socialist Party. Its members included Felix Dzherzhinsky, Julian Marchlevsky and several others who later became leading communists in Russia. Migrating to Germany, she had made it her mission to energize the S.P.D., Europe's largest, most disciplined, but most impotent Socialist party.

Steeped in Russian literature and revolutionary history, she never ceased to ridicule the Germans (she called them 'Swabians') and especially Berlin—'the most repulsive place, a real barracks, and the charming Prussians with their arrogance, as if each of them had been made to swallow the very stick with which he got his daily beating.'

Such opinions did not endear her to her fellow-socialists, in whom the German contempt for Poles (and particularly Polish Jews) was never far below the surface. Moreover she was a woman, and a woman who despite her almost dwarfish stature and slight hunch-back, possessed, with her olive skin and velvety, almond-shaped eyes, great personal attraction, and a passionate nature which she indulged in a series of tempestuous liaisons. The swing and bite of her writing made Marxism vital and exciting to a vast readership. But she remained an outsider, feared and distrusted. The Bolsheviks resented her attacks on Lenin's narrow fanaticism. Her intellectual superiority exasperated practical politicians, often of working-class origin. Her fiery militancy ('everything but revolution', she said, 'is mere bilge') drew their patronizing irony.

Imprisoned, like Karl Liebknecht, during the war, she had endured agonies of impatience. Leo Jogiches arranged for the printing and distribution of Spartacist literature, and she smuggled out a series of pamphlets. There must be an end, she wrote, to the patronization of the workers by pseudo-socialist politicians ('Up-wards from below. The broadest mass of comrades in the party and the trade unions must be reached. The handcuffs of the bureaucracy must be cracked wide open. The party must be recaptured from below by a mass rebellion.'). She recalled with loathing the futile high-mindedness of the pre-war socialist round. Whatever happened, she vowed, after the war she would never take part in that smug, mock-militant farce. 'No more meetings, no more conventicles. Where great things are in the making, where the wind roars about the ears, that's where I'll be in the thick of it.'

She welcomed the Russian revolution as a hurricane of fresh air in the stifling atmosphere of carnage and hypocrisy. The great problem had at last been formulated in action. The Bolsheviks had dragged it out of the debating chamber. 'In this sense,' she wrote, 'the future belongs to Bolshevism everywhere.' But she deplored the suppression of the Constituent Assembly and the outlawing of political opposition. She was determined to fashion in Germany a revolutionary movement which, while uncompromisingly militant, would also be sternly opposed to dictatorship *over* the proletariat.

In November 1918 Rosa Luxemburg returned to Berlin, her body wasted and her hair turned white, but as game as any Kiel sailor to set the world on fire. Leaving to the ebullient Liebknecht—an ally of

necessity rather than choice—the public appearances and public
oratory, she devoted herself with sleepless fervour to the blue-
printing of her own kind of Marxist society. The S.P.D., in its
newspaper *Vorwärts*, sneered at her, contrasting the 'pathological
instability' of Spartacus with their own 'clear-headed and sensible
calm.' Ebert, Scheidemann and Noske regarded the efforts of
Luxemburg and Liebknecht to rouse the masses as so much sentimental madness. Yet this madness was more attuned to the mildly
saturnalian mood of Berlin—the pogrom of epaulettes, the mutilation and overturning of Hohenzollern statues in the Siegesallee—
than the S.P.D.'s flourishing of wet blankets. Some seventy thousand
troops were milling around, careering through the streets in trucks
with red flags, roughing up officers. Loyalist snipers fired from
roof-tops and frolicking 'rebels' fired back. At the railway terminals
Spartacist workers met troop trains to beg or buy rifles and machine
guns. There were occasional scuffles with the police. Berlin was a
strange mixture of violence and carnival.

On November 9th Liebknecht toured Berlin in a motor-lorry
surrounded by armed guards and festooned with garlands of red
carnations. 'Comrades,' he cried, 'the red flag flies over Berlin! The
proletariat is marching. The workers of Berlin have not led the way
in the revolution, but it is for them to make it a communist revolution. The abdication of a couple of Hohenzollerns is a mere nothing.
The putting of a few sham socialists at the head is also nothing. The
civil and military power, the factories, the banks, the transport
combines, must all be taken over by the workers!' Armed workers,
soldiers and sailors stormed the Admiralty, locking up over a
hundred officers, including several admirals. The Moabit Prison was
opened. Police headquarters were occupied and weapons taken from
there and from army barracks, which put up little resistance.
Liebknecht in his lorry led a huge mob through the gates of the
Imperial Palace. 'The reign of capitalism, which has turned Europe
into a graveyard, is over,' he proclaimed. 'We must summon our
strength to build a new government of workers and peasants, to
create a new order of peace and happiness and freedom not merely
for our brothers in Germany but for the whole world. Whoever is
resolved not to cease from the fight until the Free Socialist Republic
and the world revolution shall be realized, let him raise his hand and
swear!'

'We swear!' thundered the crowd.

The bells of the cathedral were rung. A crimson carpet was torn from the floor and flung over the parapet of the balcony upon which Liebknecht stood.

'Long live the first President of the German Soviet Republic!'

When news of Liebknecht's presumption reached Ebert and Scheidemann in the restaurant of the Reichstag, where they were discussing how to fit the Kaiser, or at least a Hohenzollern, into the new scheme of things, Scheidemann rushed on to the balcony to save *his* revolution. 'Workers and soldiers! The enemies of the people have been swept away! Government by the people for the people! The old, rotten monarchy has collapsed! Long live the German Republic!'

Under the bellies of the bronze horses on top of the Brandenburg Gate workers with machine-guns blazed away at the rear lights of cars, mistaking them for advancing 'enemy' trucks. All was confusion. But one thing was clear. The Hohenzollerns had gone. The Kaiser and the Crown Prince had fled to Holland. The Crown Prince had flown a red flag on his car. Prince Heinrich, the Kaiser's brother, had taken the precaution of sewing a red badge on his sleeve. Nobles and princelings had cleared out, too, or were in hiding or despair. 'Baroness Röder and her husband came to see us,' wrote Princess Blücher in her diary. 'They had been spending the summer in Switzerland and were exceedingly surprised to find what a state Germany is in. He, poor man, looked quite crushed. He was Master of Ceremonies and for more than fifty years a faithful courtier. Now at one stroke the whole structure of his existence dissolves. There will probably be no pension forthcoming and so the future is a perfect blank to them.' The Crown Prince of Saxony was living under an assumed name in two small rooms in Breslau. The King had taken refuge in a remote hunting lodge in the midst of a Silesian forest. The Duke and Duchess of Croy trudged to the Dutch frontier at night and crawled under the barbed wire with knapsacks on their backs.

On November 10th the first government of the German Republic was elected by the Berlin Workers' and Soldiers' Councils. It consisted of six men: three Majority Socialists (Ebert, Scheidemann and Otto Landsberg), and three Independent Socialists (Hugo

Haase, Wilhelm Dittmann and Emil Barth) with the misleadingly revolutionary title of the Council of People's Commissars. Only the Majority Socialists, by virtue of their understanding with the High Command and the state bureaucracy, had any real power: and they were determined that a National Assembly should be elected as soon as possible and the Councils dissolved. The Independents wanted the council system to be made permanent, functioning as a people's watchdog alongside the central government. But they were a feeble opposition, ignored by Ebert and despised by the Spartacists and militant workers for collaborating with him. Spartacus and the Revolutionary Shop Stewards declared that parliamentary democracy would be fatal to the interests of the proletariat ('the way to a National Assembly', said Richard Müller, 'is over my dead body'), and that the Councils should *be* the government. U.S.P.D. rebels occupied the premises of three right-wing newspapers and produced their own versions. Spartacus did the same with the *Lokalanzeiger*, which reappeared as *Die Rote Fahne* (Red Flag), edited and largely written by Rosa Luxemburg. Contributors, apart from Liebknecht, included Wilhelm Pieck, boss of the East German Communist Party after the second world war. 'Civil war', wrote Luxemburg, 'is only another name for class war, and the idea of socialism without a class struggle, socialism by a majority decision of parliament, is a ridiculous petit-bourgeois illusion. The alternative before us is not democracy or dictatorship. The dictatorship of the proletariat *is* democracy in a socialist sense. It does not mean bombs, putsches, riots and anarchy as the agents of capitalism pretend. It means the use of political power for the introduction of socialism and the expropriation of the capitalist class.'

Spartacus had organized a Red Soldiers' League. Thousands of workers were armed. But Rosa Luxemburg shrank from violence. She hoped that the Councils, by a massive rejection of the revolution-stiflers, would make it unnecessary. Shocked that Dzherzhinsky, her former colleague, was now unleashing a bloody terror, she longed for German workers to show that they could establish order 'without dominance', and expected 'the highest idealism in the interests of all, the strictest self-discipline and the most active civic sense on the part of the masses', to be the moral keynote of the new order. In fact the Soldiers' Councillors, as opposed to the hordes of demoralized but rapidly demobilized troops which had provided Spartacus with a transient illusion of strength, had from the start shown every sign of wanting to shed their authority and get out of politics. The Berlin Congress of Councils contained only ten Spartacus representatives. An application for Luxemburg and Liebknecht to be co-opted as members was rejected on the ground that they were not workers.

Encouraged by these developments the S.P.D. intensified its anti-Spartacus propaganda. Luxemburg and Liebknecht were, according to the conservative press, 'human beasts' coldly scheming to 'drown society in blood'. They were sexual maniacs planning to nationalize women and encourage erotic orgies, in which they themselves liked to take part. They were, said *Vorwärts*, traitors to the Fatherland, lusting after personal power. Spartacus was sneered at for its absurd pretensions and inflated into a Red Bogey which was used to frighten the Allies and hold firm the bizarre common front of Ebert, Groener and Foch. It was impotent and it was almighty; riddled with perversion and a model of revolutionary discipline; a few mad generals without an army and an army of untold strength with a few sinister generals; the hope of all true revolutionaries and the target and darling of reaction.

To all this Rosa Luxemburg, torn between her desire for action and her dislike of dirty, unadult violence, replied in the *Red Flag*: 'Whenever a window-pane crashes or a tyre bursts in the street, the Philistines look over their shoulder and whisper, their hair standing on end: "Aha! Here comes Spartacus!" The whole thing is planned to create an atmosphere of pogrom.' By December *Vorwärts* had openly joined those who demanded the assassination of Liebknecht and Luxemburg. Both went into hiding. But Rosa, fired by news of a wave of strikes—for workers' control—in the provinces, claimed that the revolution was 'brushing aside the cardboard scenery of ministerial change … and stepping before the footlights in person.'

After the Congress of Councils had voted overwhelmingly in favour of dismantling the council system, granted wide emergency powers to the provisional government, and set January 19th, 1919, as the date of elections for the National Assembly, Spartacus may well have clutched at the hope that the provinces would once more set the pace. But the situation in Berlin suddenly took a dramatic turn. On December 23rd the People's Marine Division, half-revolutionary, half-mercenary, decided to take action for increased wages. One detachment stormed the office of the S.P.D. City Commandant, Otto Wels, took him hostage when he refused their demands, and occupied the building. Another reoccupied the Imperial Palace, which the Division had recently evacuated under government pressure. Yet another seized the Chancellery and took control of the switchboard. Republican troops ordered to attack the rebels obeyed half-heartedly, and were confused by counter-orders from the three U.S.P.D. 'commissars', who resigned from the government. The U.S.P.D. leadership was now edged into an awkward alliance with Spartacus and the militant workers. The supporters, however lukewarm, of proletarian democracy had been forced to drop all pretence of legality. The second revolution would have to be fought out in the streets. Noske, appointed to co-ordinate operations against this new threat, made contact with the Freikorps, groups of well-disciplined, well-equipped soldiers who had kept together after the armistice. Led by officers who were anything but socialist, they awaited the call to defend the Fatherland against 'Bolshevik' traitors with an eagerness whetted by the humiliation of defeat by the Allies. Civil war loomed. Karl Radek, disguised as a returning prisoner-of-war, appeared in Berlin to give the German revolutionaries the benefit of Russian experience.

Vienna, too, was in turmoil. Emperor Franz Josef's whole life, his whole regime, had been conditioned by fear of the people, hatred of the Abyss. He had never forgotten the revolution of 1848, the terrifying emergence of the proletariat — emaciated, unkempt creatures seen for the first (and, he resolved, the last) time outside their foetid slum-warrens. As a protection against this obscenity he had woven around himself a threefold cocoon of Bureaucracy, Army and Church. The Habsburg bureaucracy was of an almost unbelievable ramification, containing in its lower reaches the concierges of Vienna, all of them police agents. The army was pampered and exalted as the personal possession of the Emperor. The top layers of the army and the Civil Service were stuffed with the scions of an aristocracy notorious for its arrogance and incompetence. The partnership of Church and Throne had always been peculiarly close in an empire which had been the soul of the Counter-Reformation and the bulwark of Christendom against the Turks. The Church thundered against atheistic socialism, sponsored an anti-semitic Christian Socialist Party, and encouraged peasant illiteracy and superstition.

The slashing of this cocoon, the throwing away of the frightened bundle of reaction at the heart of it, was a necessary act of social hygiene. But the old Emperor, dying in 1916 at the age of 86, was spared at least this disaster. It fell upon his great-nephew and successor Karl, a flummoxed young man of 29 who spent his short reign intriguing with the Allies for a separate peace and offering Czechs, Poles, Yugoslavs and Rumanians ever wider autonomy in an effort to salvage something from the total wreck of the Habsburgs. He was hopelessly outbid when President Wilson and the Allies made the independence of the subject races of his empire a specific war aim, and republicanism a basic necessity. The Slav provinces of the south merged with the new Yugoslav nation. The Czechs claimed the whole of Bohemia and Moravia. West Galicia joined other Polish sectors to form a new republic. In Silesia Poles, Czechs and Germans squabbled over the coalfields. Smouldering racial animosities, deliberately fanned by Allied propaganda, burst into ugly flame. It was foolhardy to speak German in Prague, forbidden to take Austrian newspapers over the Yugoslav frontier.

Austria was balkanized to make Wilsonian largesse — and a string of 'successor' states gratefully responsive to the whims of the map changers. German Austria now consisted of barren Alps, beautiful, but as yet commercially unexploited, a few provincial towns — and Vienna, which contained nearly a third of a total population of eight and a half million. The city had lost its imperial *raison d'être* and sources of supply. Behind new, spiteful barriers lay the coal of Silesia and Bohemia, the oil of Galicia, the port of Trieste, the agricultural areas of Moravia and Southern Styria — and of Hungary, which, grappling with its own nationalist jackals, left Vienna to its fate. Stranded there was a bureaucracy which had been excessive for the needs of twenty-five million people. Railway terminals with swollen staffs now served stump lines at most fifty miles long.

Karl gave it up as a bad job. 'Filled now as ever with unchangeable love for my people, I will no longer set my person as a barrier to their free development,' he proclaimed on November 11th, and departed hopefully for Budapest. The Austrian Social Democrats, the most united and talented in Europe, entered into their fearsome inheritance. Overwhelmingly socialist in sympathy, Vienna was encircled by a triple ring of hostility: an Allied blockade, greedy new nations, anti-socialist peasants. Czechs and Poles held up and pilfered supplies intended for Vienna. Food rations fell below subsistence level. Two Jewish army subalterns — Julius Deutsch and Julius Braunthal — worked desperately at the War Office to create a politically reliable *Volkswehr* to fight off plundering Slavs and Magyars. General Segre, head of the Allied Military Commission, extorted the surrender of war material, railway stock, valuable works of art, even cash payments by threatening an Italian military occupation.

Workers and soldiers demonstrated violently, formed a Red Guard, seized ammunition wagons and food stores. Utterly dependent on Allied charity, and in any case firmly opposed to violence, the Social Democrats launched a crash propaganda campaign to explain the limitations of a revolution of beggars. Prominent in this was Friedrich Adler (the son of the founder of the Austrian S.P.D.), a popular hero as the result of his assassination of Count Stürgkh, the Austrian Chancellor, in 1916. In prison Adler, a mathematician of the first rank, had been working on a critique of Einstein's theory of relativity. Now he used his powers of reasoning to demonstrate the categorical imperative of restraint.

The Social Democrats fought to revive and protect their Socialist way of life, for Viennese socialism *was* a whole way of life. The benign, omnipresent activities of the party took in music, drama, holidays and travel, sport and education as well as politics. Its celebrated daily paper, the *Arbeiter Zeitung*, had reached a level of cultural and political journalism unrivalled even in pre-1914 Europe. Its grip on the workers of Vienna was strong. But the pressures upon that grip were terrible. Small wonder that 'Red' Vienna looked anxiously upon the vicissitudes of revolution in Berlin and vehemently urged the economic necessity of an *Anschluss* (union) with Germany. It also waited eagerly for news of events in Budapest.

Victor Adler had described the Habsburg regime in Austria as 'a despotism mitigated by slovenliness.' The despotism of the Hungarian ruling classes was unmitigated. There was no pretence of liberalism in their attitude to peasants, workers or subject races. They regarded themselves as the anti-democratic conscience of the Dual Monarchy. 'I should be a Socialist of the deepest magenta if I were a worker here,' Lord Carnock, British Consul in Budapest, had confided. Three hundred and twenty-four landowners owned twenty per cent of the arable land, with an average of more than

40,000 acres each. Prince Esterhazy alone accounted for 570,000 acres. Their sense of privilege reached almost sublime heights. 'Do gentlefolk die too?' a 17-year-old Esterhazy asked his tutor. Hunting-lodge guests expected not only stags to kill but fresh, plump peasant wenches to sleep with.

For nearly two decades the Parliament in Budapest had been dominated by Count Istvan Tisza. Only six per cent of the population voted—and they had to run the gauntlet of open balloting. In an assembly of 414 members the non-Magyar races—Serbs, Slovaks, Rumanians—were allotted an average of ten seats, though more than half the population was non-Magyar. The Hungarian Labour movement was politically impotent. Any significant opposition to the regime had to come from the grandees, and few indeed were those whose consciences stirred in their feudal slumber. Count Alexander Károlyi was one of the exceptions. He was convinced that if only his fellow-nobles would take their responsibilities more seriously, or even realize that they *had* responsibilities, they as well as their employees would benefit both morally and economically. He impressed his ideas upon his nephew, Michael Károlyi, and gave him a copy of *Das Kapital* to read—to show him how vile un-redeemed bourgeois greed could be.

A sickly boy, suffering from a cleft palate, Michael Károlyi grew up to be a horseman and a gambler reckless even by the exacting standards of his social equals. But in other respects he was odd, infuriating his father by actually reading the books in the vast ancestral library, refusing to take part in the rape of village maidens or the slaughtering of birds, foxes and stags, and showing an unaccountable disinclination to box the domestics' ears. The estate he inherited was valued at £25 million. It included 25,000 acres of forest, 35,000 acres of meadow and arable land, a coal mine, a spa and a glass factory. The Károlyi mansion in Budapest had seventy-two rooms. He enjoyed and squandered his wealth, but openly condemned the arrogance of his class and even, as an Independent Liberal member of Parliament, challenged the awe-inspiring Count Tisza to a duel. Hoping to use the war as an excuse to overturn the Tisza clique, he opened secret but unsuccessful negotiations with the Italian government for an alliance of 'liberal' Hungary with Italy and Rumania. In summer 1918, when the Central Powers were faced with defeat, Count Tisza promised, 'if we have to go, we will bring down everything in ruins.' Railwaymen and

factory workers who went on strike were shot down. At the front
discipline crumbled despite mass executions. In Parliament Károlyi
pleaded for concessions to the workers and a sweeping suffrage
reform, and demanded the replacement of the government by men
who would make a separate peace before it was too late.

In Moscow Bela Kun, the son of a village notary, who, with Tibor
Szamuelly, the son of a Jewish grain merchant, had been groomed to
make revolution in Hungary, seized hopefully upon these signs of
revolt. These, he claimed in *Pravda*, were not just hunger riots, but
harbingers of revolution—a revolution which should be regarded as
a duty. 'Soviet Russia', he wrote, 'has done so much for the liberation
of the workers of all countries that the workers of the world will
never be able to discharge their debt of gratitude. The western
proletariat cannot evade its historical destiny. It must become
revolutionary ... Against the wall with the little shopkeeper, the
petit-bourgeois peasant, as well as with the great landowners and the
bloated tyrants of industry!'

Kun and Szamuelly, both ex-prisoners-of-war, were not only
seasoned journalists and propagandists. They had played a prominent
part in the fighting in Moscow during the July 1918 revolt. But it is
doubtful if at this stage Count Károlyi knew of the existence of his
low-born rivals. At the end of September, labouring for a Danubian
federation of eighty million people, he held talks with Slovak,
Rumanian, Serb and Croat leaders in an effort to forestall a mad orgy
of nationalism. He headed a National Council composed of members
of his own Liberal group and of the Hungarian Social Democratic
Party. On October 24th a mob of students, soldiers and workers
burst into the royal palace in Budapest and nailed the programme of
the National Council to the gilt and stucco walls of the grand salon.
The government resigned. Ex-Prime Minister Count Wekerle's
country house was pillaged. In the Astoria Hotel in Budapest the
National Council sweated to control the violence. But dead and
wounded littered the streets when an attempt was made to storm the
Archduke's palace. A general strike was called. Mutinous troops
threatened to bombard the palace unless the Emperor appointed
Count Károlyi Prime Minister. Karl gave way, and immediately the
Astoria was besieged by generals, politicians, industrialists, businessmen, and even the Archduke Josef, all clamouring to take the oath
of loyalty to the people's government, together with soldiers,
sailors, railwaymen, civil servants and factory workers. The League

of Landowners hastily offered to hand over part of their estates 'to satisfy the claims of the non-landowning classes.' Imperial escutcheons were smashed from the walls. Officers tore the Imperial rosettes from their uniforms.

When, early in the morning of October 31st, Károlyi walked down the steps of the Buda Palace Gardens, he found the city *en fête*. Lorries filled with yelling soldiers and garlanded with white chrysanthemums whined past. Citizens ran up to embrace him. People danced with joy and wept with happiness. At Count Tisza's mansion in the Herminenstrasse three soldiers forced their way into the living room. Tisza, a crack shot, confronted them revolver in hand. But he did not bother to defend himself. When his whole world was exploding it seemed petty to bother about his own life. 'It had to come,' he said, as mortally wounded, he sank to his knees. Emperor Karl's hopes of keeping his job in Hungary were put to a less stoically borne death. The National Council was willing to try and employ him in some capacity. His courtiers were more realistic. If the emperor had to be sacrificed to appease the republican foibles of the Allies, then he must be made to go. Two counts, a baron and cardinal went to announce his fate. After signing the text of resignation which was thrust upon him, Karl collapsed, sobbing, into the arms of the Court Chamberlain. He and his wife and five children, departed into exile in seven cars from which the Imperial crown had been carefully erased.

On November 16th the National Council officially took over the functions of government and Count Károlyi was installed as President of the Hungarian Republic. In the Domed Room of the Parliament Building an assembly of workers, peasants, red-rosetted soldiers in ragged uniforms, and—strangest of all—women delegates, greeted his appearance with roars of enthusiasm. But the Council faced a situation almost as forbidding as that which tormented the Socialists of Vienna. The Hungarian Social Democrats were obstructive, and opposed Károlyi's plans to redistribute the big estates among the peasants (which they regarded as encouraging the petit-bourgeois mentality). The runaway nationalism of the former subject races wrecked Károlyi's hopes for a Danubian federation. The aristocracy soon began to intrigue with Colonel Vix, head of the French Military Mission in Budapest, who readily acted as the mouthpiece of reaction.

Armistice demarcation lines were constantly encroached upon by Czechoslavaks, Yugoslavs and Rumanians. By December the London *Daily News* was reporting that 'the Hungarian problem may soon be solved in the sense that there will *be* no Hungary. Unless the peace conference acts it looks as if historic Hungary will be reduced to Budapest and the Plain.' Károlyi hurried to Belgrade to plead with General Franchet d'Esperey, commander of the Allied Army of the East, for an observance of the armistice lines. He also argued that the war had not been brought about by the Hungarian people but by 'the old feudal autocratic government of the monarchy in alliance with Prussian militarism'. Wasn't it in the interest of the Allies (and in accordance with the Fourteen Points) to foster democracy in the vanquished nations? Franchet d'Esperey, strutting about in a pale-blue uniform and glistening top boots, sneered at the notion of a 'good' Hungary. 'You suppressed the minorities and made enemies of them,' he shouted. 'I hold them in the palm of my hand. A word from me and they will annihilate you.'

This was distressing for Károlyi, with his long record of anti-militarist, anti-German liberalism. But to Kun and Szamuelly, who, with false passports, had slipped into Budapest on November 19th, the situation looked decidedly promising. Károlyi's bourgeois brand of democracy discredited, a Socialist party scared to take power, a people's revolt raging against the foreign jackals of the Allies and the class enemies who welcomed them – the omens were fair for a bold Bolshevik coup.

Of all the surgent or resurgent nationalisms which battened upon the twitching corpses of the Habsburg and Romanov Empires, the most bizarre and grotesquely ambitious was that of Poland. Partitioned since 1772 between Russia, Prussia and Austria, Poles had fought in the armies of all three Powers, each of whom had dangled a half-promise of independence when victory had been won. After the armistice the Polish National Committee in Paris, representing the most reactionary elements in a land whose huge estates had produced a breed of aristocrats at least as feudal as the Magyar magnates, vied with the ad hoc government of Josef Pilsudski in Warsaw for Allied recognition. Civil war between Pilsudski's Legionaries and Polish units from the western front under the leadership of General Haller (the National Committee's 'man') seemed imminent. Around Posen, German and Polish troops were fighting over the frontier.

The German army of occupation, joined by 100,000 soldiers slogging home from the Ukraine, lived off the ravaged country by methods of terrorism. They were said to be selling arms to 'Russian agents'. It was feared that these desperate freebooters would unite to take over Poland completely. 'Poland', warned the correspondent of the London *Times*, 'is a corridor by which Bolshevism may creep into the very heart of Europe.'

Only one man possessed the authority, the daring and the following to cope with this anarchy. Josef Pilsudski had spent his life in the struggle to liberate Poland from the tyranny of Russia. By 1912, after years of guerrilla activities and a period of exile in Siberia, he was the acknowledged chief of the ragtime Polish Legion, armed with reject rifles from the Austro-Hungarian Army. The Legion fought with the Central Powers against Russia, but Pilsudski disbanded them in 1917 when he realized the hollowness of German promises of independence. Arrested and imprisoned in the fortress of Magdeburg, he had become, by the time of his release in November 1918, a figure of heroic legend. He hastily formed a provisional government and, in a peremptory radio message, informed the Allies of the existence of 'an independent Polish state uniting all Polish territories'. The National Committee, headed by Roman Dmowski (an intimate of the late Tsar and a rabid anti-semite), put in a counter-claim as the true government of Poland. The French were ready to recognize it. The British, unwilling to provoke almost certain civil war, refused.

And so the preposterous figure of 58-year-old Jan Paderewski, the most spectacular virtuoso pianist of his time, society lion and amateur diplomat, entered the troubled scene. Paderewski's father, a landowner's steward, had been imprisoned for taking part in the Polish national revolt of 1867. Paderewski himself, slaving for up to sixteen hours a day to perfect his technique, and making his money and reputation outside Poland, had spread his country's fame but had certainly not suffered for its sake. During the war, on behalf of the National Committee, he went to America to conduct a strenuous personal propaganda campaign for Polish independence. After playing the piano at a soirée in the White House, he had deeply impressed President Wilson with an impassioned plea for Poland's right to 'moral and spiritual self-determination'. In the Presidential election of November 1916 he had helped to deliver the Polish-American vote, with the help of which Wilson scraped home for a second term. The thirteenth of Wilson's Fourteen Points required an independent Poland with access to the sea.

In December 1918 Paderewski resolved to return to his native land in triumph. In London, to the astonishment of his friend, Foreign Secretary Arthur Balfour, he demanded the use of a British warship. He was offered a special train, even an aeroplane, but insisted on a warship – in return for his services in patching up some kind of truce between Dmowski and Pilsudski. After a stormy crossing of the North Sea in H.M.S. *Concord* (during which he gamely played some Chopin on a tuneless piano in the officers' wardroom), Paderewski reached Posen. Here he got a warning of troubles to come. Germans and Poles were skirmishing in the streets, and a stray bullet smashed the window of his hotel room. Then came an exhausting whistle-stop train journey to Warsaw. There he was nearly involved in a plot, led by Prince Sapieha, to overthrow Pilsudski. When his shattered nerves had been somewhat restored by his tigerishly devoted wife, he reappeared to make a fantastic if occasionally epigrammatic press statement. Bolshevism, he said, was 'war on the toothbrush,' an insult to all decent, civilized values. Why didn't the Allies send officers to train, and material to equip, the Polish army in a crusade against Bolshevism? Such anti-semitic feeling as existed in Poland was, he explained, due to the bloodthirsty agitation of Jewish Bolsheviks. The Polish ruling classes had, according to him, been grossly misrepresented as a gang of merciless reactionaries, whereas in fact they had 'always been liberal and humane to the peasants'.

Pilsudski's dislike for this dilettante patriot was deepened by the contempt of a real aristocrat who had gone among the masses for an upstart near-peasant who gave himself airs and was identified with the well-born riff-raff who supported Dmowski. Paderewski was tormented by terse phone calls at all hours of the night summoning him to 'conferences' in the General's small, spartan office in the Belvedere Palace. Pilsudski smoked and played chess or patience while the terrified conciliator, convinced that he was on trial for his life, talked volubly. But he was not to be liquidated, only used. Pilsudski tolerated him because of his influence with Allied statesmen. He appointed him Prime Minister and Foreign Secretary, allowed him to make flowery speeches ('it behoves every loyal citizen that we should be considered as a people worthy of the liberty whose radiance now illuminates the land'), smiled grimly as

Paderewski tossed on the cross-currents of party politics, made him Poland's chief delegate at the Peace Conference, packed him off, a picture of chastened relief, to Paris, and continued his talks with General Denikin, Bolshevik envoys—and anyone from whom territorial or other advantages might be wrung.

6. Red Dawn or Dark Age?

The squalid deadlock of the European war was followed by a gallop of utopianism. 'Change everything,' wrote the Russian poet Alexander Blok, 'renew everything. Let the falseness, the filth and the weariness of our life disappear. Let it become free, just, pure and beautiful ... Anything less, more moderate, is rebellion, revolt, insubordination. Only this is revolution. Revolution is like a blizzard or typhoon. It can drown good men, can wash up the evil, but these are only details. The ambition of the Russian revolution is to envelop the whole world. A real revolution can have no lesser goal.'

In London a jubilant *Herald* greeted the hoisting of the red flag. 'It is actually flying in Petrograd, in Moscow, in Budapest ... Its shadow, brighter than the daylight, is over Berlin. Sooner or later, as the symbol of the awakened and united proletariats of the world, it will fly in every city. The democracies cannot be kept down, cannot be kept back. Their day is here.' In Holland the normally cautious Socialist leader Pieter Troelstra kicked over the evolutionary traces of a lifetime and called upon the Dutch workers to rise. They rose in a series of tumultuous strikes. For several days Rotterdam was virtually in their hands.

In Switzerland the Red Menace had a direct bearing on the choice of a venue for the Peace Conference. President Wilson favoured a nice, quiet Swiss town—Lausanne, perhaps, or Geneva. He over-looked the fact that in the Swiss village of Zimmerwald Lenin had first issued his call to turn the imperialist war into an international civil war; and that Zürich and Geneva had for long been the chief havens of exiled revolutionaries, world centres of subversion. When Swiss Social Democrats, led by Robert Grimm and Fritz Platten, staged mass rallies to celebrate the first anniversary of the Bolshevik revolution, and organized a one-day general strike 'against military and bourgeois dictatorship' that brought the major cities to a halt, the authorities—urged on perhaps by hoteliers and restaurateurs desperate not to lose the huge custom that the Peace Conference would bring—called out the army and struck hard. But too late.

President Wilson acknowledged his mistake and accused Switzerland of 'harbouring the most poisonous elements in Europe'. There was even talk of Allied intervention and blockade. For if quaint, picture-postcard Switzerland went Red, where would the rot end?

Tired of the long, hopeless haul of persuasion, bored with the sound of their own civilized voices, some members of the liberal-progressive intelligentsia hailed the joys of direct action and admired the audacity of the Bolsheviks. Bertrand Russell paused, in the midst of his scrupulous juggling of probabilities and rationalities, to admit that violent revolutions *might* be necessary and even salutary. 'If the Russian revolution had been accompanied by a revolution in Germany,' he surmised, 'the dramatic suddenness of the change might have shaken Europe out of its habits of thought ... If once the idea of fraternity between the nations were inaugurated with the faith and vigour belonging to a new revolution, all the difficulties surrounding it would melt away, for all of them are due to suspicion and the tyranny of ancient prejudice.'

Maxim Gorky wrote half-approvingly about the Bolsheviks, the Men he Hated to Love. 'Our children and grandchildren', he asserted, 'will wonder at their energy, surrounded as they are by an atmosphere of suffocating hostility ... I fight against them, but I defend those whose honesty and personal honour is known to me ... I know they are making a terrible experiment on the body of the Russian people, that they have made many and great mistakes. God also made a great mistake when he made us more foolish than we should have been.' As correspondent of the *Manchester Guardian*, Morgan Philips Price (the son of a wealthy English landowner, educated at Harrow, and Trinity College, Cambridge, former, Liberal candidate for Gloucester) became a fervent admirer of the Soviet spirit. The Russian people, he claimed in a pamphlet issued early in 1919, had dared with the courage of lions to face a world in arms against them and to cry aloud to all mankind across the frontiers of the censors: 'Oh, ye conventionalities and insincerities, ye crowns of Emperors and Kings, so-called democratic parliaments, hypocrisies of the Churches, respectable mediocrities, intriguing profiteers! Behold! Ye are one and all a Gigantic Lie! But our life, our wretchedness, our hunger, is not a lie. Therefore we call all nations of the earth to witness that in Russia at any rate ye shall be abolished and, naked and starving, isolated and spurned, pariahs though we are, we shall begin to work for realities ... for those new forms of society which alone can make life worth living ...'

Arthur Ransome (the future best-selling author of children's books), educated at Rugby and the son of a distinguished academic, expressed his delight at the vitality of Bolshevism in an article called *The Truth About Russia*. He did not claim that the Bolsheviks were angels. But he did ask that people should 'look through the fog of libel that surrounds them and see that the ideal for which they are struggling is among those lights which every man of young and honest heart sees before him somewhere on the road.' The Bolsheviks, he claimed, were writing a page of history 'more daring than any other which I remember in the story of the human race, writing it amid showers of mud from all the meaner spirits in their country and in America and Britain ... When in after years men read that page, they will judge your country and mine by the help or hindrance they gave to the making of it.'

The spectacle of the Bolsheviks, sparkling with ideas and ideals, working against a flood of ignorance and reaction caused an epidemic of conversion amongst journalists and missioners of various kinds. Major Raymond Robins, head of the American Red Cross Mission in Russia, had, when he showed signs of sympathy for the Reds, been hastily recalled. 'If I tell the truth,' he protested, 'and do not lie and slander folks, I am a Bolshevik! I am perfectly willing that the Russian people should have the kind of government they want whether it suits me or not. I would never expect to stamp out ideas with bayonets. The only answer to the desire for a better human life is—a better human life.' René Marchand, correspondent of the conservative *Figaro*, was highly critical of Allied intervention in Russia. The Soviet government, he maintained in a much-publicized 'Open Letter to President Poincaré', had raised itself, under the very pressure to which it was being subjected, 'to the level of a GOVERNMENT, a revolutionary government without a doubt, but no longer anarchically or helplessly so—*really* revolutionary in the classic, administrative sense'. Pierre Pascal and Jacques Sadoul, members of a French military mission sent to Russia in 1916, accused France and Britain of fomenting the anti-Bolshevik revolt of July 1918 with the deliberate intention of provoking a Red Terror that could be used to justify all-out intervention. For any person willing to help in the great work of construction, the Soviet regime, they claimed, offered careers thrillingly open to talent. Bolshevism, far from being the enemy of civilization, was the only hope for a higher moral order—'the springtime of a new world'.

The springtime of a new world. In no single book or pamphlet were the implications of this phrase so exuberantly and optimistically explored as in *Towards New Horizons*. Written by an English novelist and free-swinging feminist, Mary Patricia Willcocks, it was a compendium of progressive hopes and fallacies. Self-determination, insisted the author, must be interpreted in the widest sense, giving free discipline to the child and the open road to the prisoner, as well as autonomy to Poles, Irishmen and Hindus. It was, in fact, the latest unfolding of the spiritual element in mankind. 'Men are longing to dream together. It is an instinct like that which warns the birds of the coming of dawn even before the first beam of light has tipped the horizon ... From the Russian peasants to the organized workers of Berlin, Vienna, Lyons or Manchester, from the Clyde to the Black Sea, the voice of longing rises.' The brotherhood of the workers, which had seemed the most tragic, colossal casualty of the war, had, it now appeared, been immensely strengthened. 'Guards learn of their prisoners, prisoners of their guards, Austrian troops go over to the Russian armies, while our West country troops learn what Ireland thinks of them.' In this sense the war had been 'the Grand Tour of Labour—a process of wholesale internationalization'.

Liberalism was the real casualty, with its fear of radical change, its identification of 'civilization' with the habits of a few wealthy, cultured, vaguely guilt-ridden people. Socialism would 'tear down all the high garden walls'. The fact of the class war, of the longing for workers' control, could no longer be blinked. It was an act of divine retribution. For the people had been the first creators, had scratched the first symbols of community on cave walls, expressed the first feelings of religious awe. The capitalist industrial revolution had robbed the people of their dignity, made them slaves of the machine. But the workers were 'real', their latent vitality the one force capable of demolition and reconstruction.

As the battle of reconstruction opened, the stage army of progressives blazed away with a wealth of noisy, if blank, ammunition. 'Labour politics', announced the *New Statesman* (chillingly described by its originators, the Webbs, as the organ of conservative collectivism), 'has but one passion—to make the world a better place

for those who inhabit it ... The world of mean streets and mean
ideals in which we live is no less intolerable as a permanent home for
human beings than the charnel-house world of the trenches ...
Labour seeks a world in which every citizen shall be able to attain
to his full moral, mental and spiritual development.' It might seem
a ludicrous thing to some people to suggest the possibility of a social
system 'in which one might find oneself sitting beside one's cook or
one's dustman in a stall at Covent Garden during a performance of
Tristan.' Yet the cultural ghettoes had to be destroyed, the boundaries
of civilization expanded. It was not proposed to compel anyone 'to
go and see Shakespeare who had rather go to a horse race, or to
force him to travel to Italy if he had rather sit on the Palace Pier at
Brighton.' But it was scandalous to shy away from the idea of a
world in which the *choice* was there for everyone.

The Bolsheviks' manful onslaught on illiteracy and religious
superstition magnified the itch for action. Long before 1917 they had
studied the full range of advanced educational theory. Krupskaya
and Lenin had drafted a programme designed to break down over-
specialization in schools. It envisaged 'free, compulsory and polytechnical education for all children of either sex up to the age of
sixteen.' Instruction was to be 'closely linked with socially productive
labour.' Visits to factories and farms were to supplement classroom
theory. The immediate aim was to ensure at least a nucleus of
skilled industrial workers, but formal education was accompanied by
literacy and basic knowledge drives in villages, factories, the army,
theatres, newspapers and museums. Members of the Communist
Party were told that they had a special responsibility to broaden and
deepen their culture. Divorce had been made swift and accessible
to all, the stigma of illegitimacy removed, the assumption of male
superiority ridiculed. No hindrance to the full mobilization of
human resources was tolerated. Alexandra Kollontai, Commissar
for Social Welfare, longed for the day when communism would
revitalize human relationships and sweep away the 'selfish, morally
diseased wreck' which capitalism called 'the family', when the
'collective woman', capable of feeling affection for any child, would
crown the socialist creation.

Conventional notions of marriage, the family and education were
under a barrage of criticism. Dr Maria Montessori condemned the
classroom Massacre of the Innocents and urged parents and teachers
not to force upon young children a knowledge of the shabby

compromises of a society rotten with fear. Her insistence on the liberation of the child was matched by the demand of a new-style feminism—most eloquently voiced by Dr Marie Stopes—for sexual equality. 'Often and often,' lamented Bertrand Russell, 'marriage hardly differs from prostitution except by being harder to escape from.' In America the flamboyant Russian-Jewish anarchist Emma Goldman, in England Sylvia Pankhurst, preached that true comradeship between the sexes could only come as the result of a communist revolution in morals. Love, they insisted, must be free, the marriage bond must be broken. Some enthusiasts fancied that proletarian emancipators would brush aside bourgeois inhibitions like so many cobwebs. 'The working man', asserted Miss Willcocks, 'is in the procession of life ... In sex questions the rule of a class that is not too fine for nature will work a revolution beneficent and vital.'

A similar belief in the vitality of a new proletarian culture inflamed Bolshevik intellectuals. The dramatization of the revolution enabled those who for long had rebelled against the insipidity of bourgeois art to give official vent to a buccaneering futurism—in which machines were more significant than meadows, the surge of collectivism than pallid lovers' idylls, the smoke and grime of great cities (hosts to the machine, spawners of the proletariat) than the unsullied air of the countryside. Bolsheviks and Bohemians did, for a few years, despite Lenin's misgivings, combine in what seemed to be a common assault on Philistinism.

In Moscow and Petrograd Expressionist and Futurist painters decorated whole streets and squares for revolutionary anniversaries and labour celebrations. Red arrows chased white blobs across acres of canvas. Squares and rhomboids clashed in bleak combat on the boarded façades of bourgeois mansions. Triangular-eyed faces appeared everywhere. Lorries draped with abstract allegories throbbed in the streets. The bewildered masses were treated to an avant-garde orgy. Peasants crossed themselves before the unholy creations and muttered: 'They want us to worship the devil!' Those who could read scratched their heads as they spelt out militant decrees signed by the poet Vladimir Mayakovsky and his Committee of Futurists. 'Henceforth, together with the destruction of the Tsarist regime, the imprisonment of art in those lumber rooms of human genius—viz. palaces, picture galleries, salons, libraries and theatres—is hereby abolished ... You find a White Guard—against the wall with him! But have you forgotten Raphael? It is time for bullets to spatter museum walls. Shoot down the past! Why is Pushkin not yet under fire?'

Mayakovsky supervised the staging of factory-siren symphonies. Literature trains, vivid with revolutionary scenes and symbols, went to the villages and the fronts. Troupes of actors trained by Stanislavsky and Meyerhold took plays (sizzling with the excitement of writers who suddenly found the world their audience) conceived in the simple heaven-and-hell terms of medieval mysteries, to convert the peasants.

Soviet Russia was full of echoes from the classic land of Futurism, Italy, where arch-iconoclast Filipo Marinetti had declared total war on the past. 'Poets, painters, sculptors and musicians,' he had exhorted, 'you must fight against inertia and slumber. The world needs only heroism. Hurry to remake everything. Write over the doors of academies, museums, libraries and universities—TO THE EARTHQUAKE, THEIR ONLY ALLY, THE FUTURISTS DEDICATE THE RUINS OF ROME AND ATHENS!' Marinetti had welcomed the war as 'a box of dynamite for all the venerated ruins.' In 1918 he refurbished and re-trumpeted his manifestoes, adding the proposal that the government should sell the art treasures of Italy lock, stock and barrel in order to finance a large army and merchant navy, speed industrialization, clean up malarial zones, liquidate illiteracy, and abolish taxes for twenty years. This, he said, would 'prove to the world that we are a people sure of its own future.' It would be a 'highly patriotic deed by which Italy, bursting traditional and sentimental chains,' would 'transform her paintings, textiles and marbles into useful, swift and lordly steel.'

Benito Mussolini had, since his break with the Social Democrats in 1914, kept pace with Marinetti in the violence of his public utterances. He flayed the ritual pacifism of his former colleagues. He hailed the war, which would, in his opinion, create a tough proletariat of the trenches ready, when the national foe had been defeated, to purge Italy of cowardice in all its forms. 'Everything from the act of thought to that of accomplishing the slightest action', said Mussolini, 'is struggle and war against something or somebody … If ever the era of a perfectly pacific and idiotic paradise should begin, I wish the ludicrous apostles of a universal camaraderie to know whom they should assassinate … It is *blood* that gives motion to the clanging wheels of history.' With insolent logic he had argued that since all the workers of Europe had gone to war, 'the principle of international solidarity demands that the Italian proletariat shall do likewise.' As for Parliament, he was convinced that 'for the welfare of Italy a dozen or so deputies should be shot in the back. The Italian Parliament is the noxious boil which poisons the blood of the nation.'

Gabriele d'Annunzio, too, demanded that the nation should remain under arms to clear out dirty, treacherous politicians and make sure that Italy was not cheated of her rightful spoils at the Peace Conference. Italy, he said, had fought *with* the Allies, but she had not fought *for* them, and especially not for the aims of the ghastly President Wilson — whom d'Annunzio, in a widely relished *mot*, characterized as 'full of false words and false teeth.'

The reactions of the self-styled defenders of civilization could be as extravagant as anything which the exploding underworld could devise. Tisza was ready to topple the pillars of society and bury everyone, rebel and divine-righter alike, in the ruins. Baron Roman von Ungen-Sternberg, a German Balt aristocrat and ex-Tsarist officer, found in the mad swirl of counter-revolution the perfect outlet for his psychopathic personality. Pale and effeminate in appearance, with ash-blond hair and a reddish moustache, he operated from Mongolia with a force composed of White Russian officers, Mongolian bandits, Chinese troops and Japanese secret-service agents. He married a Mongolian princess, dressed himself in robes of yellow silk, and announced that he was a reincarnation of Jenghiz Khan. He was acknowledged as the counter-revolution's supreme artist in atrocity, not merely torturing, mutilating and massacring Jews and peasants, but leading his horsemen in gruesome nocturnal terror rides, when human torches were dragged along at full gallop. He was, he said, the implacable foe of 'decadent democracy and Jew communism'. He would, he promised, 'make an avenue of gallows that will stretch from Asia across Europe'.

By the end of 1918, largely due to the efforts of Russian émigrés, anti-semitism and anti-Bolshevism were inseparably linked. Newspapers in Europe and America had already spread the idea that the Bolshevik revolution was fundamentally a Jewish plot financed from Germany. This was now amplified with the whole range of anti-semitic literature that had flourished in Romanov Russia. The

Jews were represented as omnipotent in evil. They had, by their usury, corrupted a golden age of idyllic feudalism, had engineered the French Revolution and the revolts of 1848, had been 'behind' Mazzini and Garibaldi and the Paris Commune of 1871, had caused the 1914-18 war through the machinations of Jewish financiers in London, Paris and Berlin, and had instigated the Russian revolutions of 1905 and 1917. The *Protocols of the Elders of Zion*, manufactured in Paris during the Dreyfus Affair at the bidding of the Okhrana (the Tsarist secret police), purported to be an account of the Jewish world conspiracy as expounded at a meeting of the Jewish 'secret government', the elders of Zion. Copies of this document were sent to newspapers and circulated among delegates to the Peace Conference—a manoeuvre which may not have been without effect in the hectic atmosphere of early 1919. If what was happening in Russia was the culmination of a centuries-old Jewish plot to smash Christendom, intervention could be seen as a Christian duty, a genuine crusade.

Just as wild as these anti-semitic fantasies, but even more effective, was the fable that Bolshevism planned to 'nationalize' women and make free love compulsory (a contradiction in terms which came easily to journalists who habitually treated the terms 'anarchist', 'communist', 'Bolshevik' and 'socialist' as interchangeable). This juicy story, which persisted, with endless elaborations, throughout 1919, was based on two sources, one dubious and both misinterpreted. The first was an article in the local *Izvestia*, or news-sheet, of a soviet at Khvalinsk. Signed 'Feodorova', it outlined a (quite possibly facetious) scheme whereby: (i) every woman above the age of 18 should be declared the property of the state; (ii) every woman over 18 and unmarried should be obliged to register at a Bureau of Free Love attached to the Commissariat of Social Welfare; (iii) women so registered should have the right to select a 'husband' from male citizens aged from 19 to 50 (the consent of the man—or of his wife if he had one—not to be essential); (iv) the Bureau of Free Love should keep a list of Men Free For Selection; (v) men too should have the right to select a 'wife'; (vi) selection should not take place more than once a month; (vii) any children born of such liaisons should become state property. In conclusion, Feodorova piously urged the local authorities to put this scheme into operation as soon as possible in order to abolish 'the age-long evils of prostitution and vice.' Her article, featured by an anti-Bolshevik paper in Moscow in April 1918, was picked up six months later by the scholarly but rampantly anti-Bolshevik London journal, *New Europe*, which omitted the last sentence, claimed that it was a decree 'published in the official Soviet organ, *Izvestia*', and added that 'it would be superfluous to comment on this and similar attempts to substitute prostitution for marriage.'

The second source was a decree said to have been promulgated by the Free Association of Anarchists in Saratov. This document, which (the anarchists protested) must have been invented by their enemies to discredit them, since it violated the most elementary libertarian principles, in fact appeared in the town of Samara, near Saratov. It proposed to 'end the bourgeois monopoly of beautiful women' by communalizing all females between the ages of 17 and 32, except those with five children. Male citizens were to have the right to 'use one woman not oftener than three times a week for three hours.' Each man wishing to use 'a piece of public property' would have to show a certificate proving that he was of working-class status. Non-proletarian males who wanted to enjoy equal rights would have to pay a monthly fee into public funds. 'Former owners' would have the right to use their wives without waiting their turn. Women would be paid an adequate monthly allowance and released from 'state duties' for four months during and just after pregnancy. Children would belong to the state.

These two 'decrees' were mentioned during the I.W.W. trial in Chicago, used to discredit Labour ('Bolshevik') candidates during the British general election of 1918, and luridly deployed in a pamphlet—possibly the work of Christabel Pankhurst—entitled *A Warning to British Women*. 'We must', it said, 'barricade our national doors against this Bolshevism (that is, Anarchy) as we should barricade our house-doors if a savage tiger was prowling round the garden. There are many worse things than death itself, and Bolshevism practises every note of the Scale of Horror.' Excerpts from the Saratov Decree, and from the *Protocols of the Elders of Zion*, were distributed among the White Russian armies, and among Allied expeditionary forces and military missions in Russia.

Compared with the inventions of the anti-semites (Robert Wilton, the *Times* correspondent in Russia, alleged that a statue of the Jewish 'hero' Judas Iscariot had been erected in Moscow) and the 'revelations' of the Saratov Decree, the less titillating laments of academic exiles and of libertarian Socialists caught beneath what

Trotsky called 'the broad and glittering blade of the revolution' had
little impact. In an Open Letter to the Bolshevik Central Committee,
written in November 1918, Spiridonova accused the Bolsheviks of
betraying the proletariat, substituting state capitalism for the
socialization of industry, and perpetuating a system of terror. 'A
time will come', she predicted, 'when a protest will arise within
your party itself against a policy which stifles the spirit of the
revolution. There will be a cleansing, an upward swing will take
place. You can only eliminate me and my party from the revolution
by killing us. We have no home except in the Socialist revolution.
We are slandered and persecuted like the Jews. But just as the future
of humanity ripens in the souls of the Jews, so does the renewal of
socialism ripen in our movement.' Moving, magnificent stuff. But
hardly comparable, for news and smear value, with Feodorova's
Bureau of Free Love.

Even among those who followed the course of the Bolshevik
revolution with critical attention, the denunciations of Spiridonova
and her like were discounted. After all, there *was* a civil war on. The
Allies *were* virtually invading Russia. This was no time for libertarian
scruples. And the Bolsheviks were, for the most part, spitting on the
right plates, eliminating, on the whole, people who richly deserved
elimination. Bill Haywood announced, after due deliberation, that
the Bolshevik revolution was 'the I.W.W. all feathered out.'

'Brothers,' wrote the Russian poet Osip Mandelstam, sorrowfully
acknowledging the sombre yet heroic necessity of the Soviet ordeal,
'let's try. A vast, clumsy and creaking turn of the helm. The earth
is afloat. Cleaving the ocean as with a plough, we shall remember
even in Lethe's cold that for us the earth has been worth a dozen
heavens.'

7. Bulwarks of Civilization

Other voices, cooler, mocking, precious, began to make themselves heard in the great post-war babel. Arch-aesthete Ronald Firbank returned to London after spending the four years of the Great Emergency ('that awful persecution') in Oxford. In his novel *Valmouth*, published in 1919, he imagined a Bolshevik Member of Parliament, Sir William West-Wind, circulating elegantly among the erotomaniacal exotics of a strange, utterly apolitical constituency. Logan Pearsall Smith set the tone of the 'twenties in his witty, quasi-philosophical *Trivia*. 'They sit for ever around the horizon of my mind,' he wrote, 'that Stonehenge circle of disapproving elderly faces ... Faces of the Uncles, the Schoolmasters, and the Tutors who frowned on my youth ... In the bright centre and sunlight I leap, I caper, I dance my dance; but when I look up they are not deceived. For nothing ever placates them, nothing ever moves to a look of approval that ring of bleak, old, contemptuous faces.'

The war, in the opinion of ex-artillery officer Percy Wyndham Lewis, Britain's prime Futurist, had been 'a giant with the brain of a midge'. Its epic proportions were grotesquely out of scale, since it meant nothing and had settled nothing. Couldn't it be allowed to sink out of sight like the anonymous horror that it was? Must there be more bleatings about Allied Unity, more claptrap about Gallant Belgium and Bestial Huns? Did one have to endure the self-righteous charade of what d'Annunzio called the Obscene Old Men of Versailles?

Despite the sneers of the smart set, the hostility of the press and the venom of Tory and Liberal diehards, the Khaki Election of December 1918 — the first in Britain for eight years — was a personal triumph, and virtually a personal plebiscite, for Lloyd George. There was no real alternative to him. As Minister of Munitions and chief wartime labour conciliator he had gained an unrivalled knowledge of the industrial scene and an almost mesmeric control over official trade unionism. He had developed a technique for bullying or circumventing generals, admirals and permanent civil servants. He showed as much contempt as any syndicalist for the traditions of parliamentary democracy (Sidney Webb complained that his brand of Direct Action in Parliament was encouraging Direct Action in industry). He was, in fact, a dynamic modernizer whom Lenin recognized as a peer and held up to his own left rebels as a model of political realism and efficiency. With his flowing white locks, cocky, leg-braced stance and air of quivering vitality, he looked the part he loved to play—Man of the People, Man of Destiny—and managed to make even the compulsory undertaker's uniform of the statesman seem like a suit of working clothes. His six months at the Peace Conference were, he later admitted, the happiest of his life.

President Wilson too had had his share of criticism. His decision to attend the conference as chief American representative had been heavily opposed. He would be more detached, and therefore more effective, argued his critics, if he stayed in Washington. No other American President had broken this rule. He would be the only head of state among the Big Four. But Wilson was set on going. He informed a sullen, silent Congress that he conceived it his duty personally to 'complete the good work so many American boys have given their lives for and to redeem America's pledge to mankind'. Lenin had told an interviewer that it was not a question of Russia, he spat on Russia—whose revolution was merely the opening gambit in the communist salvation of the world. To some Americans it seemed that Wilson, the Hope of Mankind, came perilously close to this mentality. Yet his main contribution to the idea of a League of Nations was a determination that he alone should bring it to birth. Frenchmen, Englishmen, Italians, and finally the busy, bogus colonel (House had been given his 'rank' by a Governor of Texas, grateful for his services as a political fixer), had shaped it. Wilson stole it and held it aloft like a personal grail.

The spectacle of America stifling basic civil liberty, let alone New Freedoms, may have stiffened Wilson's resolve to return from Europe as a global saviour and, with that undeniable advantage, set the nation to rights. He had predicted that entry into the war would unleash an assault on anything that was faintly radical and progressive. His prediction had been amply fulfilled. Press censorship was stringent. Thousands of men who had escaped the first draft were, in

September 1918, briskly rounded up. Alleged 'slackers' were seized on sidewalks, dragged out of street cars, milk wagons and lorries, bundled into vans, driven to barracks, and later, if they were lucky, released without apology. Four Russian immigrants were given sentences totalling 285 years for distributing pamphlets against intervention in Russia. One man was sent to the workhouse for six months for saying that he preferred the Kaiser to Wilson. Similar sentences were imposed on three people for singing 'The Watch on the Rhine' on their way back from a saloon in the early hours of the morning. Eugene Debs had been jailed for ten years, yet, as the *Nation* pointed out, Karl Liebknecht had only been imprisoned for four on a charge of high treason – in 'tyrannous' Germany.

Clemenceau awaited the coming of the Archangel Wilson with exasperation mitigated by a certainty that his moral pretensions would soon be cut to ribbons. Wilsonian cant made his hackles rise. His premiership of 1906–9 had been marked by a savage onslaught on the syndicalist unions. France, he had declared, was founded on 'property, property, and more property'. Premier again since November 1917, his ruthless methods of shoring up French morale had made him more hated and feared in France than in Germany. A solitary and ill-tempered old man, his only confidants were his Jewish private secretary Georges Mandel and his valet Albert, and even they lived in terror of his rages. Compared with Wilson and Lloyd George, his intellectual range was wide. It was not simply that he spoke English, whereas neither of them had another language (unless one counted Lloyd George's Welsh). As a drama critic Clemenceau had been among the first to appreciate and promote Ibsen. As a political journalist his vitality, ferocity and influence had been unrivalled. He was an intimate friend of Claude Monet and other Impressionist painters. He had commissioned Toulouse-Lautrec to illustrate one of his books and Fauré to write music for one of his plays. 'Only the artists are on the right path,' he was fond of saying. 'It may be that they can give this world some beauty, but to give it reason is impossible.'

Perhaps the most remarkable thing about the Big Three was that each, in the name of unity, had established, and hoped to prolong, a personal near-dictatorship. The ideological gap which, on paper, yawned between the Bolsheviks in Moscow and the democrats in

Paris was narrower than it seemed. Wilson, Lloyd George and Clemenceau temporarily escaped the prevailing distrust of 'dirty' politicians because none of them was 'really' a politician. One was a Saviour, one a convention-breaking buccaneer, one a national institution, the very personification of *revanche*. They had assumed (for the good of the people) powers of which no ordinary politician would have dared to dream. Bernard Shaw claimed, only half-facetiously, that if Bolshevism meant facing the fact that 'the masses are governable only by a mixture of cajolery and coercion dressed up in fine phrases and applied by an energetic minority (which knows what it wants and means to have it) ... we are all Bolsheviks now. Three cheers for Bolshevism!'

The Big Three, dictators at heart and as far as they dared in practice, were themselves outmatched by a Quaker engineer who was probably the most powerful single figure to emerge in the first desperate months of the Armistice. Herbert Hoover's life had been an awesome, uninterrupted escalation of success. There seemed little reason to doubt that, with a little co-operation, he could have run the world like a vast supermarket. A technocrat of technocrats, his sober Christian faith was welded to a fundamentalist belief in the virtues of the American way of life. Born in Iowa, his father a blacksmith, his mother much moved by the Spirit in meetings, he had been reared in an atmosphere of archaic speech, Quaker-grey clothes and distrust of worldly pleasure. As an office boy in the Oregon Land Company he decided that he wanted to be a mining engineer. By 1914 his own company had branches in San Francisco, New York, London, Melbourne, Shanghai and St Petersburg, and Hoover was internationally in demand as an efficiency expert. At Broken Hill in New South Wales he had invented a method of extracting zinc from slag-heaps of lead and silver. At Kyshtim on the western slopes of the Urals he had reorganized copper and iron mines. In Turkestan he had constructed railways and smelters. In seventeen years of purposeful roaming he had become rich in diplomatic experience as well as money, negotiating with the Tsarist bureaucracy, juggling spheres of influence in China, calming imperial sensibilities in Africa, coping with evanescent regimes in Central America.

During the war Hoover had turned himself into an engineer of survival. The Belgian Relief Commission, created by him, was the largest single enterprise ever undertaken by a private citizen or organization. Its budget reached 25 million dollars a month. It fed ten million people and provided mid-day meals for 2,300,000 children. By 1918 Belgium was easily the best-fed nation in Europe. This achievement had been made possible by dogged negotiation. Even at the height of the U-boat campaign Hoover's food ships were allowed through. His Commission became virtually a separate Power, issuing its own passports, flying its own flag, enjoying diplomatic privileges, briefing its own envoys.

By 1917, as head of the United States Food Administration (U.S.F.A.), Hoover was responsible for feeding not only the American Expeditionary Force in France, but, to an increasing extent, France herself, Britain, Italy and the neutral countries. With a total clientele of more than 200 million people he was the Food Dictator of Europe. His power, and his problems, increased when at the end of 1918 President Wilson assigned him to deal with all questions of provisioning under the armistice agreement. At his headquarters in Paris Hoover checked out his colossal task. It would not now be such a straightforward piece of social engineering. The U.S.F.A. was in the front line of the fight against Bolshevism. No need for guns, no need for violence. A plain Quaker *argumentum ad abdomen* would do the trick if, as Hoover suspected, Bolshevism was primarily a symptom of starvation. At his suggestion a Supreme Economic Council, on which all the Powers were represented, was set up early in January 1919. Fat-starved Europe – and American farmers who at his command had reared pork on an unprecedented scale – looked to him as to a god.

But for the moment it was not Hoover with his pork but Wilson with his talk who hogged the European limelight. He was the fairy godfather from over the seas and far away who had promised that, if people would be good and kind and do as he told them, the result would be not merely a peace treaty but Peace Eternal – and ever more blissful and loving and prosperous. No need, on the fraternal stroll to a New World, to wade through the bloody rivers of class war – as Lenin, the sado-utopian of Moscow, required. Only relax, get together, remember the Golden Rule, and trust in America (or Wilson).

On December 13th, 1918, in the chilly, narrow streets of Brest, behind the lines of spectators in Breton costume, the walls had words: LE PRESIDENT WILSON A BIEN MÉRITÉ DE L'HUMANITÉ.

Along the railway track to Paris peasants knelt in prayer for the success of his mission. In Paris the heavy chains under the Arc de Triomphe had been unhooked for the first time since 1871 to allow the two Presidents, Wilson and Poincaré, to drive through, preceded by the clattering, brass-helmeted horsemen of the Garde Républicaine. WILSON LE JUSTE, said the posters. Some of the two-million-strong crowd had swarmed into the trees bordering the Champs Elysées. People hurled flowers into the open carriage.

In London on December 26th the Wilsons were driven to Buckingham Palace in the royal carriage. Banquets at the Guildhall and Mansion House were followed by a sentimental dart north to Carlisle to attend Sunday morning service in the town where the President's mother had been born, in the church where his grandfather had worshipped. Next came a speech in the Free Trade Hall, Manchester, the Mecca of Liberalism. THE INDUSTRIAL CAPITAL OF ENGLAND, ogled a banner slung along the side of the Royal Exchange, HAS A WARM CORNER IN ITS HEART FOR YOU.

Liberal and radical journalists piled praise and exhortation on their champion. E. D. Morel, founder of the Union of Democratic Control, expected him to slay the dragon of Secret Diplomacy and make sure that the Peace Conference would witness 'the last spasm of a perverted statecraft'. The London *Nation* hoped that Wilson, by opposing a vengeful peace, would stand between Europe and Revolution. 'You alone, Mr President,' said Romain Rolland in an open letter, 'among all those charged with the doubtful honour of directing the policies of the nations, enjoy a universal moral authority ... Heir of Washington and Lincoln, take up the cause not of a party or a people but of all! Call the representatives of the peoples to a Congress of Humanity! The world hungers for a voice over-passing the frontiers of nations and of classes. May the future salute you with the name of Reconciler!'

Noble sentiments, great expectations: and as Wilson, nightly on his knees before his Maker, realized, great temptations to a pride that might well go before a mighty fall. There had, in any case, been disturbing as well as uplifting omens and incidents. At Brest the authorities had prevented working-class delegations from meeting him. In Paris the police had headed off a large procession of trade unionists which he had been expecting to harangue from the balcony of the Hôtel de Murat. The French government, he complained, was getting between him and the French people. It had been the same in Rome, where police dispersed cheering crowds before he could address them. In Milan his Presbyterian conscience had been outraged when he was manoeuvred into attending a performance of *Aïda* at La Scala on a Sunday. In London, during a meal at 10 Downing Street, Mrs Wilson had been shocked by the behaviour of Margot Asquith, the wife of the former Prime Minister. Not only had she smoked incessantly (striking matches on the seat of her dress), but announced, with flippant insolence, that she was dying to meet the President because she had never yet met an American with brains.

Margot Asquith was no doubt — confronted with the Worth-gowned, orchided, hyper-bourgeois Mrs Wilson — being deliberately provocative. For more than a year 150 highly intelligent Americans (the team of the Inquiry, under the general supervision of Colonel House) had been beavering away in the premises of the Geographical Society in New York. They had collected and collated a mountain of data bearing, so it seemed, upon every conceivable problem which might have to be solved by the Peace Conference. French experts, though discouraged by Clemenceau's notoriously low view of their opinions, had also gathered a formidable background dossier. The Foreign Office in London had prepared a series of Peace Handbooks, each written by an authority, covering a vast field and drawing elaborate parallels between the Vienna Congress of 1815 and the Paris Peace Conference of 1919. Lloyd George was as certain as Clemenceau that the whirlwind of events would soon wreck the paper castles and the meticulous timetables. What significant parallel could there be between 1815 and 1919 except that between those two crankily idealistic bores, Tsar Alexander and Woodrow Wilson? Even that was doubtful, since the Tsar had been a thoroughgoing autocrat able to put force behind his fantasies. In 1815 the Allies had controlled most of Europe and were represented by a group of powerful aristocrats in complete agreement about their aims. In 1919, as Churchill put it, there was 'a turbulent collision of embarrassed demagogues' harassed by the need to placate party and public opinion.

Even Wilson, who had almost pleaded with the Inquirers for guidance ('Tell me what's right to do, and I'll fight for it'), was forced to forget their beautifully ordered documents: forced not only by sheer lack of time but by his basic, if subconscious, decision to make concessions to the world in the treaties if only the League could be saved – to revise the treaties. Lloyd George reported to the War Cabinet his impression that the League was the only thing that Wilson really cared about. The Cabinet decided to make it the first item on the conference's agenda, since 'this would ease other matters, such as the question of the freedom of the seas, disposition of German colonies, economic issues, etc.'

The President hoped to find in Europe new scope for his New Freedoms, so elegantly outlined by the *New Republic*, of whose principles and projects the Inquiry was hardly more than an interminable elaboration. The *New Republic*, founded in 1914 and graced by Walter Lippmann (then just graduated from Harvard), dispensed the smooth cream of American progressivism. It was, said Lippmann, 'socialistic in direction' but broadly humanist, balancing theory and practice, noble dream and hard reality. Its aim was to 'raise little insurrections in the realm of human convictions'. It swung like an aloof crane above the sweating, confused masses. It was said to be so much the mouthpiece of Wilson and House (or was it the other way around?) that speculators tried to bribe the printers for advance proofs in order to play the market effectively. Wilson draped some rhetorical flesh and blood on the dry bones of New Republicanism. But even his most demagogic appeals were conditioned by a Lippmannesque distaste for violent change. Faced with a choice between revolutionary left and counter-revolutionary right, Wilson (in the belief that reaction was a *stage* on the way to liberal democracy, whereas Bolshevism had passed beyond redemption) always chose the latter. He was inexorably drawn to the defence of the kind of people who (like the Hungarian grandees) were willing to ditch their monarchs but hated bourgeois democracy as fiercely as any communist.

To John Reed, also a graduate of Harvard, New Republicanism stank of bourgeois condescension. He wrote for *The Masses* which, under the editorship of Max Eastman, had set out to flay rather than redeem the philistines. Romantic rebellion, a pathetic fallacy to the *New Republic*, was its lifeblood. 'We don't ever intend to conciliate our readers,' warned Reed. 'The broad purpose is to everlastingly attack old systems, old morals, old prejudices, the whole weight of outworn thought that dead men have saddled us with.' When he had dragged a reluctant Lippmann to the scene of an I.W.W.-run strike

in Paterson, New Jersey, Lippmann had remained a spectator. Reed
got involved and went to jail. For him the contest between Labour
and Capital was a simple confrontation of Good and Evil. His
experiences as a war correspondent in Europe had intensified this
belief. He only hoped that 'the people' would see through the
sickening fraud of it and rise against their exploiters. Lippmann's
plans to democratize industry and enlighten imperialism, his
obvious fear of revolution, exasperated Reed. Lippmann, on his part,
made fun of Reed's notion that 'the working class is not composed
of miners, plumbers and working men generally, but is a fine,
statuesque giant who stands on a high hill facing the sun.' In Russia,
in the fabulous days of the October revolution, Reed had fallen in
love with Bolshevism. Here was the great, boiling chaos which the
New Republic so loathed, but which he saw as the very stuff and
precondition of a new creation. While Lippmann laboured, un-
molested and omniscient, on House's Inquiry, Reed made rabble-
rousing speeches in the streets. 'I consider the Soviet government a
more democratic government than ours,' he told a Brooklyn
audience (and a hundred watchful policemen) late in 1918. 'The war
is finished, comrades, and where in hell is democracy? The government pretended it was a war between two ideas, democracy and
autocracy. It was just a war between two sets of capitalists. But a new
war is beginning, and this time it *is* a war between two ideas.'

Everywhere at the end of 1918 the romantic revolutionaries were on
the march. The end of a war of imperialisms intersected, thrillingly,
with the start of that era (or aura) of universal civil war in which we
still live. A handful of beggarly Bolshevik intellectuals with nothing
to lose and a world to gain had grabbed the initiative. It was this,
perhaps, which made Alexander Blok, in a famous poem, imagine
that he saw the shape of Christ the Lord at the head of a weary,
tattered, blaspheming patrol of Red Guards. It was this that gave the
lie to Spiridonova's charge that the Bolsheviks had distorted the
spirit of her noble liberators. They had (with the help of White
generals and Allied blockade and intervention) filled several hundred
thousand committed communists with something closely resembling
that spirit. They had forged an idealist-terrorist society which
bothered and frightened western pluto-democracy just as the tiny,
apathy-shaming band of Social Revolutionary terrorists had bothered
and frightened the Tsarist regime. Individually and collectively the

Big Four in Paris — Britain, France, Italy and America — spent more time on the Bolshevik Question than on any other single issue. In various forms, in various crises, they repeated the anxious query of King George V: '*What* should we do about Russia?'

II

THE FOUR MAD MONTHS

---

1. *The Rape of Riga*

A sharp warning of the impact of Bolshevism on bourgeois civilization came in the early days of the New Year, when the Red Army marched into Riga, the capital of Latvia. In 1917 socialist revolutions in the Baltic States had been crushed by German armies. Socialists had been forced into exile. Puppet regimes had been set up ready for a final absorption of the Baltic States into the German Reich. After the armistice 'democratic' governments had been hastily elected, and immediately opened negotiations with Britain, and with the remnants of the German armies under the leadership of General Rüdiger von der Goltz, for their defence against Bolshevism. The Soviet government had stated its intention of reclaiming the Baltic States. 'The end of the German occupation', wrote Lenin in *Pravda*, 'places before Soviet Russia the task of liberating the Baltic territories ... Soviet Russia must gain access to the Baltic coast and replant the Red Flag of the Proletarian Revolution ... Soviet troops must occupy Lithuania, Latvia and Estonia. The Baltic must be a Soviet sea.'

Von der Goltz, who had his own plans for re-establishing German control in the area, played a waiting game. Into the vacuum of power rushed the Red Army, a hastily assembled multi-national force only about 10,000 strong, composed of Latvian infantry, Bashkir, Kirghiz and Kalmuck cavalry, and a motley unit of Bolshevized German, Austrian, Polish and Czech ex-prisoners-of-war. The ancient Hanseatic town of Riga, a European conclave essentially German in culture and sentiment, was a juicy target for proletarian spite. Its merchants (inventors of Kümmel liqueur and aromatic bitters) were noted for their gourmandizing. Plump salmon from the River Dvina, in vast quantities, formed their staple diet, washed down with copious draughts of Rhenish or Madeira wines. As the

Red Army approached they rushed for places on the few over-crowded ships fleeing south to Lithuania and the protection of von der Goltz. The risk of wreck in the ice and minefields of the Baltic seemed preferable to the certainty of the vengeance which sat on the saddles of the much-feared Tartar horsemen.

On January 3rd, 1919, the Red Army appeared in the streets, terrifying in its very dirtiness and raggedness (rifle slings made of pieces of string, greasy red banners with unintelligible inscriptions, a military band whose instruments, musicians and music produced an impression of almost incredible dilapidation and cacophony). The sight of a detachment of women soldiers, rumours of whose more-than-male ruthlessness had flown ahead of them, struck a special chill to bourgeois hearts. Were not these Bolshevik gunwomen said to be recruited mainly from the ranks of strumpets and ungrateful domestic servants? Did they not symbolize the Bolshevik assault on those precious decencies which were the heritage of centuries of Christian civilization? Proclamations in Lettish, Russian and German, posted up at the street corners, were gloatingly explicit about the shape of things to come, hyper-optimistic (but in the absence of other information, how could this be known?) about the prospects of world revolution.

'We shall begin without delay', they said, 'to construct in Latvia a new Socialist Proletarian State. We shall exterminate the social traitors of this as of other countries. Behind us stands the Russian Soviet State, with which we shall henceforth remain intimately united. Behind us too stands the Communist Revolution, which soon will change not only Germany but the rest of Europe into a Federation of Soviet Socialist Republics, of which we shall be a constituent part. From the Rhine to Vladivostock, from the Black Sea to Archangel, the great civil war rages. Soon it will smash down the ramparts raised by victory-drunk Imperialism. In France, in England, in Italy the first mutterings of the Proletarian Revolution are already heard ... To Arms! Long Live the Soviet Government of Latvia! Long Live the World Revolution!'

Peter Stutchka, the head of the new Soviet regime, came of a prosperous Latvian family, and had for many years been a lawyer in St Petersburg. Gentle and scholarly in manner and appearance, with long white hair and a Schweitzer-like face, he nevertheless, surrounded as he was by a task force of professional Bolshevik revolutionaries, issued decrees in which soaring utopianism mingled with bloodcurdling threats. The *Red Flag*, henceforth the only authorized newspaper, drove home his message with Mayakovskyan zest:

> We are the modern Barbarians,
> Marching forward for humanity
> In unconquerable hordes,
> In ever-swelling hordes!
>
> We are the Vandals of Justice,
> We are the Barbarians of Right,
> We carry freedom on our shields,
> The Freedom of the Human Race!
>
> There is a trembling and a groaning
> Through the empty spaces of worn-out civilization.
> There is thunder and lightning where we step,
> And fertility rises like vapour from our tracks.
>
> We are the modern Vandals,
> Wandering with heavy tread
> In iron-spiked sandals
> Along the Highway of the Future!

The legal profession was abolished and revolutionary tribunals soon began to supply the firing squads with human targets in the form of 'counter-revolutionary' landowners, farmers, lawyers, bankers, businessmen, clergy and students. Houses were constantly raided and clothes, underwear, boots and bed-linen seized for the Red Army. Bank deposits were limited to 10,000 roubles, and any surplus confiscated. There was a frantic thrusting of note-rolls under floorboards and cellar flags, into wardrobes, vases and the trays of bird-cages. But all to no avail. Even if the prying squads of gun-women, now strengthened by the whores and slaveys of Riga, failed to locate the hidden treasure, Stutchka threatened to make it worthless. Money, too, was to be abolished. As soon as it was out of circulation swindling and thieving would vanish, murder dwindle. 'Money has not always existed,' lectured Stutchka. 'In the earliest days of humanity, in the age of primitive communism, money was unknown. We are beginning again in the present age of transition with the original barter of goods. Later each person who works will simply receive from the state the quantity of food and manufactured goods necessary for the maintenance of his capacity to work. Money is now living in the last days of its domination! Be this our slogan—AWAY WITH MONEY!'

In order to 'root out the parasitical bourgeoisie, bring them into closer relations with proletarian circles, and accustom them to socially useful work', all bourgeois were ordered to register themselves within five days on penalty of death. Soon was seen the grotesque sight of formerly prominent burghers, together with their wives, children and elderly relatives, dressed in the shabbiest clothes they could borrow or contrive in an effort to avoid the draft yet qualify for workers' rations. One possibly prejudiced observer (a refugee from the Red Terror in Petrograd) stated that he had seen a dung-cart drawn through the streets by a human team composed of a former mayor, a retired general, a bank director, a lawyer, a wealthy businessman, and an elderly clergyman— shuffling along, lashed by the whips (and tongues) of liberated prostitutes and domestic servants. The entire staff of Riga University was sacked and its faculties opened to all boys and girls over sixteen of working-class origin. Religious instruction in schools was forbidden. On Sundays churches could be used for 'religious purposes', but for the rest of the week were to be available for communist youth clubs, workers' concerts, and public dancing.

Among the clergy of Riga, too, established values and reputations were overturned. Most of the pulpits were silenced. Only one preacher enjoyed official favour. Edgar Model, pastor of the Evangelical Church, long scorned and persecuted for his socialist opinions, now preached to large captive audiences. 'Communism', cried this pale, thin, fanatical young man, 'must triumph! Property is of the Devil! Because men have built their whole culture on this evil foundation, it must perish for ever. The twilight of the present age precedes an era of sunlight, harbingered by a red dawn.' Jesus Christ, he said, had been the first communist. The husbandmen of the Russian vineyard had been punished because they withheld the fruits from those who laboured in it. 'A fearful judgment fell upon them. Everything which they considered to be their property, sacred and inviolable, was taken away from them and given to those who had no portion. Woe to all those in other lands who hoard the fruits of the vineyards as their property! From them also will the vineyard be taken away!'

When the southward advance of the Red Army into Lithuania was halted, the Riga Soviet talked of stepping up the class war. A *Red Flag* gasconade threatened:

> We will not yield!
> Though we have to pile the corpses up to Heaven!
> You shall never snatch the Red Town from our grip,
> The town so closely bound to us proletarians
> By innumerable bleeding wounds!

Meanwhile the mud and snow in the streets, despite the efforts of inept bourgeois shovellers and sweepers, piled up. Houses and shops were shuttered. Desolation reigned. As firing-squads shot their way through the lists of social traitors it seemed to the diminishing band of bourgeois in Riga that their tortured city, in normal times only a day or two's journey from Copenhagen, Stockholm or Berlin, had become fantastically isolated, abandoned and forgotten. Bolshevism had transformed Riga, the pride of the medieval merchant adventurers, into some wretched overgrown village in the depths of Siberia. Their bottles of Kümmel, their aromatic bitters and fine Rhenish wines, after an outburst of looting and drunkenness, had been smashed by order of the commissars. Their servants deserted them, informed upon them, shot them. Even their favourite whores had turned against them. They were prisoners of the great claustrophobia of 1919, groping in a darkness of ignorance shot through by hunger pains and mad gleams of Bolshevik propaganda. The Night of the Abyss had encompassed them, and there seemed no reason why it should ever end.

2. The Soil of Despair

The Allies' naval blockade of the Continent had done its job. By the end of 1918 Central and Eastern Europe were in desperate straits. But the Germans could, after all, have negotiated an earlier peace rather than persist in organizing famine, spinning out their genius for ersatz to its last artificial threads, robbing the home front to feed the armies. To force them to do so had been the declared and legitimate object of the blockade. But when it was applied to Bolshevik Russia as a counter-revolutionary tactic its legitimacy was questioned. When it was maintained against Germany, the Republic of Austria and the Soviet Republic after the armistice, it was assaulted by every argument, every statistic, at the command of socialists, progressives and plain humanitarians.

The effects of war and blockade could be measured by the needs put before the American Federal Food Board by Herbert Hoover late in 1918. Help, he said, was vital to boost the food supplies of 125 million people in Britain, France and Italy; to supply most of the food necessary to keep 100 million Belgians, Serbs, Rumanians, Greeks, Czechoslovaks, Poles and Yugoslavs alive; to snatch some 50 million people in north Russia from the brink of famine; to assist European neutrals, all of whom, except Denmark, were on short rations; and to save the 'enemy peoples', some 90 million of them, from a mass grave.

In Europe alone, on Hoover's reckoning, about 200 million people were in danger of real starvation in the winter of 1918–19. In Czechoslovakia a million children were totally deprived of milk: in industrial districts fifty per cent of babies were stillborn. In Poland three million Jews were starving and a million children. In Poland and Lithuania hundreds of thousands of people had as their daily meal a bowl of 'soup' consisting of water with one-third of a small potato floating in it. In Germany and Austria the staple diet of the national kitchens was potato and cabbage gruel. Hoover's investigators reported that in German Bohemia, of forty-seven schoolchildren asked what they had eaten for breakfast twelve had had nothing, thirteen only black ersatz coffee, four ersatz coffee with milk. The rest had breakfasted on a dish of wild herbs gathered in the fields. Every day in Germany 800 people were dying of deficiency diseases. Infant mortality had soared. In 1914 in Vienna, births had exceeded deaths by 10,000; by 1918 there were 20,000 more deaths than births. In Berlin, during the first months of 1919, thirty per cent of babies perished within a few days of birth. In Düsseldorf, where the milk shortage was specially severe, the figure was eighty-five per cent.

Rickets — known in Germany as 'the English disease' — was universal. Spotted typhus, due to lack of soap and the most elementary hygiene, was spreading west from Russia and Poland on a tide of lice. Hundreds of thousands of children could not go to school for lack of clothes and boots. Millions were dressed in rags or bits of old sacking in temperatures ten to twenty degrees below zero. In Rumania babies, who seldom survived more than a few hours, were born hairless and without fingernails. In some Rumanian villages there were no children under twelve, in some Polish villages none under seven. In Berlin 700 cattle and 17 pigs were brought in for slaughtering, compared with a pre-war weekly average of 6,000 cattle and 25,000 pigs. Vienna had four consecutive meatless weeks. Breakdown of transport made distribution impossible when there was a store of food. Large quantities of grain which could have relieved the populations of Petrograd and Moscow were rotting in the granaries of the Volga provinces. Throughout Russia and Europe lack of lubricants and spare parts was immobilizing locomotives and rolling stock. In March 1919 Oswald Garrison Villard, editor of the New York *Nation*, reported from Germany that there would be no trains running at all within six weeks unless lubricants were made available.

Hospitals were tragically overcrowded and under-equipped. They had few or no drugs, no anaesthetics, no heating, hardly any milk, in many cases no bed-linen, no bandages, no cotton-wool, no drainage-tubes or stethoscopes, no teats for feeding bottles, no soap, no disinfectants. The diet consisted of potato, cabbage, turnip or pumpkin gruel. New-born babies were wrapped in rags or sheets of newspaper. Patients weak from illness or surgery had to walk about unheated wards to keep warm. Lice swarmed in filthy mattresses. Henry Nevinson, an English journalist, described his horror at seeing rows of skeletal infants in a Cologne hospital: 'They had no weight, no growth, no sense. Their limbs were as thin as sticks, shapeless and boneless.' The mothers had no milk, the French had requisitioned large numbers of cows, and those that remained gave unwholesome milk. Even where milk was available the babies could not drink it, as there was no rubber for the teats of the bottles and they could not suck the substitutes of bone. Konrad Adenauer, then Burgomaster of Cologne, commented: 'We are too exhausted even to hate.' George Young, Berlin correspondent of the *Daily News*, described a visit to families living in tenement basements condemned as unfit for human habitation but crammed with people because of an acute housing shortage. Men who had work were constantly away ill with stomach trouble. Young boys lost their jobs because they were always collapsing. A mother was struggling to feed a family of five on a weekly ration of five pounds of potatoes, five pounds of bread, half a pound of meat, small quantities of skim milk, and one pound of vegetable jam — when (in a terrifying inflation which made nonsense of wages) she could afford it.

In Vienna children swallowed coal-dust to stifle hunger pangs, in the People's Kitchens sawdust and wood-shavings were mixed with the gruel to bulk it out. In eastern Poland, the most grisly area of all, post-mortems on hunger victims revealed stomachs filled with sand and half-masticated wood. The thought of suicide, not merely as a personal release but as a public duty, was common. In Vienna men and women over sixty volunteered to commit suicide so that the children should have more to eat. A relief worker in central Russia told of the arrival of some refugee children at his camp — in the care of one woman, who died within a few days. They were the last of a party of about a hundred people fleeing from the Polish front. They had stumbled eastward with their stock of food dwindling. The oldest men of the party proposed that the men should eat nothing. When the men had all died, the grown women made the same resolution. So it was that a handful of children, conducted by one dying woman, arrived in Samara.

In the Polish-Russian borderland east of the River Bug, the zone of the old Jewish Pale of Settlement, roving correspondent H. N. Brailsford found the most unsurpassably dreadful suffering. During the 1915 retreat the Russian army had devastated the villages and Jewish quarters and forced such Orthodox peasants as they found to leave the area. During the war the Jews had crept out from the starving towns to till the land. After the armistice the deported peasants had made their way back to ruined farms and villages. Germans, then Ukrainian nationalists, then the Red Army, then Poles and Russian White Guards had fought over and pillaged the land. People were fainting and dying of hunger in the streets. 'Old women came crying round me like gibbering Homeric ghosts,' wrote Brailsford, 'there were children with white lips, pinched faces, and transparent hands.' The villages had no hope of relief. Most of them lay far from the railroad, and such locomotives and rolling stock as were serviceable had all been commandeered for the war against the Bolsheviks, the war to expand Poland to its 'historic boundaries'. Locomotives had to be watered by hand with thawed-out ice. Young Polish troops marched away in the teeth of a knifing east wind, greatcoatless, their feet and bodies swathed in rags. The only adequately dressed and physically presentable group Brailsford saw was a patrol of Russian White Guards, all of them officers. 'They sang as they goose-stepped slowly through the streets of Brest-Litovsk, a haunting, melancholy Russian chorus. For them too in this town of misery one tried to spare pity. They have lost everything save the hope of vengeance.' Such was the reality of Clemenceau's *cordon sanitaire*.

The huge barracks at Brest-Litovsk were filled with refugees from the east and the returning survivors of forced labour in Germany. There was no pretence of medical care. It was a plague centre of typhus, cholera, dysentery, a veritable Belsen of disease, emaciation and cruelty. Polish army doctors refused to attend Jews, who were forced to clean out the barracks and perform the dirtiest tasks without pay or food. Roman Dmowski's agents were plugging anti-semitism in Poland's first 'free' election, so eloquently wheedled for by Paderewski, so paternally granted by Woodrow Wilson. Brailsford saw a National Democratic Party van decorated with Allied flags, scattering anti-Jewish leaflets. 'Itself the party of the big landed interests,' he commented, 'it has used anti-Jewish prejudice as a demagogic appeal, to win the masses from the Socialist and Peasant parties.' Dmowski also relied on anti-semitism to divert attention from the need for agrarian reform, which meant the break-up of the huge estates. Never, said Brailsford, even in Turkey or western Ireland, had he seen farm labourers living in such squalor. Polish landowners lavished care on blood horses and pedigree cattle. But they did not bother about their employees. Families of up to nine people lived in one room of a cottage with a floor of beaten clay. Pigs and hens slept with them for fear of robbers. There was no drainage, no sanitation. Yearly wages were enough to buy two shirts.

Much of the famine and poverty in Central Europe was traditional. The war and the blockade had, however, aggravated it beyond the bounds of even a Polish peasant's fantastic powers of endurance. Some manor houses had been sacked, some sour land seized. Yet it was in a manor house in these borderlands that Brailsford, a crusading progressive of wide culture, had his most moving experience. In this isolated place, surrounded by untilled fields and burned-down villages, itself almost without furniture after being looted successively by Poles and Bolsheviks, lived a Polish landlord and his son. Their only food came from a small potato patch. But the house was filled with books, including some beautiful sixteenth-century Elzevir editions of Greek and Roman classics and the writings of the Fathers. The man sat up with Brailsford half the night, handling the books, talking about them, speaking of Cicero and Carlyle, reciting the prayer in Latin verse ascribed to Mary Queen of Scots. When he said goodbye to his host Brailsford reflected that this culture, so forgotten, so lovingly preserved, was 'a thing more gracious and dignified by far than the monstrous births of our age'. Another decade of wars and blockades and revolutions, and 'every relic of learning and humanity may be swept away from the Rhine to the Volga ... There must have been, when the barbarians surged over the Roman provinces in the twilight centuries, lonely villas left standing amid the ruins of the Empire in which old men survived, conning Greek manuscripts in pillaged rooms ... Not all at once, nor without the flicker of a false dawn, did the darkness compass them round. But their sons lived like barbarians. Their sons' sons were barbarians born ... '

Such wistful regrets, such luxury fears, were buried beneath the sheer weight and volume of the misery in Europe and Russia. In Vienna alone, largely due to the famine of raw materials for the factories, 100,000 men were idle, representing, with their women and children, perhaps half a million human beings in despair – one quarter of the city's population. 'Has the Labour Party', agitated the *Herald*, 'given a thought to those millions of starving and work-less? Has the Triple Alliance dreamed of using a little of its strength to demand that the blockade be lifted? If faith in the Socialist International is to live, British labour must act. Our capitalists have "locked out" the workers of Central Europe. The cruel policy is nothing but a move in the game to capture the world's markets. The League of Nations is a ghastly mockery while this wickedness continues.' What it amounted to, thundered Norman Angell, was that child massacre was being used as a political weapon. 'It would have been more merciful', commented Robert Smillie, Secretary of the Miners' Federation of Great Britain, 'to turn the machine-guns on these children.' Brailsford warned of the farce of expecting a nice, quiet Wilsonian democracy to grow from such soil. Blockade had made the very name of democracy stink.

Bitterness against France, reported Villard, was growing among Germans because of the well-known backing of Clemenceau and Foch for the blockade. In the opinion of the *Echo de Paris* both the continuance and the lifting of the blockade had disadvantages: 'If a state of order exists in Germany her influence over Russia will be strengthened. If order is absent revolution will be encouraged and may spread to France.' It was a nice problem, best solved by 'keeping Germany equally removed from political health and disease by dosing her and controlling her food supply'. E. D. Morel and the *New Statesman* raged against the economic insanity of pauperizing one's enemies and then expecting them to pay reparations. Instead of pouring arms and French military advisers into Poland, wrote Brailsford, 'let the Allies pour in food and raw materials. Let them meet the scourge of hunger and unemployment by ample grants and loans of money. To Poland they can give only one fatal gift — the means of embarking on an imperialist career.'

Miss Eglantyne Jebb, founder of the Save the Children Fund, was imprisoned for displaying a poster with a searing photograph of an emaciated 'enemy' child. Hoover, too, was having his diffi-culties. It had taken much argument to persuade the British, French and Italian governments not to cancel their orders for American pork. Farmer ruin was still imminent if the blockade was maintained. That ruin, he warned, might well go on along the line — first the farmers, then the country banks, then business in general. He tried to get agreement for a plan to allow the northern neutrals — Holland, Denmark, Norway and Sweden — to import food and exchange it for German products. This was vetoed by the Allied Blockade Council. In February 1919, impressed by Hoover's reasoning (and possibly by an urgent telegram from Wilson: 'Food relief is now the key to the whole European situation and to the solution of peace. Bolshevism steadily advancing westward, poisoning Germany. It cannot be stopped by force but it can be stopped by food'), Congress approved a grant of 100 million dollars for the provisioning of Europe. The House of Commons, despite the furious grumblings of the jingo brigade, approved a grant of about half the size. 'We really do not like to imagine', chuckled the *New Statesman*, 'the state of mind of those who thought that they were voting at the election to make the Huns pay, when they discover how much they are going to pay for the Huns! To keep two or three hundred million people alive for several months, even at famine relief rations, will, as Mr Austen Chamberlain' (the Chancellor of the Exchequer) 'has already had to realize, cost something not far short of continuing the war for that time.' Soon Britain would be asked to share the cost of supplying German, Austrian, Polish and Czechoslovak factories with raw materials, to enable them to revive their export trade to Britain! 'So painfully do we have to learn that we are, economically, members of one another.'

It was one thing to get approval for the U.S.F.A. programme, another to get it moving freely. Foch insisted that to abandon the blockade was to abandon all military control of the situation; Clemenceau, in no hurry to ease German suffering, agreed that it must be maintained until the peace treaty had been signed. An immense merchant navy was needed to carry the saviour fat from America. Yet after the armistice the American merchant fleet, until then controlled by an international council, had been diverted by its owners to the South American and other lucrative routes. In Britain influential members of the government were suspicious of Hoover's motives. Cecil Bisshopp Harmsworth (younger brother of the press barons Northcliffe and Rothermere), recently appointed Acting Minister of Blockade, was one of them. In February 1919 he wrote to Lord Robert Cecil, chief British delegate on the Supreme Economic Council: 'I regard the blockade as the easiest and cheapest method of applying pressure to Germany if pressure should be required ... The most formidable influences working against it are Mr Hoover and our own trade community.' Care should be taken, he told Sir Auckland Geddes, to put the case for blockade as moderately as possible, or else 'the Yanks will agitate for uncontrolled export of industrial raw materials, as well as food, to Germany.'

Harmsworth's concern about the effect of dollar imperialism on the balance of power in Europe and possibly in Russia was shared by socialists who had nothing else in common with him. President Wilson's approaches to Soviet Russia, said the *Call*, were the manoeuvres of the chief travelling salesman of American capitalism. Hoover's proposal to commission Nansen, the eminent Norwegian explorer, to assess the relief needs of the Russians and the willingness of the Soviet and White governments to make a compromise peace was also seen as an attempt to corner the Russian market for American pluto-democracy. French and British hostility killed the idea. Hoover battled away in Paris with what Geoffrey Keynes called 'the air of a weary Titan'. On February 19th, in a confidential memorandum to the American Peace Delegation, he complained that 'up to date not a single pound of food has been delivered to Germany. The uses to which the blockade is being put are absolutely immoral. I do not feel that we can with any sense of national dignity and honour continue to endure this situation ... I wish to solemnly warn the conference as to impending results in the total collapse of the social system in Europe.' A few weeks later his arguments were unexpectedly buttressed by a telegram from General Plumer, commanding the British Army of Occupation on the Rhine. The morale of his troops, he reported, was being badly undermined by the sight of the suffering of women and children. His men were already sharing their rations with German civilians. He demanded an immediate supply of food to Cologne to be distributed from army headquarters.

Lloyd George, disturbed by the loss of several by-elections and the growing hostility of labour to blockade and intervention, made aggressive use of the Plumer telegram (though Plumer himself was relieved of his command). The blockade was breached. Powered by Hoover's fanatical anti-Bolshevism and bulldozing humanitarianism the U.S.F.A. went into top gear. Hoover kept hammering away at the conference and the Supreme Economic Council. His envoys reasoned or threatened away the newly-erected barriers between the new nations, fixing ad hoc treaties to open up railways and canals, arranging for the exchange, across closed borders, of surplus foodstuffs for coal, raw materials, even manufactured goods and railway equipment. More than 1,500 engineers and other technicians were seconded from the American Army. Railways, locomotives and rolling stock were repaired. A system of telegraphic communications was set up, reaching from Helsingfors to Constantinople, with main stations at Paris, Berlin, Prague, Warsaw and Vienna. Cargoes of wheat and pork sped to the Baltic States. To combat cold and unemployment Hoover's army distributed coal as well as food, fed factories as well as bellies. To fight typhus Hoover borrowed experts from the Red Cross and the U.S. Army Medical Corps and commandeered delousing equipment from all the armies, including the German. His relays were the chief runners in the race to catch up and head off revolution.

3. *The Crop of Revolt*

Poland at least presented no serious ideological problems. It was too preoccupied with nationalist wars on four fronts, too lacking in a liberal or socialist tradition, too under-industrialized, too absorbed in the struggle with an archaic Jewish state-within-the-state. The war against the Bolsheviks was part of the war to push Poland out to its 'natural' frontiers and to annex land which could be thrown to the peasants to avoid the break-up of the big estates. Dmowski's assertion that all Jews were Bolsheviks at heart was a propaganda lie. Most of the Jews in Poland were so Talmudically conservative that they hated anything new. The Catholic Church had a firm grip on all classes, partly because of its identification with the long underground resistance to foreign rule and foreign religion. Even in Lodz, the largest industrial centre, the Workers' Councils, after frightening a few factory owners by putting them under house arrest and demanding a war bonus to buy a few warm clothes and blankets, had faded rapidly away. There was no single focus for action. Catholic, Socialist and Jewish trade unions, Catholic, Socialist and Jewish Labour Parties—the whole sectarian muddle against which Rosa Luxemburg had raged—soon began to quarrel. Racial and religious prejudice prevented common action. Lancers and police with fixed bayonets patrolled the streets of Lodz, but they were superfluous. The real guarantor of patience and patriotism was the Madonna on the walls of stinking tenements in which families of ten slept on bare boards. She could stifle the urge to rebel and teach the worker to hug his chains. She could perform every miracle except one—to touch the consciences of Polish industrialists.

In Warsaw there were some workers' demonstrations, with red banners and slogans about the dictatorship of the proletariat. But there were no renegade bourgeois to make a revolution. Rosa Luxemburg and Leo Jogiches were in Germany; Dzherzhinsky, Marchlevsky and Radek in Russia. Those who passed for the Polish intelligentsia were no danger to anyone except perhaps themselves and a few pedestrians as, gold-braided, side-whiskered and horn-blowing, they galloped, cloaks afloat, over the cobblestones to wienerschnitzel and whipped-cream rendezvous in red-plush cafés. 'It is not fair', wrote the correspondent of the New York *Nation* in an ironic despatch, 'to deprive Poland of its impulsive romantic youth. Poles need a decade at least of mid-Victorianism before they turn sober twentieth century and begin to wrestle with the prole-tarian problem.'

In Austria the revolution of beggars defied threats of Italian military occupation and the blackmail of the U.S.F.A. and the British Food Commission in a series of desperate protests. In February, along railway tracks on which coal-conserving locomotives crawled at little more than walking pace, young soldiers held placards appealing to passengers to Vote Red. The elections produced sweeping Socialist gains in Vienna and other industrial districts: but since the Catholic Clerical Party carried the countryside the final result was a Socialist-Clerical coalition in which Socialists held all the main government posts. The republic, as orators tirelessly emphasized, was hopelessly split, humiliatingly impotent. Yet, largely due to the activities of communist agitators striving to link Vienna, Munich and Budapest in revolutionary alliance, their pleas were not always heeded. In April a demonstration of twenty thousand unemployed workers, returned prisoners-of-war and disabled ex-soldiers marched down the fashionable Prater to the Reichsrat. There they listened to speeches about the treachery of Social Democrats and amused themselves by tying red ribbons round the necks of pseudo-classical statues, draping a bronze effigy of the late Emperor Franz Josef in a red cloth, and running a red flag up the flagstaff.

Their mood changed suddenly when a deputation was turned back. Undeterred by a desultory cavalry charge, they battered at the doors and smashed windows. When police fired into the crowd, there was a great cry of 'Murderers!' and a passing coal cart was overturned to make a barricade. Lumps of coal were hurled at windows, but most of it vanished into the pockets and aprons of the rioters. Petrol was siphoned from politicians' cars to set fire to the wood-work of the building ('What do we want with Parliament? All power to the Soviets!'). War cripples on crutches danced round the flames. A detachment of the Volkswehr, the people's army, appeared on the scene and urged the crowd to order. 'Comrades, don't push.

Comrades, give way, please.' The comrades obeyed. The flames were put out. The demonstration dispersed, pausing to hack the flesh off a police horse which had been shot in the charge. Within a few minutes only the skeleton and the saddle remained—and five naked corpses (stripped of their clothes by beggarly comrades)—and the memory of a pertinent question which had punctured the violent bombast of an agitator from Budapest. 'If Vienna makes a revolution, can Budapest send us twelve trains of daily bread?'

In Italy, despite a dampening dependence on Britain and America for fuel and food, revolutionary prospects seemed livelier—to judge by the pronouncements of would-be revolutionaries. The war had blown up in the government's face. Neither Prime Minister Vittorio Orlando nor Foreign Minister Baron Sonnino had desired or visualized the complete disintegration of the Habsburg Empire. A reclamation of the lost lands of Trento-Trieste would have suited them, with Vienna remaining as the guardian of the Danube and the civilizer of the Balkans. The multi-nationalist mêlée along the northern frontier, the Yugoslav occupation of Dalmatia, frightened them. A wave of romantic neo-imperialism threatened to engulf them. Marinetti continued to demand the removal of King and Pope and the selling, burning or dynamiting of Italy's treasures. D'Annunzio, haranguing huge crowds, spoke of his nausea at 'the stench of peace' and urged his audience to blow up Parliament and its pitiful rabble of bourgeois lawyers.

As poet, novelist, playwright and assiduous libertine he had trampled profitably on convention. His short-story themes included the rape of a spinster schoolmistress by a drunken water-carrier and the coupling of the widow and brother of a dead man in the presence of his decomposing corpse. He had made a cult of swash-buckling neo-barbarism:

> Would you fight? Kill? See rivers of blood?
> Great mountains of gold? Flocks of captive women?
> Slaves? Or other prey?

He now called upon his compatriots to defy the Anglo-Saxon tyranny of the Peace Conference, drive the Yugoslavs from Dalmatia, and inaugurate, under his leadership, a grand holocaust of bourgeois philistinism.

The time had come, said the nationalist paper *Politica*, for Italy to resume her imperial mission. The change from nationalism to imperialism was one from petty rights to great duties, from the stagnancy of the pool to the frothing grandeur of the waterfall. In March 1919, at a meeting of the first *fasci di combattimento* in Milan, the slogan was 'Fight for the Revolutionary Fruits of a Revolutionary War.' Mussolini, for whom socialism was synonymous with indecision and platform orthodoxy, had changed the sub-heading on his *Popolo d'Italia* from 'A Socialist Daily' to 'A Daily for Fighters and Producers'. The revolution begun by the war, he insisted, was not over. 'We have no formal principles,' he said. 'We accept whatever means may be necessary. We are realists, realizers. We have to accept the principles of the labouring classes. We are syndicalists. During the war we all realized the incapacity of those who were governing us. We know that we won only by virtue of the efforts of the Italian people. We are forming *fasci*, bodies capable of creative action, of going out in the squares and crying: "It is we who have the right to govern".' The Fascists demanded Fiume and Dalmatia; an Italian republic; universal suffrage for men and women; the abolition of the Senate; workers' control in industry wherever possible; a heavy capital levy and death duty; the confiscation of church property and eighty-five per cent of war profits, and the abolition of clerical privileges.

His main object was, without committing himself to any definite line, to encourage a revolutionary atmosphere, a contempt for the past which would include old-fashioned socialists as well as old-fashioned liberals. Both he and d'Annunzio began to think of a spectacular march of 'new Romans' on the effete ditherers in Rome. Only the Social Democrats did not consider such a possibility. They decided to leave the discredited Second International, issued stern manifestoes about their unalterable determination never to share power with bourgeois politicians, spoke about the inevitability of a socialist revolution—but showed every sign of finding the explosive situation as alarming as Orlando or Baron Sonnino.

The Fascists underlined their scorn for mummified Marxism when in April 1919 they burned down the Milan office of *Avanti*, the socialist daily of which Mussolini had once been editor. Peasants began to occupy idle land on the great estates. Crowds angered by rising prices looted stores and beat up shopkeepers. The *Popolo d'Italia* urged its readers to string up profiteers and food hoarders to the nearest lamp-post or 'smother them under their own potatoes and bacon.' EVVIVA LENIN! signs were whitewashed on church walls. In country towns the victory speeches of landowning mayors were interrupted by raucous heckling and the bawling of a socialist anthem:

> Forward O people to the attack,
> The Red Flag will triumph!
> Forward O people, the cannon thunders,
> Revolution, revolution, we shall make!

All Italy seemed to be in the streets and squares, shouting, gesticulating, paying off old scores. The lines were drawn for civil war in which it seemed certain that liberalism and bourgeois democracy would go to the wall, unwanted and unlamented.

But it was the second revolution in Germany that fixed the attention of the world and its press. In office the Independent Socialists, led by Hugo Haase, had curtly rejected Lenin's offer of food trains, telling him to keep his grain for the starving Russian workers (and knowing that the scrapings of Soviet granaries could not compete with Hoover's bounty). They had also resisted demands for the reopening of the Soviet Embassy in Berlin, whose staff had been sent packing in November 1918. Out of office, the Independents showed no more fondness for Bolshevism. 'There is no rapid road to Utopia,' cautioned Karl Kautsky. 'The seizure of factories and other industrial concerns is sheer anarchy. The will of the people as shown in the forthcoming elections must decide. One cannot countenance the thrusting of socialism on an unwilling country. First the desire for socialism, then its achievement. We must repudiate anti-democratic Bolshevism absolutely.'

For Rosa Luxemburg and Karl Liebknecht there had *been* no revolution, only a flurry of 'democratic' scene-shifting for the benefit of the Allies and at the bidding of the High Command. Both abominated a return to ritual Marxism as much as Mussolini. Both felt that its sins of complacency and cowardice had to be expiated in blood. Both had been rejected as bourgeois intellectual nuisances by the militant workers. Both, but especially Rosa Luxemburg, realized that Spartacus was a symbol rather than a mass movement, that it owed its notoriety to the vicious publicity of the nationalist and Majority Socialist press rather than to its own strength. She was proud that anyone with a spirit of revolt and an

itch for action called himself a Spartacist. She was filled with sadness
as well as exaltation by the prospect of armed rebellion and the near-
certainty of its failure. 'Because we are the socialist conscience of the
revolution,' she wrote in the Spartacus Programme, 'we are hated
and maligned by all the open and secret enemies of the revolution...
Spartacus does not want to attain power over or through the masses.
It is the self-conscious part of the proletariat, pointing out to the
broad masses their historic tasks ... The proletarian revolution can
only battle its way to clarity and maturity along a Golgotha path,
through bitter experiences, many defeats and victories. The triumph
of Spartacus belongs not to the beginning but to the end of the
revolution. It is identical with the triumph of the great mass of
workers. Up, proletarians! Arise to battle! You are about to conquer
a world and to fight against a world. In this last great class war for
the highest goal of humanity, our slogan must be—thumb in eye
and knee on chest!'

On December 29th a conference of about a hundred Spartacist
delegates voted to make a complete break with Social Democracy
and to found the German Communist Party (K.P.D.). Two days of
stormy debates attended its birth. Karl Radek delivered a long,
optimistic speech. 'When the news of the German revolution reached
us,' he said, 'a veritable tumult of joy seized the working class of
Russia ... which knows well that without a socialist revolution in
Germany it would not have sufficient strength to build anew on
the ruins of capitalism.' Civil war, he soothed, was not so awful as
was sometimes thought. It did not destroy the possibility of socialism. A whole year of civil war in Russia had destroyed fewer
people and less property than a single day of international war.
Russia had created a network of elementary schools unequalled
anywhere in the world. The finest music and works of art were
freely available to the masses. The Red Army was growing daily
more formidable. The Bolshevik regime was not a reign of terror.
It stood for the will of the people and its defence against counter-
revolution. 'What we are now carrying out in Russia is nothing but
the great unperverted teaching of German communism. The
Council of People's Commissars of Europe will yet meet in Berlin.
Spartacus will conquer. It is destined to seize power in Germany.'

Karl Liebknecht, always more headstrong than Rosa Luxemburg,
cried: 'The open recognition of the class struggle symbolized by
the formation of the K.P.D. is decisive. We do not want a lemonade

revolution. We have to hasten the internationalization of civil war.'
Rosa, suspicious of Radek's glibness, hostile to Radek himself
(whom she had known and disliked since they had clashed in the
early days of the Polish Social Democratic Party), remained cool.
Much work was needed, she stressed, before K.P.D./Spartacus could
claim to have any mass following: it had not begun to make an
impact on the peasants, or to link with left socialist groups in the
provinces. She vehemently opposed a resolution condemning K.P.D.
participation in the elections. At this stage, she thought, every effort
should be made to infiltrate existing institutions. 'Comrades,' she
reasoned, 'you take your revolution too lightly. Despite the stress and
urgency of the moment we must not lose our ability to analyse the
situation. When the National Assembly was forcibly dismissed in
Russia the government of Lenin and Trotsky already existed. We are
still governed by Ebert and Scheidemann. The Russian proletariat
has been through a long series of revolutionary struggles. We are
only at the beginning of ours. We must ask ourselves: What is the
surest way to educate the masses?' But the wild youngsters outvoted
her. Reluctantly, with a kind of maternal loyalty (bourgeois senti-
mentality in the opinion of later communist leaders), she accepted
the verdict, and tried to identify herself completely with the lost
cause of gutter Spartacism.

Not even her superb but overtaxed intellectual machinery could
work fast enough to keep pace with events. For some days leaflets
demanding the murder of her and Liebknecht had been circulating.
They changed lodgings every night, staying now at cheap hotels,
now with various friends and sympathizers; strolling, when they
had time, in the streets, to listen to the heated discussions of the
crowds, sometimes taking part in them. On January 4th the government announced its intention of removing the self-appointed
'revolutionary' police chief, Emil Eichhorn. Armed Spartacist
groups easily fought off lukewarm attempts by republican troops to
storm police headquarters, skirmished with soldiers guarding the
Chancellery, and for the second time occupied the offices of *Vorwärts*.
The unreliability of the government forces and rumours that naval
units at Spandau and the military garrison at Frankfurt were ready
to march to the aid of the rebels brought excitement to fever pitch.
The Spandau factory workers downed tools, and demanded action.
The hour of Spartacus seemed to have struck. Even the Independent
Socialists and Revolutionary Shop Stewards, united mainly in

distrust of Spartacus, were swept away—into the formation of a revolutionary committee representing all three groups, but still wrangling about whether to call for a general strike and mass demonstrations or to put themselves at the head of an armed insurrection. K.P.D./Spartacus tried to force the pace. Once more Liebknecht pushed through a sea of agitation in a red-flagged lorry, orating incessantly. 'The time for action has come! Let the Socialist Republic be no longer a dream but a reality! Today begins the socialist revolution which will spread through the whole world!' Germany, commented Luxemburg in *Die Rote Fahne*, had always been the classic land of organization, but 'the organization of revolutionary action ... must be learned in revolution itself, as one learns swimming in the water.' Still Richard Müller, leader of the Shop Stewards, hesitated. The Independents went to Ebert with an offer of mediation. The leaderless mob began to drift away. Only the Spartacist guerillas held on at police headquarters and in the *Vorwärts* building.

The moment of truth had come, too, for Gustav Noske and his strange allies. The Freikorps (free companies) represented the solid core of the Imperial army. They had refused to disband after the armistice, convinced that they had been let down by an incompetent High Command and cheated of victory by the collapse of the civilians on a home front undermined by Jewish socialist propaganda. There were more than 150 of them, an eager democracy of reaction created and led by professional patriots whose rank ranged all the way from private, first class, to general. Freikorps commanders were natural leaders in the full sense, approved by the harsh sifting of the front line. They expected and received complete loyalty. Their first assignment had been to fight against Poles on Germany's eastern frontier and Bolsheviks in the Baltic States. Now they were to tackle the internal enemies of the Reich. It was a task which some of them approached with scrupulous restraint, some with a cruel relish sharpened by the psychological need for victory, however cheap, however fratricidal: a task which, thanks to good pay and special rations, they were in good physical shape to perform.

The reconquest of Berlin had been entrusted to Lieutenant-General Freiherr von Lüttwitz, commanding a force composed of the ultra-reactionary Guards Cavalry Rifle Division, the Landesjägerkorps, and the Marine Brigade formed by Noske himself in Kiel. By January 7th the Freikorps had fought their way past the amateur opposition of Spartacist snipers to a position of strength in the centre of the city. The *Rote Fahne* office in Wilhelmstrasse was machine-gunned, the K.P.D./Spartacus office in Friedrichstrasse blown up, Emil Eichhorn and his supporters driven from police headquarters. Liebknecht renewed his appeal for militancy. 'Workers! Soldiers! Now the last fog has cleared. Ebert and Scheidemann have openly called the bourgeoisie to arms. It is necessary to fight to the end. To war! Come out of the factories! To the general strike! To arms! On to the streets for the last fight and victory!'

The Freikorps captured the railway terminals, closed in on the *Vorwärts* building in the Lindenstrasse, and called for surrender. The Spartacists inside refused. Von Lüttwitz drew a cordon round the area. Troops were posted in the rooms and on the roofs of surrounding houses. A Spartacist sally was driven back by heavy machine-gun fire. Four-inch artillery guns and mine-throwers were trundled into position. The *Vorwärts* building vanished under a cloud of smoke, dust and debris in a series of tremendous explosions. Soldiers moved forward to hurl grenades into the screams and yells of the defenders. Surrender was still refused. More mines were thrown on to the roof. In the complete silence that followed, the Freikorps, ignoring a flag of truce, rushed the building under a machine-gun barrage. The Spartacist survivors filed out, men and women, with their hands above their heads. Some were sobbing with shock. So ended the six-day Spartacist occupation of *Vorwärts*, which the Spartacists of 1919 and their successors regarded as the very emblem of sham-socialist treachery. So ended the January revolution: a hundred rebels dead, about four hundred wounded — Freikorps casualties thirteen dead, about twenty wounded.

But the personal resistance, the potent myth-making, of Liebknecht and Luxemburg, continued. Still they wrote articles for *Die Rote Fahne*, still it was printed. On January 12th and 13th the two stayed in the working-class suburb of Neuköln. On the 14th, together with Wilhelm Pieck, they moved to an apartment in the select residential district of Wilmersdorf. AN EYE FOR AN EYE! screamed a headline in the right-wing *Deutsche Tageszeitung*: and *Vorwärts*, reissued in an improvised edition, joined in the hue and cry:

> Five hundred corpses all in a row.
> Liebknecht, Rosa, Radek & Co —
> Why are they not there also?

At Wilmersdorf Rosa and Karl wrote their last testaments. ORDER REIGNS IN BERLIN was the title of hers. The revolution had failed, she admitted. But it was a constructive failure, an honourable defeat. 'The masses were up to the mark. They have forged this defeat into the chain of those historical battles which are themselves the strength and pride of international socialism ... "Order Rules in Berlin." You stupid lackeys! Your order is built on sand. Tomorrow the revolution will rise again, in a blare of trumpets, to announce "I was, I am, I always will be!" ' Liebknecht too, in an article headed IN SPITE OF ALL, looked beyond the corpses of the fighters. 'Hold hard. We have not fled. We are not beaten. For Spartacus—that means fire and spirit, heart and soul, will and deed of the workers' revolution. For Spartacus—that stands for all the longing for achievement, all the embattled resolution of the class-conscious proletariat. Whether or not we survive, our programme will live. It will dominate the world of liberated peoples. In spite of all.'

On the evening of January 15th a detachment of soldiers burst into the Wilmersdorf apartment. Rosa was resting. She packed a small suitcase, putting in some books, expecting to go to prison. Liebknecht was driven away first. Rosa followed in another car with Wilhelm Pieck. All were taken to the Eden Hotel, Freikorps headquarters in the centre of Berlin. Jeered at, spat at, pushed and struck in the lobby, they were given a lengthy interrogation, during which Rosa's sarcastic replies visibly enraged her questioners. Liebknecht was led out from a side door into the street, where a soldier called Runge slammed him hard over the head with his rifle butt. Bundled into a car and driven a short distance, he was forced to get out and shot in the back. Official version (accepted by *Vorwärts*): shot while trying to escape. Rosa Luxemburg, that ardent spirit in a crippled cage, hobbled (one hip had been permanently injured in a childhood accident) to her triple martyrdom as woman, Jew and communist. She was again beaten up in the lobby of the hotel, then rifle-butted by Runge, then dragged, half-dead and bleeding profusely, to a car, shot in the head by an officer, and dumped into a canal. Official version: that an angry mob had stopped the car and taken the prisoner away to a destination unknown. With Rosa's corpse into the canal went the last hope of socialist unity, the only hope of a republic which was to be anything more than a breathing-space for German nationalism. The blood of Liebknecht and Luxemburg

trickled, a small but impassable barrier, between the Social Democrats and the Left.

The Spartacist leaders had been murdered: but Spartacism—the
spirit of revolt—was livelier than ever. In Berlin Noske's soldiers
were assaulted by angry mobs. During the funeral of Liebknecht
inner Berlin was cordoned off. Cannon and machine-guns were
stationed at every street corner. Soldiers with fixed bayonets lined
the route of the procession.

Berlin subsided into an uneasy, ominous sullenness. There were
riots, strikes and demonstrations in Bremen, Hamburg, Düsseldorf,
Essen and Wilhelmshaven. A militant left wing began to emerge
in the hitherto docile workers' and soldiers' councils. In Bremen
bourgeois newspapers were closed down and threats made to
socialize all factories and banks. The miners of central Germany
struck for the socialization of their industry. In Stettin the Workers'
and Soldiers' Council forced the resignation of the Governor of
Pomerania, ex-Reich Chancellor Michaelis, who had refused to fly
flags at half-mast on the day of Liebknecht's funeral. In Stuttgart
the Majority Socialist newspaper office was seized, the town hall
raided, the burgomaster kidnapped, the councillors thrown out, and
the municipal cigars and champagne liberally sampled. A Spartacist
plot to derail a train on which Scheidemann was travelling was said
to have been narrowly foiled. The Soldiers' Council of the 8th
Army Corps at Altona threatened to 'blockade' Germany by preventing the unloading of food ships at Hamburg—in protest against
the 're-Junkerization' of the army.

The Majority Socialists were successful in the elections for the
Constituent Assembly. But it was moved from Berlin to Weimar,
and even then had to be given heavy Freikorps protection. The
Leipzig Workers' and Soldiers' Council issued an appeal for a
general strike to which twenty-three towns responded. The Councils
in Brunswick planned a federal republic with a constitution similar
to that of Switzerland. Embers of rebellion flared and flamed all
over the Reich. The fire-brigade Freikorps had a tough job ahead.
The second revolution, assumed to have died in the ruins of the
Vorwärts building, seemed to have acquired another lease of life.

At an open-air rally in Petrograd in honour of the murdered Spartacist leaders, effigies of Ebert and Scheidemann, clad in evening

suits and bearing the legend, THUS DIE ALL TRAITORS, were suspended from mock gallows. For Lenin the mere fact of the founding of a Communist party outside Russia, and especially in Germany, was an encouragement. 'When the German Spartakusbund with its world-renowned leaders broke with the social chauvinists who for ever dishonoured themselves by their open alliance with the imperialist robber bourgeoisie of Germany,' he wrote in an Open Letter to the Workers of Europe and America, 'when the Spartakusbund called itself the Communist Party ... then the foundation of a really international, really revolutionary Third International became a fact.' In Moscow as in Paris the slender strength of Spartacus was made to bear a towering structure of fantasy.

While the struggle between the first and the second, the republican and the socialist revolutions went on in the rest of Germany; while the Weimar Assembly, complete with model constitution, opened its deliberations; while the Junkers of the High Command sacrificed the monarchy and the Majority Socialists sacrificed the workers' councils—the Bavarian revolution proceeded on its idiosyncratic way.

Kurt Eisner continued, with fitful brilliance, to exploit Bavarian pride. Munich, he pointed out, had completed its republican revolution before Berlin. Its Independent Socialists had made earnest efforts, with no bloodshed and commendable orderliness, to develop a dual parliamentary-soviet system of government in which the Councils were encouraged to play a full part. The Bavarian revolution represented (at least in the opinion of Eisner—who was Chairman of the Congress of Workers' and Soldiers' Councils as well as Head of the Provisional Government and Minister for Foreign Affairs) the finest flower of Social Democracy. It was firmly opposed to Bolshevism and violence, it repudiated Prussianism, openly derided the hypocritical window-dressing of Ebert and Scheidemann, and regarded Spartacism (though refusing on principle to repress it) as the unwitting tool of reaction. It had been careful to woo and win the support of the peasants. It was firmly backed by the republican army. It had the full support of the industrial workers. With a little encouragement from the Allies, Bavaria could, he considered, become a model democracy-in-depth for the rest of Germany. He badgered the Allies to give this encouragement. When Clemenceau, whom he persisted in regarding as an ardent liberal, exasperatedly refused several requests for a personal meeting, he peppered Woodrow Wilson with urgent appeals.

'We do not want', said Eisner, addressing the State Soldiers' Council, 'to create a formal electoral democracy in which a slip will be dropped into a ballot box every few years and then everything left to the politicians. That is actually the opposite of democracy. The new democracy should be such that the masses themselves directly and continuously assist in the affairs of the commonwealth. The restoration of the old parliamentary system means the elimination of the council system. This I will try to prevent as long as I have power to do so. I see the hope of Germany in the unfolding strength of its members, not in their amputation.' But his much-vaunted Bavarian unity soon began to crack under a variety of pressures. An obstructive but indispensable bureaucracy (a hazard which all revolutionaries have to face); the political inexperience of the Councils; and above all the familiar post-war poverty and economic chaos. With factories at a standstill, 45,000 unemployed, coal supplies from the Saar cut off by French occupation, and the Allies (deaf to his pleas) continuing to strip the country of locomotives and rolling-stock and to insist on heavy financial reparations, Eisner was forced to admit the uselessness of socializing industry when there was nothing to socialize. An eight-hour day, increased unemployment insurance and better working conditions were decreed —on paper. Members of the Workers' and Soldiers' Councils received a payment which amounted to little more than unemployment relief. Erhard Auer, the Majority Socialist Minister of the Interior, considered the Councils ludicrous toys, and did all he could to disband and discourage them. Spiralling inflation raced ahead of wages. Elections for the promised National Assembly were imminent, and there was every sign that Eisner and the Independent Socialists would not triumph at the polls.

The Catholic-dominated Bavarian People's Party began to make insinuations about 'certain atheistic elements of international Jewry with a predominantly Russian colouring.' The bohemian radical fringe of Eisner's supporters (led by Gustav Landauer, an anarchist philosopher, Erich Mühsam, an anarchist poet, and Ernst Toller, a Prussian Jewish writer who, though nominally socialist, was anarchist by temperament) became increasingly restless. They wanted action, an idealistic clearing of an atmosphere which was heavy with impotence and indecision. All three were founder members of the original Revolutionary Workers' Council (which, unlike its counterpart in Berlin, was liberally seasoned with bourgeois intellectuals). Landauer, summoned from his village retreat by his friend Eisner, was soon agitating against any survival of parliamentary rule – 'the damned National Assembly means the perpetuation of the foulest party politics.' Mühsam and Landauer formed their own group, the Union of Revolutionary Internationalists of Bavaria (V.R.I.), which called for 'the salvation of the world in the renaissance of a radical, concessionless socialist-communist International', and talked of following the example of 'our Russian comrades'.

Outré threats and pranks flustered Eisner, frightened the more solid citizens, set Munich laughing, and were gravely reported in the foreign press as examples of 'Spartacist terrorism'. The Archbishop of Munich was warned that he would be hanged from a bell-rope in the cathedral. Four men shinned up a drainpipe into Eisner's office with a V.R.I. ultimatum. Others interrupted a wedding service in a village church, arrested the bridegroom (the son of a wealthy Munich 'counter-revolutionary') and whisked his tearful bride away. In two simultaneous night raids, one gang led by Mühsam broke into Auer's house and forced him (at gunpoint, shivering in his nightgown) to write out his resignation, another occupied the offices of several leading newspapers, evicted the editorial staff, and awarded control to the terrified typesetters. Eisner refused to take action against the V.R.I., since the whole incident, as he put it, was 'in the spirit of Mardi Gras'. More serious was the emergence of K.P.D./Spartacus as a force in Munich. Under the leadership of Max Levien and, later, Eugen Leviné, both Russian-born revolutionaries of considerable experience, the K.P.D. became the focal point for Bavarian radicalism. K.P.D. policy, proclaimed by a local *Rote Fahne* under the slogan 'All Power to the Soviets of Workers, Soldiers and Peasants', denounced the elections and demanded an end to Eisner's beloved parliamentary-soviet system.

Eisner and the U.S.P.D. went down to crushing defeat in the elections of mid-January 1919. The Bavarian People's Party won thirty-five per cent of the total poll, the S.P.D. thirty-three per cent. The Independent Socialists came almost bottom of the list with a mere two-and-a-half per cent. Eisner himself failed to get elected, (though he had put himself forward as a candidate in twenty-five constituencies. But at the first post-war meeting of the Second International, held in Berne, he delivered a rousing attack on Prussian

militarism and Weimar pseudo-democracy and lauded his own conception of 'dual control'. Back in Munich in mid-February, Eisner
ignored the clamour for his immediate resignation and made a final,
confused bid for popular favour. On February 20th, the day before
the National Assembly opened, Eisner addressed the last session of the
Congress of Councils. 'The bourgeois majority', he said, 'is now to
implement bourgeois policies. The Councils should therefore continue their task of constructing the new democracy. Tomorrow
the Landtag opens. Tomorrow the activity of the Councils should
also begin anew. Then we shall see where are to be found the force
and vitality of a society consecrated by death.' This, though Eisner
continued publicly to abhor violence, was virtually an incitement
to civil war.

Eisner himself was abruptly delivered from his somewhat ludicrous agony of indecision. Early on the morning of February 21st
he went to his office in the Foreign Ministry to prepare a statement
announcing the resignation of himself and the other members of the
provisional government. At ten o'clock he put the text in his brief-
case and, accompanied by two secretaries and two armed guards,
set out for the Landtag, his face haggard, his bushy beard sunk low
on his chest, his hair straggling untidily over his collar, the very
picture of an idealist intellectual dejected by the vulgar brawl of
power ('I long for the time', he had told the Congress of Councils,
'when Socialists will cease to rule and again become the opposition').
As he turned the corner into the Promenadestrasse, a young man in
a trench coat, Count Anton Arco-Valley, stepped forward, fired two
shots into Eisner's head, and was himself wounded by a shot from
one of the armed guards. Eisner collapsed and died on the pavement.
As the news of his assassination spread through Munich Alois
Lindner, a member of the Revolutionary Workers' Council, rushed
into the Landtag and fired point-blank at Auer, who was taken to
hospital in a critical condition.

The delicate bloom of Eisner's democracy withered in the blasts
of violence released by his death. Workers menaced bourgeois in
the streets, shaking their fists and yelling 'We'll get even with the
aristocratic bastards who shot our Eisner!' At the site of the assassination a kind of shrine was set up, surmounted by photographs
of the martyr and piled high with the wreaths of mourners.
PROLETARIANS! HATS OFF BEFORE THE BLOOD OF KURT
EISNER, read a sign. Ranks of peasants in native dress walked in

the funeral procession on February 26th. The Rathaus was draped in black, state and city officials walked behind the hearse, the bells of the churches were tolled by Catholic priests (sometimes at gunpoint). At the graveside Gustav Landauer, weeping, pronounced a final eulogy: 'He was one like Jesus, like Huss — *o sancta simplicitas* — who were put to death by stupidity and greed.'

A Central Committee of Workers', Peasants' and Soldiers' Councils took over the government. Newspaper offices were occupied and a three-day general strike called. Fifty prominent citizens were taken as hostages. The workers were armed. Aeroplanes flew over the city dropping leaflets. Bits of white paper ordered a seven o'clock curfew. Bits of bright red paper proclaimed a state of siege. Truckloads of armed workers patrolled the streets. The Central Committee, dominated by the fiery oratory of Max Levien, sent a sharp note to Weimar: 'It is time that a word of warning was spoken to Weimar and Berlin. Let Scheidemann and Noske understand once for all that we will allow none of their Prussian interference in Bavaria. Whatever may happen in Munich, we say "Hands Off!" ' When, at a mass rally on the Theresienwiese meadow, republican security guards opened fire and killed three people, it was taken as the final proof of S.P.D. treachery. 'In the whole of natural history,' said Landauer,' 'I know of no more disgusting creature than the Social Democratic Party.' Johannes Hoffmann, S.P.D. Minister of Education, was made Acting Premier. But the Landtag, ignored and threatened, adjourned itself on March 19th. Thousands of unemployed demonstrated nightly in the streets, which, to add to the general impression of fantasy, were piled high with snow after freak falls. Eugen Leviné (who had fought as a student in the Russian revolution of 1905) was under orders from Paul Levi, the new K.P.D. chief, to purge the Munich party of its anarchist and U.S.P.D. elements and associations, and to restrain the masses from premature revolt. The first assignment he performed ruthlessly, the second he found beyond his power.

On April 4th, in the cellar of the Löwenbräu beer hall, a large and smoky Councils meeting approved a resolution urging the elimination of parties, the unity of all workers, the proclamation of a Soviet republic, and alliance with the Russian and Hungarian proletariat. 'Then no power on earth will be able to prevent full and immediate socialization.' On the night of April 6th, despite

Leviné's refusal to take part, members of the Central Committee and the Revolutionary Workers' Council and a group of left-wing Independent Socialists gathered in the former Wittelsbach Palace. In a mood of hilarious confusion People's Commissars — including Toller, Landauer and Mühsam — were elected. On Monday morning, April 7th, shivering Munichers stared at new posters which informed them, BAVARIA IS A SOVIET REPUBLIC. A red flag streamed over the palace. The men of the First Life Guards renamed their barracks after Karl Liebknecht. Edicts announced the socialization of the press, the arming of the workers, the formation of a Red Army, and state control of housing and food supplies. The Hoffmann government fled north to Bamberg. Leviné called the new regime of bohemians 'the Pseudo-Soviet Republic'.

But the fact remained that parliamentary democracy, bourgeois interests, and the basic conservatism of the Bavarian peasants had now been drastically challenged, Weimar and Berlin defied in deeds as well as words. The mad, romantic plunge had been precipitated by news of martial law in Stuttgart, riots in Frankfurt, strikes in the Ruhr. Food riots and street fighting had flared in Vienna. A Soviet republic had been proclaimed in Hungary. A tidal wave of revolution seemed to be curling westward.

Count Károlyi, despised by his own class, humiliated by the Allies, faced by the same problems of economic and social dislocation, distrusted by the Social Democrats on the National Council, experienced the same pangs and prestige-crumbling as Kurt Eisner. Unlike Eisner, he was not granted the escape of apotheosis by assassination. He was forced to watch the demolition of liberal democracy and publicly to acknowledge the inevitability of it.

By promising ruthless action to the hordes of unemployed, refugees and jobless soldiers in Budapest, Bela Kun and Tibor Szamuelly had gained a large following. Their newspaper, *Vörös Uszag*, and *Nepszava*, the Social Democratic daily, flayed each other in print. On February 20th Kun made a move which was almost a ritual for revolutionaries (whether communist or fascist) in 1919. He led an attack on the handiest symbol of Social Democratic 'treachery'. During the storming of the *Nepszava* offices seven people were killed and eighty wounded in a clash with police and security guards. 'Social Democracy is our Number One Enemy,' shouted Kun. 'We must destroy it to clear the road to communism. Down with the Social Democrats! Down with the *Nepszava*, that lackey of the bourgeoisie!' Károlyi ordered the arrest and imprisonment of Kun, who was savagely beaten by the police. Next day all the newspapers blamed Károlyi for such uncivilized behaviour. The Catholic Church aligned itself with the aristocracy—and the Social Democrats—in hostility to Károlyi's 'third force'. Both rejoiced openly at the fall of the provisional government. When Catherine Károlyi appealed to her father, Count Julius Andrassy (who had fled to Switzerland), to support that government in its threefold struggle against reaction, Bolshevism and the succession states, he replied that his only wish was that the situation should become worse, provoking armed counter-revolution backed by the Allies.

Károlyi had time for one conscience-easing gesture before he accepted defeat. On a gloomy day of heavy rain in March he performed the ceremony of redistributing his own lands. The peasants stood under large umbrellas, 'their deeply furrowed faces lifted up to me in indescribable amazement, wonder and suspicion. I felt as if a great weight had fallen from my heart, for I had always felt the guilt of possessing such wealth. The order of things had been restored ... ' But Károlyi, never a demagogue, could command little gratitude or support in Budapest. On March 20th Colonel Vix presented a new ultimatum. Hungarian troops must be pulled back from the eastern frontier to allow the Rumanians to occupy several thousand square miles of Hungarian territory. Károlyi refused to accept the ultimatum: but it had the effect of focusing hopes for national resistance, even sheer survival, on the one force which had not yet been tried—the communists. Budapest was loud with mass meetings demanding the release of Bela Kun. Sigismund Kunfi, leader of the Social Democrats, hurried to interview Kun in prison, and agreed to a Communist-Social Democrat merger to be known as the Socialist Party of Hungary. *Nepszava* printed Károlyi's statement of resignation, although in fact he had not signed or even written it. The Public Prosecutor, a rabid opponent of Bolshevism, personally released Kun from prison.

Károlyi was put under house arrest in a villa in the hills above Budapest. Kun, still scarred and bruised from his beating, hurried to form a government. Alexander Garbai, a stonemason and trade union leader, was made President—though Kun, as Commissar for

Foreign Affairs, was the recognized head of the regime. Tibor Szamuelly became Commissar of the Interior. Josef Haubrich, leader of the metal workers, was appointed Commandant of Budapest. The brilliant economist Eugen Varga was Commissar of Socialization, Matyas Rakosi Commissar of Trade, journalist Sigismund Kunfi and philosopher Georg Lukacs Commissars of Education. Eugen Hamburger, a German physician who had settled in a Hungarian village (where he preached the Tolstoyan simple life and doctored the peasants free of charge), became Chief Commissar of Agriculture. Julius Helvesi, an engineer, was Commissar of Social Production. Vilmos Boehm — a rarity as a socialist general — took over command of the hastily-recruited Red Army. Kun's government contained a glittering array of socialist intellectuals as well as solid, if slightly bewildered, proletarians. Twenty-five of the thirty-two commissars were Jewish, a fact which provoked the London *Times* to scream about the iniquity of this latest manifestation of 'the Jewish Mafia'.

Edicts ordered the socialization of housing, banks, retail distribution and the land, the ploughing up of racecourses, and the rigorous suppression of black market activities. 'Proletarians!' said the proclamation of the Soviet Republic on March 22nd. 'Enough of words, the time for action has come … By seizing power the Hungarian proletariat has become an outpost of the World Revolution…' At press conferences in his office in the former royal palace 33-year-old Kun (by no means the youngest of a remarkably youthful government) was kept busy denying that he intended to socialize women or 'bolshevize' marriage and the family. The French, British, Italian, Yugoslavian and Rumanian Missions left Budapest in a concerted huff. But some foreign observers enjoyed the vigour, virtuosity and idealism with which the new broom was wielded.

H. N. Brailsford, travelling from Austria to Hungary, found the move one from darkness and depression into light and hope. 'Debts and mortgages, loans and share capital, all the old lumber had gone. Men walked with quicker steps because they were facing a new life.' Even some of the bourgeois had accepted the logic of the situation. 'Does one battle for respectability when one's wardrobe is reduced to the last three-year-old suit? Does one fight for property when its measure in currency has sunk to twenty per cent? When every bourgeois knows that he is already ruined, who is going to rush the

Bolshevik barricades?' Counts had new visiting cards printed without their titles. Bankers and factory managers wore red rosettes in
their lapels. Women of noble birth found that their services as
teachers, translators and musicians were in demand. They had been
emancipated overnight, and quitted their empty lives with little
regret. Waiters returned forbidden tips with a gesture of outraged
virtue.

Kun, with his chubby face and ready smile, was a brilliant
publicist: and his government had contrived, by calling in *avant
garde* writers and artists, to sustain a mood of exuberant gaiety.
Leading actors and actresses recited revolutionary poems at the
street corners. Favourites of the opera sang in the service of the
new order. 'One had the irresistible feeling,' wrote Brailsford, 'in
those bright days of spring, as the music of these festivals floated
on the lilac-scented air over the Danube, that youth and art and
talent and creative impulse were with this spirited movement.' True,
the socialized press was filled with little but stern decrees—about
the confiscation of all jewellery above 3,000 kronen in value, for
instance—disobedience to which carried a death penalty. But, as
one commissar explained, chuckling, the bourgeois press had done
such a fine job of spine-chilling overstatement about the Red Terror
in Soviet Russia that everyone was being very co-operative. And
where in Europe or America would one find such a theatrical spread
as in Budapest, where plays by Shaw, Schiller, Shakespeare and
Molière were all running simultaneously? Would not Broadway be
better off for such a cultural dictatorship? The general belief was
that when the Entente tried to impose crushing peace terms, the
whole of Europe would seek escape in communism. Why not,
when in Hungary at any rate it was so clearly on the side of the
angels? Dr Lukacs had recognized the social value of teachers by
giving *all* of them, whether in university or village school, the
maximum monthly salary of 3,000 kronen. He announced his intention of raising the school-leaving age first to sixteen then to eighteen,
and providing a wide and free range of further education. He hoped,
he said, to recruit teachers from the lawyers who had been thrown
out of work by the new People's Courts.

After a visit to Budapest H. G. Alsberg, the correspondent of the
New York *Nation*, grew positively lyrical. 'We have wrongly read
the spirit of the proletarian revolution,' he reported. 'We have read
too much about class warfare and too little about brotherhood.

Yet its spirit is the essence of brotherhood ... By the magic of changing the direction of human thoughts and hopes, the people of Hungary have purified the well-springs of their humanity.' One got the
same food to eat in a luxury hotel or a workmen's café. 'Even at
afternoon tea at the Ritz the high-rouged ladies in near-Paris gowns
and the begaitered *jeunesse doré* who have learned nothing from recent
events can get nothing save a few crackers and an unsweetened cup
of near-tea.'

Lenin brooded over this latest and most promising Bolshevik
infant. 'The great commander of this revolution', wrote Alsberg,
'is a man called Ulianov, alias Lenin. When the history of this period
comes to be written Lenin, I am inclined to think, will be its greatest
figure, with nobody a bad second. Daily, from his headquarters, he
issues his commands by wireless, and his Hungarian followers,
sitting in the castle of monarchy, make notes and follow instructions.
Couriers travel back and forth to the seat of the internationalist
caliphate for orders, aeroplanes wing across the mountains to fetch
his behests. He advises when to be firm and when to yield.' Lenin
had already sent a telegram to the Munich 'Soviet' asking what it
proposed to do when the Bavarian peasants started to withhold
supplies. He was anxious that, for the time being, the Hungarian
Soviet leaders should go easy on the issue of collectivized agriculture—even as he had been forced to temporize.

Paris was as electrified by the Hungarian Bolshevik coup as Moscow. Hoover made it clear that Hungary could expect no relief
until Bela Kun had been bounced. But at the beginning of April a
special train containing an international mission headed by General
Jan Smuts was speeding to Budapest with offers of negotiation. In
his villa in the hills Count Károlyi reflected, sadly but not without
a certain bitter amusement, that though Bolshevism had bounced
him, it had at least forced the Big Four to recognize Hungary's
existence and to treat her with a semblance of respect.

4. *Direct Action*

The Bolsheviks showed great ignorance about the potentialities for social revolution in Britain and America. But they never made the mistake of addressing their appeals to the official socialist parties which, in their dullness, had been the despair and the laughing-stock of the Second International, and were rated even lower by the architects of the Third. Trotsky, during his brief stay in the United States, had rapidly come to the conclusion that Eugene Debs, though a shoddy Marxist, was the only leader of the American Socialist Party (A.S.P.) who had any guts at all. The typical American socialist leader, thought Trotsky, was a ghastly kind of Babbitt who 'supplements his commercial activities with dull Sunday meditations on the future of humanity'. Morris Hillquit, a much-respected moderate A.S.P. man, he saw as 'a Babbitt of Babbitts – the ideal socialist spokesman for successful dentists'.

Lenin and Trotsky would no doubt have agreed with Beatrice Webb's estimate of the Parliamentary Labour Party. Composed almost entirely of trade-union officials (twenty-nine of them ex-miners), it was led by a middle-aged Scottish nonentity called William Adamson. Pious, domesticated, a total abstainer, Adamson typified the average British worker's dislike for anything resembling intellect or ideology. According to Beatrice Webb he fumbled in politics 'as we should fumble in the dark recesses of a mine, and gets about the same output as we should do.' For anti-revolutionary, anti-Bolshevik fervour there was little to choose between Samuel Gompers (who maintained that socialism 'destroys personal initiative, wipes out national pride, and plays into the hands of the aristocrats') and his counterparts in Britain. J. H. Thomas, the railwaymen's leader, remarked that the Kaiser was 'morally superior' to the Bolsheviks.

Bolshevik propaganda was, therefore, aimed at the workers in uniform (chafing for demobilization and infected with trench cynicism) or at the small but, it was hoped, influential syndicalist leavening in both countries. During the war the rank-and-file revolt in industry had reached formidable proportions. The question was:

how far was it capable, after the armistice, of seriously challenging the government?

'That figure of Nobody in sodden khaki, cumbered with muddy gear, its precious rifle wrapped in rags, no brightness anywhere about it except the light of its eyes ... its face seamed with lines which might have been dolorous, which might have been ironic, with the sweat running from under its steel casque, looms now ... huge, statuesque, silent but questioning, like an overshadowing challenge,' said the London *Nation* on November 16th, 1918. Would the workers in uniform, trained to wholesale slaughter, make common cause with the militant workers in the factories in a violent attack on profiteers, politicians and rack-renting natural rulers? The mere possibility, alleged the *Herald*, had millionaire industrialists quaking in their high-buttoned boots. The government took care not to clot the country with too many returning heroes. In the two months after the armistice only 750,000 of the $3\frac{1}{2}$ million men serving in the Imperial British armies were demobilized, many of them 'starred' high-grade workers with jobs waiting. Discontent mounted to mutiny among the rest. Winston Churchill was appointed Secretary of State for War and Air to deal with a threatening situation.

In a single week in early January 1919 more than thirty cases of insubordination involving nearly 100,000 men occurred in England and Scotland. Some units told their officers that they had formed themselves into soviets and intended to march to the nearest town to 'fraternize' with the workers. Drivers withdrew their services and immobilized their vehicles. Officers furiously bicycled down lanes to intercept their men and urge them to come to their senses. Generals sallied forth from Whitehall armed with soothing oratory. At Folkestone 10,000 troops refused to parade and marched to the town hall. 'For Officers Only' notices were torn down, the harbour had to be closed temporarily as an embarkation port, and troopships left for Boulogne half empty. At Dover the mayor, faced with a similar demonstration, commandeered a cinema to keep the rebels occupied while a deputation went to the town hall. The Mayor of Brighton had to pacify 8,000 angry Guardsmen. Lorry-loads of mutineers from army camps around London drove to Whitehall demanding a categorical assurance that they would not be sent to fight against Soviet Russia. At Rosyth men of the mine-sweeping flotillas refused to put to sea. On February 8th some 3,000 soldiers, exasperated by inadequate transport and transit accommodation, marched on the War Office from Victoria railway station. A reserve battalion of Grenadier Guards surrounded them with fixed bayonets. Two troops of the Household Cavalry were alerted.

Though on this occasion Churchill was agitated ('a very grave issue had arisen at the physical heart of the State') the army mutinies in England were soon dealt with. 'Tell me the old, old story' or 'Why are we waiting?' were sung more often than the Red Flag or the Internationale. More serious were reports of the formation of soldiers' councils among the troops in Egypt, and a large-scale disturbance at Calais, where, at the end of January, army ordnance and mechanical transport detachments mutinied and persuaded troops returning from leave to join them. For four days, until encircled by the bayonets and machine-guns of two specially drafted divisions, they controlled the town. Since this turbulence happened to coincide with a period of great industrial strife, the government was easily persuaded that sinister forces were at work. The reports of secret agents who had insinuated themselves into various tiny Marxist groups helped to confirm this assumption. 'The present unrest in the Army occasioned by the difficulties of demobilization', alleged one report, 'is in grave danger of spreading and of taking the form of an alliance between the soldiers and the extreme section of the workers ... The ultimate end of this manoeuvre would be Revolution and a Soviet form of government ... '

The *Herald* emphasized the need to strike hard before the government of businessmen had time to deliver its blows. The election results, it argued, had proved nothing. Only half the electorate had bothered to go to the polls and matters had been so arranged that barely twenty-five per cent of the forces overseas had registered their vote. The government must be brought down. Labour demanded not reform but revolution – a peaceful one if possible, but a revolution, a complete remaking of society. 'Today must be our battle of the Marne. If we can break their onslaught there is hope for the future. If we fail – God help us!' The *Call* derided 'the feeble futilities of the go-slow brigade ... municipalizing this service and nationalizing that – always buying out the other people, of course – and always leaving them in possession of what we have paid them for, and making it necessary to continue the buying-out process for centuries.' The militant Left was almost solidly anti-parliamentarian. 'Comrades,' wrote W. F. Watson (a cockney lathe-minder who had left school at the age of ten) in the *Workers' Dreadnought* (edited by Sylvia Pankhurst), 'comrades, keep your eyes off what William Morris aptly describes as a dung-hill – that is, Parliament. Keep your minds off the relative merits of piecework, bonus, or day-work. Concentrate your energy and activities on the complete overthrow of capitalism! Russia has started and Germany is following. France, Italy, Spain, the Argentine and even America are seething with revolt. Shall it be said of British workers that they alone lifted their chains and kissed them?'

The armistice had freed employers for a campaign against war-time 'socialism'. National factories were sold. Employees – and especially 'troublemaking' employees – were sacked. 'Inflated' war-time wages came under review – or attack. Official trade-union leaders, smarting from a four-year tussle with the rank-and-file, eagerly joined the Government of Businessmen in its fight against the 'anarchists' of industry. The trouble with trade unionism, re-marked Churchill at a meeting of the War Cabinet, was that there was not enough of it – that is, of the sound, patriotic kind. Infuriated by the attitude of their own leaders, frightened by mounting unemployment (by February 600,000 were jobless), despairing of help from the Parliamentary Labour Party, the workers turned to direct action in defence of their interests.

The first really menacing move came in Belfast and Glasgow, the great engineering centres most affected by the running down of the war machine. Defying the Amalgamated Society of Engineers, which had negotiated a 47-hour week with the government, the men struck in Belfast for a 44-hour, in Glasgow for a 40-hour week, with no reduction in wages. The object, they explained, was to minimize unemployment and to make way for demobilized soldiers. The workers of Belfast acted first – on January 25th – and stayed out longest. Twenty-six unions were represented on the General Strike Committee. Employees of the municipal transport and electricity services joined the strikers. All factories save those which generated their own power were closed. In the abattoirs butchers had to use pole-axes since the mechanical killers would not function. Theatres and cinemas were closed. No ships could move into or out of the harbour or dry docks without permission of the strike committee. Only hospitals were given exemption from the electricity fade-out.

'It is syndicalism pure and simple,' raged the *Belfast News-Letter*. 'The strike leaders are not relying on the strength or justice of their demand. Their weapon is the paralysis of the city's daily life.' On January 30th strikers paraded through the streets to Donegall Square North, where they were harangued by Charles McKay, Chairman of the Strike Committee. 'The city has been ours since Saturday,' he told them. 'The workers simply go down and show themselves and the municipal staff come out either on principle or for safety' (laughter). 'The employers know the workers' cause is just. The government intervened quickly enough during the war in the so-called national interest when there were any disputes. Why don't they intervene now? We can't rely on the government. We can't rely on our unions. We have to rely on ourselves. The little tin gods over there' (pointing to the city hall) 'know we are right, though there is not a man among them who has the courage to say so.' The nearest approach to violence, however, came when a delegate from Dublin who expressed some vaguely revolutionary sentiments was knocked off the platform to the accompaniment of howls of 'We want no Papist Bolsheviks here!' There was an almost total absence of class-war feeling. When the managing director of Harland & Wolff (a firm which employed most of the rebels) died during the strike, a contingent of strikers marched in the funeral procession. Direct action in Belfast scrupulously observed the bourgeois decencies.

In Glasgow, where for years Marxism had been preached and studied as a secular, but still predestinarian, religion, it had a more ideological tinge. This, said the orators of the Clyde Workers' Committee, was the first class strike of any significance that had taken place in Scotland. At last a whole complex of unions, normally concerned only with the interests of their own members, had united in a straight fight with capitalism. 'Into it then, comrades,' urged William Gallacher, 'as never before. Let this be the class war started at last. Too long have we been groping about in the dark. Now at last we begin to see the light, and come what may we must sustain the fight until we emerge into the full, bright day of the Socialist Republic.' Emanuel Shinwell, then boss of the radical Glasgow Trades Council, directed the 40-hour agitation and approved an emergency plan to sabotage Glasgow's electricity supply. By January 29th, the third day of the strike, 70,000 men were out. A deputation, headed by Shinwell and Gallacher, spoke to the Lord Provost, telling him to ask the government – of which, in Lloyd George's absence in Paris, Bonar Law was the acting head – to intervene in the dispute. Bonar Law, after a telephone conversation with the Prime Minister, refused.

On January 31st a crowd estimated at 100,000, composed of Clyde-side strikers and unemployed from all over western Scotland, assembled in George Square in front of the City Chambers. The strikers' deputation entered the building to hear the government's verdict. The Lord Provost kept them waiting while he concluded a meeting of the Magistrates' Committee. Word of this insolent delay reached the crowd. A huge red flag was unfurled over an ocean of cloth caps. A tram was overturned. Mounted police joined the foot police surrounding the square. A baton charge was made. A general scrimmage began. David Kirkwood, a member of the deputation, ran down the steps to see what was happening, and was bludgeoned down from behind. Gallacher assaulted the Chief Constable and was also batoned. The Lord Provost read the Riot Act. Gallacher, Kirkwood and Shinwell were arrested. Windows were smashed. The Chief Constable was hit on the head by a bottle, shrapnel from which cut Sheriff Mackenzie's hand. 'The bottle-throwers', reported the *Times* correspondent, 'turned and fled into side-alleys, panting and gasping … Later the unruly element rallied sufficiently to smoke cigarettes and discuss the situation in the foulest language I have heard for years.'

The Rt Hon. R. Munro, Secretary of State for Scotland, insisted that this was not just a strike, but 'a Bolshevist rising'. General Sir William Robertson gave a summary of the Scottish troops available to restore order in Glasgow. Sixty tanks and a hundred lorries were sent north by rail. The tanks were garaged in the meat market. Highland regiments garrisoned all the major public build-ings and patrolled the main streets in full battle order. The City Chambers were ringed with barbed wire and machine-guns. The men began to drift back to the shipyards and factories. Troops broke up the strikers' 'terrorist' pickets around the power stations. But the Joint Committee's *Strike Bulletin*, still selling briskly, looked on the bright side. The underground motormen and electrical workers of London were ready to take up the battle. 'London is now in the turmoil of a new strike movement, the profiteers of Belfast are still helpless before the united forces of the workers … the surrender of the employers and the government is only hours away. No one knows better than they do that they are beaten to a frazzle by the greatest strike movement this country has ever seen.'

The London strike rapidly fizzled out when threatened with special legislation and mass prosecution. In Belfast a military occupation of the city hastened the end of the strike, which came on February 20th—by which time the last of the Glasgow rebels had surrendered. There still remained what promised to be the most serious onslaught of all. The miners, nearly 200,000 of whom had already downed tools in Yorkshire and Lanarkshire, threatened a general strike in support of their demand for a six-hour day, wage increases, and workers' control of the industry. On February 12th the miners refused a government wage offer. There was talk of the railwaymen and transport workers making it a Triple Alliance occasion. Coal stocks were low. Secret War Office circulars were issued by Churchill asking for information about the reliability of troops if strike breaking should become necessary. The answers were pessimistic. Even the police could not be counted upon without reservation. The War Cabinet's Committee of Industrial Unrest redoubled its efforts to create volunteer motor pools and reserves of special constables. *The Times*, *Daily Telegraph* and *Morning Post* were full of appeals for middle and upper class unity 'in the defence of the nation'. For the situation had taken an even more sinister turn when the Triple Alliance decided to canvass its members about their willingness to make 'Hands Off Russia' one of the aims of direct action. Most of the workers, said *The Times*, were sound enough at heart, but were 'the unconscious instruments of a planned campaign drawn up by intellectuals in the background who desire to emulate Lenin and Trotsky and the Spartacus leaders in Germany.' The *Saturday Review* criticized 'the growing belief in labour circles, first that force alone counts, and secondly that no other class than their own exists. "*L'État*", they cry (or would cry if they knew French), "*c'est Nous*".'

In a confidential report to the War Cabinet, the Home Secretary solemnly asked what action he should take in the case of David Ramsay, a shop steward of the Amalgamated Society of Engineers who, during a Herald League rally in a Croydon cinema, had declaimed: 'In a short time this country will be engaged in a general strike for the overthrow of capitalism. I am proud to call myself a Bolshevik. I am prepared to use every means from the bomb to the ballot box ... If the master class is not prepared to give way, see to it that you are not too squeamish in your attitude to them.' Home Office snoopers, busy opening letters from Glasgow to America, turned up some alarming items. One writer described the I.W.W. as 'the only union that matters'; another was 'ready to take part in a revolution tomorrow'; another insisted that 'the only solution for unemployment is Bolshevism'.

Lloyd George hurried over from Paris. By the end of February a National Industrial Conference had been set up. On this, representatives of management and labour continued to discuss, with decreasing urgency (and until well on in 1921), a number of mild reforms which were duly referred to the government for a decision. That took care of all the unions outside the Triple Alliance. For the miners Lloyd George produced a flattering safety-valve in the form of a Royal Commission presided over by Mr Justice Sankey. There followed the diverting spectacle of six capitalists (three coal-owners and three 'independent' industrialists) pitting their wits against six miners' champions (three miners' officials headed by Robert Smillie, and three Fabian intellectuals – Sidney Webb, R. H. Tawney and Sir Leo Chiozza Money) and getting much the worst of it. The Commission sat in the Robing Room of the House of Lords, a piquant setting for a trial of high-born villains. Smillie, Secretary of the Miners' Federation, took the initiative. Mine-owners' profits, he proved easily enough, had trebled during the war. 'If the mine-owners have sunk their capital,' commented the *Herald*, 'the miners have sunk their lives. Three men are killed in the mines for every day of the year. A third of them are injured more or less seriously. *There is blood on all the coal we burn.*' Here was 'the whole tragic drama of a million men shut out in more senses than one from the light of the sun. It is a drama worthy of a great actor, and he has been found in Robert Smillie.'

But while, for the next four months, Smillie acted his simple heart out in the Royal Robing Chamber, the revolution was bundled off the stage and out of the headlines. Gallacher fired a last journalistic shot: 'Every man or woman must make a choice, to cringe at the feet of the employers and offer up body and soul as a sacrifice on the unholy altar of Mammon, or fight as a true-hearted champion of their class ... Your Trade Unions, your Constitutions, are a bugbear and a hindrance to working-class unity. Away with them to the scrapheap. Come together as workers. Fight together as workers ... for a new Britain.' He, Shinwell and Kirkwood went to prison. So did David Ramsay and W. F. Watson. 'I stand before you,' said Watson at his trial, 'proud of the fact that I am a revolutionary socialist, thoroughly convinced that only by the complete over-throw of the present system of society can we ever hope to find the great white bird of truth.'

After the collapse of a dockers' strike in London, Harry Pollitt, then a branch secretary of the Boilermakers' Society, told an East End audience bitterly: 'We could have had a revolution a month ago if our so-called leaders had not been afraid of prison.' But that, he said, was not all. The working classes, in their abysmal, capitalist-sponsored ignorance, cared only for beer, tobacco and horse-racing. It would, he reckoned, take twenty years to educate them. From the sad, toy wreck of Britain's revolution, Gallacher and Pollitt drew the conclusions which made them prominent and passionate advocates of an international revolutionary movement controlled by the Russian Communist Party. 'We revolutionaries, as we called our-selves,' wrote Pollitt later, 'not only lacked experience: we were also eaten up with rival jealousies. Each little group thought itself right and everybody else wrong. The workers were begging for leader-ship, which we could not give. I look upon this period of golden opportunities, when we failed to provide the workers with real leadership, as one of the blackest and most tragic in the whole of my experience.'

In the United States, where employers were busily exploiting the wartime mood of national hysteria, the mere desire of the mass of unskilled workers to organize in unions was represented as un-American. As William Z. Foster had predicted, the end of the wartime truce and of federal control of industry meant a declaration of war not only on I.W.W. extremists but—despite its frantic declarations of loyalty to the Constitution—on the A.F.L. and any hint of blasphemy against the Divine Right of Capital. In this battle neither Big Business nor Government had any scruples about using force. There was no need for anxious enquiries about army loyalty. Most Americans, however poor, had been made to feel that the fight for the Open Shop and the Dictatorship of the Boardroom was somehow a fight to preserve their 'liberty' against ravening foreign collectivists. In the new American Civil War there were to be no neutrals. Every worker who had ever dared to force rather than wait for a pay rise was assumed to have taken sides. Even Gompers was hustled out of no man's land into the back trenches of 'Red' unionism.

The first clash came in the Pacific North-west, an area of almost traditional I.W.W. sentiment. Wobblies in and around Seattle had been active in lightning wartime strikes and in creating a general atmosphere of militancy among shipyard and lumber men. On January 21st, 1919, 35,000 Seattle shipyard workers struck for higher wages and shorter hours. The Emergency Fleet Corporation, insisting that the men's contract had two months to run, refused to negotiate. The Central Labour Council, representing all organized labour in the city, had already expressed sympathy with the Russian Workers' Republic. Now it decided to back the shipyarders' action by a general strike—the first in America. The stated object was 'to promote labour solidarity against the growing militancy of employers.' On February 3rd, while newspapers were still full of denunciations of the 'Bolshevik revolution' in Glasgow and Belfast, the strike began. Sixty thousand workers, covering almost every trade, walked out. The Strike Committee's 'inner circle' of fifteen members, led by I.W.W.-sympathizer James Duncan, granted special leave for the functioning of garbage trucks and laundry and milk vans, and for emergency food, coal and electricity supplies.

Drugstores, groceries and department stores were besieged by citizens intent on stocking up for a state of siege. They bought guns as often as canned food. The local and national press fanned the panic. 'This is America, not Russia,' wailed the Seattle *Star*. The *Post-Intelligencer* ran a front-page cartoon which showed the Red Flag flying above the Stars and Stripes, with the caption NOT IN A THOUSAND YEARS. All over America headlines screamed REDS DIRECTING SEATTLE STRIKE—TO TEST CHANCE FOR REVOLUTION. In Seattle, said the Cleveland *Plain Dealer*, 'the Bolshevik beast has come into the open.' It was 'only a middling step from Petrograd to Seattle,' warned the *Chicago Tribune*. The restraint and efficiency of the Strike Committee's administration made it hard to mount a reactionary counter-attack with any show of reason. But Ole Hanson, the Mayor of Seattle, was not the man to be bothered by such a detail. Recently foiled in an attempt to get elected to the U.S. Senate, this political weathercock (he had switched from Taft to Theodore Roosevelt to Wilson), ex-grocery-store-owner, ex-realtor, ex-advertising-copywriter, ex-investment broker, the very epitome of opportunist dollar democracy, saw the chance to cover himself with glory. He took it with both hands and a ready flow of naive but widely-accepted fantasy.

According to Hanson the strike was part of an I.W.W. plot to start a 'revolutionary holocaust' throughout America. The time had come for the people of Seattle to show their patriotism. On their behalf he ordered federal troops into action, and at dawn on February 6th, in a large automobile draped in the Stars and Stripes, himself headed their entry into the city. With soldiers and policemen posted in strategic positions, Hanson called upon the Strike Committee to end their putsch, or see it crushed by force. Scared by this threat, worried by frantic appeals from Gompers, most of the A.F.L. representatives climbed down. On February 10th the Committee capitulated. 'The rebellion is quelled,' roared Hanson. 'The test came and was met unflinchingly.' 'FULL STEAM AHEAD,' whooped the Seattle *Star*, 'today this Bolshevik-sired nightmare is at an end.' OUR FLAG IS STILL THERE, captioned the *Post-Intelligencer* beneath a cartoon showing a tattered Red Flag drooping beneath a majestically streaming Old Glory. 'From Russia they came, and to Russia they should be made to go!' shouted Congressman Albert Johnson, referring to the strike leaders. Hanson emerged as the man of the hour, a fighter 'with a backbone that would serve as a girder in a railway bridge.' The Seattle Clown (as the radical press christened him) set off on a lucrative, nation-wide anti-Bolshevik career. His decision to resign as mayor in order to concentrate on this 'patriotic duty' was rewarded in the next seven months with earnings of 40,000 dollars.

The inauguration of a One Big Union campaign at a convention of Western Canadian labour radicals at Calgary a few weeks after the Seattle strike was seen as another outcropping of I.W.W. Bolshevism. The socialist rally of December 1918 in Winnipeg had been followed by talk in the *Western Labour News*, journal of the city's Trades and Labour Council, of a Dominion-wide strike in defiance of the government. 'In Germany the workers are shooting,' orated R. J. Johns, a prominent member of the Council, in January 1919. 'In Winnipeg we are still fighting with ideas—but we shall soon be fighting with rifles.' The *O.B.U. Bulletin*, spearhead of the drive for industrial unionism, stressed the class war as the central reality. The Russian Soviets, it argued, were essentially trade councils federated in One Big Union. If the Dominion government did not tackle the problem of unemployment with radical determination, Bolshevism was bound to spread, warned the *Western Labour News*.

When the workers took control, they would 'form a dictatorship which will give the same order to the owners of Canada as Lenin gave to the capitalists of Russia: Obey or starve!'

The Calgary conference referred to the Central Committee of the projected O.B.U. as 'the Central Soviet'. Regional committees were to be known as 'Provincial Soviets'. As if this provocative terminology was not enough, the dominating figures at Calgary and in the Winnipeg Trades and Labour Council could almost all be classified (at a Red Scare pinch) as foreign agitators. Johns was a 29-year-old Cornishman who had emigrated to Canada in 1912. Bob Russell, a 30-year-old machinist, was from Clydeside. William Pritchard, an eloquent young Welsh Marxist, had settled in Vancouver in 1911. John Queen, a cooper by trade and a Winnipeg Town Councillor, was a Scot. Abraham Heaps, another councillor, had been born in Leeds, Yorkshire, of Jewish parents. William Ivens, editor of the *Western Labour News*, was a Warwickshire man who had come to Canada in 1896. He had worked first as a market gardener then as a well-known preacher on the Methodist circuit—until his socialist views obliged him to quit the pulpit. 'There are men, *real* men,' wrote Ivens in 1919, 'who believe that there is something in Bolshevism that is essential to a free democracy and to civilization.'

The Ottawa Parliament, alarmed by the ferment in the west, planned to deport the 'British Bolsheviks.' It was feared that their message might find a receptive hearing among the 60,000 Russians, Ukrainians, Poles and Scandinavians who formed nearly a third of the population of Winnipeg.

In the Pennsylvanian coal belt the A.F.L.-backed drive to organize the steel workers faced stiffening opposition. In company towns where for sixty years union organizers had been met at the railroad station and given the alternative of leaving town or going to jail, it needed real courage to buck the system. It was impossible to hire a hall. Open-air meetings were often broken up by a baton charge of the 'Black Cossacks'—the mounted police of the Pennsylvania State Constabulary. But a 'flying squadron' of eight intrepid organizers fought on grimly in an area which was in effect a huge industrial jail. Company detectives noted the names of workers who attended the meetings, and they were summarily fired. Not going to meetings was no guarantee of safety. In a policy of deliberate, terrorist victimization, specially vulnerable employees were sacked—men with large families, even old and half-crippled men. One mechanic discharged as a 'union agitator' was deaf and dumb and could neither read nor write.

The Iron and Steel Organization Committee's efforts were hugely outmatched by the National Security League (N.S.L.), financed by J. P. Morgan, John D. Rockefeller and Coleman Dupont. The N.S.L., with voluntary speakers in every major town, held over a thousand meetings in 1919, reaching at least 375,000 people. Local Chambers of Commerce, the Boy Scouts, the wildly conservative Sons and Daughters of the American Revolution, were its close and willing allies. N.S.L. literature, playing endless variations on a basic theme of 'when you hear a man trying to discredit Uncle Sam—that's Bolshevism', was circulated among schoolteachers, clergy, businessmen and government employees. The National Civic Federation (N.C.F.), founded in 1901 with the declared aim of fostering greater co-operation between capital and labour, had for years made the I.W.W. its chief target. Backed by Judge Gary and department-store tycoon Everit Macy, it featured a few tame union representatives on its executive board. In spring 1919 the *N.C.F. Review*, famed for its wartime patriotic extravaganzas, ran a series of lurid exposés of 'Bolshevism' in schools, universities, the press, churches and trade unions, and led a rapidly growing demand to search school textbooks for un-American lapses. Reprints of articles were syndicated to business magazines and right-wing A.F.L. journals. The *Open Shop Review*, sponsored by three national employers' associations, took the line that unionism 'ranked with Bolshevism as the greatest crime left in the world'. At the bottom of each page readers were reminded that at least three million workers believed in 'the insidious and radical principle of the Closed Shop'.

Supposedly impartial federal investigations of radicalism did nothing to cool fevered brows. The 1,200-page report of the Overman Committee of the United States Senate was nothing but an anthology of Red Scare fables. The Red Army, it alleged, was composed mainly of criminals; the Russian revolution was led mainly by former East Side Jews; the Bolsheviks were establishing hundreds of Free Love Bureaus. The press let rip with tales of nationalized womanhood, atrocities and massacres. Any decent Russian citizen, it seemed, was liable to be roasted, scalded, hacked or torn to pieces. Soviet Russia was a country in which raving maniacs stalked the streets and starving people fought with starving dogs for gutter carrion. That was what America would be like if the radicals were given a chance. RED PERIL HERE, bannered the head-lines, REDS PLAN BLOODY REVOLUTION.

Under these circumstances, the persistence of Foster's flying squad must rate as one of the most heroic actions of 1919. 'We are going to see whether Pennsylvania belongs to Kaiser Gary or Uncle Sam,' 89-year-old Mother Jones told her equally heroic audiences. 'Our Kaisers smoke 72-cent cigars and have lackeys bring them champagne while you starve ... They have stomachs two miles wide and two miles long, and you fill them. If Gary wants to work twelve hours a day, let him go into the mill and sweat it out. What we want is a little leisure, time for music, a decent home, books, and all the things which make life worth living.'

All round the world the evident determination of businessmen's governments to get back to their idea of normalcy set off flares of workers' resistance. In Johannesburg, in April 1919, workers took over the town hall and prepared to administer the city. In Australia a One Big Union campaign for industrial solidarity was started. A massive strike of miners and seamen in New South Wales turned into a trial of strength with the whole complex of government, arbitration courts and reformist trade unionism. In Italy the workers of Milan, Genoa and Turin, though deluged with anti-Bolshevik propaganda by jittery managements, talked of occupying the factories. But it was in Spain, with its treacherous playboy king and grotesquely unrepresentative Cortes, that the workers' rebellion burst out most spectacularly.

Perhaps only the tremors of the Bolshevik-inspired revolutions in Europe could have nerved the anarcho-syndicalist C.N.T. to yet another challenge in 1919. It went into battle with a millennial fervour inconceivable to the welfare-minded militants of Britain, France or even America. Though loosely linked in regional and national federation, anything resembling a permanent bureaucracy was so hateful to the C.N.T. that it employed only one paid official and maintained no strike or benefit funds. Yet all of the 100,000 C.N.T. workers in Barcelona struck in February 1919. The city went without light. Factories ground to a halt. Amazingly, though thousands were arrested and heavy sentences passed, there was little violence. Amazingly, too, the strike lasted for a month, and ended in an uneasy truce. Such solidarity without strike pay was a truly impressive achievement.

From Barcelona the revolt spread south, causing large-scale strikes in Seville and Granada, and a new surge of militancy among the peasants on the huge estates of Andalusia. Many of them had joined the C.N.T. They now demanded increased wages and the provision of work for unemployed day-labourers and ruined smallholders – until such time as the land was 'handed over to peasant syndicates, to be worked by them in common'. Fifty towns in Andalusia had anarchist newspapers of their own which acted as a forum for the views of contributors who were often barely literate. The peasants, though excited by reports of the revolution in Russia, were not in any sense Marxist. They dreamed, rather, of reviving a golden Middle Age when peasant communes, unpestered by kings, nobles and grasping merchants, had worked the land in fraternity and peace. But to grandee landowners this *was* Bolshevism. Terrified, they granted whatever the peasants asked and fled to the towns.

Foreign observers were equally alarmed. 'A wave of Bolshevism is passing over Andalusia,' reported a correspondent of the Paris *Temps*. 'At San Luccar a few days ago agricultural workers burned their barns to show their discontent at inadequate wages.' Anarcho-syndicalism, said the London *Times*, had not only 'yoked the political aspirations for Catalan home rule to the fiery chariot of Bolshevism', but was making a serious effort to capture the whole country. Señor Merry del Val, the Spanish ambassador in London, insisted that it was 'only the continental form of Bolshevism'. This interpretation at least had the virtue of hastening the flow of foreign aid. A British government loan of £3 million was soon under negotiation. Most of it was probably used to wipe off some of the chronic pay-arrears of the Spanish army, to which the refugee landowners of Andalusia and the industrialists of Barcelona now looked for salvation.

For all their simplicity, ideological confusion and lack of clear-cut leadership, the mutinous workers of Britain, North and South America, Spain, South Africa and Australia, and the rebellious peasants of Spain and Italy, had done the Bolsheviks – or the shining myth of the Russian Workers' Republic – proud. The mere fact that they had confronted governments infinitely more powerful and subtle than the decayed bureaucracy of the Romanov Empire was in itself an alarming portent. As interpreted by the plutocratic press and plutocratic politicians—who, after all, were without benefit of hindsight—it appeared as a gigantic upseething of the Abyss which had carried the frontiers of the Bolshevik revolution to Milan, Barcelona, Glasgow, Belfast, Pittsburgh, Seattle, Winnipeg, Buenos Aires and Sydney, as well as to Berlin, Munich, Vienna and Budapest.

5. *Capitals of the World: Paris*

Lenin insisted that industrialization must take priority over dreams of social redemption. Economically crippled Russia was, as Hoover realized, the perfect field for Americanization. The Bolsheviks realized this too. But their cries for machinery and technical missions were cancelled out by bellows of outraged Marxist virtue. America, so eager to propel the world into its version of the twentieth century, and Soviet Russia, so eager for a wicked imperialist world to hoist it into *its* version of the twentieth century, were like ideal mates whose fruitful coupling is prevented by a tragi-comic ideological incompatibility. In 1919, from Paris and Moscow, those self-styled capitals of the world, the clamour of their mutual frustration filled the air with shrill remonstrance.

'There are American principles, American policies,' Woodrow Wilson had said in 1917. 'We stand for no others. They are the principles of mankind and must prevail.' Since then the Bolsheviks had brilliantly staked a similar claim for *their* principles. Apprehension mingled with pride in Wilson as – a high-minded truant from the White House – he approached Paris. 'It is to America that the whole world turns today,' he told George Creel, head of American Information Services, 'not only with its wrongs but with its hopes and grievances. The hungry expect us to feed them, the homeless look to us for shelter, the sick of heart and body depend upon us for cure. All these expectations have in them a quality of terrible urgency. There must be no delay ... '

But delay there had been. The Peace Conference, originally scheduled to begin in mid-December 1918, was not formally opened until January 18th, 1919. The soldiers – Foch, Sir Henry Wilson, Weygand and Pétain – had pressed for a quick imposed peace with Germany to release its forces (and the armies of the Allies, before the rot of demobilization set in) for a grand anti-Bolshevik campaign. But Lloyd George had to make sure of his parliamentary majority. Wilson went on his three-week spree of acclimatization and People-sounding. The professional diplomats preferred to wait awhile in the hope that the Bolshevik government might collapse, that the confusion in Germany would sort itself out, that the governments of the new nations would have time to acquire a semblance of authority. The conference opened on a note of anti-climax, dwarfed in news value by Spartacus, the accelerating social revolutions in Bavaria, Austria and Hungary, the miraculous revival of the Red Army, the Riga Soviet, army mutinies and rumblings of industrial revolt. When the sleek black motor cars carrying the arbiters of Europe purred importantly up to the wrought-iron gates of the Quai d'Orsay, a small and apathetic crowd, estimated at less than five hundred people, watched their arrival.

In France, too, there was trouble brewing. Victory had not anaesthetized proletarian memories. Clemenceau, the butcher of French syndicalism, was vehemently loathed, especially by the railway workers. In the sheds at Batignolles an effigy of him was placed in a coffin and a mock funeral service held, with cries of *'En voilà un de moins!'* and a singing of the Internationale. On February 19th an attempt was made to realize the railwaymen's death-wish. At nine o'clock in the morning, as the car taking Clemenceau from his house in the Rue Franklin to his office slowed to turn into the Rue Delessait, a young man called Emile Cottin emerged from behind a public urinal and fired nine revolver shots. All the bullets save two were absorbed by the cushions upon which the old man was leaning. One penetrated the right shoulder blade, the other was rumoured to have pierced the lung. In court Emile Cottin, thin, slight, fair-haired, the pallor of his face heightened by the bruises of the beating he had received from passers-by and the police, calmly described his motives and background. He was an anarchist, he said, the son of bourgeois parents. He had been three times imprisoned for anti-militarist agitation while in the Army. He hated violence. His room was filled with books—Homer and Marcus Aurelius as well as Bakunin and Kropotkin. What, though, was the use of noble, liberating ideas, if brigands like Clemenceau ruled the world? When millions of men had died for nothing was it not just that one old tyrant should be shot in the name of freedom? Cottin's death sentence was commuted to life imprisonment. His deed rang round the world, but his quarry lived. Clemenceau, after ten days' enforced rest, rose again, a little shorter in temper, a little wearier in manner, his chest-cough deeper and more gurgling than before, to dominate the Peace Conference. He was not the only victim of the great Parisian brouhaha. Arthur Balfour, Britain's Foreign Secretary, was seen with his right arm in a sling. Vittorio Orlando, the Italian Premier, was driven to the verge of nervous breakdown by his efforts to make sure that Italy got her rightful share in 'the work of civilization'. Major Herbert O. Yardley, of United States Military Intelligence, claimed to have uncovered a plot to assassinate President Wilson by 'giving him the influenza in ice'.

Almost anything could happen in the *Ville Lumière* in 1919. Behind the Paris of the press photographs, in which the Big Four tended to look like a group of baffled family physicians, behind the bromide press statements ('It is true', murmured Balfour, languorously crossing and uncrossing his long legs, 'that there is a great deal of discussion going on, but there is no real discord about ideas or facts. We are agreed on the principal questions, and it only remains to find the words to embody the agreements') — lay a turmoil of crazy, conflicting ambitions. Every hotel flew the flag of some foreign potentate, or several. In the Hotel Continental in the Rue de Rivoli the Emir Feisal and Colonel T. E. Lawrence (Paris was full of speculations as to what really *had* happened to him on that traumatic night in Deraa) held court. So did the aged Empress Eugénie, impressing upon anyone who would listen the vital necessity of so crushing Germany that she could never again threaten the peace of Europe. The cheaper *hôtels meublés* were crammed with representatives of every nation, minority, enclave and tribe on the Eurasian continent. Greeks, Macedonians and Montenegrins; Serbs, Croats, Slovenes, Czechs, Slovaks, Transylvanians, Galicians, Poles, Ukrainians, Lithuanians; Estonians and Latvians; Arabs from Palestine, Arabs from Mesopotamia, Kurds, Persians, Syrians, Moslem Lebanese and Christian Lebanese, Armenians, Azerbaidjanians, Georgians; Jewish Zionists and Jewish anti-Zionists; an envoy from the Duchy of Teschen, missions from Luxemburg and Lichtenstein; a Danish delegation demanding the return of Schleswig-Holstein and a Swedish delegation asking for the Aaland Islands. Any decision, however circumspect and conscientiously researched, trod on a dozen corns, provoking yelps of rage and warnings of Bolshevism.

Patriarchal beards, turbans and fezzes, mitre-like headgear,

flowing mantles, garish military uniforms designed for the embryo-
nic armies of new nations, snow-white burnouses, helped to create
an impression of dreamy fantasy. Around the fringes of the horde of
delegates hovered another horde of adventurers hawking dubious
oil, coal, timber and manganese concessions, pretenders to thrones
or dukedoms, cranks offering a plethora of panaceas, secret agents,
private detectives, refugees with heirlooms or secrets to sell, bogus
art dealers, procurers, pimps and an international army of prostitutes.
An august member of the lunatic fringe was Lord Northcliffe,
proprietor of *The Times* and the *Daily Mail*. Maddened by the refusal
to appoint him one of the British peace delegates, he installed himself at Fontainebleau to co-ordinate a virulent anti-Lloyd George
campaign in his own and the French press. Exasperated beyond
endurance by Northcliffe's guerrilla warfare, the Prime Minister
pulverized him in the House of Commons. 'When diseased vanity is
carried to the point of sowing dissension between great Allies whose
unity is essential to the peace of the world,' he said, 'not even that
kind of disease is an excuse ... In France they still believe that *The
Times* is a serious organ. They do not know that it is nothing but a
threepenny edition of the *Daily Mail*. I want them to know.'

It was tough at the top in Paris: but it could be entertaining.
Guests at Lloyd George's flat in the Rue Nitôt enjoyed his baiting of
Paderewski about Poland's inflated claims ('What can you expect',
he had said, 'of a country that sends a *pianist* to a peace conference?')
and his indiscreet criticisms of the French *cordon sanitaire* and its
puppet politicians (he described Eduard Benes, the Czech Foreign
Minister, as 'that little French jackal'). They were also liable to meet
Sarah Bernhardt, haloed with reminiscences and an enormous gold
wig, or to be diverted by the impersonations of Ruth Draper, the
singing of Leila Megane (a Welsh soprano), a glimpse of Clemenceau
nibbling tea-time *langues de chats*, or the sight of American sentries
driving irate pedestrians from the pavement outside the mansion
in which President Wilson was quartered.

Augustus John, one of the artists commissioned to record the
conference, threw a series of parties celebrated for their wild
abandon. President Wilson (who as Princeton's most popular
professor had once convulsed select audiences with his female
impersonations), though sitting out a performance of Rameau's
Castor and Pollux at the Opéra National, found time to attend a
sprightly revue, *Hullo Paris!*, with Arthur Balfour and Lord Derby.

The Hotel Majestic, which housed the British delegation, was the scene of much boisterous democratic jollity. 'The domestic staff', reported the *Daily Mail* on March 12th, 1919, 'held a very successful dance ... The ballroom was a medley of plenipotentiaries and chambermaids, generals and orderlies, Foreign Office attachés and waitresses. All the latest steps were to be seen, including the jazz and the Hesitation Waltz.' There were, of course, more recherché get-togethers, such as the dinner party for Balliol men in the British delegation. 'At least sixty per cent of the civil staff were at Balliol,' noted Harold Nicolson in his diary. 'We feel proud.'

High society, *nouveaux riches*, delegations – everyone was giving and going to balls. *Le Matin* contrasted Lucullan banquets, opulent luncheons and all-night parties with the lot of ordinary French people waiting in line for small rations of bread, sugar or meat at inflationary prices. While all this heartless extravagance and dissipation was going on, 'the corpses of many gallant soldiers' lay unburied 'on shell-ploughed battlefields a couple of hours' motor drive from Paris.' The most lavish hospitality of all was dispensed at the Hotel Lutétia, by the Chinese delegation. Superb banquets were followed by indigestible speeches about China's grievances delivered by Lou Tseng-Tsiang, the Minister for Foreign Affairs. At night the streets were dense with soldiers on leave, all hell-bent on having a good time. American troops, with a lack of inhibition induced by higher pay and more drink, were the liveliest, a fact immortalized in the words of a popular song:

> How you gonna keep 'em down on the farm
> Now that they've seen Paree?

For journalists the problem was how to get word out of the gay city. The telecommunication service was so inefficient, or overtaxed, or censored, that an estimated forty thousand dispatches were held back every day. Most of them, complained the *New York Herald*, were never delivered, and the rest distributed only after news-killing delays. To use the telegraph, the mails or the telephone, grumbled the correspondent of the *Philadelphia Public Ledger*, was 'an exhibition of childish faith'. Paris, he added, was no place for an idealist. Greed and incompetence had combined to make it a huge fleecing machine, where the sums of money spent by foreigners were said to exceed the total French revenue from foreign trade.

If the centre of Paris resembled a cross between a bazaar and a clip joint, the conference at the heart of it was a mad, harsh auction, with Clemenceau wielding the hammer as delegates of minor powers (often diplomats of immense subtlety and legendary experience) put their country's case. The official interpreter, M. Paul Mantoux, had to speak through a buzz of conversation, comment and laughter. The Territorial Committees, charged with the detailed re-mapping of Europe, did not start serious work until late in February, and then laboured with frantic, unco-ordinated urgency. The results of twenty-six local investigations and the recommendations of hundreds of experts had in the end to be channelled through the increasingly tired minds of the Big Four. No priorities had been fixed. All the peace treaties, and all the territorial adjustments involved, were tackled in a serial nightmare of illogic. 'Maximum' clauses were inserted on the mistaken assumption that they would be modified by later consultation. 'It is Archangel and Murmansk one moment,' moaned Colonel House, 'the left bank of the Rhine the next, next Asia Minor, the African colonies, the Chinese-Japanese difference, the economic situation as to raw materials, the food situation ...' Harold Nicolson complained that the strain of constantly focusing on geographical minutiae had driven him to a point where even the rain-puddles on the pavements began to look like frontiers, salients, corridors, neutralized channels and demilitarized zones.

President Wilson developed a constant twitching of the left side of his face: perhaps not surprisingly in view of the kind of schedule which, as a conscientious world saviour, he attempted to fulfil. On one sample day in April he received, at fifteen-minute intervals, over a period of three and a half hours, the following medley: Dr Wellington Koo, presenting the Chinese delegation; the Marquis de Vogué and a delegation from the Congrès National Français, to present their view as to the disposition of the left bank of the Rhine; an envoy with a message from the Assyrian-Chaldean peoples; a delegation from Dalmatia to present the results of a plebiscite in those parts of Dalmatia occupied by the Italians; M. Bucquet, Chargé d'Affaires of the Republic of San Marino, to inform the President that he had been made an Honorary Citizen of the Republic; M. Coloner, Swiss Minister of Foreign Affairs; two delegates of the National Women's Trade Union League of the United States; the Patriarch of Constantinople; Essad Pasha, delegate of Albania; M. Coromilos, Greek Minister in Rome; Mr Herbert Hoover;

M. Bratianu, chief Rumanian delegate; Dr Alfonso Costa, Portuguese delegate; Boghos Nubar Pasha, head of the Armenian delegation; M. Pasich of the Serbian delegation; and Mr Frank Walsh
of the Irish-American delegation.

Wilson was everyone's scapegoat. He was blamed for his presence
in Europe, for his temporary absence from Europe; for trading
punches, for pulling punches; for his obstructive idealism and his
concessions to realism; for trying to wreck the Balance of Power
and for merely camouflaging it; for being arrogantly American and
arrogantly un-American; for not being God and for acting as though
he were God; for having his head in the clouds and for trying to
keep his feet on the ground. Literary liberals like Romain Rolland,
Henri Barbusse and Anatole France piled him high with heavy
tasks and thrashed him with compliments. George Bernard Shaw,
in his *Hints to the Peace Conference*, advised him to look into the great
chasm which stretched between American claptrap and American
reality. Feudal barons were not so much worse than beef barons, nor
Hohenzollerns or Habsburgs than railway, steel or kerosene kings,
that Wilson could 'offer a substitution of one for the other as a
contribution to the emancipation of the human race'. The most
convincing democratic asset Wilson had to show was himself ('and',
commented Shaw, 'he may feel some delicacy about harping upon
that'). Mere dogmatic republicanism would change the ramshackle
unity of the Habsburg Empire into an anarchy of warring tribes.
It should be Wilson's task to create a federation of republics, not to
sponsor a chaos of anachronistic nationalisms.

Wilson may have been the only One to receive such lessons (the
Son of God Himself had been forced to listen to the homilies of
worldlings on the relativity of truth): but he was not the only one.
All over Paris aspiring young diplomats were being put wise to the
fact that diplomacy, like politics, is the art of the possible. When
young Harold Nicolson ventured to say that Britain had no moral
right to Cyprus (which, given the chance, would choose union with
Greece), that *one* of the Big Powers must make *some* attempt to take
the principle of self-determination seriously, his boss, Sir Eyre
Crowe, sharply replied, 'Nonsense, my dear Nicolson. You think
you are being logical and sincere. You are not. Would you apply
self-determination to India, Egypt, Malta and Gibraltar? If you are
not prepared to go as far as this, you have not the right to claim that

you are logical. If you *are* prepared to go as far as this, then you had better return at once to London.'

When the Big Four took over the direction of the conference, leaving the nineteen junior nations ('Powers with special interests' was the euphemism) meagre representation on various committees, experienced statesmen such as Paul Hymans of Belgium, Eleftherios Venizelos of Greece and Eduard Benes of Czechoslovakia vehemently criticized such arrogance and waste of political talent. To which Clemenceau replied flatly that the five Great Powers had had twelve million men under arms at the time of the armistice, and their dead could be counted in millions. The junior nations were represented at all only by grace of the Big Five. They were free to state their case. But the final decision must remain where the real power lay. Wilson's already weakening protest was brushed aside with the comment that if America wished to colonize Europe she would have to spend billions of dollars on garrisoning hundreds of thousands of troops in the Old World. Did Wilson really want that, or imagine that an isolationist Congress would stand for it? The original Council of Ten (the Big Five and their foreign secretaries) was soon reduced to a Council of Five. Even that could be, and was, whittled down to a Council of Three. When one got down to brass tacks, Italy and Japan were only 'Powers with special interests'.

Pressing the logic even further, America too (more interested in the Great Red Scare and the Monroe Doctrine) came into this classification, except in so far as she was misrepresented by an individual with a special obsession. Wilson, however, persisted in claiming that his was the Voice of America. 'You can imagine, gentlemen,' he told a plenary session of the Peace Conference on January 25th (what time vast and enthusiastic American crowds were listening to denunciations of his attempt to involve America in the affairs of Europe), 'the sentiments and the purpose with which representatives of the United States support this great project for a League of Nations. We regard it as the keystone of the whole programme which expressed our purposes and ideals in this war and which the associated nations have accepted as the basis of the settlement. If we returned to the United States without having made every effort to realize this programme, we should return to meet the merited scorn of our fellow citizens ... We have no choice but to obey their mandate.'

Italian, French and British as well as American drafts for a League of Nations were in existence. The final Covenant and Articles, accepted with cynical haste at a plenary session on February 14th, were an amalgam of the American and British drafts, with a dash of idealistic 'warmth' added by Wilson. Despite the fact that neither Germany nor Soviet Russia was in the League, and that the unanimous consent of its members (an unlikely happening) was required for their inclusion, Wilson was happy. He had salved his conscience. He had created the means of grace. The concessions and expedients to which he had been forced to stoop would be justified. The press censorship, the retreat to secret diplomacy, the whole tragi-comic Dance of the Fourteen Veils, would be seen, at the last, as a noble strategy. Now he had buckled on, and had forced his tormentors to buckle on, the armour of God. He had bettered, or substantially supplemented, the teachings of his Master. 'Why', he asked an incredulous Clemenceau and Lloyd George, 'has Jesus Christ so far not succeeded in inducing the world to follow His teaching in these matters? It is because He taught the ideal without devising any practical means of attaining it. That is the reason why I am proposing a practical scheme to carry out His aims.'

Back in America for the closing of the 65th Congress, Wilson slammed the isolationists. If they gained the upper hand, he told an audience in Boston, America would be cheated of a great destiny. 'She would then have to keep her power for those narrow, selfish, provincial purposes which have been so dear to some minds which have no sweep beyond the nearest horizon.' His tendency to talk as though Boston, New York and Washington were mere suburbs of Paris (or of Geneva, the prospective home of the League of Nations) infuriated many Americans. Conscious of this hostility, Wilson returned to Paris in a mean mood. Not only did he reaffirm the central importance of the League in the long-term resettlement of Europe, but fought tenaciously against French designs on the Rhineland and inflated reparation demands. He vetoed Italian claims to Fiume and the Dalmatian coast (the recognition of which Orlando saw as the only hope of averting a socialist revolution), composed a high-toned message to the Italian People, and, early in April, threatened to leave the conference. The Italian delegation actually did leave. But this flurry of pugnacity soon ended in that alarming psychosomatic collapse which had been Wilson's characteristic response to the major crises of his career. Wearily he allowed

Clemenceau and Wilson to hand him down from his high moral horse, and returned to the pedestrian agony of condoning evil that good might come.

Wilson, in a schizophrenic *tour de force*, might contrive to justify his trading of the Fourteen Points for the League of Nations, but the now-snarling pack of progressives saw it in a different light. Wilson had failed as the freelance champion of liberalism. He was now reviled as its prime saboteur. His League of Nations was nothing but a revamping of the infamous Holy Alliance of 1815, his facial twitching probably an outward and visible sign of his inward and spiritual identification with the spasms of perverted statecraft. The most cardinal of all his sins was his failure to come to the rescue of Soviet Russia. In his opening address to the Paris Peace Conference, he had proclaimed: 'There is ... a voice calling for definitions of principle and of purpose which is, it seems to me, more thrilling and more impelling than any of the many moving voices with which the troubled air of the world is filled. It is the voice of the Russian people.' Yet American aid to Russia had been channelled solely to the camps of reaction – troops to Archangel and Siberia, a hundred invaluable locomotives shipped via Vladivostock to Admiral Kolchak.

Wilson's optimism about a Russian settlement had understandably faded. In Washington he had found it expedient to present the League of Nations as essentially a league of democratic defence against Bolshevism. In Paris he heard only the anti-Bolshevik voice of the Russian people, as represented by the so-called Russian Conference, a 'sacred union' of émigré groups. Headed by Prince Lvov, its most influential members were Serge Sazonov, the former Tsarist Foreign Minister, and Boris Savinkov. They still maintained that the Bolshevik regime was tottering. In February Winston Churchill, the most outspoken opponent of what he called 'the foul baboonery of Bolshevism', hurried to Paris to confer with Sazonov and Savinkov. In the absence of Lloyd George and Wilson he vigorously appealed to the Council of Ten for the dispatch of 'volunteers, technical experts, arms, munitions, tanks and aeroplanes' to the White armies. In the following months White Russian emissaries received a warm welcome in the War Office in London. As grand co-ordinator and supplier of the anti-Bolshevik crusade, 'Gallipoli' Churchill was in his element.

Such behaviour, reasoned the progressives, was inevitable, even forgivable, in Churchill. Clemenceau's callous plan for the economic strangulation of Soviet Russia was consistent with his whole character. Lloyd George's weathercock veerings were only to be expected. But that *Wilson* should in effect make common cause with this gang of cut-throats was insufferable. John Reed, in a satirical playlet, *The Peace that Passeth Understanding*, captured the mood of outraged progressive fury. The Big Five are shown in conclave at the Quai d'Orsay, spellbound at the feet of Wilson, the world champion of hypocritical phrase-mongering. 'I suggest', says Lloyd George, 'that we get to work on what our American colleague has called the solemn and responsible task of establishing the peace of Europe and the world' (laughter). 'I don't want to be late for the Folies Bergères.' Wilson then explains away his Fourteen Points (Open covenants of peace openly arrived at? 'Well, gentlemen, everybody knows that we're holding a Peace Conference.' Absolute freedom of navigation upon the seas, except as the seas may be closed by international action? 'What could be more international than England, Scotland and Wales?'), and asserts that 'select classes of men no longer direct the affairs of the world. The fortunes of the world are now in the hands of the plain people' (laughter). 'It was', comments an admiring Baron Makino, 'worth coming all the way from Japan just to hear him.'

Wilson's intellectual, as well as his moral, pretensions were sneered at. Precious little *he* knew of what, before he left America, he had called 'the intellectual feast of Paris'. While he was applauding *Hullo Paris!*, cultured underlings were meeting Marcel Proust, Jean Cocteau, André Gide and Paul Adam. Poor old Wilson. He was just a professorial American philistine after all. He was, take him at any level, a failure and a fraud. He now experienced the bitter fulfilment of the prophecy he had made to George Creel on the *George Washington* in December 1918: 'People will endure their tyrants for years, but they tear their deliverers to pieces if a millennium is not created immediately.'

The real beneficiaries of the Peace Conference were the landlords, hôteliers, restaurateurs and food retailers of Paris. Already in December 1918 hotel prices had been prohibitive. But they were raised several times – in fact almost quintupled – during the conference. Large consignments of meat and vegetables were allowed to rot (alleged journalists) in order to force up prices. All this, though shocking, was understandable. France had been attacked. Part of France had been occupied. Over a million Frenchmen had been killed. It was natural that the survivors should be something less than scrupulous. But Someone had profiteered in ideals, battened on the emotions of decent, impotent progressives of all nations. That could not be forgiven. So President Wilson, the pseudo-saviour of democracy, emerged as the true villain of the Parisian piece. The thwarted fellow-travellers of the Western world now turned, with what remained of their utopian illusions, to Lenin.

6. Capitals of the World: Petrograd and Moscow

On January 30th, 1919, Arthur Ransome set out from Stockholm, travelling with the thirty members of the Soviet Legation, headed by Maxim Litvinov and V. Vorovsky. Sweden had broken off diplomatic relations and the Russians were going home. On the train through Finland, unperturbed by the latest report put out by the émigré Russian news agency in Helsinki (that the Semyenovsky Regiment had risen against the Bolsheviks and seized Petrograd), the whole party played chess. Escorted by sentries down a lane deep in snow, they crossed the Russo-Finnish frontier. At the Soviet sentry-post Nina, Vorovsky's little daughter, began talking to the Red Army soldier, who bent over to let her touch his cap-badge, the hammer and sickle emblem of the Workers' and Peasants' Republic.

There were no porters at the dilapidated railway station. The buffet tables were bare. The scene was bleak and the cold biting. But everyone was joyful. The Russians walked about the village of Bielostrov, singing and playing with the children. On the unheated train they kept themselves warm by dancing to the music of a balalaika. The five children ran about excitedly, catching the mood of the grown-ups, revolutionaries returning to their revolution, to a country which was not just home, but the Hope and Bane of the world.

The evicted diplomats and their families were plunged into a fantastic situation in which squalor, misery, disease, class hatred, military encirclement and near-total economic dislocation was matched by feverish intellectual exuberance, soaring optimism about the prospects of revolution in Europe, and superbly defiant propaganda. 1919 was the year of Soviet Russia's completest isolation. Foreign diplomats had left. Soviet representatives abroad had been told to leave. Soviet Red Cross missions were interned, deported, even murdered.

Petrograd, the Metropolis of World Revolution, and Moscow,

capital of the Soviet Republic since the government's flight east in March 1918, were being blockaded not only by the Allies and the Whites, but by the exasperated peasants. Pitched battles were fought between villagers and requisitioning squads from the cities. The population of Petrograd had fallen from 1,200,000 to 700,000 as workers were drafted into the Red Army or fled to the villages. The dictatorship of the proletariat was exercised in a country where its basis and raison d'être was melting away. The socialization of basic industries, banks and shops, soaring inflation, and a plethora of currencies ('Kerenskys', Soviet notes, notes issued by Kolchak, Denikin and every nationalist or guerrilla leader), had brought the Soviet economy to barter level. Wages often took the form of extra food rations issued through regimented trade unions. Moscow and Petrograd starved and muddled on in a deathlike commercial trance. Houses crumbled. Streets split open. Sewer pipes broke and over-flowed. Water pipes cracked and water had to be fetched from the river. Typhus was endemic. Statisticians calculated that there were seventeen cartloads of disease-spreading refuse for every house in Moscow.

The plump, strutting pigeons of Moscow and Petrograd had vanished: all had been slaughtered for food. In the canteen of the Petrograd Soviet Zinoviev and other commissars ate watery soup with bleached shreds of horse-flesh floating in it, and considered themselves fortunate to get a tablet of saccharine from Ransome's phial with which to sweeten their tea. The famished crows of Moscow attacked the bony, staggering cab-horses and forced their way through hotel ventilators to peck at any scraps they could find. The Keeper of the Kremlin Archives worked in an old sheepskin coat, periodically standing up to flog the blood into his hands like a frost-menaced cabby. M. Pavlovich, President of the Committee of Public Works, complained that the fearful cold in unheated offices was decimating his staff. Two of his assistants had collapsed, he told Ransome, in 'something like a fit'. His own right hand had been crippled, the fingers swollen and rigid like the roots of a vegetable. Lecturers suffered from frostbite after touching the icy metal of scientific instruments during demonstrations.

Education—on paper—was free and universal. But classrooms, teachers, books—and a necessary minimum of warmth—were lacking. In the winter children came to school just to be fed, to be issued with felt boots, to sing and dance. Until the summer arrived classrooms could be little more than relief centres. On paper all workers were guaranteed two weeks' paid holiday every year and an eight-hour day, and no one under 16 was allowed to work in a factory. But in the emergency of civil war no one got a holiday, everyone worked all hours, and many a worker was under 16. Hordes of *besprizornye* (war orphans) roamed the streets, robbing, murdering, scraping a living as child prostitutes.

Lenin gave away the gifts of food, fuel, even stoves, which peasant admirers brought to the Kremlin. Frustrated academics made despairing little jokes about the breakdown of the apparatus of civilization ('In ten years we shall be running about on all fours'). Chaliapin, the enormously popular bass singer, when told that star artistes were to receive the same wage as scene-shifters at the State Opera Theatre, threatened to work as a scene-shifter. But the masses, to whom the Bolsheviks had in 1917 promised peace, bread, and work, did not have the luxury of refusing gifts or the power to bend the rules, nor were they able to muster a mood of wry detachment. The main—perhaps the only unalloyed—satisfaction that the revolution had to offer to them was that the rich and the mighty had been brought low. The Soviet press did not neglect to blare this negative achievement. 'Where are the wealthy, the fashionable ladies, the rich restaurants and private mansions, the lavish entertainments, the lying newspapers, all the corrupt golden life?' asked *Pravda* in January 1919, and answered: 'All swept away. You cannot meet a rich *barin* (gentleman) in a fur coat strolling down the street reading the *Russki Vedemosti* (a well-known liberal newspaper). 'There is no *Russki Vedemosti*, no fur coat for the *barin*. He has fled to the Ukraine or the Kuban. Or he is exhausted and emaciated from having to exist on a third-class ration. He has lost even the appearance of a *barin*.'

But Petrograd and Moscow were remarkable for ideas, fun, idealism and a wild ingenuity in making virtues out of the dire necessities of war communism, as much as for class hatred, misery, revenge and fear. Lenin boasted that even the most minor Bolshevik leader would have headed the government in any country in Europe. It was this intellectual exuberance that most impressed Ransome. He could not escape, he wrote, from 'the feeling of the creative effort of the revolution'. Commissars' salaries were fixed at two-thirds of the rate for the highest category of industrial technicians. But they

were the happiest artist-politicians in the world, slapping away at
their collective canvas, smudging, erasing, re-stating, at a pace
which left no time for regrets. It was a far, and to some observers,
a blessed cry from the high, hot, gilt auction rooms of the Quai
d'Orsay to the workshops of the Russian revolution where the action
painters of Bolshevism were slashing out the sketch of a new society.

Nicolai Bukharin, the nimble theorist of the revolution, with his
high-pitched voice, almost constant state of voluble excitement,
half-running from one conversation to the next, epitomized Bolshevik bravado. The League of Nations, he told Ransome, was really
a kind of capitalist syndicate, dominated by America, with other
countries as small shareholders. Chicherin's offers to the Allies of
economic concessions ('tell us what you think and we are ready to
buy you off'), which had so angered the Big Four with their 'cynicism', Bukharin regarded as realistic. He thought there would be a
fifty-year period of revolution before the whole world was socialized.
When the civil war was over and agriculture had been knocked into
shape Soviet Russia, together with a Soviet Hungary and a Soviet
Rumania, would be able to supply grain for the Workers' Republics
of Europe. When Britain went Red, the United States would probably take over her colonies. Then America would succumb. The
final struggle might well be to overthrow a last stronghold of capitalism in 'some bourgeois republic in South Africa'. A. Rykov,
President of the Supreme Council of National Economy, claimed
that blockade and civil war were actually lessening Russia's dependence on foreign imports. The shortage of salt, for example, had
forced the creation of a new industry which could supply not only
Russia but the whole world with salt. The coal shortage had been
beaten by the discovery and exploitation of huge peat deposits.
N. Krestinsky, Commissar for Finance, argued that the currency
crisis was a blessing in disguise, since it would lead to a moneyless
economy. Once the factories were able to supply the manufactured
goods needed by the peasants there was no reason why this should
not be possible. In the cities the wage system was already being
replaced by payment in kind. 'You can fairly say that our ruin or
salvation depends on a race between the decreasing value of money
and an ability to do without money altogether.'

Early in 1919 the Soviet Government was discussing limitation of
the powers of the Cheka, a halting of the Terror, and a modification

of its peasant policy. Discussions were opened with representatives of opposition parties about relaxing the veto on their activity. Almost every section of the opposition condemned Allied intervention and admitted the need for at least temporary support of the Bolsheviks.

Brilliant libertarians volunteered their services to the regime, though not without reservations. Gorky waged a one-man war against the inhumanities of Bolshevism and the absurdity of blank anti-Bolshevism. Making good use of a direct telephone line to Lenin, he founded a Commission for the Protection of Monuments of Antiquity, a Committee for Freedom and Culture, homes for starving scholars, writers and artists, and, grandest of all, an Institute of World Literature. While Gorky agitated on the fringe of politics, Angelica Balabanov—Balabanova—took her broom of idealism into the very corridors of power, replacing Spiridonova as the spiritual conscience of the revolution. The daughter of a wealthy Ukrainian businessman, she had studied intensively in four European universities, seeking not degrees but the Truth. From the Belgian anarchist Élisée Reclus and the Italian socialist Antonio Labriola she had caught a vision of the masses as the potential saviours of mankind, creators of a finer and more humane society. Fluent in six languages, she became the official interpreter at congresses of the Second International, perhaps its most beloved figure, and certainly its most devoted servant. The collapse of the International and Lenin's sneers at its impotence had deeply grieved her. But she reasoned that the Bolsheviks alone had (though by abhorrent force) cleared a growing-space for socialism. Solicitously, tenderly, she returned to Russia to help it to grow nobly—or perish nobly: for, like Spiridonova, she preferred a beautiful failure to an ugly success. Many Bolsheviks found her embarrassing. But Lenin sensed that, tiresome as she could be, she might have her uses. He made her an honorary member of the Bolshevik Old Guard by giving her a nominal twenty-five years' seniority in a party to which she had never belonged.

Victor Serge, when he arrived in Petrograd early in 1919, was even less of a Marxist, though much more of a revolutionist, than Balabanova. His parents had fled from Russia in the 1880s after his father had been implicated in the terrorist plots of the People's Will. Serge, born in Brussels in 1890, had been brought up in an atmosphere of poverty and high ideals: on the lodging-house walls

portraits of terrorist heroes and heroines, on his parents' lips constant
talk of the necessity for revolt, for the blasting of a mean and sordid
system, no matter what the cost. He became an anarchist and,
moving to Paris, lived among the gangster anarchs of the slums who
took the brawling, bourgeois-baiting Albert Libertad as their
model. 'Don't be sheep. Don't wait for the revolution to solve all
your problems,' Libertad told his disciples. 'Make your own revolution here and now. Be free men and live in comradeship. Let the
old world go to hell.' They defied that world by stealing, shooting
policemen, committing suicide as a last gesture of freedom. Serge's
girl-friend, a midwife, had abandoned her profession rather than
help to bring any more lives into a capitalist prison. His closest
comrade, a young Belgian, turned to reporters and yelled from the
scaffold just before his execution: 'Nice to see a man die, isn't it?'
He himself had been sentenced to five years' solitary confinement.
The news of the revolution in Russia thrilled him with a feeling that
a huge tunnel to the future was at last opening.

In Petrograd Serge found an ambience after his own heart. Bill
Shatov, a Russian-Jewish ex-Wobbly, was in charge of the defence
of the snow-shrouded, half-depopulated city. Serge, who had barely
read Marx and was not even a socialist, was nevertheless welcomed
as a godsend. He joined the staff of the Northern Commune (the
administrative organization of the Petrograd Soviet). He also taught
adult education classes and gave lectures to militiamen – who at the
end of a session would reward him with a hunk of black bread or a
precious herring. Here was a whole society stripped down for the
right kind of war, a city in which the police were on the right side.

The revolution could still attract plenty of unorthodox, unlikely
champions. Ivan Bakayev, chief of the Petrograd Cheka, had holes
in his boots and looked like a village minstrel in the embroidered
smocks which he habitually wore. Vladimir Mazin, Serge's most
intimate new friend, had been a Social Revolutionary terrorist.
Imprisoned for ten years after an attack on a Treasury van, he had
studied Marx and written a book called *Goethe and the Philosophy of
Nature*. Both he and Serge were highly resourceful as well as highly
literate and temperamentally romantic. As honorary Bolshevik
jacks-of-all-trades they needed to be. One of their assignments
was to arrange for the purchase of weapons from dealers in Helsinki.
To pay for them they printed stacks of Tsarist notes bearing the
image of Catherine the Great and the signature of a director as

non-existent as his bank. In furtive silence, in a dusky fir-wood on the Finnish frontier, the exchange was made. This was gangsterism with a purpose, a relish, and a hope – the hope of the revolutionary breakthrough that Serge's comrades in Paris had died longing for and despairing of.

War communism had not killed the theatres of Moscow or stifled the exuberance of the avant-garde. The demand for theatre seats was so enormous that both Lenin and Balabanova – united at least in a determination not to accept preferential treatment – were turned away one evening from the Arts Theatre, where a Stanislavsky production of Chekhov's *Three Sisters* was playing. In February 1919 Moscow offered two operas, Saint-Saëns's *Samson and Delilah* and Rimsky-Korsakov's *Sadko*; three plays adapted from Dickens (*The Cricket on the Hearth*, *A Christmas Carol* and *Little Dorrit*); one Shakespeare (*Much Ado About Nothing*) and two Molières (*Le Misanthrope* and *Georges Dandin*); a Maeterlinck (*The Miracle of Saint Anthony*); a Gorky (*Starik*); and an Ibsen (*Rosmersholm*). Audiences were solidly proletarian, dressed in shabby clothes topped by threadbare overcoats to keep out the teeth-chattering cold. Young Red Army officers provided the only splash of smartness. Orchestras were dressed in a mixture of military tunics and civilian trousers or breeches. Only the conductors wore frock coats.

In the streets Mayakovsky stuck posters lampooning the Entente, the White generals, Lloyd George, Clemenceau, Capitalism (pot-bellied, top-hatted, cigar-smoking). The symbolist poet Valeri Bryusov, now head of the Literary Department of the People's Commissariat of Education, was the proud originator of a wall-chart featuring squares, rhomboids and pyramids which represented networks of cultural endeavour. Marc Chagall was busy illustrating children's books and decorating the foyer and interior of the State Jewish Theatre in Moscow with magnificent friezes. The icono-clastic babel of the pre-revolutionary cafés was reproduced in the form of public debates sponsored by the Department of Fine Arts.

Vladimir Tatlin, who for some years had been 'composing' in tin, wood, iron, glass and plaster, proclaimed that paints and brushes were outmoded tools. The aim of his 'constructivist' movement was to transform the environment instead of decorating or imitating it. While Tatlin and his disciples designed for industry or the stage (Tatlin also designed utility suits for workers), the 'suprematists' Kasimir Malevich and Alexander Rodchenko declared war on such degrading functionalism. For them the canvas was not outmoded. Its business was to mirror the progressive liberation of the human soul. Malevich's 'White on White', Rodchenko's 'Black on Black' abstract sequences were accompanied by aphoristic manifestoes. 'All utilitarian art is of no account,' declared Malevich. 'I am only free when my will can create new phenomena out of what merely exists ... I have broken the blue boundary of colour limits. I have invented the semaphore of Suprematism. I have torn away the coloured lining of the sky. Comrade pilots, swim with me in this new element! Swim! The free white sea, infinity, lies before you!'

The argument as to whether art should be a form of social engineering or a personal metaphysic was fought out in the field of literature by the poets Vladimir Mayakovsky and Sergei Yesenin. They shouted at each other in black-market cafés and abused each other in public debate in Moscow's Polytechnical Museum. Mayakovsky, a Bolshevik since the age of fourteen, was an extreme, though romantic functionalist. 'I, who have superseded the soul,' he wrote, 'shout about things necessary for the revolution.' Yesenin, a handsome, golden-haired young peasant, a member of no party and no school, continued to write poems about birchwoods and waving corn, his old mother, animals, and the splendours and miseries of alcoholism. A kind of Russian Dylan Thomas, success had come to him early, and deservedly. Fame had gone to his head. But his talent was unimpaired. The marvellously tender lyrics of the man who a few years later was to marry that other muddled alcoholic anarch, Isadora Duncan, were more popular than Mayakovsky's braggart Futurism.

Yesenin, not Mayakovsky, was the king of the poets' cafés in Tverskaya Street. Here Victor Serge, shocked at first by the toleration—in a Moscow otherwise so bleak—of a decadent bohemianism 'entangling its homosexuals and exotics with our militants', found him surrounded by sheer glory. The noisy drinkers hushed when, dressed in a white silk smock, Yesenin mounted the platform to declaim his poetry—which at other times he would chalk on the walls of the secularized Monastery of the Holy Passion. Ilya Ehrenburg, newly returned from Paris, found that the bohemian ferment of Moscow outvied that of the cosmopolitan pre-war rebels of the

Rotonde — Modigliani, Vlaminck, Diego Rivera, Cocteau, Léger, Picasso, Apollinaire. Yesenin wore a shiny ex-capitalist top hat, and when drunk yelled of a revolution of cataclysmic destruction in which a surge of mounted peasants from his own province, Ryazan, would gallop over the face of the earth setting fire to everything. Poets and painters dyed their sheepskin coats vivid greens and reds and yellows. The women wore old army greatcoats, hats cut from emerald billiard-table cloth, and dresses made of purple curtain material enlivened with suprematist squares and triangles snipped from furniture coverings.

Lenin, exasperated by what he regarded as the noisy, pose-striking irrelevance of the cultural revolution, grudgingly accepted the assurances of Gorky and Lunacharsky that Mayakovsky, Yesenin, Malevich and Tatlin were 'good', that their activities had prestige value and were, in some incomprehensible way, important. He preferred Socialist Realism himself, as typified in the 'proletarian' jingles of Demyan Byedny —

> My hard, sharp verse is hammered out, a workaday engagement,
> You, my own folk, you workers, grasping all my rage meant,
> Only your judgment do I count as true,
> You are the only critics who speak straight and try no ruses,
> You, of whose hopes and feelings not one jot my verse refuses,
> You of whose rat-hole corners I'm the trusty watchdog, you!

— and saw to it that they were given a huge circulation.

Yet it was Tatlin who was commissioned to design a monument to the Third International. Straying far beyond his brief, he obliged superbly. His was to be a working monument, housing and inspiring as well as commemorating. It was to be a world-beating constructivist triumph — a leaning tower, twice the height of the Empire State Building in New York, with a special iron framework based on asymmetrical axes and cradling a glass cylinder, a glass cone, and a glass cube. The various components would move continually at varying *tempi*. The cylinder, intended for lectures, conferences and congresses, would make one revolution a year; the cone, filled with executive offices, would complete one revolution a month; the cube, surmounting the whole structure, was to execute one full revolution a day (enough to satisfy even Zinoviev) and to contain an information centre to end all information centres. This would constantly transmit news bulletins, proclamations and manifestoes by telegraph, telephone, radio and loudspeaker. A vast exterior screen, floodlit at night, would rivet the attention of the people. A special projector would flash words upon the sky in cloudy weather.

Intense curiosity surrounded the Moscow studio where, with three assistants, the secretive designer began to build his models of wood and wire. His own concepts were more fantastic than the wildest rumours. In Tatlin's Leaning Tower ingenious machinery would dethrone the tiresome body, glorify and liberate the mind. Already the Lord of Constructivism, to whom politicians and ideologies were mere accidents ('Neither to the Right nor the Left, but to the Needed,' he proclaimed), was roughing out his house rules. 'Least of all must you stand or sit in this building. You must be mechanically propelled up and down, carried along willy-nilly. Before you will flash the firm, laconic phrases of an announcer-agitator. Further on the latest news, decree, decision, the latest invention, will be announced. Creation, only creation!'

The illusions and manipulations accompanying the foundation of the Third International bore a closer resemblance to the world of the Marx Brothers than the dialectics of Marx. When Victor Serge arrived in Petrograd in January he found the Bolsheviks unshakable in their certainty of the imminence of world revolution. 'What', they asked, 'is the French proletariat waiting for before it seizes power?' Once strikes and soviets took hold in Britain, Lenin told Ransome, capitalism there was doomed. 'Put Russia under water for twenty years and you would not affect by a shilling or an hour a week the demands of the shop stewards in England. Twenty years ago I had abortive typhoid and was going about with it. England, France and Italy are like that. England may seem to you untouched, but the microbe is already there.'

The Berne conference, presided over by Hjalmar Branting of Sweden and starring such Lenin *bêtes noires* as Karl Kautsky, Friedrich Adler, Kurt Eisner, Eduard Bernstein and Ramsay Mac-Donald, was denounced as the Yellow International, a gathering of enemies of the working class. On January 24th 1919, Foreign Commissar Grigon Chicherin had sent out invitations to an international conference to be held in Moscow early in March. It was as though a new company with immense ramifications had been launched in the midst of a bankruptcy hearing. The invitation, drafted by Trostky, analysed the components of the Second International into right-wing 'social-chauvinists', fit only for contempt and unsparing opposition; Centre Socialism, typified by Adler, Kautsky and Turati, to which must be applied a policy of 'splitting off the most revolutionary elements and unsparing criticism and exposure of its leaders'; and a 'left revolutionary' wing which would obviously join a Communist International. The purpose of the Moscow congress was to establish 'a fighting organization for permanent co-ordination and systematic leadership ... subordinating the interests of the movement in each particular country to the interests of the revolution on an international scale.' The summons was issued in the name of the Central Committee of the Russian Communist Party; the exiled or questionably existent Polish, Hungarian, Austrian, Latvian and Finnish Communist Parties; a shadowy Balkan Revolutionary Social Democratic Federation (as represented or invented by Christian Rakovsky); and the Socialist Labour Party of America (as represented by Boris Reinstein in Moscow). Among the thirty-nine groups invited to send delegates were such hostile or debatable quantities as the I.W.W., the 'revolutionary elements' in the Czech, Belgian, Spanish and Portuguese Socialist Parties, the Irish nationalist movement, the Socialist Party of America, and the Shop Stewards' movement in Britain.

Few delegates managed to make the long and dangerous journey to Moscow: only one from Germany, France, Norway and Switzerland, none from Britain or Italy. America was 'there' in the person of the émigré Boris Reinstein. The Russians—Lenin, Trotsky, Zinoviev, Stalin, Bukharin and Chicherin—inevitably dominated the proceedings, having also drummed up delegates with full voting rights representing the American Communist Party (as yet unformed) the 'Communist Party of the German Colonies in Russia', and the 'United Groups of the Eastern Tribes of Russia'. Apart from the thirty-five full delegates there were sixteen 'consultative' delegates. Holland, the Socialist Propaganda League of America (composed mainly of Slav immigrants) and Japanese 'communist groups' were all represented, consultatively, by a Dutch–American engineer named Rutgers, who had once briefly visited Japan. Fineberg, consultant for the 'British communist group', was a Russian ex-political exile now working in the Commissariat for Foreign Affairs. Jacques Sadoul stood in for the French communists. The Korean Workers' League and alleged communist groups in Turkestan,

Turkey, Georgia, Azerbaidjan and Persia each had one consultant, and the Chinese Socialist Labour Party two. Balabanova appeared in her capacity as Secretary of the Zimmerwald Commission. Add the fact that the official language of the conference was German and that there had been little attempt (or time) to prepare an agenda, and the stage was set, when the first congress of the Third International opened in the Kremlin on March 2nd, 1919, for an exhibition of pure, robust farce.

The room was carpeted and decorated in red. LONG LIVE THE THIRD INTERNATIONAL banners in many languages draped the walls. On the dais, behind a long table, Lenin sat in the middle flanked by Eberlein and Platten. Trotsky, in black leather uniform and fur hat with Red Army insignia, frequently disappeared into another room to work on the draft of a New Communist Manifesto and to dash off articles extolling the ragtime congress. 'The tsars and the priests, those former lords of the Kremlin,' he wrote, 'never foresaw that within its hoary walls would one day gather the representatives of the most revolutionary part of humanity ... In one of the halls of the Palace of Justice, still haunted by wan ghosts of the criminal paragraphs of the Imperial Code, at this moment the delegates of the Third International are in session. Verily the mole of history has dug his tunnel well beneath the walls of the Kremlin.' Before 1914 the Russian revolution had been represented by exiles, towards whom the opportunist leaders of European socialism had adopted an attitude of ironical condescension. 'The bureaucrats of parliamentarianism and trade unionism were filled with certainty that the miseries of a revolution were to be the lot only of semi-Asiatic Russia, while Europe was assured of a gradual, painless, peaceful development from capitalism to socialism.' But the imperialist war had brought forth a proletarian revolution. All questions had become revolutionary questions. The upheavals in Germany, Austria and Hungary, 'the strong tide of sovietism and civil war that has poured over Europe', showed that the destiny of Europe was the same as that of Russia. 'We are witnesses of and participants in one of the greatest events in the history of the world. What happiness—to live and fight at such a time!'

The immediate problem was to overcome the obstinate resistance of Hugo Eberlein, the K.P.D./Spartacus delegate, to a fake International trumped up and manipulated by Moscow. Such a development would, in his and Levi's opinion, make doubly difficult the growth of communism in Europe. 'Real communist parties', he protested, 'exist in only a few countries. In most they have only come into being in the last few weeks. In many countries where there are communists there is no organization. What is missing is the whole of Western Europe—and America. Not even Platten can speak in the name of his party!' One after another the Russians explained that the new international was intended to *provide* organization and to share experience, that the siting of its headquarters in Moscow and Petrograd would, they hoped, be temporary, that they would be only too pleased if future congresses could be held in Vienna, Rome, Berlin, Paris and London. That, however, depended upon how well the proletariat and its leaders understood their duties and did their work of revolution. In the meantime ... But still Eberlein refused to budge. The Chinese, Turkish, Turkestanian, Korean and Persian delegates were speechless and bewildered extras. Balabanova wanted to sink through the floor, especially when Lenin tried to pressure her into announcing the affiliation of the Italian Socialist Party.

The deadlock was dramatically broken when, on the third day, in the midst of further fruitless wrangles, the door burst open and a bearded man in Austrian military uniform—Hubert Steinhardt, alias K. Gruber—rushed into the room, announcing himself as the delegate of the Austrian communists. Producing a knife, he slit open his greatcoat, extracted his 'mandate', slammed it on the table, and made a long speech in which he declared, in tones of ringing conviction, that the whole of Central Europe was on the brink of revolution. Eberlein was effectively isolated. On the next day, March 4th, a resolution proclaiming the establishment of the Communist International (Comintern) was unanimously adopted— Eberlein having been persuaded to abstain from voting in order not to mar the harmony of the occasion. Trotsky's manifesto and a set of Lenin theses denouncing bourgeois democracy and exalting the dictatorship of the proletariat were approved. An Executive Committee (E.C.C.I.) was elected, with Zinoviev as President and (surprisingly, since he was in prison in Berlin) Karl Radek as Secretary. To her astonishment, Balabanova was asked to act as Secretary in Radek's absence. Lenin, though maddened by her refusal to face or 'create' facts, believed that her association with Comintern might help to recommend it to 'idealistic' waverers.

That night the State Theatre was packed for a special meeting to celebrate the occasion. After Kamenev had made the official announcement the audience roared and stamped and sang the Internationale with a fervour not heard since the early months of the revolution. Lenin's speech was drowned in wave after wave of hero-worshipping applause. He repeated the message of the *Appeal to the Workers of All Countries* just approved by the congress. This expressed a proper gratitude to 'the Russian revolutionary proletariat and its leader, the Russian Communist Party of the Bolsheviks'. But, stressed Lenin, it was not enough to admire from a distance Russia's heroic struggle. It was the plain duty of the working masses everywhere to force their governments to withdraw their armies, to resume diplomatic and commercial relations, and to send 'hundreds, even thousands' of engineers, technical instructors and skilled workers to help in the tasks of reconstruction.

The *New Communist Manifesto* brilliantly sustained the note of urgency and shaming scorn. The aim of Comintern, it said, was 'to generalize the revolutionary experience of the working class, to cleanse the movement of opportunism and social-patriotism, to mobilize all genuinely revolutionary forces, and hasten the victory of the communist revolution throughout the world.' The toy whips of Kautskyan criticism must be laid aside. 'Unless it renounces itself and its future, which is the future of all mankind, the working class must give blow for blow.' It must not think in terms of a millennium of leisure and comfort, but rather of stern discipline and universal labour conscription. It must ignore attempts to paralyse its militancy: for only over the corpse of reformist pseudo-socialism could the International of Action march to victory.

Balabanova, who resigned from the secretaryship of the International of Action after a few conscience-raping weeks, was horrified by the lengths to which Lenin was ready to go to discredit the Socialist Centre, and especially its leaders in Italy. No slander was too outrageous, no agents too vile, to hustle these sincere but obstructive men from power. Balabanova protested when she discovered that two hastily bolshevized prisoners-of-war were being rushed to Italy with large sums of money to open the campaign against her beloved comrades. 'These men', she said, 'are merely profiteers of the revolution. They will damage us seriously in Italy.' To which Lenin replied: 'They are quite good enough for the destruction of Turati.' When word came that they had squandered the money in the cafés and brothels of Milan, more funds and fresh agitators were dispatched. When counter-emissaries from Italy were due to arrive in Moscow, Balabanova was sent on an urgent but, as it turned out, quite superfluous mission to the Ukraine. When she came back, fuming and expostulating, Lenin was all solicitude. She was tired, she was overwrought. Why didn't she go to a Soviet sanatorium for a nice long rest?

With Tatlin's Tower still in the mind of its creator (alas, it never did get any further) the offices, working conditions and even working clothes of the executive staff of Comintern did not match the grandeur of its manifestoes. For some time Serge and Mazin *were* the executive of the Third International, whose Secretary-Designate was in jail in Berlin, whose Secretary-Substitute had resigned. They were given a large, unheated room in the Smolny Institute, with two hard chairs and a wooden table as their only furniture. Both were unshaven. Serge wore a tattered suit and a shabby overcoat; Mazin a curious out-at-elbows pale blue uniform. Their first job, as they sat there shivering and cursing, was to design a seal for Zinoviev. They scoured Petrograd in an ancient coughing motor car to recruit staff, wheedle string and paper out of government departments, and arrange for the printing of the *Communist International*. This appeared in bad type on shoddy paper, with an aggressively conventional cover showing a giant worker with a large hammer striking the chains off a globe of the world.

Serge and Mazin, despite special rations of greasy soup with shreds of horsemeat in the Commissars' canteen, were constantly gnawed by hunger pains and had to resort to the black market — where Serge also managed to buy a fur- (and flea-) lined riding jacket. One of their biggest successes was the discovery, in some wardrobes in the former Austro-Hungarian embassy, of some officers' uniforms in excellent condition. These were used to clothe new staff members. The worst trial, especially for Serge, with his knowledge of realities in Europe, was Zinoviev himself. Flabby, puffy-faced, curly-haired, wreathed in smiles and drugged with fantasy, he presided over meetings of his weirdly attired, haphazardly recruited staff in a smug, euphoric haze. His plump fingers toying with the silken tassels which he wore instead of a tie, Zinoviev would cap every resolution with the remark: 'Always provided that new revolutions do not come along to upset our plans.'

Like an ideological pawnbroker this laggard of the October

Revolution rubbed his hands behind the counter of Comintern, awaiting an inevitable queue of clients. Things seemed, undeniably, to be going his way. The Spartacists were rising again in Berlin. Bela Kun's takeover in Budapest was greeted with a frenzied E.C.C.I. *Manifesto to the Workers and Soldiers of All Countries.* 'Comrades! In Hungary all power has been transferred to the working class ... Gritting their teeth, the Hungarian bourgeoisie had to yield ... The Entente imperialists burned their fingers. Their rapacious pressure only hastened the birth of the Socialist Soviet Republic ... When the Hungarian bourgeoisie thus confirmed their inability to save their country from ruin they gave clear proof that their historic rôle has been played out, and that their gravedigger, the proletariat, has come to take their place.' The proclamation of the Landauer-Mühsam-Toller Soviet in Munich at the beginning of April rated a shorter but still roseate *Message*: 'I send my warmest greetings ... We are deeply convinced that the time is not far off when the whole of Germany will be a Soviet republic. The Communist International is aware that you in Germany are now fighting at the most responsible posts, where the immediate fate of the proletarian revolution throughout Europe will be decided.'

'Surely,' said Lenin to Ransome shortly after the founding of Comintern, 'they must have learned by now that sending troops to Russia is like sending them to a communist university?' Bolshevik propaganda—shot from guns, dropped from aeroplanes, shouted from trenches, distributed by agitators—had already helped to demoralize the German Army in the Ukraine. Now, in the fertile soil of French, British and American expeditionary forces fed up and far from home, it began to bear fruit an hundredfold. In Odessa General Franchet d'Esperey ('General Désespéré' as Victor Serge, now heading the Romance Language Section of Comintern, christened him) fumed at the indiscipline of his troops. On the Archangel front British and American soldiers refused to go into the firing line. Perhaps they wanted to digest and discuss their copies of Comintern's star propaganda leaflets—*The Shame of Being a Scab, Say, What Are You?* and *The Work of the Soviets*. 'Is there', asked the first of these, 'a more contemptible creature in the world than the one who deserts his fellows and helps to defeat his own side? Are you aware, American and British soldiers, that you are earning such contempt for yourselves?' They were, it explained, scabbing on the Russian revolution, which was in essence a strike on a huge scale.

'Say! American and British soldiers!' taunted the second leaflet. 'What are you? We are standing on the threshold of a new age. It is the time of which poets have dreamed. Are you not stirred by the throb of new life that is pulsing in the veins of your fellow-workers? Are you just dull clods? Are you satisfied to resume the life of endless toil, of dull monotony and the pauper's end? Do you want to condemn your children to the same stunted, purposeless existence?' *The Work of the Soviets* offered a wide survey of the educational and cultural revolution. Particular care, it stressed, was being lavished upon working-class women and children. In Petrograd free food was provided for children up to the age of 14. Former country houses of the aristocracy, palaces and castles of the Tsar and the Grand Dukes, had been converted into children's residential centres and places of public instruction. 'The Winter Palace now gives shelter to no less than three thousand children and Tsarskoe Selo, the Village of the Tsar, is now Dietskoe Selo, the Village of Children.' Unsparing efforts were being made to open up the 'limitless intellectual and moral resources of the masses'. In Moscow and Petrograd ballet companies were 'giving incessant pleasure to thousands, no longer idlers in frock coats and bedizened society women, but men and women of toil and action.... It is for them that Chaliapin sings every evening....'

Seldom if ever had mass propaganda so mingled shrewdness and naivety, realism and romanticism. Libertarians who, like Serge, meant business could feel that Trotsky was right, that these were great times, that a bold, sometimes bloody, but always spirited attempt was being made to usher in the springtime of a new world. In 1919 the revolution was still many things to many men, full of potentialities, a bedraggled but a many-splendoured thing.

7. A Spectre is Haunting Europe

In Paris as in Moscow attention was still focused on the situation in Germany. British secret agents and War Office fact-finding teams presented an alarming picture. A wide-ranging report turned in by Agent V.77 at the end of February 1919 stressed that even if German nationalists were using Bolshevism as an excuse to revive militarism, even if (as was rumoured) Hindenburg, Junkers and wealthy industrialists were contributing to K.P.D./Spartacus funds, that did not mean that German Bolshevism was a mere stunt.

The Spartacist organization, said V.77, had much improved, both in Berlin and the provinces. Funds were getting through from Russia. Agitators drew large audiences and were even distributing subversive leaflets among the Allied armies of occupation. Squads of unemployed workers (and there were three million unemployed in Germany) were being trained as agitators and sent from one trouble centre to another to foment strikes. The Berlin garrison was honeycombed with disaffection, and the loyalty of some of the Freikorps was questionable. In Mannheim the garrison had made little resistance to a Spartacist mob which, during a demonstration held soon after Kurt Eisner's death, had helped themselves to arms and ammunition from the barracks, stormed the castle, burned the income tax records and stolen five million marks from the Treasury. V.77 claimed to have talked to workers in cheap cafés and beer halls. 'In nine cases out of ten they say: "We are not Spartacists, but if we don't get food very soon we'll smash everything up, plunder the rich, plunder the farmers, join the Russians and plunder Europe".' 'The masses', he warned, 'are like people wandering through a fog ... Prolonged undernourishment has produced a condition of nervous irritability and an incapacity to undertake any organized action ... Their temper is becoming more and more dangerous. If some ray of light does not very soon pierce the gloom, it is absolutely certain that in the shortest possible time complete and universal anarchy will break out, every industrial centre will be destroyed, the rich will be robbed of everything they possess, and the state of

Germany will be at least as bad as that of Russia.' The report of the
British Officers' Commission told much the same tale. Brigadier-
General H. C. Rees, Lieutenant-Colonel J. H. Cornwall, Captain
W. E. Hinchley-Cooke and Lieutenant A. Campbell showed a
distinct sympathy for the workers' and soldiers' councils, in their
opinion the best hope for democracy in the land. Yet the Weimar
Assembly seemed determined to smash them. Berlin, they said, was
'a fair representation of the mood of the people ... Dirt, disorder,
dancing and death. Once the cleanest city in the world, it is now
filthy ... Every dancing-hall in the city is filled to overflowing, and
almost within sound of the orchestras Spartacists and government
troops shoot each other down.'

In the Weimar Assembly Gustav Noske ('a rugged, simple
figure,' according to Churchill, 'a son of the people acting without
fear in the public cause') accused the U.S.P.D. of being financed by
the Bolsheviks. Weeks of industrial strikes, food riots, provincial
breakaway movements and Freikorps punitive expeditions culminated, at the beginning of March, in a second Spartacist revolt in
Berlin. The Congress of Workers' and Soldiers' Councils demanded
new elections to reflect a growing militancy, a sense that their loyalty
had been abused by the government. Independent and even Majority
Socialist members of the Councils joined Richard Müller in calling
for a general strike to force the government to socialize key industries, raise unemployment relief, grant sweeping measures of
workers' control, guarantee the permanence of the Councils as part
of the machinery of government, and disband the Freikorps. The
railway between Weimar and Berlin was cut and government troops,
moving north, had to fight past rebel snipers and barricades in
Halle and Leipzig. Wealthy Germans increased their smuggling of
assets abroad — by plane to Switzerland, by motorboat to Denmark.

The government, appealing for calm, alleged that it was hurrying
to enact measures of socialization. Every strike, it warned, brought
Germany nearer to economic ruin. The Red Army hordes on the
eastern frontier were ready to roll west while Germans were
fighting each other. The spread of insolent rebellion in Eastern
Prussia, fumed the *Tägliche Rundschau*, was disgraceful. In Königs-
berg Herr Seidel, a Spartacist greengrocer, had incited the workers
to break up reactionary meetings with foghorns, mouth-organs and
penny trumpets. 'When we have silenced them, we will take the
platform. Down with militarism! The death penalty for Hinden-

burg? No! That is too easy. Put a crank in his hand and make him a tramway conductor. Then he will know what it is to work. Then he will have a chance to show his famous powers as a leader. And we must make the Kaiser a miner. Let him see what bread cards are!'

On March 3rd workers left the factories on the outskirts of Berlin and once more converged on the centre of the city, demonstrating, looting, smashing nightclubs and gambling halls and black-market restaurants. Joined by the remnants of the People's Naval Division and over a thousand soldiers of the Republican Defence Corps, their numbers were put at fifteen thousand. They occupied railway terminals and some police stations. Yet still, as in January, they lacked a sense of real purpose. They were hungry, bitter, grey-faced men, pathetically set on showing that they *were* men. It was more like a mass prison breakout than a rebellion, a concourse of convicts shuffling through the streets not knowing what to do with their freedom, waiting to be rounded up or, almost mercifully, killed. Among the marchers was a leavening of Cavalier intellectuals. George Young of the *Daily News* spoke to one of them — 'the handsomest and most intelligent man I've met in Germany, a film actor by profession. The last time I saw him, with a rifle slung over his shoulder and stick bombs in his belt, he said he was glad to have a life to offer to the right side.' That was the authentic note of the second Spartacist insurrection: a sacrifice of one's life because it was the only decent thing to do. Woodrow Wilson, said the film actor, was a dreary fool. How could internationalism be based on national governments or even national parliaments? An international soviet of washerwomen would have more significance and vitality than the League of Nations. With which remark he walked away, waving his hand, and two days later got killed. It was all, Lenin would have said, very amateurish, very self-indulgent, very bourgeois. But it kept Zinoviev happy and Paris in a dither, and forced Noske to rush back from Weimar, declare martial law in Berlin, and set forty thousand Freikorps trouble-shooters in motion.

After five days of tough house-to-house skirmishing — cannon, machine-guns and strafing aeroplanes against rifles and grenades — Noske ordered that every person who was captured, arms in hand, fighting against the government was to be shot immediately. The rebels, driven into the industrial suburb of Lichtenberg, were surrounded. A ring of howitzers and mine-throwers bombarded them by day. Flare-dropping planes bombed and machine-gunned

them by night. Freikorps brutality brought reprisals. Some Freikorps prisoners were beaten up, some shot. Rebel 'punitive' squads
appeared in the streets of central Berlin, where fashionably dressed
men and women were forced to strip naked and run for their lives
while (amid yells of 'Down with the bourgeois!') grenades were
lobbed at them. Government bulletins not only credited the insurgents with batteries of field guns but announced that they had
massacred hundreds of prisoners and hostages. *The Times*, under the
headline WOMEN SPARTACISTS' VENGEANCE, hinted at obscene
atrocities ('revolting stories are told of the frenzied attacks of these
depraved furies upon government soldiers who fall into their hands.
Compared with the women of Berlin the Bolsheviks of Petrograd
took their vengeance cold'). The *Manchester Guardian* carried a
report of bourgeois victims being scalped and thrown into the
gutters to bleed to death.

By March 16th the fighting was over. More than a thousand rebels
had been slain, thousands more wounded (compared with 100 dead,
150 wounded for the Freikorps). Yet 'Spartacism' still persisted.
Strikes broke out again in the Ruhr. In Dresden the Saxon War
Minister, Herr Neuring, was thrown into the Elbe and shot at as he
tried to reach the bank. In Bremen and Hamburg seamen refused
to man the ships which were to carry the first large consignments of
Hoover's pork. Berlin, reported *The Times*, was a maelstrom of
plots and counter-plots. Masked Spartacist gangs were terrorizing
the nightclubs and cafés, running a lucrative protection racket.
Twenty-five thousand Russian agents were flooding the country
with counterfeit banknotes. The Ebert-Scheidemann government
was helpless, caught between the extremists of Left and Right.
Only a Noske dictatorship, backed and controlled by Allied military
occupation, could provide stability. Provincial rebels continued to
form short-lived independent republics. In Oldenburg and East
Frisia Stoker First Class Kuhnt, one of the roaring boys from Kiel,
led the separatist movement. The Workers' and Soldiers' Councils
of Rhine Hesse, Oberhessen, the Palatinate, Hesse-Nassau and
Würtemberg voted to amalgamate in a Hessian Republic. The
Freikorps in those parts—whose leaders included General von
Lettow-Vorbeck, the hero of East Africa, and Captain Rommel, the
future hero of North Africa—made ready for another series of 'For
Law and Order against Spartacus' operations.

Germany was in chaos. Hungary had gone Red. 'Bolshevism is gaining ground everywhere,' wrote Colonel House in his diary. 'Hungary has just succumbed. We are sitting upon an open powder magazine and some day a spark may ignite it.' Lloyd George seized the chance to put in a sensational plea for realism in the treatment of Germany. 'I cannot conceive', he said in a confidential memorandum circulated among Peace Conference delegates on March 25th, 'any greater cause of future war than that the German people ... should be surrounded by a number of small states, many of them consisting of people who have never before set up a stable government, but each containing large masses of Germans clamouring for reunion with their native land.' The same criticism applied to the balkanization of Hungary. Reparations ought to be scaled down, raw materials and world markets made available. 'The greatest danger that I see ... is that Germany may throw in her lot with Bolshevism. The present government is weak. Its authority is challenged. The Spartacists offer to free the German people from their indebtedness to the Allies and to their own richer classes ... If Germany goes over to the Spartacists it is inevitable that she should throw in her lot with the Russian Bolsheviks. Once that happens all Eastern Europe will be swept into the orbit of the Bolshevik revolution, and within a year we may witness the spectacle of nearly 300 million people organized into a vast Red Army under German instructors and German generals, equipped with German cannon and German machine-guns and prepared for a renewal of the attack on Western Europe. The news which came from Hungary yesterday shows that is no mere fantasy ... '

On the night of April 1st, 1919, the Paris-Bucharest train left the Gare de l'Est with a long special carriage coupled to its rear. Travelling in it were General Smuts, Harold Nicolson and Allen Leeper (both members of the British delegation, both Balliol men), two British officers, a French officer, and an Italian officer. Their destination was Budapest; their mission, while offering to fix an armistice line between the Hungarians and the Rumanians, to assess the durability of the Kun regime. 'A curious business,' commented Field-Marshal Sir Henry Wilson in his diary, 'that a Welshman is sending a Dutchman to tell a Hungarian not to fight a Rumanian.' The Mission arrived in Budapest early on the morning of April 4th. Soldiers with fixed bayonets and scarlet brassards were drawn up along the platform in drenching rain. Kun arrived, together with Josef Pogany, Deputy Commissar for Foreign Affairs. While Kun, accompanied by an interpreter, was shown into General Smuts's compartment, Nicolson talked to Pogany. Nicolson (the son of that Lord Carnock who, as British Consul in Budapest, had said that if he were a Hungarian he would be 'a Socialist of the deepest magenta') was rather disgusted by his first contact with Bolshevism. Kun he described as 'a little man with a puffy white face and loose wet lips. He has the face of a sulky and uncertain criminal.' Pogany was 'a little oily Jew — fur coat rather moth-eaten — stringy green tie — dirty collar.' Plump, pinkly complexioned, wearing impeccable linen and an expression of quizzical Balliol poise, Nicolson listened to Pogany chanting the praises of communism in bad German. Communism, said Pogany, meant happiness, culture for the masses, free education, free medical care, free concerts, decent housing, and the triumph of the machine. ('I ask him what machine?' noted Nicolson. 'He makes a vague gesture embracing the whole world of mechanics.')

After this uneasy encounter the bland young diplomat escorted Kun and Pogany to the barrier at the end of the platform. The Red Guards, he noticed, did not salute. They stared at the black-suited, shiny-shoed super-bourgeois as he strolled gingerly past, like an expensive physician shepherding two odd clients of doubtful sanity and social standing from his consulting room. An engine driver ran forward to ask them for a light. Kun held out the stump of the cigarette he was smoking. A natural enough gesture, but one hardly likely to occur on a state occasion at the Gare de l'Est or Victoria Station. Nicolson described it sarcastically. 'The engine driver returns to his engine puffing a proud, comradely cigarette. Bela Kun darts little pink eyes at me to see whether I am impressed by this proletarian scene. I maintain an expression of noble impassivity.' On the following day Nicolson was driven to the Hotel Hungaria, now the Soviet House, for afternoon tea. He decided that the people sipping tea and lemonade in the foyer — while an orchestra played dashing gipsy tunes — were all bourgeois extras rounded up at gunpoint or released from prison for a few hours. 'Not a word do they speak to each other … If one looks up one catches countless frightened eyes, and at the back of those eyes a mutely passionate appeal.' Not even Nicolson was immune from high emotion if circumstances pushed the right class button. Smuts, perhaps wisely, refused to leave the train.

Two more visits from Kun, this time accompanied by Alexander Garbai and Sigismund Kunfi, ended in stalemate. Kun would not accept Smuts's truce line. He would not bargain. So, with a 'goodbye, gentlemen!' and a courteous salute from Smuts, the special train slid from the siding. But the fact remained that the Allies had been willing to make concessions, had even suggested a formal meeting in Paris. Kun, however, demanded that the meeting should take place not in Paris but in Vienna or Prague. SMUTS PROPOSALS REJECTED, whooped the communist press. 'Our magnificent example has given Bolshevism a new impetus. Hungarian events have, like a stiff sea breeze, filled the sails of Bolshevik craft in other countries. Our example will prove contagious. It will rouse the sleepers, encourage the irresolute.'

In Paris on the brilliant spring afternoon of April 11th, Harold Nicolson met William Bullitt at a luncheon party at the Meurice. Bullitt, a rich, idealistic young member of the American peace delegation, talked enthusiastically about Soviet Russia. Nicolson blinked politely ('He probably thinks me a lousy official. Better blink therefore. He did not like my saying that Bela Kun was a silly little man'). Bullitt was in no mood for the supercilious. Late in February he had set out, with Captain W. Pettit of U.S. Military Intelligence and the celebrated American journalist Lincoln Steffens, to bring back a report on conditions in Soviet Russia and the kind of peace terms which might be acceptable to the Bolsheviks. Bullitt had taken with him a list of questions jotted down by Philip Kerr, a Lloyd George aide, Steffens a list compiled by Colonel House. British consuls had speeded the three envoys on their way through Norway, Sweden and Finland: and though theirs was a 'sounding' mission which was not to commit anyone, it was understood that if its findings were favourable they would be used to persuade Clemenceau to join Wilson and Lloyd George in a summit parley with the Bolsheviks.

All three had been immensely impressed with the vigour and intelligence of Lenin, Trotsky and other Bolshevik leaders, by the sweep of their programme and its evident hold on the imagination and loyalty of a majority of the Russian people. Without Allied support, they concluded, the counter-revolution would collapse overnight. The Red Terror was abating. The commissars had the same rations as a soldier or an industrial worker. Contrary to the absurd stories in the European and American press, family life had not been changed. 'I have never heard', wrote Bullitt, 'more genuinely mirthful laughter than when I told Lenin, Chicherin and Litvinov that much of the world believed that women had been "nationalized".' The Soviet government had done more for the education of the people in a year and a half than the Tsarist regime had done in fifty years. Captain Pettit indignantly contrasted the Soviet spirit of sacrifice for an ideal with the lies and sordid intrigues of 'the despicable hordes of Russian émigrés who haunt Stockholm, Helsingfors and Paris'. He urged recognition of the Soviet government and every possible economic aid. He was, he said, 'so convinced of the necessity for us taking a step immediately to end the suffering of this wonderful people' that he was willing to stake all he possessed on converting ninety out of every hundred American businessmen whom he could take to Petrograd for two weeks. According to Steffens's summary the revolution, if left alone, was ready to enter into its constructive phrase. There was a wonderful freshness about Bolshevism. 'In Russia *all* legislators are young or new. It is as if we should elect in the United States a brand-new set of men to all offices, from the lowest county to the highest Federal position, and as if the election should occur in a great crisis, when all men are full of hope and faith.' The aim was not political democracy but a radical economic democracy based on occupation, not on artificial geographical constituencies. The attempt to create an economic democracy was the essence of the revolution. 'It is this that has startled the world: not the atrocities of the revolution but the revolution itself.'

The Soviet government, keen to buy time, was willing to accept an armistice on the lines of demarcation at present occupied by the contending armies, and to grant economic concessions: but it insisted that the blockade should be ended and a conference arranged with the Entente. Immensely excited and elated, the three missioners sat down in Paris to write their reports, upon the favourable reception of which — in Bullitt's estimation — the fate of the world, and of a superb and courageous social experiment, hinged. Here was the chance for a real breakthrough, the chance too for President Wilson to redeem himself and revive the wilting loyalty of his supporters. 'The following conclusions', Bullitt summarized, 'are respectfully submitted ... (1) No government save a socialist government can be set up in Russia today except by foreign bayonets ... The Lenin wing of the Communist Party is as moderate as any socialist government which can control Russia. (2) No real peace can be established in Europe or the world until peace is made with the revolution. This proposal of the Soviet government presents an opportunity to make peace ... on a just and reasonable basis – perhaps a unique opportunity.' He added a canny, Hoover-like rider – '(3) If the blockade is lifted and supplies begin to be delivered ... a more powerful hold over the Russian people will be established – the hold given by fear that this delivery may be stopped. Furthermore, the parties which oppose the communists in principle but are supporting them at present will be able to begin to fight against them.'

Pettit went around in a mood of almost religious exaltation. Though the hunger, the disease, the manifold physical sufferings of Petrograd were appalling, he said, the spirit of hope and creation was so high and beautiful that one could not be depressed – except by the stupidity and crass ignorance of the so-called statesmen of Paris. Steffens, when someone asked him: 'So you've been over into Russia?' made his famous reply: 'I have been over into the future, and it works.' He contrasted the purposeful flexibility of Lenin with the sad flaccidity of Wilson. Lenin admitted that concessions to peasant conservatism had driven the Communist land policy off course, but added: 'We will get back on the right lines one day.' That was the advantage of having a *plan*, of *knowing* that you were wrong. Wilson would never make such an admission. He was too busy justifying his compromises. Lenin was a navigator, Wilson a mere sailor.

The Bullitt Report got no welcome from Wilson. He refused even to see it, or its enthusiastic compilers. Lloyd George saw it and them, but within a few weeks repudiated both and denied all knowledge of the mission. The news from Hungary had changed the whole climate of thinking in Paris. The policy now was to give maximum aid to Denikin, Kolchak and Yudenich, in the certainty that their efforts, whether or not they succeeded in overthrowing the Soviet regime, would prevent the Red Army from spilling into Europe and enable the French *cordon sanitaire* in Europe and the British *cordon sanitaire* in the Baltic to patch up their quarrels and defences. Mutinies among the Allied troops in north and south Russia had proved the futility of direct intervention. The French expeditionary force in the Ukraine had already been ignominiously routed. The Bullitt Report was overshadowed by the news from Odessa as well as the news from Hungary.

From the moment when the first French contingents from Salonika disembarked at Odessa on December 19th, 1918, there had been trouble. General Denikin resented Franchet d'Esperey's tendency to order him around. Franchet d'Esperey's efforts to present the French expedition as a humanitarian task force were laughed at. The distribution of leaflets recalling the 'treachery' of Brest-Litovsk and maintaining that Lenin was a German agent (the word 'Bolshevik' was said to be derived from 'Boche'), failed to produce a fighting spirit. Franchet d'Esperey's French, African, Polish, Greek and Serbian troops were inadequately clothed for the fierce Ukrainian winter. Bolshevik propaganda played on their natural desire to get home as well as the shame of fighting profiteers' battles. French troops were soon writing articles for *Le Communiste*, an illegally printed Bolshevik news-sheet. 'Forgive us, comrades, brothers! Don't look upon us as murderers! We did not understand why we were here.' Other contributions (either written by or attributed to *poilus*) cursed Clemenceau — 'the big dictator'.

On January 30th, 1919, a battalion of the 58th Infantry and two batteries of the 2nd Mountain Artillery fell out of an attack on Tiraspol in Bessarabia, cutting the wires of the field telephones and taking their guns with them. On March 7th two companies of the 76th Infantry refused to march to Kherson, thus weakening a front mainly held by Greeks. The Red Army captured the town. Units of the 4th and 37th Colonial Regiments refused to open fire on the Red Army. Early in April the 1st Zouave Regiment and the 19th Artillery refused to harness their horses to artillery limbers during a Red Army attack on Odessa. On April 5th Odessa had to be evacuated. Greek soldiers were ordered to encircle and disarm mutinous French troops, but refused. Men marched out of the city singing the Internationale.

Franchet d'Esperey appealed for fresh, picked troops. But the revolt of the French fleet in the Black Sea destroyed such hopes. On April 16th the battleships *France* and *Jean Bart* and the heavy cruisers *Vergniaud* and *Waldeck-Rousseau* sailed from Odessa to Sevastopol to bombard the Red Army, then besieging the city. A landing party was put ashore and Vice-Admiral Amet gave his routine speech. 'You are faced with abominable bandits. They kill women, children and old people. We have been sent here to stop their crimes. I hope that you will do your duty.' Next day most of the crews failed to answer the bugle call to battle posts. The Admiral was booed.

There were threats to throw the officers overboard. On the *France* the Master-at-Arms was butted in the stomach. 'What are we doing in Russia?' roared the sailors. 'We don't want to fight our brothers.' When the Vice-Admiral came aboard from the flagship, the *Jean Bart*, he was greeted with the Internationale and cries of 'Death to the tyrant! Get hold of the stupid bastard!' Amet explained that Sevastopol would soon be evacuated, but that the men must remember that they were 'faced with abominable bandits' etc., etc. Pandemonium broke loose.

'You're Number One Bandit yourself! You condemn sailors to five or ten years' hard labour for nothing!'

'Lies! Lies! He's trying to sing us a lullaby!'

The Admiral changed his tone. 'My children, I entreat you to maintain order.' A delegate presented the seamen's ultimatum — (1) An end to intervention and immediate return to France. (2) Leave. (3) Relaxation of discipline. (4) Better food. (5) More letters. (6) Rapid demobilization. (7) Otherwise the ships would be turned over to the Reds. Across the water came the sound of singing on the *Jean Bart*, where a red flag was already flying from the bowsprit. A radio message from the *Waldeck-Rousseau* put the same ultimatum, and added that the officers were under armed guard. Amet capitulated ('So I have a crew of Bolsheviks, it seems'). Soldiers deserting from the forts joined a procession of sailors in a march to the Sevastopol Town Hall, where the Chairman of the Revolutionary Committee, who spoke fluent French (having once worked in the Galeries Lafayette in Paris), thanked them for their support. When Greek soldiers opened fire on the demonstrators, French gunners began to shell the Greek battleship *Kilkis*. Ammunition boxes were hurled off the quays into the water.

Even in the puppet-states of the French *cordon sanitaire* gratitude to their sponsors was not always what it might have been. General Franchet d'Esperey's appeal to the Rumanian government to order a general mobilization of troops to fight in the Ukraine was ignored. On April 15th at a mass meeting held in a Prague brewery, socialist speakers derided the manoeuvres of America, Britain, France and Germany to offload war guilt upon each other. 'The American dollar rules the world markets today,' said one orator. 'If America wants to make peace with Russia it is only to gain new markets and sources of raw materials. One fact is clear. The American army is not going to fight in Russia, nor will the English or French. The Allies are always telling us what they have done for us. It is high time that we told them what we have done for them.' The National Assembly and a majority of the government were against intervention in Russia, yet the Prime Minister, Dr Kramar, was bargaining with the blood of Czech soldiers (yells of 'He owns large estates in Russia!'). The meeting demanded the recall of the Czechoslovak Legion and an end to intervention in Russia and Hungary. It also warned the government that 'we do not consider the development of the Czech republic as final, since the ideal of the Czech workers is a socialist republic, for which we shall work with all our means and might.'

In Poland socialism was dormant, if not defunct. But Pilsudski was not inclined, any more than nationalist leaders in the Baltic States, to risk troops in all-out collaboration with White Russian generals whose aim was to restore the rule of Russia over her lost provinces. Lenin sent special envoys to Warsaw to press this point, and to suggest that if agreement could be reached about the Russo-Polish frontier, Pilsudski's soldiers might be better employed in helping the Red Army to put paid to General Denikin.

In Munich the Soviet Republic, inspired by that delightful libertarian trio — Gustav Landauer, Ernst Toller, and Erich Mühsam — provided entertainment rather than apprehension. Levien and Leviné continued to denounce it and to work for its downfall. Landauer sent a postcard to a friend: 'I am now the Commissar for Propaganda, Education, Art, Science and a few other things. If I am allowed a few weeks of time I hope to accomplish something. But there is a strong possibility that it will be a couple of days.' Mühsam concentrated on filling the soviet's newspaper with *avant-garde* poems and woodcuts, and promising the workers that he would arrange performances of *Parsifal* for them at cheap prices. (The *Morning Post* described Mühsam as being the despair of his respectable Jewish parents. 'His mode of living and habits of drug-taking were no secret, and he was the dirtiest, shabbiest and most unkempt customer of a bohemian café in Berlin. He borrowed money from everyone, including, it was said, the waiters.') Ernst Toller, President of the Central Council, was overwhelmed by a stream of eccentric petitioners: women who wanted a quick divorce, tenants who did not want to pay rent, ideologues demanding the arrest of their own particular enemies, and a rich flow of cranks – some of whom believed that the root of all evil was cooked food, others the gold standard, others unhygienic underwear, or machinery, or the lack of a universal language, or birth control, or multiple stores.

Nor were the cranks confined to Toller's ante-room. Some of them, in the chaos of the 'elections' in the Wittelsbach Palace, had become commissars. Señor Silvio Gezell, an Argentinian of unknown background, had talked his way to the head of the Department of Finance. An equally mysterious Czech had emerged as Minister of Communications. Most remarkable of all, however, was Dr Franz Lipp, People's Commissar for Foreign Affairs. Heavily bearded, resplendently frock-coated, and (though this did not become known until later) only recently discharged – not for the first time – from an expensive lunatic asylum, Dr Lipp was a learned eccentric on the grand scale. His first telegram, recalling the Bavarian representative in Berlin, began: '*Opus primum sed non ultimum* …' Another dispatch assured the Papal Nuncio that 'I shall make it my Holy Duty to guarantee the safety of Your Reverence.' Puzzled post-office clerks showed Toller the text of a telegram to Lenin: 'Proletariat of Upper Bavaria happily united. Socialists plus Independents plus Communists firmly as one, together with the Farmers' Union. Liberal bourgeoisie completely disarmed as Prussian agents. Cowardly Hoffmann, who took away the key of my W.C. in his flight, now established at Bamberg … Receiving coal and food in tremendous quantities from Switzerland and Italy. We want peace for ever. Immanuel Kant *Vom Enigen Frieden* 1795, Theses 2–5.'

When Toller sent for Lipp, the Foreign Commissar was thoughtfully filling the typists' room with red carnations. He agreed to resign but a few hours later was back in his office with more flowers for the typists and more telegrams to dictate. When, on April 13th, disillusioned Republican security guards, deciding to end the six-day spree and recall the Hoffmann government from Bamberg, broke into the Palace, they found Lipp still at large, and arrested him, Toller and Mühsam. Posters announced the deposition of the Central Council. 'Workers and soldiers, certain swollen-headed agitators foreign to this country have sought their selfish ends while pretending to unite the proletariat. Fellows like Lipp have been entrusted with your fate … Today Munich is completely cut off from the whole country and stands alone … Bavarians, support the lawful government. Order and quiet bring work and bread. Food trains are standing ready outside the city. Protect yourself against reaction by supporting the Socialist government.'

At this point Leviné and Levien, throwing caution to the winds, decided to form a 'real' soviet and make *their* bid to save the honour of the revolution. At a stormy gathering of the Workers' and Soldiers' Councils in the Hofbräuhaus, Eugen Leviné was elected Chairman of the new Central Council. At last, he said, the proletariat was to be properly led. 'Finally today Bavaria has also erected the dictatorship of the proletariat! The sun of world revolution has arisen! Long live the world revolution! Long live the Bavarian Soviet Republic! Long live communism!' Ernst Toller, released from captivity, burst into the hall, shouting that a communist coup would alienate whatever peasant support remained and condemn Munich to starvation. 'Do you want to go to war about every gallon of milk?' He was re-arrested and bundled into the cellar, but released again by the troops who had arrested him only a few hours earlier. Leviné called a general strike – mainly in order to release all able-bodied workers for service in the Red Army. Fighting between armed workers and Republican guards ended with the former regaining control of the main railway terminal at a cost of twenty dead and more than a hundred wounded. 'The socialization of the world', proclaimed a K.P.D./Spartacus manifesto, 'cannot be accomplished by officials, commissions and parliaments. It can be brought about only by the strong hand of the people. Such', it concluded, in a précis of Rosa Luxemburg's original Spartacist Programme, 'is the will of Spartacus, and because of this all open and secret enemies of the revolution hate it and slander it. Spartacus does not wish to gain power over the proletariat; it is simply that part of the proletariat which has become politically conscious. Rise up, proletarians! Stand to arms! There is a world to conquer and a world to fight! It will be a fight to a finish!'

The Hofbräuhaus was to be the 'parliament building' of the new regime. Bourgeois bank accounts were confiscated. The police force was disarmed and replaced by Red Guards. Rudy Egelhofer, one of the leaders of the Kiel sailors' revolt in 1917, became Commander-in-Chief of the Red Army. But at a meeting of armed workers at an inn in Karlsberg the reluctant, violence-abhorring Toller was elected commander of the forces in the field ('the chief thing is that we all know you'). Toller formed a 'staff' from a handful of ex-Imperial Army officers, including a 19-year-old subaltern who led the infantry in an attack on Hoffmann's troops in Dachau. This was successful largely because the 'Whites' had no stomach for civil war. There were no casualties, but Toller found himself with forty-one prisoners on his hands. Disregarding an order from Egelhofer to shoot the officers, he released them all. Fighters for humanity, in Toller's view, were under an obligation to act humanely. But, ignoring his appeal for voluntary discipline, his troops got very drunk. Toller's worst moment came when he was summoned to a house where a young woman had been raped by twenty of his fighters for humanity. Somehow he nerved himself to order an advance to Hollanderau, where friendly peasants were ready to supply food. But Egelhofer, jealous of the non-Bolshevik 'Hero of Dachau', countermanded his order.

Toller returned to Munich filled with nausea and anger. After making a speech in which he accused Levien and Leviné of exploiting the ignorance of the people and the glamour of the Russian revolution ('In Russia we did it differently—this phrase is constantly used to demolish commonsense and kindness. But we are Bavarians, not Russians'), he was once more arrested. On April 27th, after a vote of no confidence by the Councils, Levien and Leviné resigned. Hoffmann, now under orders from General von Oven (the commander of the Freikorps whom he had reluctantly summoned to his aid), refused an offer of negotiation and demanded unconditional surrender. Toller was again released, Egelhofer began to organize a last-ditch defence, and Leviné plastered the walls of the city with another manifesto: BETWEEN HEAVEN AND HELL THERE IS NO COMPROMISE—BETWEEN COMMUNISM AND CAPITALISM NO NEGOTIATION.

The Freikorps were in a grim mood. They had been told that Munich was in the throes of an orgy of terrorism, that innocent bourgeois were being rounded up and used as living targets for proletarian rifle practice, that in a few days not a single 'decent' person would be left alive. In fact, Egelhofer had ordered the taking of ten hostages. Indiscriminately including a railway official, a sculptor and an artist, as well as Prince Gustav von Thurn und Taxis, Countess Hella von Westarp, Freiherr von Seidlitz and Lieutenant Freiherr von Teucher, they were executed on April 30th in the Luitpold Gymnasium in retaliation for Red Army casualties in the fighting on the outskirts of Munich.

In April, Lloyd George had a lively time of it in a House of Commons described by Harold Nicolson as 'the most unintelligent body of public-schoolboys which even the Mother of Parliaments has known'. Three hundred and seventy M.P.s, led by Colonel Claude Lowther, Lieutenant-Colonel Walter Guinness and Brigadier-General Page-Croft, had sent a telegram to the Prime Minister pointing out that the British public expected him to honour his election pledges about stern treatment of Germany. They had also, they said, been alarmed by rumours of secret negotiations with the Bolsheviks. On April 9th, in a Commons debate on recognition of the Soviet government, the diehards (quoting heavily from a White Book, *Bolshevism in Russia, or Revolutionary Socialism in Practice*, which was little more than a compendium of lurid atrocity tales) had their fling.

Brigadier-General Page-Croft maintained that atrocity reports in the newspapers were mild compared with the reality. 'An Hon. Gentleman says "No! No!", but does he realize that in all the churches and cathedrals which the Bolshevik regime holds they are dancing day and night in those churches, which have become the homes of the harlots of Russia?' The entire Bolshevik movement, in the opinion of Horatio Bottomley, was 'part and parcel of German propaganda ... It stands for anarchy, despotism, enslavement of the working classes, murder, pillage, rapine, lust, every conceivable crime which you can find in the devil's calendar.' The government must never deal with 'this body of inhuman scoundrels'. If Russia wanted Bolshevism, reasoned Lieutenant-Colonel Guinness, it would not be necessary for the Bolsheviks to 'have these cold-blooded murders of whole sections of the population in order to maintain their rule'. Home Secretary Edward Shortt assured the House that 'every single day that passes I sign a certain number of orders getting rid of emissaries of Bolshevism'. John Jones, M.P. for Silvertown in the East End of London, had difficulty in making himself heard when he argued that it was easy to vilify Lenin and Trotsky, but what about Ireland, where forty thousand troops were needed to keep four million people in subjection? And why was it that, when it was agreed that the spread of Bolshevism in Europe depended upon the spread of starvation in Europe, hon. members supported a policy of starvation?

On April 16th, forewarned and forearmed, Lloyd George made one of his infrequent appearances in the House of Commons. He opened with an explanation of the difficulties of peace-making which was perfectly attuned to the niggers-begin-at-Calais mentality of most of his audience. No conference in the history of the world, he said, had been faced with 'problems of such complexity, of such magnitude and of such gravity'. How many members, for instance, had heard of the Duchy of Teschen? 'I had never heard of it, but Teschen very nearly produced an angry conflict between two Allied states.' Soviet Russia? Of course there was no question of recognizing a regime which had committed crimes against Allied subjects and was at this very moment 'attacking' our friends in Russia. 'But intervention, my friends?' asked the Prime Minister, and piously answered himself: 'We cannot interfere to impose any form of government on another people, however bad we may consider the present form of government to be.' Russia was a country very easy to invade but very difficult to conquer, as Napoleon had found out. She would have to be redeemed by her own sons. 'Therefore we are not sending troops, we are supplying goods ... I do not in the least regard it as a departure from fundamental principle that we should support General Denikin, Admiral Kolchak and General Kharkov' (Lloyd George here mistook the name of a Ukrainian town for that of a White general: but no one corrected him). This aid, he stressed, was essentially for purposes of containment. Russia was a volcano still in fierce eruption — 'the best you can do is to provide security for those who are dwelling on its slopes, and arrest the devastating flow of lava so that it shall not scorch other lands.'

William Bullitt and his mission were ruthlessly disposed of. 'We have had no approaches at all,' said the Prime Minister in answer to a direct question. 'Constantly there are men coming and going to Russia of all nationalities, and they always come back with their tales of Russia ... There was some suggestion that a young American had come back with a communication. It is not for me to judge the value of this communication, but if the President of the United States had attached any value to it he would certainly have brought it before the conference, and he certainly did not.'

Having passed that buck, Lloyd George argued the case for a just, but not vindictive peace with the Central Powers. He thought it possible that hon. members did not fully realize the extent of the starvation in Central Europe. Perhaps a little illustration would help. Two British soldiers were crossing a square in Vienna. They saw a hungry child. They took out a biscuit and threw it to the child. Then, suddenly, 'hundreds of children came from nowhere. They clamoured for food, and it was with difficulty that the two soldiers escaped with their lives.' In the glow of personal triumph, and perhaps too in the knowledge of the latest, exaggeratedly optimistic, bulletins from Denikin and Kolchak, the Prime Minister ended on a note of rhetorical compassion. 'The Central Powers and Russia', he said, blithely laying the awful spectre he had raised in his Memorandum of March 25th, 'have overtaxed their strength ... They are lying prostrate, broken, and all these movements of Spartacists and Bolsheviks and revolutionaries ... are more like the convulsions of a broken-backed creature crushed in a savage conflict.'

The temper of the parliamentary blimps had not been improved by the persistent needling of the *Herald*, the growing influence of the 'Hands Off Russia' movement, and a series of rip-roaring anti-Establishment pamphlets by J. T. Walton Newbold.

Novelist-playwright Israel Zangwill, the son of a Russian-Jewish immigrant, launched the 'Hands Off Russia' campaign with a scathing speech at the Royal Albert Hall in February. If the Allies had recognized Lenin's government as they had recognized Kerensky's, he argued, the Bolshevik revolution might have been comparatively bloodless. But it had been forced to 'stand with its back to the wall against the whole world'. This animal was very spiteful: when it was attacked it defended itself. If anti-Bolshevik propaganda was only half true, if Lenin and Trotsky *were* ruining Russia, paralysing agriculture and industry, and hated by ninety per cent of the population—why intervene to destroy what was destroying itself, why, like Gilbert's Mikado, make suicide a capital offence? The fact was that Bolshevism, by undermining German morale, had saved the West from German militarism: and the fear of Bolshevism was the beginning of wisdom. It had so frightened Capital that everywhere wages were rising, even in the Army and Navy, and the Peace Conference was offering Labour an International Charter. Only on one condition could the Big Three presume to interfere in internal politics—if they did so all round: in Egypt, India, Ireland and the southern states of America, where Negroes were being terrorized and prevented from voting. When the Allies presumed to lecture the Bolsheviks, they were entitled to reply, 'Mind your own bloody business!'

Zangwill warned that the Bolsheviks had to a large extent succeeded in turning the imperialist war into a class war. Walter Newbold typified the fury of Marxist militants at the refusal of the

Labour Party and the I.L.P. (with its harping on moral rectitude and good will) to recognize this. In his pamphlet *Bankers, Bondholders and Bolsheviks* he sought to drive home the lesson that intervention in Russia was part of the class war and motivated by financial interests. He did not confine himself to generalities, but named names. Prominent bankers such as the Barings, Hambros, Lazards and Rothschilds, and private houses like Hoares and Coutts, with their royal and aristocratic connections, were, he argued, particularly concerned to reimpose their tribute of four to five per cent per annum upon the Russian people. 'It is not enough for their parasitic clients that for twenty, forty, sixty, even eighty years they have drawn interest out of the peasants and workers, and that six million Russian soldiers have died fighting Germany in their cause. They, in common with French moneylenders and American financiers ... clamour for the principal and for continuing years of regular interest.' The desire of Rockefeller's Standard Oil to keep an eye on the Caucasian and Persian oil fields explained 'the humanitarian propaganda for a United States "mandate" under the League of Nations to care for the tormented people of Armenia.' Was it to be marvelled at that Minister of Transport Sir Eric Geddes (a large shareholder in the Kyshtim Mining Corporation), First Lord of the Admiralty Walter Long (a shareholder in the Anglo-Russian Trust) and Chancellor of the Exchequer Austen Chamberlain (a former director of the Russian & English Bank) should be 'in favour of burdening the British Treasury with advances to Tsarist generals, one of whom returned the Spassky mine to its exploiters as soon as he recovered it from the Soviets?' What else could the workers expect from 'the golden hog, capitalism' but to find it 'rooting and grunting in search of human flesh?'

In the Middle East and Asia as well as in Europe imperialism seemed to be threatened by the Bolshevik ogre. The nationalist agitations in Egypt and India were freely attributed to Bolshevik prompting. The *New Communist Manifesto*, after referring to 'a series of open risings and revolutionary unrest in all colonies', observed that the purpose of the League of Nations was 'merely to change the label of colonial slavery'. The liberation of the colonies could, it said, only be achieved by the liberation of the working classes in the metropolitan countries. 'Colonial slaves of Africa and Asia! The hour of proletarian dictatorship in Europe will strike for you as the hour of your deliverance!' At the Eighth Congress of the Russian Communist Party Bukharin had been cynically explicit: 'If we propose the solution of the right of self-determination for the colonies, the Hottentots, the Negroes, the Indians etc., we lose nothing by it ... The most outright nationalist movement, for example that of the Hindus, is only water for our mills, since it contributes to the destruction of English imperialism.'

Even as Lloyd George, in the House of Commons, was describing the European revolutionary movements as 'the spasms of a broken-backed beast', India was erupting. The very limited measures of self-government proposed in the Montagu-Chelmsford reforms did not satisfy the demand for Home Rule, or seem an adequate reward for the efforts of the 1,215,000 Indian troops who had served overseas (of whom more than 100,000 had been killed or wounded). The passive-resistance movement founded by Mahatma Gandhi in 1915 reached massive proportions. To check the rising tide of political discontent, the Rowlatt Act was passed, giving the police wide emergency powers. It was furiously resented. Gandhi's hold over his followers was not yet strong enough to prevent outbreaks of violence. In the Punjab railway lines were torn up, railway stations attacked, telegraph wires cut. In Lahore the mob was dispersed by cavalry charges and rifle fire. On April 10th during riots in Amritsar, buildings were burned and several Europeans, including a woman missionary doctor, murdered. Three days later Brigadier-General Rex Dyer hearing that, despite a ban on political meetings, a large crowd had gathered in an enclosed space known as the Jallianwala Bagh, took drastic action, ordering a detachment of fifty troops to fire on the crowd without warning. In less than ten minutes 379 men and boys were killed and 1,500 wounded. It was the worst scene of bloodshed in the whole period of British rule in India. Dyer, like many other British officers and civil servants, was convinced that the Punjab 'revolt' had been timed to coincide with an invasion from Afghanistan: and that both were master-minded from Moscow.

In February Amanullah, the young and would-be progressive Amir, had demanded formal recognition of Afghanistan as a sovereign state. Getting no reply from the Viceroy, Lord Chelmsford, he prepared in April to launch an invasion of India. Casting about for support, he sent a flowery oriental letter to Lenin – 'the High-Born President of the Great Russian Republic' – proposing diplomatic relations. The so-called Professor Barkatullah, a characteristic throw-up of 1919 (that year of eccentric international flotsam), arrived in Moscow describing himself as the head of the Afghan delegation. A native of Bhopal, he had during the war been appointed Foreign Minister of a puppet provisional government of India set up in Berlin. Based in Kabul, Barkatullah's colleagues distributed leaflets in northern India urging the Muslims to rise, kill the British, tear up railways and cut telegraph wires. Now it seemed that some were responding to the call.

Wearily, at a moment when British troops were impatient to be repatriated and the loyalty of Indian troops was strained, the Sahibs prepared for yet another punishing campaign in Afghanistan. Zinoviev, whose activities had so far been almost exclusively concentrated on Europe, began to realize that Stalin's oft-repeated slogan, *ex oriente lux*, might have to be taken seriously. The Sahibs, and ex-Viceroy Lord Curzon, were convinced that it had already been taken seriously. Gandhi broke off relations with the British. 'It is not without a pang', he wrote in a letter to Lord Chelmsford, 'that I return the Kaiser-i-Hind Gold Medal granted to me by your predecessor for my humanitarian work in South Africa, the Zulu War Medal for my services as an officer in charge of the Indian Volunteer Ambulance Corps in 1906, and the Boer War Medal for my services as Assistant Superintendent of the Indian Volunteer Stretcher-Bearer Corps ... I can retain neither respect nor affection for a government which has been moving from wrong to wrong in order to defend its immorality ... The government must be moved to repentance. I have therefore ventured to suggest non-cooperation.' Taken in conjunction with the veiled threats of the *New Communist Manifesto* and Bukharin's amoral remarks, this declaration acquired sinister undertones. Could it be that the saintly Mahatma had, wittingly or unwittingly, become the tool of the fiends in the Kremlin?

III

MAY DAYS

---

1. *Don't Count Your Soviets*

In 'Perspectives of the Proletarian Revolution', an article which
appeared in the May issue of the *Communist International*, Zinoviev
reached his peak of excitement. 'The Third International already has
as its members three Soviet republics – in Hungary, Russia and
Bavaria. But nobody will be surprised if by the time these lines appear
in print we have not three but six more.' The victory of communism
in Germany was wholly inevitable. There might be a few isolated
defeats: but the revolution was spreading with such speed that one
could predict with certainty 'that in a year's time the whole of
Europe will be communist'. Capitalism might contrive to exist in
America and perhaps in Britain for a year or two – 'but for any length
of time such a symbiosis is impossible.'

Comintern produced a swingeing *May Day Manifesto to the Working People of the Whole World*. 'Communism has come out on to the
streets ... In France huge demonstrations have begun ... In Italy the
struggle has reached boiling point. In England strikes are epidemic.
Here and there workers' soviets are being formed. In America the
proletariat is getting ready for the decisive conflict.' The attempt to
revive the corpse of the Second International had failed. Social
Democracy had been exposed as a feeble fraud. 'The storm is
rising. The flames of proletarian revolution are spreading all over
Europe. It is invincible. The moment of which the best of mankind
dreamed is becoming reality ... The last hour of our oppressors
has struck ... In 1919 the great Communist International was
born. In 1920 the great International Soviet Republic will come to
birth.'

'In all nations', Lenin claimed in a Red Square speech, on May 1st,
'the workers have started on the path of struggle with imperialism.
The liberated working class is celebrating its anniversary freely and

openly not only in Soviet Russia but also in Soviet Hungary and Soviet Bavaria.'

Even as Lenin spoke and the *Communist International* came off the press they were out of date. The second German revolution, already quelled in Berlin, took a sharp drubbing in the rest of the Reich as the Freikorps carried out another and more drastic mopping-up operation. The Munich Soviet was in its death throes. On May 1st, bursting through the flimsy outer defences, General von Oven's troops entered Munich. Several days of confused and obstinate fighting served as a further excuse for a savage White Terror. Seven hundred people were shot, thousands arrested. Leviné and Engelhofer were shot after drumhead courts-martial. Gustav Landauer was rifle-butted from his cell into the prison yard, the walls of which were spattered with blood and brains. An officer struck him in the face. 'Dirty Bolshie! Let's finish him off!' Clubbed to the ground, he somehow struggled up and tried to speak. 'This damned carrion has nine lives,' said the officer. 'He can't even die like a gentleman.' Shot in the back, Landauer's body still twitched. It was trampled to death, then stripped and thrown into a wash-house.

By Sunday, May 4th, the firing was over. Noske sent a telegram to von Oven expressing his pleasure at 'the discreet and wholly successful way in which he had conducted operations'. 'The result of the Soviet episode at Munich, so far as at present can be seen,' summarized a memorandum compiled by the Political Intelligence Department of the British Foreign Office, 'is to strengthen the cause of law and order throughout Germany, and to discredit Spartacism and Bolshevism with the masses. It was only in Munich, with its atmosphere of reckless and irresponsible bohemianism, that an experiment of this kind could have been made.' Toller – 'the King of Southern Bavaria' as Leviné had sarcastically called him – the most responsible and high-minded bohemian of the bunch, was found hiding in the house of an artist friend. Even his grim-faced discoverers laughed when he tumbled out of a wardrobe with his hair dyed a vivid red. On his way to the Stadelheim Prison he noticed the change that had come over Munich. Monocled, carefully groomed officers were strolling and flirting with smartly dressed women. The bourgeoisie was on top again. Over the prison gates was scrawled in chalk: THIS IS WHERE WE MAKE SAUSAGES OF SPARTACISTS. REDS EXECUTED FREE OF CHARGE. The day before his trial Toller's hair, now piebald, was cut. The barber wrapped up the red ends. They were to be used by the Public Prosecutor to demonstrate to the court to what lengths of deceit the prisoner had gone to cheat the law. Hugo Haase, a well-known barrister as well as the leader of the Independent Socialists, argued that it was ridiculous that one set of revolutionaries should be sitting in judgment on another set. Toller had not been in Munich when the revolution began. He had simply accepted the situation — like Field-Marshal Hindenburg and General Gröner — and offered his services to the new regime.

Brushing aside these well-meaning sophistries, Toller declared: 'I would not be a revolutionary if I did not allow that force must sometimes be used to change existing conditions. Revolution is not an abstract theory. It is made up of the determination of millions of working men. It cannot die until the hearts of those men have ceased to beat. I have heard it said that the revolution was a purely mercenary movement. Gentlemen, if you went among the workers for one day you would see for yourselves why these men must satisfy their material needs before they do anything else. But they are also struggling with all their energy for the things of the mind. They desire most earnestly to know something of art and culture. The struggle has begun and not all the persecution of the united capitalist governments of the world can stop it.'

Fortuitously but felicitously, it had fallen to an Independent Socialist with piebald hair and a compassionate, unideological heart to say the last word about the strange parabola of the Bavarian revolution. When Toller, sentenced to five years' imprisonment, left Munich railway station, a crowd of workers including booking clerks, porters and engine drivers, shouted good wishes. His police guards offered him cigarettes and food and apologized for the dirty work they had to do. In prison Toller was reunited with Erich Mühsam, serving a fifteen-year sentence, and a whole cross-section of their former comrades. He and Mühsam were appalled by the bitter socialist sectarianism. It reminded them of the Middle Ages, when men went to death for the sake of a word or a letter. They were abused when they declined to believe in the likelihood of a great workers' uprising and criticized the proletarian play-acting which had inspired one man, an ex-Imperial Army officer, to slash his splendid greatcoat into tatters. Politics divided men. But the sexual urge broke down all barriers. In some this

showed as homosexuality, reaching a fantastic climax when prisoners formed themselves into a Court of Love in which lover and
beloved had to defend themselves, each case being submitted to
ardent arbitration. Others pored for hours over girlie magazines,
and conveyed notes to the women prisoners on the floor above.
One incident stayed in Toller's memory. Left alone for a short time
by her warder, a girl prisoner, recognizing her 'lover' from smuggled descriptions, jumped back from the barred window of the
laundry where she was working, unbuttoned her coarse grey dress,
and showed him her body, laughing and weeping for joy.

So ended, or so continued, the bohemian revolution in Bavaria. It
was not, and never had been, exactly what Lenin and Zinoviev had
in mind.

The facts of the situation in Austria were hardly more encouraging.
The Social Democrats went as far as they dared in supporting the
Hungarian revolution. They agreed to trade manufactured goods for
foodstuffs, winked at the activities of sympathizers who smuggled
arms across the frontier, and elected to meet the activities of the
Hungarian Embassy, a notorious centre of agitation, with arguments
rather than bullets.

More they could not do, even if they had wanted to. Outside
Vienna the peasant provinces had formed their own provisional
governments and armed forces. One needed a passport to travel
from one province to another, and the Home Guards were as
likely to be used against the Volkswehr as against external enemies.
The ultra-democratic Volkswehr had its work cut out to repel
land-grabbing Czech and Yugoslav invasions which cost over 300
dead and nearly 1,000 wounded. Its battleworthiness was suspect.
Officers were appointed on probation for a month, after which the
Soldiers' Councils decided if they 'enjoyed the confidence of the
men'. Lectures were given in barracks on such themes as 'The Idea
of Class Warfare' and 'The Teaching of Karl Marx'. The War
Ministry depended on the Central Executive Committee of the
Soldiers' Councils to transmit orders after prolonged discussion.
'Militaristic' discipline was abjured, but 'proletarian' discipline,
though in some ways very strong, could be distinctly eccentric.
The soldiers' council of a battalion sent to guard a railway on the
Czech-Austrian frontier objected to the assignment and ordered the
battalion back to Vienna. During a skirmish with the Yugoslavs,

a battalion commander ordered all those whose consciences might be violated by the coming affray to fall out. This reduced his unit to 140 men. A second earnest appeal made minutes before going into action reduced the total to eighty.

It was not surprising that when Julius Braunthal, the Deputy War Minister, went to Berlin to confer with Gustav Noske, he was less than courteously received. Couldn't Noske do something, he asked, to democratize the Freikorps? Did he have to encourage them to murder their fellow-countrymen? Couldn't he, in a word, make them more like the Austrian Volkswehr? 'Mind your own business!' shouted Noske. 'Leave it to me! The leaders of the Freikorps are better Germans than the revolutionaries!' Noske was not interested in an *Anschluss* with Austria. He had enough to do keeping order in Germany, he said. The conversation was constantly interrupted by orders, barked into the telephone, to send out more troops to crush disturbances in various industrial centres. 'There you have your workers' councils,' sneered Noske. 'They're making trouble everywhere. They're ruining Germany.' After half an hour of heated argument, Braunthal left the office of the defender of the November revolution wondering if he had ever met such an appalling bully.

If Noske and Braunthal could have changed places, Zinoviev's predictions might not have proved so wildly wide of the mark. An authoritarian Red Guard in Vienna, a humanitarian Volkswehr in Germany, and things might have been different. As it was, despite the lashings and the lies of Kun's agitators (according to whom the Russian and Hungarian Red Armies were for ever on the point of joining forces), the most, perhaps the only, effective act of social rebellion in Austria occurred in the provincial town of Graz—where the maidservants decided, when addressing their mistresses, to cut out the time-honoured greeting: 'I kiss your hand.'

Eagerly the *Arbeiter Zeitung* praised 'these courageous girls' and called upon other citizens to follow their example of emancipation. But not even Zinoviev could make much of a Soviet of Maidservants in Graz.

In Britain the National Industrial Conference and the Coal Commission continued to dissipate such militancy as there had been in the labour movement. An interim report of the Coal Commission, issued in March, had conceded wage increases, promised a seven-hour day, and condemned 'the present system of ownership'. Bonar Law, in reply to a query from the Miners' Federation, wrote reassuringly: 'I have pleasure in confirming my statement that the Government are prepared to carry out in the spirit and in the letter the recommendations of Sir John Sankey's report.' In April the Commission had resumed its sessions. All through May Robert Smillie continued to cross-examine royalty owners on what work they did for the enormous sums of money they drew from the industry. The Dukes of Durham, Northumberland and Hamilton, the Marquis of Londonderry, the Earls of Stafford and Bute, Lord Tredegar, and their agents went to the witness box to be 'roasted' (as the *Daily Herald* put it). There was a great deal of badinage about how many vans or railway carriages would be needed to convey the peers' accumulated land titles to London if the Chairman required to see them.

But if this was the best that Britain's largest single industry could do in the way of 'mauling the capitalists' and pressing the case for permanent and radical socialization, the performance of the Parliamentary Labour Party was even feebler. It kept quiet about socialization, and agreed with Brigadier-General Page-Croft that Soviet Russia was ruled by bloodthirsty criminals. Bonar Law had little difficulty in fobbing off delegations which came to protest about intervention. He knew that they only did so to put up a front for the Triple Alliance. He knew, also, that the Triple Alliance was so divided in its counsels that it would be nothing short of a miracle if the strike threat was carried out. And with every week that passed the government was strengthening its strike-breaking organization.

France, with the Black Sea revolt, a May Day strike of transport workers in Paris which ended in clashes with the police and casualties on both sides, and a deepening schism between evolutionaries and revolutionaries in the unions and the Socialist Party, came nearer to a show of militancy. In Italy the socialists, paralysed by internal feuds, were being taunted by Mussolini for their impotence. President Wilson's veto on Italy's Adriatic claims was the main topic of the time. How dare this hypocritical Quaker (as d'Annunzio persisted in calling him) prefer ignorant Slavs to the heirs of the grandeur that had been, and still, if Italians would only rise to the hour of destiny, could be Rome? Many socialists, disillusioned by the sectarian squabbles of their party, and convinced that Wilson was backing the Slavs only because he expected them, in return, to

Plate 1. Moscow, the Kremlin, March 2nd, 1919. *Left to right:* Eberlein (Germany), Lenin and Fritz Platten (Switzerland) during one of the sessions which resulted in the launching of the Communist Third International.

Plate 2. Makhno and his entourage foreshadowed, sartorially and ideologically, the hippie-style freedom-fighters of the 1960s.

Plate 3 (*left*) Liberated proletarian giant smashes 'capitalist' chains on a globe of the world—the cover of the first issue of the *Communist International*, published in Petrograd in several languages, May 1919.

Plate 4. (*right*) Budapest, May Day 1919. Michael Biró's famous Worker Giant poster

Plate 5. (*below*) Overloaded trains in Petrograd railway station, September 1919.

Plate 6. (*facing page*, *top*) Fiume, October 1919. Gabriele d'Annunzio, the 'Dictator' of Fiume, harangues his legionaries.

te 7. (*right*) Bolshevik
ders in Hungary. *Left to
t:* Joseph Pogany,
ismund Kunfi and Bela
n.

"Come On!"
(Cartoonist Murphy in the San Francisco Examiner)

THE CRISIS IN ESSENCE

RAIL
STRIKE
GOVT
OBDURATE

CALL OUT
THE ARMY
THAT REFUSED
TO FIGHT THE
GERMANS

ERIC: "Russia is nothing to this, Churchill, my boy! Now w
this nonsense of an 'England Fit for Heroes' once and for a

Plate 8. (*left*) Cartoon which appeared in the San Francisco *Examiner* at the height of the 1919 Red scare.

Plate 9 (*right*) Napoleonic Churchill. A cartoon by Will Dyson in the *Daily Herald*, September 1919, at the time of the English rail strike.

Plate 10. (*below*) President Wilson arrives in Paris, December 1918.

Plate 11. Berlin, November 1918. A statue of Kaiser Wilhelm I overturned by revolutionary mobs in the early stages of the German revolution.

Plate 12. (*left*) Karl Liebknecht, son of a founder of the German Social Democratic Party. He became a leader of the Spartacus movement, and was murdered in Berlin in January 1919.

Plate 13. (*right*) Rosa Luxemburg, leader of the Spartacus movement which formed the nucleus of the German Communist Party (K.P.D.). She was murdered in Berlin in January 1919.

Plate 14. (*left*) Berlin riots, November 1918. Red flag carried through the streets.

Plate 15. (*right*) October 1919. A snatched press shot of the exiled ex-Kaiser exercising in the grounds of Amerongen Castle, Holland.

Plate 16. Berlin, March 1919. Troops escort prisoners during the second Spartacist revolt.

Plate 17. Belfast, January 1919. The car of the Lord Mayor menaced by demonstrators during the general strike.

Plate 18. Glasgow, January 31st, 1919. Strike leader William Gallacher and others being arrested and given first aid by the police.

Plate 19. London, October 1919. Class war in Britain: gentlemen volunteers attacked by workers during the great rail strike.

Plate 20. Mrs Fannie Sellins, Trade Union Organizer, killed by Steel Trust gunmen in West Natrona, Pennsylvania, on August 26th, 1919.

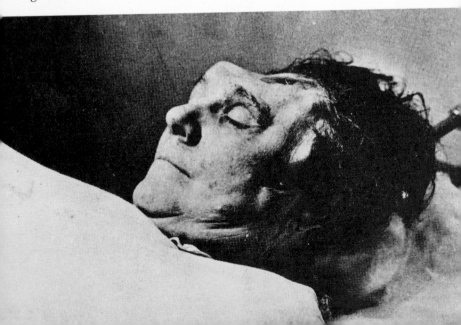

do his anti-Bolshevik bidding in Hungary, turned to d'Annunzio, who on May 4th told a huge nationalist rally in Rome: 'Our epic May begins. I am ready. We are ready. I repeat that today only Italy is great, that today she alone is pure. Against us I see only big and small merchants, big and small usurers ... the same obscene côterie of bankers.'

D'Annunzio's *sacro egoismo* and his scorn for a money-grubbing, philistine bourgeoisie had a much wider appeal than the wooden dialectics of the Socialist Party. D'Annunzio and Mussolini were the only two possible catalysts of revolution in Italy. But they could not be fitted into any known or conceivable Comintern category.

By May it was a question of whether the Hungarian Soviet Republic could survive—and fan such embers of revolt as were still glowing. Frequent, searching and imperious were Lenin's catechisms. 'Please inform me', he telegraphed, 'what real guarantees you have that the new Hungarian government is really communist and not merely bourgeois socialist.' 'Dear Comrade Lenin,' replied Kun, 'the difficulties with us are much greater than they were with you in Russia ... Yet I believe that no objection can be made to our actions even from the point of view of pure principle ... The members of the extreme right have been pushed out of the party and the old trade-union bureaucracy is gradually being sifted out. I beg you to keep your confidence in me. I will never go to the right, but we are standing so far to the left that a further move in that direction is out of the question ... '

There was some justification for this claim. Kun's team of effervescent Jewish intellectuals had, at breakneck pace, transformed Budapest into a powerhouse of progressive radicalism. The legal profession had been replaced by a system of revolutionary tribunals. Hundreds of pending lawsuits had been abandoned when the plaintiffs were threatened with a fine for obstruction of business. Proletarian defendants were informed that 'the Revolutionary Tribunal promises you exemption from punishment and has ordered all the documents relating to your case to be burned. A new regime, rooted in the purified ethics of universal brotherhood, admonishes you to avoid all criminal actions in future and to devote yourself to the service of the Dictatorship of the Proletariat.' Monasteries and convents had been suppressed. Nuns were forced to serve as army nurses, but forbidden to proselytize. Fanatical young Jewish Marxists scandalized the peasants by atheistic propaganda campaigns in the villages. As in Soviet Russia the stigma of illegitimacy was officially abolished. All those of both sexes who earned a living by 'work useful to society' had the vote. In the schools the inculcation of socialist virtues was combined with anti-religious instruction, sex education for boys and girls from an early age by means of specially prepared films and illustrated lectures, and a system of 'children's soviets' which were to maintain discipline in consultation with the teachers. The worst offence, ruled the Commissariat of Education, was 'any utterance or action in school or outside it directed against society as a whole'.

All factories employing more than twenty workers were socialized. All estates of more than a hundred acres were to be socialized immediately, and as soon as possible all holdings of more than twenty acres (a decision taken against Lenin's pointed advice). The Commissariat of Housing restricted upper and middle class tenants to a maximum of three rooms in their own houses or apartments, and wrestled with the problem of accommodating not only workers and their families but key specialists such as doctors, dentists, writers and painters, who were all to have an extra room for their work. It also supplied newly married couples with basic furniture and kitchen utensils, and organized day nurseries for working mothers. By May houses in twenty-eight villages around Budapest had been socialized and plans made to extend this measure to the main provincial towns. All banks were socialized. The maximum sum for any account was 100,000 crowns, doled out at the rate of 2,000 crowns per month—the equivalent of an industrial worker's wage. But spiralling inflation made commissar-economist Eugen Varga think in terms of a 'fully communist', moneyless economy based purely on labour values and labour vouchers. 'In the economic life of a new society', he announced, 'the expropriation of a great bank has little importance ... for in the last resort what is a bank but a building with many desks and a mass of paper?'

The old regime, however, had possessed one great virtue. Everyone had known exactly where he stood. Now each day brought a new batch of decrees and supplementary instructions from Budapest. When provincial councils complained that they were bullied both by the workers and the government, Minister of the Interior Szamuelly sharply replied: 'Comrades complain that they are being trodden upon from below and above. In my opinion leading members of the councils who not only omit to read the decrees of the government but would not understand them if they did, deserve not merely to be trodden upon but kicked out.' Szamuelly had no time for fools and laggards, especially as all this bold experimentation went on against a near-background of invasion or threatened invasion by Rumanians, Czechs and Yugoslavs. In April the Hungarian army had suffered a series of crushing defeats, and at the end of the month the Rumanians were rapidly advancing on Budapest. At this point the proletariat of Budapest rose *en masse* to defend their country and their revolution. Many anti-socialist ex-officers (supervised by a hastily recruited force of political commissars) volunteered, in a rush of patriotism, to serve under the command of the socialist general Vilmos Boehm and a new convert to communism, Colonel Aurel Stromfeld.

At this point, too, Budapest staged its most brilliant display of revolutionary solidarity. The direction of the May Day carnival had been entrusted to Szamuelly. He called in the *avant-garde* painters and sculptors who, as in Russia, had swept traditionalists from the art schools, and now celebrated their own and the people's liberation. For sheer emotional impact and aesthetic merit the Soviet posters of Budapest were unsurpassed. Giant fists smashed through palace windows and smote the banqueting tables of the rich, scattering crowns and courtiers. Beautiful, Henry-Moore-like files of statuesque soldiers summoned men to the ranks of the Red Army. Peasants fell on their knees in fields before the unearthly effulgence of a red star. A grinning skeleton gibbered above the slumped form of a worker clutching a tumblerful of (now forbidden) alcoholic poison. Michael Biro's immortal figure of a giant proletarian with upswung hammer dominated street after street in hypnotic reiteration.

'Workers! Attire yourselves, your souls, in the red tint of joy,' conjured the *Nepszava*, 'lave yourselves in the crystal waters of the new spirit, for we are preparing for a festival such as the world has never seen ... Our May is the spirit that ever surges forward, ever aspires upward, a spirit reddened by proletarian blood and proletarian joy!' There were triumphal arches, dancing-booths, ice-skating on a rink in the main park, gymkhanas, music on all the bridges, a gala performance of the orchestra of the Opera House, forty brass bands in procession, even (by special dispensation) an eating contest. Streets were garlanded, houses draped, in red. A statue of Karl Marx, fifteen feet high, was erected on Coronation Hill. Plaster busts of Lenin and Liebknecht fronted the House of Soviets. A large statue of Engels, dwarfed by a thirty-feet-high effigy of Lenin, appeared in the park. The employees of the socialized cinema industry had devised their own procession. In front came a film-roll of enormous dimensions on a chariot drawn by six white horses. Star actors and actresses walked behind in the costumes of their best-known rôles. A rout of women in blood-red blouses with red ribbons in their dishevelled hair rushed past behind a tumbril and guillotine screaming and gesticulating in the traditional manner of the furies of the French Revolution. The carnival ended with a tremendous firework display and the illumination – in red – of the chief buildings.

It was a great success. But Bela Kun was unable to enjoy it. The strain of the last five weeks, and not least of Lenin's peremptory solicitude, had told upon him. On May Day Count Károlyi, visiting the Hotel Hungaria, found Kun flopped out on a couch in a state of complete nervous prostration, with his wife in anxious attendance. Kunfi and Szamuelly were left to make the call to arms. But within a few days the resilient, emotional Kun had recovered. The workers' army had, incredibly, won the first of a series of victories over the Rumanians, driving them back far beyond the original armistice line. The factories of Budapest, like those of Petrograd and Moscow, had been almost stripped of workers. Commerce barely existed. Yet Alice Riggs Hunt, an American journalist, found Budapest an exciting city. The posters (PROLETARIANS! DON'T DRINK, WORK!), the earnest-looking crowds, gave her the impression that she had 'landed in a New England town on a Sunday', and that the people strolling along the banks of the Danube were 'good Puritans'. Kun received her only an hour after she had requested an interview, and painted a rosy picture of bulging granaries and factories turning out vast quantities of agricultural machinery. The commissars, in fact, talked until they dropped. At twelve specially arranged meetings they tried, under a barrage of indignant heckling, to explain to the women of Budapest why their men had been taken from them, why there had to be war, why there were food shortages and irksome queues. Never, perhaps, had a government, and certainly not a dictatorship, committed itself to (or indulged itself in) such a non-stop orgy of democratic self-justification.

Miss Hunt found the comradely frankness of the commissars a welcome change from the politic evasions of Paris. In the canteen of the Soviet House she heard them discussing the problems of the hour with (and over the same food as) clerks, typists, window-cleaners and chauffeurs. In the Budapest Soviet age and seniority did not guarantee respect. When Food Commissar Mor Erdelyi, under persistent questioning, pleaded that he had been in the socialist movement for twenty-five years, a young soldier-deputy yelled: 'That's long enough to make you a bourgeois!' The twenty women deputies were brimming with zeal. Yolan Fried, twenty-seven-year-old head of the Child Welfare Department of the Commissariat of Education, described how she had organized a chain of public baths, commissioned a new series of splendidly illustrated children's books, and converted orphanages into centres for all kinds of children – 'so that the poor orphans need not feel isolated in society.' She aimed, she said, to set up child-psychology centres where each child's abilities and preferences could be assessed and education planned accordingly. She was also establishing a children's colony on the shores of Lake Balaton (the fences round the gardens of confiscated bourgeois villas were being removed to create an open village), and had arranged to send city children to peasant families during their holidays.

In his letter to Lenin, Kun had vowed to 'chop off the head of counter-revolution wherever it shows itself'. In fact the Red Terror had been very mild. By May the patricians had rallied sufficiently to form a rival government, headed by Count Julius Károlyi, in Szeged, which had been captured by French troops under the command of the ubiquitous Franchet d'Esperey who, fresh from the fiasco of Odessa, lapped up the treacly flattery of his repulsive puppets. 'We, representatives of the real Hungary,' said Count Julius Károlyi, 'see in Your Excellency not an enemy of our land, but the saviour and champion of an oppressed people.' Yet still the proletarian terror hung fire. Despite occasional bursts of looting and violence, most of the bourgeois deaths in Budapest were self-inflicted. Several scores of men and women, depressed by the confiscation of most of their wealth, distressed by the presence of slum families complete with smelly paraffin cookers and lots of noisy, dirty children, committed suicide by shooting themselves or jumping from the roofs of their desecrated homes.

The deeply feudalized peasants refused to believe that they could be the equals of their masters. Convinced that the madness in Budapest would soon end, they treated such landlords as had not fled with special respect, hoping to avert the vengeance to come. By the end of May they had begun their own blockade of Budapest. The attempted collectivization of agriculture was hated and obstinately resisted. Peasants refused to fight except in defence of their own soil, refused to send food to the cities. The cost of living soared daily. The Red Army, having routed the Rumanians, had turned north to face the Czechoslovaks. It routed them too, and even occupied most of Slovakia. But provisioning was chaotic. A crippling fuel shortage wrecked railway transport. In an attempt to mollify the troops, the government allowed soldiers' wives to visit their husbands at the front. The women brought demoralizing tales of hardship at home. A trickle of deserters became a stream. Class loyalty began to revive among the officers. In Budapest the revolutionary posters and the effigies of Marx and Lenin were defaced. The bourgeoisie, sensing the turn of the tide, took fresh heart. The Supreme Economic Council announced that the blockade of Hungary would not be lifted until a new government 'which gives some assurance of settled conditions' was installed. The life of the Hungarian Soviet Republic hung by a slender thread.

Neither Zinoviev nor Lenin had made much reference, in their Soviet fantasies, to the Latvian Republic. It was too blatantly the result of Soviet 'imperialism'. Dutifully but with growing listlessness, it functioned in a vacuum of indifference. Pastor Model alone maintained his feverish excitement. Bolshevism, he asserted in his Easter sermon, was a far more glorious Resurrection than that of two thousand years ago in Jerusalem. 'The great Resurrection foretold by Jesus Christ is taking place now. The Kingdom of Heaven is being built on earth before the eyes of this generation in such splendour as no one has dreamed of.'

Only the eye of faith could have discerned any signs of such a development. The Red Army was being pressed back. Latvian peasants were blockading Riga and violently resisting requisition squads. Riga, once so clean and bustling, was squalid and sullen. The busiest people were the dreaded female terror units, which, in a wood near the city, shot batches of bourgeois hostages under the supervision (it was said) of a beautiful, club-footed, black-velvet-cloaked young Amazon commissar mounted on a white horse.

Compared with this Valkyrie of Terror, Peter Stutchka, the puppet President, was a grey, sad figure. On May 1st, in a soaking drizzle, Riga staged its own utility Fête of the World Proletariat. Lampposts had been painted red, a plywood Temple of Reason had been erected in the main square. Streets had been ceremoniously renamed—Revolution Street, Karl Marx Boulevard, Third International Prospect. Plaster statues of Marx, Lenin, Trotsky and Zinoviev had been imported from Petrograd. So, it seemed, had Stutchka's speech, with its routine hyperbole about the rising tide of world revolution. His damp oratory failed to arouse any enthusiasm in the sodden crowds and shivering soldiers. At night the fireworks sputtered unfestively in the rain.

The fate of Riga depended upon the whims of General Rüdiger von der Goltz, whose ambitions were proving a much more serious menace to Allied plans for the Baltic than the half-hearted operations of the Red Army. Von der Goltz was in a strong bargaining position. In December 1918 the Latvian government had appealed for German help, offering Latvian citizenship—and grants of land on the vast estates of the Teutonic Baltic barons—to all who would fight for four weeks against the Bolshevik invaders. 'Baltic fever' had swept the recruiting offices in Prussia. Eighteen Baltic Freikorps were formed. They were joined by Latvian troops, Polish mercenaries, a Russian émigré officers' corps commanded by Count Levien, and a German volunteer corps recruited by another Russian, Colonel Avalov-Bermondt. Von der Goltz, supreme commander of a force of 30,000 nominal anti-Bolsheviks, had his own ideas of how it should be used. He was not prepared to be a mere tool of the British, but dreamed of new scope for German imperialism. 'Why not', he wrote, 'revive under a new form, in agreement with the Whites, and under cover of an anti-Bolshevik crusade, our old Eastern policy? Why not work for an economic and political rapprochement with Red Russia which, having massacred its intellectuals, needs merchants, engineers, and administrators, and whose frontier provinces, devastated and depopulated, might offer a fertile land for hard-working German peasants?'

His ultimate aim was to set up a Baltic Grand Duchy with himself as ruler. His immediate plan was to allow the Red Army to create a maximum of disintegration. He would then pick his moment to act the saviour and exact his own terms. Ignoring protests from British naval and military leaders, he arrested several of them and even threatened to bombard the British fleet in the harbour of Libau. His army lived off the land, terrorizing burghers, peasants and Baltic barons alike. In April von der Goltz ordered a series of mild skirmishes with the Red Army. In May his forces began a leisurely northward advance. Stutchka ordered the shooting of more hostages. Hundreds of bourgeois 'parasites' were sent to the front to dig trenches and empty latrines. Those who were left behind were evicted from their few unrequisitioned rooms and herded into two canvas ghettoes on islands in the River Dvina. Von der Goltz shed no tears over their persecution, nor did he hurry to end it. Stutchka was his puppet as well as Moscow's.

2. Novelty Samples, Red Winnipeg

More attractive than the dull, sporadic butchery of the Riga Soviet was the utopian ferment among Latvian workers in the United States. Together with Lithuanian, Hungarian, Czech, Yiddish and Slav foreign-language federations, they ran their own socialist journal, with 'All Power to the Soviets' as its slogan and a 'real' revolution in America as its declared aim. These federations formed the left wing of the Socialist Party. In the short interval before federal and state governments began to show a crushing interest in their somewhat naive revolutionary talk, they took over where the I.W.W. had been forced to leave off as the vanguard of socialist militancy. The I.W.W., after the body blows of 1918, was barely surviving. State after state had enacted criminal syndicalist laws to pulverize what remained of its spirit and organization.

With the entire I.W.W. leadership in jail, Haywood unreservedly endorsing the anti-capitalist fight of the Workers' Republic, and a new Wobbly chorus ('If you don't like the Red Flag of Russia, If you don't like the spirit so true, Then just be like the cur in the story, and lick the hand that's robbing you') stressing the broad lines of class loyalty, the headquarters of radical socialism in America switched to an office in New York's World Tower Building. Here a German-born Marxist, Ludwig Martens, bearing credentials from Chicherin, had set up in the propaganda business.

Early in May, with the founding of the American Legion, the forces of 100 per cent Americanism were boosted by a powerful reinforcement. The Legion fulfilled the *Nation*'s hope that veteran associations would dedicate themselves to the cleansing of American democracy—but only in the sense of allying itself with the most xenophobic, anti-radical elements in the country. 'For God and country,' said the preamble to the Legion's constitution, 'we associate ourselves together for the following purposes: to uphold and defend the Constitution of the United States of America; to maintain law and order; to foster and perpetuate 100 per cent Americanism; to preserve the memories and incidents of our association in

the Great War ... to promote peace and goodwill on earth; to
safeguard ... the principles of justice, freedom and democracy.'
Ku Klux Klan racism ran riot, using the time-honoured excuse of
the 'defence of Southern womanhood against negro "Bolsheviks".'
'Not one Negro to whom I spoke in the Delta Region', reported
the *Nation*'s correspondent, 'but wished to get away. Daily life for
them is almost intolerable ... subject to every insult and abuse, not
to mention Jim Crow-ism: and they have had too much experience
of the courts to rely on them ... Convince men that they have no
stake in society and in the courts and no refuge in an enlightened
public sentiment: insult, injure and degrade them without redress, and
you create the desperation out of which springs violence.' The same
could have been said of the helot workers of the Steel Trusts. But
federal and state government, blind to such logic, continued to
foment and fight the Great Red Scare. At the end of April some
sensationally reported bombing incidents gave this a fresh impetus.
Ex-Senator Thomas W. Hardwick of Atlanta (whose coloured
maid's hands were blown off by a bomb-package addressed to him)
had been Chairman of the Senate Immigration Committee which
had proposed drastic measures to keep out aliens. The discovery
that a packet addressed to ex-Mayor Ole Hanson in Seattle also
contained a crude bomb, and the appearance of a few anarchist
posters in Chicago ('The senile fossils of the United States see red!
The storm is within and very soon will leap and crash and annihilate
you in blood and fire. You have shown no pity to us! We will do
likewise. We will dynamite you!') had been followed by an SOS to
all post offices. A hasty search in the New York parcel-post division
revealed sixteen bomb-packages marked NOVELTY—A SAMPLE.
Eighteen similar packages were found in other offices. Intended
recipients — it was said — included Frederick C. Howe, Com-
missioner-General for Immigration; Senator Lee S. Overman,
Chairman of the Senate's Bolshevik Investigation Committee;
Oliver W. Holmes, Associate Justice of the Supreme Court;
Postmaster-General Albert S. Burleson (who had barred radical
literature from the mails); Judge K. M. Landis (who had presided
over the I.W.W. trial in Chicago); Senator William H. King, a
strident critic of organized labour; Attorney-General A. Mitchell
Palmer; John D. Rockefeller Jr; and John Pierpont Morgan.

36 MARKED AS VICTIMS BY BOMB CONSPIRATORS—REDS
PLANNED MAY DAY MURDERS, said headlines. Panic newspaper

warnings caused the contents of thousands of harmless packages to be ruined by immersion in water. The police were swamped with phone calls. The press demanded vigorous action, 'or we may as well invite Lenin and Trotsky to come here and set up business at once'. Ex-Mayor Hanson ranted that if Washington did not hang or incarcerate for life all the anarchists, he would. The *United Presbyterian* urged that 'every true lover of God and his country should hit with an axe whenever and wherever appears the evil head of anarchy.' Religious revivalist Billy Sunday, in a much-quoted interview, described the Bolshevik as 'a guy with a face like a porcupine and a breath that would scare a polecat', and added: 'If I had my way I'd fill the jails so full of them that their feet would stick out the windows. Let them rule? We'll swim our horses in blood up to the bridles first!'

The bomb hysteria was worsened by lurid reporting of minor disturbances arising from traditional May Day parades solemnly dedicated to 'the Reconsecration of Our Lives to International Socialism'. In Boston one policeman was stabbed to death, three policemen and one demonstrator wounded, in a scrimmage which broke out around a Red Flag parade of the Latvian Workmen's Association. Vigilante squads thereupon wrecked the headquarters of the Socialist Party and beat up any stray 'Reds' they could find. The Russian People's House on East 15th Street, New York, was raided by soldiers who set fire to books and pamphlets and forced those present to sing the national anthem. The offices of the *Call*, which had consistently opposed as futile any attempt at revolution, were smashed by a mob of four hundred soldiers and sailors. In Cleveland, Ohio, 'loyal' soldiers who tried to break up a socialist demonstration were counter-attacked by 'Red' troops. One person was killed and forty injured in a free fight which had to be quelled by army trucks and a Victory Loan tank. Most of the mass-circulation press, claiming that these disturbances—invariably provoked by 'loyalists'—were nothing less than a dress-rehearsal for the looming revolution, clamoured for more stringent anti-radical legislation. Radical and liberal journals claimed that the bombs had been planted. 'The May Day bombs', asserted the *Liberator*, 'were a frame-up by those who are interested in "getting" the leaders of radicalism, and feel the need of a stronger public opinion before they can act.' The fact that a nation-wide police hunt failed to produce a single suspect was proof to radicals that their thesis was correct.

To others it proved the existence of a sinister and subtle foe. From now on any incident was either a capitalist 'plant' or a Red plot.

In 1919 western Canada seethed with a political passion normally confined to the French Canadians of Quebec. Even the farmers of Ontario were about to launch a Progressive Party in an attempt to upset the Liberal-Conservative see-saw (or coalition) in Ottawa and Toronto, and break the stranglehold of industrial finance capital. Alarmed by the possibility of a 'Bolshevik' alliance between farm and factory, the Dominion government reacted by a no-strike order, which was promptly defied by freight-handlers in Calgary, with the threat of a general strike if the order was enforced. Other edicts suppressed socialist societies, including the Social Democratic Party and most of the foreign-language associations, and set up a Directorate of Public Safety, headed by a Montreal lawyer-financier, which compiled a black-list of 'revolutionary' literature (including Plato's *Republic*).

When the Winnipeg metal-trades bosses, who for long had been notoriously hostile to unionism, refused to negotiate a demand for higher wages and an eight-hour day, their action was seen as part of a larger offensive which must be resisted with complete solidarity. On May 6th, at an emergency meeting in the Labour Temple in James Street, the Winnipeg Trades and Labour Council agreed that if the metal-trades' dispute was not settled within a week a vote should be taken on whether or not to call a general strike. On May 13th, with the bosses still stubborn, balloting showed 11,000 men in favour of a general sympathy strike, with only 500 against. Two days later the strike began. Thirty thousand workers, including policemen and other civic employees, made this the most thorough attempt ever made to put the O.B.U. principle of 'an injury to one is an injury to all' into practice. On May 16th unemptied garbage cans, undelivered milk and bread, no newspapers (the compositors had ceased work), no telephone, mail, freight or passenger services, shocked the city into an awareness of the implications of class war. An 'inner' strike committee of fifteen men, with Clydesider Bob Russell prominent, took over the administration.

The vans of milk and bread roundsmen carried BY AUTHORITY OF THE STRIKE COMMITTEE stickers. In cinemas and theatres, which it was decided not to close, managers were obliged to display, or to flash on the screen, the message, WORKING IN HARMONY

WITH THE STRIKE COMMITTEE. The weather was hot and
fine, morale high. 'The only thing the workers have to do to
win,' explained the *Strike Bulletin*, 'is to do nothing. Just eat, sleep,
play, love, laugh and look at the sun. There are those who are
anxious for us to do something which would provide an excuse for
putting the city under martial law. Therefore, once more, do
nothing ... WHAT WE WANT: (1) right of collective bargaining;
(2) a living wage; (3) reinstatement of all strikers. WHAT WE DO
NOT WANT: (1) revolution; (2) dictatorship; (3) disorder.' Victoria
Park was full of picnicking, sunbathing families, listening to workers' bands and socialist oratory. William Pritchard held forth at
length on the materialist conception of history and the evils of
capitalism. At open-air Labour Church services the ex-Rev. William
Ivens preached socialism, and led the congregation in a fervent
singing of selected hymns:

> When wilt thou save the people, Lord,
> O God of mercy, when?
> The people, Lord, the people,
> Not crowns and thrones, but men.

The bosses, said Ivens, were wicked. They were whited sepulchres
and grinders of the faces of the poor. Their day of doom was near.
'If you will but stand firm for a short time,' he prophesied, 'we will
bring them cringing on their knees to you, saying "What shall we
do to be saved?"'

A Citizens' Committee, functioning from the Board of Trade
building in Main Street, and headed by A. K. Godfrey, a wealthy
grain and lumber merchant, set to work, in co-operation with the
mayor, to organize emergency postal, telephone and police services
and to raise a para-military force of strike-breakers. Protesting its
neutrality and devotion to the commonwealth, it raised a fund of
more than a million dollars to combat what it called 'the James
Street Soviet'. The *Winnipeg Free Press* and the *Telegram*, which were
allowed to resume publication after a few days, persistently referred
to the strike as a revolution or THE GREAT DREAM OF THE
WINNIPEG SOVIET. Stockbrokers, lawyers, merchants and real-
estate moguls hurried daily to the barracks for rifle practice and
bayonet drill. Their anti-strike broadsheet, the *Winnipeg Citizen*,
was a classic mixture of injured innocence and clubman fury. Only
Bolshevism and 'Red Socialism', it maintained, were preventing

a great tide of prosperity from flooding Canada. Soviet despotism had been revealed in its full horror in 'the vulgar impertinence of placards upon shops and conveyances'. If revolution, disguised as the sympathetic strike, was what organized labour stood for, then 'there is just one answer—the open shop everywhere.' Alderman Abraham Heaps might deny that the strike had established a dictatorship of the proletariat. But the fact was that on May 23rd the *Western Labour News* had exulted: 'The fight is on. It overthrew the government in Russia, Austria and Germany ... Now it has Winnipeg in its grip. We shall fight until we win.'

Yet commonsense, argued the *Citizen*, would surely prevail. Winnipeg did not want any 'Made in Germany' nostrums—'this is an enlightened democracy we have in Canada, not an ignorant peasantry as in Russia nor a mechanical soldiery accustomed to dictatorship as in Germany.' How would citizens feel if the *employers* decided to paralyse the community and hold it up to ransom? Not that they would, of course, for as a far greater man than A. K. Godfrey had inspiringly said: 'Communities succeed or fail together. The unreasonable critic or agitator is the enemy of mankind, including himself. One who is controlled by selfish motives ... will never receive any lasting benefit. This applies to all classes of people and to every department of life ... If we are sincere and fair in our treatment of others, we may hope for similar treatment by them. If we are diligent in trying to ascertain the good in others, they may see good in us.' In Victoria Park William Ivens, and even the atheistic William Pritchard, appealed to the teachings of Jesus Christ. The Citizens' Committee instinctively turned, for spiritual comfort and moral authority, to Judge Elbert H. Gary.

The *Winnipeg Citizen* probably did more than any other single factor to stiffen the resolve of the strikers and to spread the spirit of rebellion. West from Winnipeg, in Calgary, Edmonton, Lethbridge, Medicine Hat, Saskatoon, Regina, Prince Albert, Brandon, Fort William, the chain of rebellion stretched clear to the coast, where, in British Columbia, a High Tory colony of retired Empire-builders and refugees from Lloyd George's pre-war budgets apopleptically coexisted with I.W.W. theories of workers' control. On May 28th, hearing that troops had been sent to deal with the 'revolution' in Winnipeg, a majority on the Vancouver Trades and Labour Council voted in favour of a general strike. It began on June 2nd, involved fifty thousand workers, bottled up industry and shipping, and lasted a month. A strike in Toronto, called for May 30th, was less wide-spread, but the fact that the ripples were reaching so far east shook Ottawa badly.

In Winnipeg tension grew. Pro- and anti-strike veterans demon-strated and counter-demonstrated. On June 6th the Dominion Parliament rushed through a bill enabling the deportation of 'any persons who do not believe in or are opposed to organized govern-ment.' The metal-trades employers refused any negotiations except on an open-shop basis. Class feeling ran so high that the board of a children's hospital indignantly rejected an offer from striker volun-teers to repair damage done to the roof during a severe storm. The appearance in the streets of revolver- and bludgeon-carrying special constables increased ill-feeling. On June 10th, during a riot on Main Street, one special was shot. A week later Russell, Johns, Ivens, Pritchard, Queen, Heaps and Armstrong were arrested on a charge of 'conspiracy to excite divers liege subjects of the King to resist laws and resist persons'. Four days later, during a noisy demonstration in front of the city hall, Mayor Charles F. Gray read the Riot Act. Royal North West Mounted Police and specials charged the crowd, firing and bludgeoning. Two strikers were killed. For several days police and troops patrolled the city. Trucks mounted with machine-guns guarded warehouses and rumbled past the Tem-ple of Labour. On June 25th the strike ended, and the Citizens' Committee prepared to dance on the corpse of trade unionism. Some of the rebel police were reinstated, but 403 postal employees, 119 telephone workers, and 53 firemen were not. After six weeks, a dream of social justice had, as the *Winnipeg Citizen* predicted, proved an inadequate substitute for wages. But the strike had also shown that the gospel of Gary and the wisdom of the Chambers of Commerce were inadequate substitutes for self-respect and the occasional catharsis of direct action.

RUSSIAN SICKNESS—BOLSHEVIK INTERIM. In the United States the Winnipeg revolt was given full scare treatment. Stories described babies dying for lack of milk and a city threatened with plague because of the breakdown in sanitation services. In mid-June the *Nation* put in a plea for calm. The outstanding fact was that in Seattle and Winnipeg, in Glasgow, Belfast and London, in Buenos Aires and Johannesburg, the workers had shown no desire to use violence. They were simply asking 'for what human beings ought to demand—decent pay and living conditions, reasonable leisure, a voice in fixing the conditions of their own life and work, and honesty and humanity in the relations of government and peoples.' For all its confusion and revolutionary appearance, the situation was one for 'hopefulness and thoughtful planning, rather than for fear and uncritical, unseeing opposition'. Wall Street *was* hopeful. 'Trouble in Europe?' said one banker at a press conference. 'It will die down when the harvests begin to come in. I don't look for any serious trouble. I think they will be able to clamp the lid down some way.'

3. *And Then There Were Two*

The draft German peace treaty caused agitation among progressives and economic realists. Herbert Hoover, convinced that its consequences would 'pull down all Europe and so injure the United States', was unable to sleep. He got up, dressed and went out into the streets of Paris at dawn. There he met two other restless spirits, General Jan Smuts and John Maynard Keynes. As they paced along they vowed to do what they could to modify the terms and make the dangers clear. Keynes was sickened not only by the cruel nonsense of sky-high reparation demands but by the way in which subtle legal minds had worked to camouflage the murder of the principle of self-determination. Instead of saying, for instance, that Austria was forbidden to unite with Germany except with France's permission, it was stated that 'Germany acknowledges and will respect strictly the independence of Austria within the frontiers which may be fixed in a Treaty between that State and the Principal Allied and Associated Powers; she agrees that this independence shall be inalienable except with the consent of the Council of the League of Nations' (which had to be unanimous). Moral obliquity and economic insanity went hand in hand.

William Bullitt and other disillusioned idealists of the American peace delegation, wondering how best to register their disapproval, turned to Lincoln Steffens for advice. 'I have seen the Russian revolution, the war, and this peace,' he told them, 'and I am sure that it is useless – almost wrong – to try to fight for the right under our system – petty reforms in politics, wars without victories. Either we should all labour to change the foundations of society as the Russians are doing, or go along with the civilization we know, only trying to keep our intellectual integrity by seeing it all straight.'

Some of the angry young men resigned in a round robin of protest. Bullitt sent his letter of resignation to President Wilson on May 17th. The treaty, he wrote, had betrayed those principles of justice and permanent peace that had induced many people of goodwill to regard the President as their leader. No real effort had been made to understand the problem of Russia. 'I am sorry', the letter ended, 'that you did not fight our fight to the finish, and that you had so little faith in the millions of men like myself in every nation who had faith in you.'

Harold Nicolson came near to resigning. Keynes did resign. The seeds of appeasement had been sown in the deep carpets of the Crillon and the Majestic and the plush banquettes of the Meurice.

On May 22nd von der Goltz finally went through the motions of capturing Riga. He allowed the 'White' Latvians to have their little reign of terror. Karl Marx Boulevard and Third International Prospect were rechristened after only three weeks of titular communism. The burghers left their island ghettoes and returned to their houses. The Soviet gunwomen were publicly executed. They spat in the faces of their captors, shouted insults at the firing squads, and even, it was said, tore open their greatcoats and shirts and pulled up their skirts in a last gesture of gutter contempt – thus joining the club-footed, black-velvet-cloaked Amazon commissar in the 1919 Chamber of Bourgeois Horrors.

Winston Churchill laboured to put heart and bite into the mangy tigers of the Russian counter-revolution. On May 5th he told General Golovin that he hoped to send 10,000 volunteers to the northern front to replace 'demoralized' British and American troops (they were for ever asking their officers why the hell they were there). Denikin, he said, could expect a sizeable 'military mission' of 2,500 instructors and technical experts. Aid worth £24 million would be allocated to the various anti-Bolshevik fronts. There should be enough equipment and weapons available for 100,000 troops, under the command of General Yudenich, to make a formidable assault on Petrograd. On his return to Omsk Golovin reported: 'Churchill is not only a sympathizer but an active and energetic friend. The greatest possible aid is assured us.'

Sazonov, too, had been busy in London. He wired Kolchak that he had seen the King in private audience and had twice conferred with M.P.s of all parties. But he stressed the need to rush out some kind of 'liberal' statement of aims for British and American consumption. On May 26th the Supreme Council sent a note to Kolchak which claimed that it had always been 'the cardinal axiom of the Allied and Associated Powers to avoid interference in the internal affairs of Russia'. They were, however, prepared to continue their assistance to loyal Russians—on certain conditions. Kolchak must hold free elections for a Constituent Assembly as soon as he captured Moscow; he must guarantee that no attempt would be made to restore the Tsarist regime; and he must recognize the independence of Finland, Estonia, Latvia, Lithuania and Poland.

Kolchak fumed at such insolent catechism. He could not risk antagonizing his supporters by agreeing to such terms. He could not answer for Denikin, still less for Yudenich who, despite threats from Churchill, persisted in referring to Estonia as part of Russia and to the Estonian government as a 'gang of criminals'. If only, Kolchak may have reflected, Churchill had possessed more power, how different things might have been. But Cabinet opposition to the cost and scope of intervention was strong: and Churchill also had to endure the checks and taunts of an impudent democracy. The Triple Alliance held the threat of a general strike over his head. The *Daily Herald* enterprisingly, and with sensational effect, published not only the secret Army Circulars about the reliability of troops for strike-bearing, but General Golovin's report. The *Nation*, after outlining the social revolution in Hungary—mansions requisitioned for the homeless, public baths for the children of the slums, galloping social equality—commented: 'If not checked this kind of thing might spread to London. Mr Churchill should see to it. Why not organize an expedition of rescue for the afflicted landlords of Buda? A battalion or two recruited from the slums of Stepney or Walworth would be just the thing.'

But Churchill, never one to be frightened by popular clamour, kept to his task. Though the guns of the British cruisers in the White Sea would have supplied more than adequate cover for the embarkation of a few thousand troops and Russian civilians in the Archangel-Murmansk area, two brigades, each of 4,000 volunteers, were sent out as 'cover' against a possible Red Army attack. Yet the Bolsheviks had several times offered an armistice to facilitate evacuation. More recklessly loyal disingenuity in a bad and hopeless cause could hardly have been shown or expected.

Reaction was in full spate. On May 9th the trial of the alleged murderers of Rosa Luxemburg and Karl Liebknecht opened at The Hague. *The Times* reported that the accused, Captain-Lieutenant von Pflügk-Harting and Lieutenant Vogel, arrived in court 'laughing, their chests decorated with medals. They gave the impression of going to a wedding rather than a murder trial.' Their cheerfulness was justified. They were acquitted.

On May 31st the corpse of Rosa Luxemberg, water-eroded and barely recognizable, was dredged up from a canal in Berlin—a fitting symbol, it seemed, of the plight of world revolution at the end of a lively, lethal month.

In a *Manifesto on the Versailles Peace Terms* Zinoviev, only two weeks after the appearance of his May Day paean, blew despairingly on dying embers. 'Down with the Versailles Peace! Long live the Communist Revolution! All illusions are destroyed. The League of Nations, at whose cradle stands the butcher Clemenceau, is exposed as a league of robbers out to crucify the labouring masses of the world. Workers of France! Workers of England! Workers of America! Workers of Italy! You must tear the knife from the bloody hands of your governments!'

Arthur Balfour, on the other hand, calmly predicted that the Bolshevik straw-fire in Russia would soon burn itself out.

IV

BOLSHEVISM AT BAY

---

1. *The Circle Closes*

In mid-June another Comintern manifesto exhorted the workers to remember that the Red Army in Hungary and Russia was fighting *their* battles. 'The fate of the world revolution is being decided in the Urals and before Red Petrograd, in the Carpathians and on the Danube.' If the League of Imperialists succeeded in smothering the revolution, proletarians everywhere would find themselves under attack. 'The E.C.C.I. summons the masses of all countries. The time for verbal protests is past. It is time to act.'

The response to this was unspectacular. In Vienna, where Hungarian agitators piled on more pressure, June was a crisis month. An attempt at armed insurrection cost many casualties. But Social Democracy weathered the storm. In Germany the U.S.P.D. was split between those who wanted to rejoin the S.P.D. and those who wanted to break away and form a separate party — or join the K.P.D. Communists were split between 'National Bolsheviks', heirs of the wilder Spartacist tradition, who hankered after a revolution in alliance with the extreme Right, and those who followed Paul Levi, the K.P.D. leader, in a policy of reorganization and penetration of the trade unions. Berlin was a festering Brechtland of crank astrologers, quack doctors, gambling hells, sleazy cabarets, fancy brothels and frenzied swarms of starving prostitutes. The revolutionary urge was mostly channelled into pornographic ('adult') films, magazines, books and newspaper serials. Even the respectable *Neue Rundschau* featured the tale of a youth who, after running away from his puritanical family, 'experienced the whole gamut of reckless passion'. The scoutmasterly Comintern appeal found few readers.

In Italy the disintegration of the Socialist Party had been deliberately accelerated by Lenin. In France the aftermath of the Black

Sea Revolt caused riots and demonstrations in Toulon and the crews
of several ships refused to sail for Russia. But the government was
not seriously bothered.

In Britain the annual conference of the Labour Party, held in
Southport at the end of June, seemed to hold some revolutionary
promise. It censured the Parliamentary Labour Party for its col-
laborationism and voted in favour of using direct action—if necessary—to force the government to stop intervening in Russia. But
it firmly rejected a motion to join the Third International, and vetoed
a proposal for a one-day Hands Off Russia general strike. Demonstrations, yes: speeches, of course. But a strike? That must await the
result of balloting—and with any luck the government would so
modify its policy as to make direct action unnecessary.

The government was in a confident mood. The Home Office
Directorate of Intelligence *Reports on Revolutionary Organizations in
the United Kingdom* were reassuring. 'There is no increase in class
war,' soothed an end-of-May summary, 'and in some places it is
certainly decreasing. No doubt the association of men of the working classes with officers and nurses during the war has done a great
deal to break down the old class barriers.' Extremist intellectuals
such as Sylvia Pankhurst (who had created a disturbance in the
Strangers' Gallery of the House of Commons) were not taken
seriously. The workers were more concerned with the beer shortage
than with forming soviets or saving them. The government's
promise of an extra six million barrels had eased the situation, 'but in
Lancashire the workers say that it is not enough. They will not be
satisfied until the Liquor Control Board is abolished.'

In the *Call* John Maclean, the most militant of Scottish Marxists,
who had been much jailed for his rabble-rousing speeches, warned
that capitalism was stronger and more aggressive than ever and
conceded that Lloyd George, as British plutocracy's chief trouble-
shooter, had done a magnificent job. 'A capitalist class that can
manoeuvre "Labour" backwards and forwards in this way shows no
sign of having lost its kick. This may be the final convulsion of
British capitalism. I hope so. But I fear not.'

On July 19th Peace Day, conceived by Lord Curzon in the spirit
of a National Squire reluctantly pandering to the desires of the lower
orders, was celebrated. Virginia Woolf stayed at home. But her

servants, she noted in her diary, had a marvellous time. 'They stood on Vauxhall Bridge and saw everything. Generals and soldiers and tanks and nurses took two hours in passing. It was, they said, the most splendid sight of their lives ... But I don't know—it seems to me a servants' festival, something got up to placate "the people".'

In the East End of London Sylvia Pankhurst wept to see the slum-dwellers stringing Union Jacks across the mean streets and forgetting all about the revolution in their hurry to get to the West End and enjoy the servants' festival.

The Peace Conference, too, ended in a welter of strutting barnyard vainglory. On June 28th, the Journée de Versailles, the wide avenue leading to the palace was lined with cavalry, their red-and-white lance-pennants fluttering in the sunshine. Gardes Républicaines in plumed and glinting helmets lined the grand staircase. In the Hall of Mirrors, in a buzz of excitement, Clemenceau sat quietly, small and sallow, his hands as always gloved to cover the eczema with which he was chronically afflicted. When the delegates arrived and began to process up the aisle towards the horse-shoe-shaped signature table, silence fell. The guards at the doorway slid their sabres into their scabbards with a loud, self-important click.

'Faîtes entrer les Allemands!' croaked Clemenceau. Preceded by Allied officers the German delegates, Herr Müller and Dr Bell, two minor ministers detailed to do the dirty work refused by their superiors, walked with eyes downcast. 'Messieurs,' said Clemenceau, after they had been led to their chairs, 'la séance est ouverte.' When the Germans had signed, the other delegates queued for their turn. Guns boomed in the courtyard, frightened pigeons whirred up, the French servants' festival crowd cheered.

When it was all over Clemenceau chanted: 'La séance est levée.' He had done his duty. He had not cheated the world of its triumph (the New York *Nation* called it 'the silly mummery of victor and vanquished'). The two Germans were marched out under military escort. 'Oui,' said Clemenceau, tears dimming his already bleary eyes, 'c'est une belle journée'. Hoisting himself to his feet, he linked arms with Lloyd George and Woodrow Wilson.

The Big Three walked along a broad path to watch the fountains spraying out the water which for days had been laboriously pumped up from the Seine.

The real tragedy of Paris, wrote J. L. Hammond in the *Nation*, was that the new world was being made by men whose imagination belonged to the old. They treated revolution in the spirit of Pitt, Castlereagh and Metternich and threatened to turn the League of Nations into a weapon for destroying any system which they disliked. During the Herreros rebellion in Africa, recalled Hammond, the Germans had cut off a tribe from the river upon which it depended for water, and shot men, women and children as they crept down to drink. 'That simile haunts me,' he said, 'when I read that the Supreme Council has decided to exercise the blockade against Hungary until she finds a government that satisfies them, or when I read Mr Churchill's speech justifying the war we are making on the women and children of Russia.'

With Germany crushed, both by the treaty and the Freikorps, with the revolutionary impotence of Austria and the socialists of the *cordon sanitaires* proved beyond doubt, the time was ripe to increase the pressure on Budapest and Moscow. The French Union of Economic Interests launched its famous poster showing a pirate Bolshevik with a blood-dripping knife between his teeth. Newspapers produced a hair-curling flow of Red atrocity tales.

Around the horizons of the two surviving Soviet republics loomed Pearsall Smith's Stonehenge Circle of elderly, disapproving faces, haters of youth and creative folly, implacable, ludicrous, but seemingly all-powerful.

2. The Throttling of the Hungarian Revolution

Hungary was first on the Stonehenge list. From Vienna Franchet d'Esperey threatened invasion by Senegalese troops unless the government was changed. The Swiss Red Cross reported that in Budapest children were dying like flies in hospitals which had no food, no drugs, no soap, no bandages, no bed linen. Those who survived were afflicted with scrofula and eye diseases. Trees in the parks were being cut down, bourgeois furniture (including grand pianos) smashed up for fuel. There was talk of a rising of Social Democrats to oust Kun and the communists. Late in June a counter-revolutionary insurrection in Budapest, during which naval monitors on the Danube shelled the city and military cadets seized the Post Office, was suppressed in savage fighting which left more than a hundred dead.

Somehow the Soviet government clung on. Bela Kun himself led the Red Guard in the street fighting of June. As in Russia, most of the leading communists and politically conscious workers were at the fronts. Kun wrestled with a deadweight of weariness, indifference and open hostility. Allied Missions deluged the 'dictator' with phone calls whenever a well-born counter-revolutionary was arrested. They warned him not to take reprisals after the June rising, since this had been 'an expression of legitimate grievances'. Only five members of the upper classes, and no leading politicians, had been shot. Bolshevism in Budapest was almost as hamstrung as Social Democracy in Vienna.

Yet still the Soviet idea ramified, putting out blossoms in the stoniest soil. On June 16th, in that part of Slovakia still occupied by the Hungarian Red Army, a Soviet republic was formed, an alliance with Hungary and Soviet Russia concluded, the socialization of industry, commerce and banking decreed, and recruiting for a Red Guard begun. In Sofia the Bulgarian Revolutionary Social Democrats resolved to withdraw its members from Parliament, to join the Third International, and to 'follow that path for the realization of the communistic ideal which the great Russian Bolshevik revolution has revealed'. Greek naval and military units at Sevastopol rebelled. The Greek Socialist Workers' Party voted to affiliate with Comintern. There was even a rumour that General von Mackensen, former commander-in-chief of the German armies in South-east Europe, had joined the Hungarians with ten thousand troops. The Hungarian revolution, like Gustav Landauer, would not die like a gentleman.

On June 25th Sir Samuel Hoare gave a gloomy interview to the *Morning Post* on his return from a visit to Central Europe. There was no doubt, he said, that Hungarians of all classes were thrilled by the victories of the Red Army. The Allies were trifling with the situation. Unless their ultimatums were backed by armed force Bela Kun ('not only a political adventurer of the worst type, but a convicted thief who embezzled trade-union funds before the war') would continue to throw them in the wastepaper basket.

In fact, the Allies had not been so idle. On June 8th they had assured Kun that Hungarian representatives would be invited to Paris and the Rumanian army instructed to keep behind the armistice line—but only if the Hungarian army evacuated Slovakia. Lenin urged Kun by telegram to earn a breathing-space by negotiating with the Allies, and added (rather superfluously): 'Do not trust the Entente Powers for an instant. They are deceiving you and only seek to gain time to strangle both you and us.' To which Kun replied: 'I am very proud to be one of your best pupils, but I think that in one point I am superior to you, namely in *mala fides*.' The telegrams were intercepted. Hoover read them out to the Council of Four in Paris as startling evidence of Bolshevik villainy—and ample justification for democratic *mala fides*.

On June 24th Kun (knowing that the Red Army was already weakened by mass desertions) ordered a withdrawal from Slovakia. A few days later the Slovakian Soviet Republic collapsed. Paris explained the previous offer as the result of a 'clerical error', and the Rumanians refused to agree to an armistice. Switching forces to the shaky eastern front, Kun, whose decision to evacuate Slovakia had cost him most of his purely nationalist support and had been heavily criticized by the Budapest Soviet, tried to stiffen morale by a mixture of threats and exhortations. Since mild treatment had not brought the bourgeoisie to see reason, it would now, if it continued its resistance, 'be suffocated in blood'. The depleted Red Army was congratulated on its glorious exploits in the north and exhorted to repeat them against the Rumanians. 'We are not retreating before the mercenary troops of the Czechoslovak imperialists. But we have to face the greatest exploiters in the world—the French, British and American money-kings, labour oppressors and peasant-plunderers.'

Since the Russian Red Army was too busy with Denikin, Kolchak, Yudenich, peasant revolts and Ukrainian nationalists to come anywhere near the borders of Hungary, Comintern weighed in with its own *Appeal on Behalf of the Hungarian Soviet Republic*: 'To all! To all! A monstrous crime is being committed ... The English and French Imperialists are attacking the Hungarian Soviet Republic from all sides, in order to drown the Hungarian revolution in blood ... Czechoslovak, Rumanian and Yugoslav workers and soldiers! Comrades! Stop playing the part of forced executioners! The workers of the entire world turn away in contempt from those who at this crucial moment fail in their duty.' The Comintern appeal was not, however, all flattery, ardent greetings and anti-capitalist diatribe. There was in its tail a sting of impatience with this, the last of Europe's ninepin Soviet experiments. 'In the year and a half of their dictatorship the Russian proletariat have often been in as grave a crisis. And still they have surmounted the difficulties. We are firmly convinced that you will steadfastly withstand the present test.'

The commissars in Budapest girded themselves for yet another orgy of oration, both in the threatened city and at the not far distant front. Eugen Varga promised that as soon as transport could be improved there would be enough food for everyone—and even a surplus for export. Sigismund Kunfi limned the utopian fields of leisure and culture which glimmered ahead, paradisal and worth any sacrifice. But Bela Kun was still the prince of exhorters ('again and again', wrote the fascinated correspondent of the *Manchester Guardian*, 'he rallied the masses by a hypodermic injection of his mob oratory'). He pictured the miseries of the White Terror which would be unleashed if the revolution was defeated. Hundreds, thousands, would be shot and tortured if the Counts got back into the saddle. There would be no mercy, no attempt at discrimination. Any worker, whether socialist or not, would be fair game. And this time there would be no protests from Paris or the Allied Missions. Culture and education would again be reserved for the rich. The poor would be treated like slaves and driven back into the Abyss from which the revolution had plucked them. There would be no children's villages.

The huge baths of the patricians, comparable in size and luxury with those of Imperial Rome, would no longer echo to the delighted cries of workers' children: they would be polluted by the bodies of a few idle parasites whose tyranny had been as foul, if not fouler, than that of Tsarist Russia. 'Comrades! Oh Comrades! Will you let this happen? Is not hardship, starvation, even death for the revolution better than the living death of the old, despicable regime?'

The 'Counts' government' at Szeged was having, for the moment, a roughish time. Imprisoned for a while by the Rumanian military authorities, boycotted by the compositors, who went on strike in protest against their presence, they relied for funds (ironically, since they were, to a man, virulently anti-semitic) on refugee Jewish financiers. Nor was this the only example of their lack of any principle save that of self-preservation at all costs. At a moment when the plebs were fighting for Hungary's very existence against Rumania and Yugoslavia, they entered into negotiation with the royalty of both states, offering the Crown of Hungary in exchange for their lost privileges. Their only solid achievement was the formation of the nucleus of a 'National Army' of 'death battalions' under the leadership of Admiral Nicholas Horthy, sworn to revenge.

When ordered to reduce the Red Army to the size prescribed by the armistice agreement, Kun cheekily replied that since the Great Powers seemed incapable of controlling their Rumanian ally, the Soviet government had been forced to do so.

Despite a sense of impending doom, which anyhow had never been absent, Budapest was still an exciting place. Nowhere outside Russia was there such progressive zeal, such liberation of talent, such class hatred and such classless comradeship, such dogmatic obstinacy and such a feeling of utopian hunger – and all swarming and gambolling in the cannon's mouth. The theatres, opening at five o'clock in the evening for proletarian convenience, continued, by plutocratic standards, to cram the masses with unwanted culture, and continued to be full night after night. In the divorce courts a professional judge was flanked by two trade-union nominees, one of whom had to be a woman. Palaces, mansions and luxury hotels were filled with proletarian families. Colonel Josiah Wedgwood, M.P. (a recent recruit to the Independent Labour Party), sent to Budapest on a fact-finding mission, was shocked by the absence of free comment. But when he returned to England he told a Labour meeting that though he disagreed with communism, he also disagreed with making war on it. The fact was that Bolshevik Budapest had its attractions. 'I liked to see the rich cafés filled with workers drinking coffee from beautiful cups and listening to bands from plush armchairs. I loved the complete absence of the idle rich and the complete freedom from class distinction. I liked the fact that there were no prostitutes in the streets.'

The sight of real social democracy in Budapest in 1919 was unforgettable (George Orwell reacted in much the same way when he came across it in Barcelona in 1936). But communism had bred civil war, a war of town against country, country against town. Every solution had to be a final solution. There was no room or time for Anglo-Saxon compromise.

To Tibor Szamuelly, the essence of scientific socialism was that one did not compromise or spare the knife, any more than a conscientious surgeon when an operation was necessary. The cancerous growths of the past had to be cut out. Bolshevism, in the conditions of 1919, was socialism in a hurry. Anyone who got in the way was an enemy of the people, a frustrater of the New Creation, the Marxist equivalent of anti-Christ. Like Dzherzhinsky, Szamuelly juggled with plans for a final solution of the class 'problem'. He was the terror of the Social Democrats, of the nobles and the bourgeoisie, of the more moderate communists, and of Kun himself. They all knew that if Szamuelly decided to take power, the Terror would *be* a Terror. The term 'counter-revolutionary' would have a very wide interpretation. Many heads would roll. Phone calls from Allied Missions would be ignored and their makers probably shot.

It was Szamuelly whom Lenin summoned to Moscow for conferences, Szamuelly whom he regarded as the watchdog of the Hungarian revolution. To upholders of the *ancien régime*, he was the devil incarnate. Small, intensely pale, with fine features and jet-black hair, he was described by reactionary journalists as 'sickly and undersized, with a diseased and degenerate air', a fiend who indulged in every form of vice as a matter of atheistic principle. If it was possible for the instincts of the wild beasts to be found in human beings, 'they were to be found in Tibor Szamuelly. To hang and torture, to inflict pain, grief and spiritual agony on others, were the breath of life to him.' He looked, they said, like 'the very spirit of the

Inquisition as, haggard and of a corpse-like pallor, he walked among his robust, thick-set terrorists.'

His fanaticism was made more frightening by extreme, even reckless, personal courage, and great administrative ability. He was a superb propagandist and a keen patron of the *avant-garde*, as much perhaps for ideological reasons (he enjoyed flouting bourgeois taste) as from aesthetic conviction. There seemed to be no chink in Szamuelly's revolutionary armour. The Social Democrats timed their attempt to seize power, the reactionaries their insurrection, to take place when he was far away from Budapest. He did not aspire to replace Kun – yet. His mere presence and legend were sufficient to deter the bold and stiffen the yielding. He had, in any case, a specific rancour and a special ambition. He hated the reactionary countryside, that bane and stumbling-block of Marxist revolutionaries, with a hatred remarkable even among his Bolshevik contemporaries. He was determined to be the Hammer of the Peasants.

Had not these stupid, obstructive creatures wrecked the chance of a communist revolution in Austria, helped to shake the life out of the Munich Soviet, and come near, in their ignorance and greed, to aborting the Russian revolution? They were the worst enemies of the people – of the only people who counted, the industrial workers and impatient socialist intellectuals of the towns. The awful, immovable mountain of their conservatism had driven Lenin close to despair. John Maclean had told audiences in Glasgow that when the revolution came in Britain farmers would have to do as they were told – or else. Maxim Gorky had argued with Lenin over his decision to 'include' the peasants in the soviet process. He thought Lenin was sacrificing 'the small but heroic band of politically educated workers and all the genuine militants among the intelligentsia,' that 'the single active force in Russia would be thrown into the vapid bog of village life, and would dissolve without leaving any trace.'

In June Szamuelly and a picked force of terrorists set out from Budapest in a vivid armoured red train to deal with the peasant traitors and provincial counter-revolutionaries of western Hungary. He approached his task with relish, and a complete disregard for his own safety. His car was shot at and shelled. Sometimes there were pitched battles, as near Dunapataj, where three thousand townsmen and peasants, armed with cannons, machine-guns and rifles, were

defeated—and nearly a hundred killed. Sometimes the villagers—
in defence of their grain, their cattle, and their hordes of thick, blue-
tinted Imperial paper money—marched to battle with pitchforks and
scythes. Always a number of them were publicly executed for the
sins of their class. The bourgeoisie of Budapest had got off lightly.
Szamuelly was resolved that the peasants should know the full
meaning of class war. In the next two months his hangmen and
firing squads saw to it that grim orchards of gallows and trenchfuls
of human manure reminded the arch-enemies of communist civilization that if they would not co-operate with the city revolution,
would not wait for their money and their machinery, they might
as well be dead, and richly deserved to die. In Szamuelly's demonology the peasants loomed as large and as loathsome as the Jews in
the demonology of the White Terror. *The Times* described him as
'smiling and smoking while his victims were breathing their last':
and perhaps it was not far wrong.

Towards the end of July Szamuelly was called to Moscow for emergency talks. If he had been in Budapest he would almost certainly
have carried out a massacre of bourgeois hostages, on the theory
that it might halt the Rumanian advance, and that even if it did not,
nothing except a few lives would be lost—for the White Terror
would not be mitigated by any gestures of moderation. The Budapest
Soviet was hot for harsher counter-revolutionary measures. There
were demands for a Red Terror, and particular fury against the
activities of the Church. 'Comrades!' said one delegate, 'I come from
a district where there are many ecclesiastical institutions. For months
these have carried on an unbridled agitation against the Soviet
Republic. Last week this reached new heights. Morning, noon and
night the monks and nuns whom we have ejected assembled in the
churches and former monasteries and convents. I propose that
tomorrow we arrest all the monks and nuns still in the capital and
load them onto a train which will take them as far as the frontier.
There we will let them loose in Austria, which is still a bourgeois
state and where they will be able to shift for themselves.' Six days
later, on August 1st, with the Rumanian army only fifty miles from
Budapest and pushing on with little resistance, no attempt had been
made to act on this suggestion. Kun had not the heart, Samson-like,
to pull down a few last pillars. In a speech to the Central Workers'
and Soldiers' Council, frequently interrupted while he fought to

control his sobs, he argued that the government must resign and hand over to a caretaker Social Democratic government with which the Entente might be willing to negotiate. He did not disguise his opinion that such a government would be treated with the same contempt as Károlyi's 'democratic front', and that it would soon be succeeded by a dictatorship of naked reaction. But ... if the workers of Budapest could not or would not make any further sacrifices for the revolution, then the motions of 'reverting to democracy' had to be made.

Kun, Varga, Lukacs, Rakosi, Kunfi, Pogany and other leading members of the Soviet government took advantage of the Austrian government's offer of asylum in Vienna, where they opened a bureau of Comintern and possibly hoped, like ex-Emperor Karl, for a come-back. Szamuelly, hurrying from Moscow, was arrested at the Austrian frontier and blew his brains out. The caretaker government, headed by Julius Peidl, a trade-union leader, decreed that the state would now be known as the Hungarian People's Republic and that elections for a Constituent Assembly would be held as soon as possible.

An Inter-Allied Military Commission appeared in Budapest to supervise the transition. The Supreme Council announced that 'conditionally upon the good behaviour of the new Hungarian government', it had decided to lift the blockade. Kun and the Soviet Republic had vanished, as a British Intelligence report had said it would, like a dream: so much so that on the evening of August 1st, workers commuting from the outer suburbs of Budapest, unable to believe the rumours of capitulation, began to sing the Internationale on the railway station—to the astonishment of carriage loads of businessmen who had emerged from hiding to return to their offices. The sequel was equally fantastic. The Ruma-nian army, ignoring the command of the Supreme Council, did not retreat to the armistice line. It marched on and occupied Budapest. With its help a new caretaker government—this time of bureaucrats and 'experts' presided over by Archduke Josef—soon ousted Peidl. The wheel had turned full circle. Bonar Law, when asked in the Commons to guarantee that no government in Hungary would be recognized unless freely accepted by the people, cheerfully replied: 'We cannot control the government of any country except our own.' American pressure, exercised through Hoover, soon brought a demand from Paris for the resignation of the Archduke, and

Hoover's man in Budapest, Captain Gregory, called at the palace
with the same ultimatum that had bounced Bela Kun – get out or
starve. On August 24th the Archduke got out. 'TO THE HUN-
GARIAN PEOPLE!' ran his farewell proclamation. 'In the fateful
hour of gravest crisis I, at your request, undertook the leadership
of my beloved Fatherland ... My person shall be no hindrance to
those who have hitherto been our enemies becoming our friends
and assisting us with the means necessary for the development of
the people ... The God of the Magyars bless my beloved nation
and cause our Fatherland to prosper.'

Having, with virtuous ostentation, repulsed the Habsburgs, the
Allies left the Rumanians, and a government dominated by viciously
anti-semitic Christian Socialists, alone. The Rumanians embarked
on an orgy of systematic looting. Factories were stripped of
machinery, storehouses of manufactured goods, offices of furniture
and equipment. Livestock was driven across the frontier. On the
ground that they were offensive weapons, ancient gem-studded
sabres, silver-mounted firelocks, medieval lances and halberds were
removed from private collections. Desperate landowners hid their
thoroughbred horses in walled-up cellars or sent them to remote
meadows or forests. The Rumanian passion for pillage knew no
class distinctions and no bounds. Only a cordon of American troops
saved the Hungarian National Museum from being plundered. In
the intervals between conducting treasure-hunts and cramming
lorries with loot, the Rumanians helped the Christian Socialists to
arrest thousands of 'Red' workers and 'collaborationist' bourgeois.
Unemployment pay was cut off. It was unsafe for any Jew to show
himself in the centre of Budapest. Wealthy Jews were forced to hide
in the warrens of the poor. Roman Catholic priests watched, with
every sign of delight, the beating and insulting of Rabbis.

The workers were driven, at bayonet point, from the palaces, the
mansions, the delectable villas on the dolomitic crests overlooking
Budapest, the luxury hotels. Even in 1911, out of a total population
of 900,000, 125,000 people had been homeless and nearly 400,000
had lived five, seven, even ten to a room. By 1919, with the wartime
expansion of industry and a rush of refugees from Rumanian-
occupied territory, the population had swelled to $1\frac{1}{2}$ million and
overcrowding had reached a point of incredible promiscuous
squalor. It was this misery that the requisitioning decrees of the

Soviet government had tried to mitigate. It was to this misery that the proletariat was now forced to return.

But they had left their own peculiar mark on the desirable residences of the master class. 'What little sleep I managed to obtain', reported the *Manchester Guardian*'s correspondent from an hotel double-starred by Baedeker, 'was won by dragging the mattress off the bed into the middle of the floor and keeping all the lights blazing. A few minutes after getting into bed my neck, arms, and body were blistered and burning. The stench of the hotel was so foul that I was shaken with spasms of nausea.' Next day he moved to another hotel, in ordinary times a favourite with the Hungarian aristocracy. It was even lousier. 'The feeling of degradation that accompanies such an experience', he commented, 'is worse than the lowering of physical condition from lack of sleep and even loss of blood. Add to that a starvation diet – no breakfast and a single plate of boiled cabbage for lunch and dinner – and multiply my experiences by as many times as there are days in four months and as there are people of a cleanly habit of life in this magnificent city, and the result will be only a faint reflection of the sufferings of the middle class of Budapest during the communist regime.'

Some of the more idealistic commissars had hoped that the intermingling of the classes might somehow 'help to awaken in the bourgeoisie the communal sympathy which they so sadly lack, and in the proletariat a taste for civilized refinement'. In fact it had left behind a legacy of class hatred that it would take generations to appease. 'The bourgeoisie hate the proletariat with a hatred that is physical. The proletariat have left the homes of the bourgeoisie with their class hatred intensified by an impossible association with a life and a code of behaviour beyond their comprehension. So long as the bed-bug exists and the use of soap has not been universalized it is dangerous to experiment with the merging of the classes.'

The new government charged Bela Kun with 'murder and robbery'. The Chief of Police proudly displayed Franz Janczik, former commander of Budapest's Red Guard, as 'the world's greatest murderer' (he was alleged to have executed five hundred people). Journalists were invited to watch Janczik, unshaven, bloodshot-eyed, faint with hunger and lack of sleep, being bullied for three hours at a stretch by a squad of detectives. What about the corpses with pinioned arms which were being fished daily out of the Danube? What about the Ukrainian officers who had disappeared in June? What about the shooting of Professor Berend, the well-known, well-loved children's doctor? ...

... What about the failure of the Allies to fight disease and suffering in Budapest? What about the shameful failure of the Inter-Allied Commissions to see that the food from the countryside and from America was fairly distributed to *all* classes? What about *this* murderous class war? asked Dr Leslie Haden Guest, a socialist attached to the British Food Commission, after a visit to the city early in October 1919. Ninety per cent of the children had to depend on relief missions for food. Twenty-five per cent of them had rickets. The mortality in children's hospitals was eighty per cent. In the slums it was nothing for five people to sleep in a damp-reeking cellar seven feet by six feet with no window, no chimney, no furniture. 'Meanwhile at the Ritz Hotel one can have a five-course meal if one has the money. Every night there is a wild orgy, lasting until dawn. It is a picture of absolute debauchery and brutality run mad.' The only hope, said Dr Guest, of decency and a modicum of social justice was that Hungary should be policed by an international force which would ensure free elections and see that the food was not stolen from the mouths of the poor.

Admiral Horthy's death-battalions put in some practice by 'clearing' the country around Lake Balaton. The Soviet children's village was raided and its teachers and administrators liquidated. Peasants who had formed co-operatives on the estates of fugitive counts, bishops and wealthy farmers were massacred. Jews were lined up and shot, or bayoneted, into mass graves. At Veszprem one Jew, a lawyer who had lost a leg during the war, was beaten to death by officers using whips loaded with lead balls.

By mid-November, when the Rumanians, glutted with loot, finally decided to evacuate Budapest, Horthy's men were in fine terrorist fettle. On November 16th, mounted on a white charger, Horthy led his National Army in the capital. Twelve thousand 'Bolshevik' workers were sent to forced-labour camps. Fifteen thousand others were jailed. Official retribution was supplemented by the operations of terrorist gangs, whose members wore a breast-ribbon lettered '*Commission Interallié à Budapest*'. The Hejjas and Pronay gangs, with headquarters in the Royal Hotel and the Hotel Britannia, specialized in killing and torturing Jews and communists and liquidating socialist editors and journalists. The Ostenburg 'detachment', which supplied a bodyguard for Horthy, specialized in 'labour problems'. After a few weeks' experience of beatings-up, executions, and mass-internment of 'trouble-makers' the mere sight of the Ostenburg killers was sufficient to 'solve' any problems: and behind the guns and bludgeons of the terrorists was another powerful argument for docility—the huge army of the unemployed.

By the end of September the White Terror had, at a conservative estimate, 'purified' the country of six thousand 'Bolsheviks'. Progressive schoolteachers and university staff were sacked and often shot; Jewish children barred from high schools; Dohnanyi, the celebrated composer and pianist, deprived of his post as head of the Academy of Music because he had held it under the Soviet regime; and the entire country placed under martial law. 'We must all endeavour', said Karl Huszar, President of the Provisional Government (in which a few scared socialists had been forced to serve as democratic window-dressing), 'to preserve the Christian and national spirit in the government. My Christianity is the essence of Christianity itself: goodness, love, self-sacrifice.' Already, praised be the God of the Magyars, the sanctity of the family and the holy dominance of the Church had been restored.

The liberal and socialist press of Britain and America rang with impotent denunciations of the throttling of the Hungarian revolution. 'This is the crowning act of Allied infamy,' charged Mrs Philip Snowden in the *Labour Leader*, 'an outrageous violation of all the professions about radical unity and national rights and self-determination ... Cannot International Socialism do *something* to prevent this iniquity?'

Hungarian communists and Social Democrats smuggled out separate manifestoes. 'In this tragic hour,' said the communists, 'we turn with a solemn appeal to the industrial workers of Italy, France and England. We beseech you—how long is your heartless indifference to last? How long will you suffer the criminal activity of your governments in establishing the blackest reaction in Eastern Europe?' Bolshevism, pleaded the Social Democrats, had been an act of desperation caused by the hostility of the Western democracies. 'We Social Democrats can only condemn the methods of the dictatorship and the Red Terror. Yet at the moment that we are in the mood to make up for past mistakes we are faced with a medieval and barbaric White Terror ... Brothers! Comrades! Use your influence with your governments to help us to preserve our fledgling freedom and our young Republic, to create for ourselves and our children some hope of economic survival ... '

The Comintern obituary on yet another Soviet republic concentrated its venom on the Social Democrats, whose treachery, it proclaimed, had been primarily responsible for the disaster. The inoffensive Peidl, forced to serve under Huszar, was, according to Zinoviev, the Hungarian Noske. 'Just as the Scheidemanns and Kautskys in Germany drowned the proletarian revolution in blood, just as the Social Revolutionaries and the Mensheviks are objectively helping the Tsarist generals, just as the Yellow Berne International is selling the working class to the predatory League of Nations, so the Hungarian social traitors have surrendered the Hungarian Soviet Republic, the pride of the world proletariat, to be torn to pieces.' But the Hungarian proletariat should not despair. Defeats were inevitable, but final victory certain if true revolutionaries would listen to the voice of Moscow.

3. The Ninth Wave, the Russian Sieve

'We are in the midst of the combat and the ninth wave of attack is now surging upon us,' claimed Chicherin in a radio message on June 16th. 'In the south Denikin's army is receiving excellent war materials from the Entente; Rumania and Poland serve as a mask for France, while England is using Estonia and Finland ... The Entente is provisioning these White Guard governments, and the English fleet is protecting the landing of troops near Petrograd ... The billows of conflict are running high. But we have held our own against all. We have drawn our strength from the revolutionary and proletarian foundation ... We are the only ones who have resisted successfully. All the capitalist states are down on their knees, impotent before the victors ... '

On the map the counter-revolution was more formidable than ever. Britain, France and America were pumping surplus war material, military missions, provisions, locomotives and rolling stock, uniforms and boots to the four fronts in enormous quantities. In Siberia foreign troops—about two thirds of them Japanese or Czechoslovakian—with smaller Polish, Rumanian, Yugoslavian, American, British and French contingents, outnumbered Russian troops by 120,000 to 90,000. The Omsk government's propaganda, though clumsy and uninspired, was having some success. 'Red Army men!' said one leaflet. 'Why do you invade Siberia, like blinkered horses, flogged by your commissars? You are driven here so that they can take refuge in the *taiga* [primeval forests] after they have been crushed in Moscow and Petrograd.' The punch-line came at the end. 'Throw away your arms, come over to our side, and you will get plenty of bread. You will also get a money reward. Corporals 750 roubles, privates 600 roubles: and for those who escape with their families the reward will be twice as large.'

But despite recognition of Kolchak as Commander-in-Chief by Generals Denikin, Yudenich (in Estonia) and Miller (at Archangel), there was no real cohesion. Vast distances separated them; the views of the Allied military missions often conflicted with those of their protégés; and Kolchak's supremacy was purely nominal, grudgingly conceded because it was thought necessary to put up a show of unity to impress London and Paris. By May, when he was catechized by the Big Four, Kolchak was, in any case, already a spent force. In July his army was in full retreat. The Allies sent him a bored letter, promising further support. He was written off as another counter-revolutionary flop, just as Moscow had had to write off what it now represented as the 'false' soviets of Munich and Budapest. If it had not been for Winston Churchill ('the Russian Gambler' as the *Daily Herald* called him) Kolchak would almost certainly have been more abruptly and brutally dropped, and the armies of Denikin and Yudenich would have melted away. In 1945 Churchill coined a (borrowed) phrase — 'the Iron Curtain': but in 1919, as the chief impresario of counter-revolution, he did more than any single person (with the possible exception of Hoover) to make the Iron Curtain inevitable.

This was one of the most remarkable — and baleful — performances of Churchill's career as the rogue-anarch of British politics. Loathed by the generals, disliked by the mass of *nouveau-riche* Tory business-men who dominated the House of Commons, distrusted as a political turncoat by Tory patricians and old-fashioned Liberals, the bluff bane of the militants of the Labour movement, a romantic individualist in an age of calculating party machines, he nevertheless continued to turn the War Office into a kind of personal empire and rival Foreign Office. There were strong parallels between him and his Bolshevik opposite number, Trotsky — at whom in later years he aimed his choicest vituperation ('Trotsky, whose frown meted death to thousands, sits disconsolate ... a skin of malice stranded for a time on the shores of the Black Sea, and now washed up in the Gulf of Mexico'). Both were brilliant and suspect outsiders; both spoke in terms of crusade; both were incurable romantics; both despised the milk-and-water, suburban ideal of 'normalcy'; both regarded the masses as material which could only acquire life and meaning under the manipulation of the artist-leader; both were protected by a thick armour of egoism against the shafts of lesser mortals; both had made themselves — to the fury of their enemies — indispensable: Churchill as the hero of the demobilization crisis and the sole hope of the rabid anti-Bolsheviks of the Commons, Trotsky as the architect of the Bolshevik coup of October 1917 and of the Red Army of 1919.

Between mid-July and mid-August 1919 there were five lengthy War Cabinet discussions of British commitments in Russia—and one lively debate in the Commons. Lloyd George returned from Paris to find that Churchill had exploited his 'containment' brief (preventing the overspill of the 'lava' of Bolshevism) up to the hilt and beyond. General Knox in Siberia, General Ironside at Archangel, were eager for an aggressive campaign in which the four counter-revolutionary armies would converge in a last effort to crush the 'usurping' Bolshevik regime. Ironside knew that, since October (just before the White Sea iced up) was the latest date for evacuation, time was running short. Yudenich knew that he would only have the support of the British fleet in the Baltic for the same period. Aid to Kolchak had been cut, but aid to Denikin had been stepped up. Thanks to Churchill's tireless badgering and the feebleness of the Parliamentary Labour Party and the Triple Alliance, London outvied Paris as the headquarters of capitalist reaction.

Wearily, and with much interdepartmental bickering, the Cabinet concluded that the expensive, unsavoury farce of intervention might as well drag on until Kolchak, Denikin and Yudenich had finished what, by almost common consent, was regarded as their futile fling. No British troops had been involved (Lloyd George was glad to say) in Hungary: but £500,000 of railway equipment had been supplied to the Rumanians. There was an argument about sending flour to Archangel to supply the population through the winter after the evacuation of the British expeditionary force. Austen Chamberlain, Chancellor of the Exchequer, complained about 'pouring money in this way into the Russian sieve'. Lord Curzon pressed for 'some measure of co-ordination' between the White leaders. Could not a British High Commissioner be appointed to keep a close political and financial check on Denikin? H. A. L. Fisher, President of the Board of Education, suggested that the Bolshevik government was 'losing some of its more objectionable features' and was the most stable government in Russia. Cossacks, he said, were not remarkable for their state-building capacity, and he had received alarming reports from British officers of the atrocities committed by Kolchak's troops. Denikin, he thought, was a waning force. Civil warfare in Russia was frustrating the economic efforts of millions. No matter what government was in power the most important thing was that trade and production should be restored. Curzon was asked to prepare a draft report on the internal situation in Russia. On August

12th this was torn to pieces by Lloyd George, who used the occasion to put on a convincing display of cool realism. Curzon's report was essentially a subdued restatement of the Prime Minister's panic March vision of a Russo-German Bolshevik alliance, and of his 'lava' speech in the Commons. Now, when that danger seemed to have vanished, Lloyd George complained that Curzon had presented Britain's helping of her 'friends' as an anti-Bolshevik campaign, and argued that it was ridiculous to 'go to war again in order to place a customs barrier between Germany and Russia'.

Facts, he said, had to be faced. France, though full of anti-Bolshevist bravado, was bankrupt and not beginning to pay her way. The earlier backing of Kolchak had been 'a legitimate risk'. Now it seemed certain that though America and Japan would remain in eastern Siberia, western Siberia would go Soviet. As for Denikin, Lloyd George felt that there was 'hardly an even chance of his reaching Moscow'. Kolchak and Denikin had antagonized the Baltic States, Poland and the Ukraine by their insistence on a United Russia. They were politically inept. Britain must clear out of northern Russia. Aid to Kolchak must cease unless America and Japan were willing to continue it. Denikin should be given one last 'packet' and told: 'You must make the most of it. You have all the coal of Russia, you will get plentiful supplies of oil, and you will soon be in possession of the main food supplies. We have carried you up to a point where you are self-supporting.' If Denikin succeeded in establishing himself in his 'sector' the Allies should aim at making peace. If both sides were fairly strong. Lenin would say, 'Denikin is powerful enough to prevent me getting any coal,' and Denikin would say, 'Lenin is too powerful to give me any prospect of reaching Moscow.'

Churchill's part in these debates was a strange mixture of submission, contradiction and reckless asides. On July 25th he was deprecating the Cabinet's urgency about Russia, since it was 'quite conceivable that the anti-Bolshevist movement may collapse ... and then a Lenin or Trotsky empire will be complete.' Four days later he thought it 'quite possible that Admiral Kolchak might retrieve his position', and reported that General Denikin was confident of success. When Sir Eric Geddes hinted that though Denikin, like Kolchak, might be a 'good man', he was surrounded by reactionaries, Churchill hotly denied that the term 'reactionary' could be applied to men who were defending the lives of their wives and

236 THE NINTH WAVE, THE RUSSIAN SIEVE

children. Nor could he agree that the results of operations in Russia had been disappointing. On the contrary, it was quite amazing what *had* been achieved. The forces of Kolchak and Denikin had been in existence for less than a year, yet between them they had pinned down three-quarters of the Red Army, and prevented Bolshevik military intervention in Europe.

On August 14th Churchill conceded that 1,200 émigré Russian officers were being trained in England to lead Russian troops 'in those areas where we have responsibilities, so as to enable our forces to withdraw'. When Colonel Wedgwood asked if the government had taken the opinion of the country on the subject, Churchill brusquely replied that the government was as good a judge of the opinion of the country as his questioner. Churchill was frustrated. Despite a hatred for half-measures, he had been forced to accept the Cabinet verdict that the North Russian theatre should be closed, and that Yudenich and Denikin were to be given their last boost. His main concern now was to make sure that the boost should be as large as possible.

This required tact and guile: but now and again the full extent of his ambition and frustration flashed out. Large sums of money, he grumbled in a memorandum written in September, and considerable forces had been employed by the Allies against the Bolsheviks during the year by Britain, France, America and Japan. Kolchak's army, mostly weaponed and equipped by Britain, had reached in May a total of nearly 300,000. Denikin's forces numbered some 225,000. Great potentialities existed in the Baltic States, Poland had built up a formidable army, Rumania, Yugoslavia and Czechoslovakia could make a further contribution now that Hungary had been disposed of. 'It is obvious from the above', concluded Churchill, 'that the elements existed which, used in combination, would easily have been successful. They have, however, been dissipated by a total lack of combination ... due to a complete absence of any decided policy among the victorious Allies. Some were in favour of peace and some were in favour of war. In the result they made neither peace nor war. If they made war on one part of the front, they hastened to make peace on another.' Promises to continue supplies to Kolchak had not been honoured. Yet it was a delusion 'to suppose that all this year we have been fighting the battles of the anti-Bolshevik Russians. On the contrary, they have been fighting ours: and this truth will become painfully apparent from the moment that they are exterminated and the Bolshevik armies are supreme over the whole vast territories of the Russian Empire.'

Lloyd George, holidaying at the Manoir de Clairefontaine near Deauville (where evening sing-songs were enlivened by Sir Eric Geddes's rendering of 'Roses of Picardy' and Nancy Astor did an apache dance with one of the Prime Minister's secretaries), was exasperated by Churchill's persistence. Churchill was sharply reminded that his job was to bury the hatchet not brandish it. Undeterred, and encouraged by the startling initial success of Denikin's drive on Moscow and Yudenich's assault on Petrograd, Churchill threw the last shreds of caution to the winds in a triumphant memorandum submitted to the Cabinet on October 15th: 'At the present time,' he exulted, 'the military situation, taken as a whole, is such that it would be prudent to count upon the collapse and destruction of the Bolshevik power and its replacement by some form of government based upon the forces of Kolchak and Denikin.' Britain, as the backbone of Russia's 'liberators', would be in a particularly strong position to influence them. They might be willing to recognize the independence of Poland and possibly Finland, but there would be no point in arguing about the independence of the Baltic States, the Ukraine or the Caucasus. Kolchak and Denikin would never agree to it. 'The practical steps which are open to us at present', urged Churchill, 'are the following. (1) To recognize the government of Kolchak and Denikin and the government of United Russia, and by so doing place ourselves in a still more favourable position to influence the course of events. (2) To continue to support all the anti-Bolshevik forces as far as our limited resources go. (3) To use our influence to the full in the direction of a broad solution of the Russian Constitution. (4) To promote an alliance between Poland and the Kolchak-Denikin Russia, and thus powerfully influence future Russian developments in an anti-German direction.'

A Special Report on Russia produced by the Home Office Directorate of Intelligence was almost as jubilant. True, it said, the Soviet government was still technically in power, but its sphere of influence was daily contracting, and signs were not wanting that the end was 'within measurable distance'. The communists, who were nearly all Jews or Latvians, were in a minority even in the large towns, and could only stay in power by the use of terror. Propaganda was their main weapon in the fight for survival, and at last the Whites were beginning to match them even here. The religious movement inaugurated at Tomsk and Krasnoyarsk was steadily gaining ground. The Old Believers, under the banner of the Cross, together with the Mohammedans under the Green Flag, had proclaimed a Holy War. Press reports indicated that General von der Goltz had decided to join Yudenich with his Iron Division. The 'Green Guard' composed of peasant deserters from Whites and Reds was said to number several hundred thousand and to have its own secret General Staff in Petrograd. If the Whites would only stop their indiscriminate shooting of captured communists and communist sympathizers, the Greens would probably join forces with them. This might well hasten the death of the Bolshevik regime. But it was in any case doomed. It had massacred the upper and middle classes without improving the social or economic condition of the masses, antagonized the peasants, wrecked industry, and failed to produce a constructive policy which was either practical or popular. Superiority in tanks, cavalry and heavy artillery favoured Denikin, and 'the Bolsheviks, having sown the wind, show by their wireless messages that the approach of the whirlwind is trying their nerves.'

4. *Lenin's Greatest Ally*

In saying that the Bolsheviks had ruined or massacred the upper and middle classes, the Home Office survey merely repeated a wishful platitude. The Soviet regime in the Lenin era was the most fabulous meritocratic outburst since the French Revolution, ravenous for talent and ambition, intellectual and executive ability, wherever they could be found. It had frightened away or driven to the wall those who were unwilling to come to terms with reality. In Helsinki such people had set up their own news agency to broadcast the prurient obsessions or fantasies of the dispossessed (free-love weeks, church-brothels, enforced prostitution for girls of good family, lustful commissars etc.), and quoted the shares of non-existent companies on their own make-believe stock exchange. In the entourages of Kolchak, Denikin and Yudenich, outcasts from their 'world' of Moscow and Petrograd, they dreamed, gentleman gangsters, of burgling their way back into 'society', and rapidly disillusioned the fugitive Social Revolutionaries and Mensheviks who had hoped to fashion a democratic counter-revolution. These ludicrous enemies of promise and intelligence, having driven the bourgeoisie to revolution in alliance with the proletariat, proceeded to drive the White generals to despair and defeat.

It was fitting that their cause should receive its first mortal blow in the icy wastes of Siberia, where the bones of Cossack officers, peasant-flogging seigneurs and worker-murdering capitalists could mingle with the remains of their spiritual ancestors, the mastodons. They had converted the civil war into a confrontation of history and prehistory. It was fitting, too, that the military commander of this muddled escapade should be an admiral. Alexander Vasilevich Kolchak, the son of a regular army officer, was a curious mixture of scientist and martinet. A distinguished oceanographer and hydrologist, he had been prominent in the reorganization of the Russian navy after its defeat in the Russo-Japanese war. Brave, capable and rigidly loyal, he had, by a near-miracle, risen to the top of his profession by sheer ability. But as commander of the Black Sea fleet, he had, with his combination of academic detachment and strict discipline, made himself a prime target for the wrath of the mutineers of 1917. The experience of sailors' soviets dictating to the officers had been a traumatic shock from which he never recovered. Casting his ceremonial sword into the sea with a melodramatic gesture, he had resigned—to wander the world in a daze of vengeful horror. Volunteering to join the British army in any capacity, he had been on the point of embarking for Mesopotamia when it was decided that he would be of more use to the Allies in the Far East. At the urging of General Knox, head of the British Military Mission in Vladivostock, he had accepted the post of Minister of War in the All-Russian Directorate at Omsk. All the 'working' generals had congregated in the Ukraine—so Kolchak, on the principle that war is war on land or sea, was welcomed as a godsend. A few months later the vagabond admiral emerged as the political dictator and commander-in-chief of the forces of reaction.

It proved an unenviable eminence. The Czechoslovak Legion, which controlled the Trans-Siberian Railway and had created such economic and administrative sanity as there was in the region, disapproved of the Omsk government—and sponsored its own puppet 'democratic' government at Irkutsk (composed of S.R. and Menshevik refugees from Omsk, including the future Soviet diplomat, Ivan Maisky). The arrival of supplies from Vladivostok depended on the mood of the Czechs—and the Japanese, who used their troops as an army of occupation in eastern Siberia and treated Kolchak with hostile contempt. The American expeditionary force, led by General William S. Graves, spent much of its time protesting against the atrocities of Kolchak's lieutenants and of Japan's Cossack mercenaries (and sometimes actually skirmished with them). General Ivanov-Rinov, the Kolchak commander in eastern Siberia, alleged that the American soldiers were infected with Bolshevism. 'Most of them', he reported, 'are Jews from the East Side of New York, who constantly agitate for mutinies ... out of sixty liaison officers and translators at American headquarters over fifty are Russian Jews.' In September 1919 Graves received an angry letter from Kolchak. The American troops, he wrote, consisted of 'the dregs of the American army ... They are a factor of disintegration and disorder. I consider their removal from Russian territory necessary.'

General Knox was one of Kolchak's few firm supporters: but even he dared not risk trying to send into battle the four thousand semi-mutinous British troops in the area. When the Red Army advanced and the Bolshevik propaganda bombardment started, Kolchak's peasant army melted away. Omsk itself was full of saloons, pilfered army store depots, moneylenders, brothels and brawls. The atmosphere was one of crude, hysterical hedonism rather than of serious military endeavour. Kolchak found himself the Supreme Ruler of a demoralized if colourful rabble, the moral offscourings of the Red Terror. His nerves gave way. He stormed and raved, pounded his desk and smashed any object which happened to be lying on it: for there lay the limit of his authority. His mistress, Mme Timireva, was his only source of comfort and almost his only conquest.

The evacuation of Omsk began on November 18th, 1919, in the depth of a Siberian winter. There had been plenty of time to prepare for it, but it was a complete shambles. Of the three hundred trains which set out on the 1,500-mile journey to Irkutsk, only about seventy arrived. The rest were left stranded without food, fuel or medical equipment. Thousands of their occupants died of typhus, and even the blazing funeral pyres, past which the 5th Red Army marched in pursuit of the eastward-chugging Kolchak, did not prevent the infection spreading. The remnants of Kolchak's armies slogged along through the snow by the side of the railway track, barely twenty-four hours ahead of the Reds. Many died of frostbite. 'The truth is', said the *New Statesman*, 'that Kolchak, because his movement focuses all that remains of the reactionary forces of the old Russia, in a form which no democrat can fail to recognize, is in reality the greatest of Lenin's allies. If there had been no Kolchak to unite the republican democracy of Russia – under the banners of a regime which is intensely unpopular – it is more than probable that there would have been no Bolshevik government in Moscow today.'

Lenin's greatest ally, huddled in a cold railway compartment with Mme Timireva, badgered by panicky officials and urgent messages from Denikin and Miller, worrying over his own future and his personal fortune of 30,000 depreciated Omsk roubles, was enduring a journey of unmitigated torment and humiliation. It took five weeks to reach Nizhneudinsk. Frozen pumps, points and signals were one cause of delay. More important, the Czechs held up progress until their own evacuation had been completed. At Nizhneudinsk, where the Czechs were fighting rebel Russian troops, Kolchak and his entourage had to wait, squabbling incessantly, in a siding for two weeks. From this siding, on January 14th, 1920, Kolchak formally resigned as Supreme Ruler and Commander-in-Chief and handed over to General Denikin. Three days later, in a shabby second-class coach covered with American, French, British, Japanese and Czechoslovakian flags, he completed the last three hundred miles of the journey to Irkutsk, where the S.R./Menshevik Political Centre had seized control and was negotiating with the Bolsheviks. At Irkutsk a Czech officer came to the train to inform him that he was to be handed over to the local authorities. 'In other words,' said Kolchak, with weary calm, 'the Allies are betraying me.' After a series of interrogations in the local prison, he and his Prime Minister, Pepelyaev, were shot and their bodies shoved beneath the ice of the Angara River: rough, but in a sense poetic justice, for in death the displaced admiral was at last returned to his element. There were a few twinges of loyalty and qualms of conscience. The Russian General Keppel challenged the Czech Commander-in-Chief, Syrovy, to a duel for insulting the ex-Supreme Ruler. Syrovy promised to fight — later. In the Foreign Office in London, a tardy memorandum recommending the abolition of the post of British High Commissioner in Siberia was placed before Lord Hardinge. He minuted: 'So ends a not very creditable enterprise,' and passed the file to the Foreign Secretary, Lord Curzon, who, erasing the words 'not very', substituted 'highly dis-'.

To Austen Chamberlain, thinking peevishly in terms of 'the Russian sieve', to Lloyd George, irritated to have his Deauville frolics disturbed by Churchill's warmongering, the Russian imbroglio was an expensive nuisance. Statesmen in Britain, America and France comforted themselves with the thought that casualties were negligible and that it was one way of using up surplus war material. Military authorities were pleased that some of their officers and men would acquire useful experience in a war of movement — and would also get a sight of the Red Army in action. Bankers and industrialists drank, regularly but with decreasing conviction, to the success of the Whites. Boris Savinkov (that most urbane and persistent of counter-revolutionary beggars), with his sallow, deadpan face, heavy-lidded eyes and constantly replenished cigarette holder, made light of the whole business. It was really, he explained, a kind of farce, played out by self-important Bolsheviks and dashing Cossacks against the eternal backdrop (and drawback) of peasant cunning and obstinacy.

Churchill saw the Russian civil war as a pale imitation of the Great War. Hundreds of thousands of men were engulfed, their efforts diluted, by distances so vast that an advance of any consequence created insoluble transport problems and spread the lines almost to vanishing point. Cavalry galloped aimlessly to and fro. Eventually came the moment when the Bolsheviks, at the centre of the enfeebled commotion, made an only slightly less feeble sally and won the ghost of a victory. There was some truth in this: but it was no consolation to Russian peasants and factory workers enduring their fifth year of war, footslogging in the lethal cold of winter and the thick mud of spring thaw and autumn rains, braving the damp, mosquito-mad vapours of the bogs and forests of the north in summer, bumping over the Siberian steppes in wooden-wheeled carts. Once again the peasants voted with their feet. In 1919, out of $2\frac{1}{2}$ million drafted into the Red Army, at least 1,750,000 deserted — and a similar proportion from the White Armies.

This was the Russian sieve in action again. But it was a horrible sieve to be shaken in, especially for the peasants. In eastern Siberia Baron von Ungern-Sternberg's horsemen set fire to them and dragged them across the steppes for mere entertainment. Ivanov-Rinov ordered the massacre of the entire male population of villages suspected of harbouring Bolsheviks. Women were raped and whipped with ramrods. One American officer, sent to investigate atrocities, begged General Graves: 'For God's sake never send me on another expedition like that. I came within an ace of stripping off my uniform and joining those poor people.' Political prisoners were treated as hostages and shot if there was any subsequent sign of rebellion in the areas where they had been arrested. On both sides ferocious mutilation was common. The leader of the revolutionary committee in Irkutsk (which was soon to order Kolchak's execution) informed the Admiral that partisan guerrillas, entering a village recently 'disciplined' by Cossacks, had found rebels lying in agony with their ears and noses cut off. The Bolshevik note was attached to a Cossack prisoner whose leg had been severed and tied to his body.

Kolchak's liquidators, tiring sometimes of direct killing and summary torture, packed thousands of prisoners into cattle trucks and sent them off, without food, water or sanitary facilities, on long, leisurely, rebel-warning trips. An American Red Cross worker saw one of these 'death trains', fifty cars long and forty people to each car, after it had been on the move for six weeks. 'In the past two days', he wrote in his diary, 'I have seen enough misery to fill a lifetime ... animals who were once human ... cars never opened save to hurl out the dead ... sixty men fighting like dogs for a piece of bread ... I have climbed into these cars at night with my flashlight ... and seen men with the death-rattle in their throat, half-naked, with lice and vermin visible upon them, just lying in a semi-conscious stupor ... and others, with the whining grin of imbeciles, holding out their hands for a few cigarettes or kopecks, gibbering like apes with glee when given them.' Lying across the threshold of one car was the body of a young boy. 'No coat, merely a thin shirt, in such tatters that his whole chest and arms were exposed; for trousers a piece of jute bagging pinned around him. No shoes or stockings. What agony that boy must have suffered before he died of filth, starvation and exposure.'

The breaking of Kolchak's rabble had cost Moscow a mighty effort. The pick of the proletariat had been drafted to the eastern front. Formed into the Karl Liebknecht Regiment they were prominent in the autumn offensive which culminated in the evacuation of Omsk. As the shock troops of the Soviet Republic they knew they could expect no mercy. On September 7th, 1919, *Der Tag*, the Berlin daily newspaper, carried an account of the fate of some who had been captured. 'The prisoners are driven into a field. A Kolchak officer shouts: "Those of you who are true communists, show your courage and step forward!" Slowly, over half the men step forward. They are told to take off their uniforms, which are needed by the Whites, and to make ready to dig their grave. Peasants, women, children and soldiers crowd into the field, huddling together like sheep in a storm. The communists stand there shivering. In the moonlight their skin appears extremely white, almost transparent. Each of them is given a pickaxe. They begin digging large common graves. At last the graves have the necessary depth. The naked condemned sigh with weariness. Many throw themselves on the soft, wet ground and rest. I ask one of them: "What made a communist of you?" He replies: "THE ACCURSED LIFE! THE WORLD NEEDS HAPPINESS!" The firing squads are ready. The communists close together, forming a white wall. Volley follows volley ... Those who are still alive cry out: "Ho there! Take better aim!"'

Such men, dying in the belief that their bodies would form the cornerstone of a new righteousness, transformed death into a sacrament, and themselves (at the moment of what was intended to be their ultimate degradation) into the most powerful apostles of the communist ideal. They were the salt of the earth which somehow, in a time of crushing physical and moral squalor, had not lost its savour. Whatever might be built upon their bones and their dreams, they were the heroic foundation. The sight of the martyrdom of a true communist was worth a million pamphlets or posters or speeches. Their presence in the Red Army did more than anything else to leaven that huge peasant lump of sullen indifference. Trotsky likened them to a caste of *samurai*. They were his missionaries among men who, taking his Red Army oath by the battalion and raising their hands at the order of an ex-Tsarist officer who did not believe in what he was reading, used propaganda leaflets (which most of them could not read) mainly to wrap herrings or roll cigarettes.

In Russia today there are many devoted party workers who had their first experience of communism and counter-revolution as village children during the civil war. Timofei Petrovich Cherkasov, now chairman of a collective farm in the Kuban, is one of them. He was eight years old in 1919 when, after a brief period of Soviet rule, Kolchak's soldiers arrived in the central Siberian village where he was born. 'I don't remember much,' he told a reporter in 1967, 'but one episode I'll never forget. Kolchak's men found out about a young lad leading the Red partisan resistance. They threatened: either he surrenders or we burn the village to the ground. And so he gave himself up to save the village. He walked to his death, singing a revolutionary song about his last days on earth. That brave, beautiful boy. I watched him. It was my first real memory. I can see him to this day, and I envy him—the way he died, and for *what* he died. This wasn't just fanaticism. It was an act of pure humanity. The way that boy died! When I hear patriotic songs today I remember that boy's song. When things are tough with me, I remember his courage. I try to live up to his example. He was the beginning of my education.'

Kolchak—or what was done in his name—was indeed one of Bolshevism's greatest allies.

5. Red Panic, Whiteslide

The efficiency of the Red Armies, already hampered by lack of fuel and lubricants (trains inched along at 1 m.p.h., guns and rifles rusted), peasant revolts, and a chronic shortage of weapons and ammunition (victories over the Whites were needed to remedy this alone), was further menaced by the running battle between Trotsky and his powerful enemies on the Central Committee. The advantage of holding the centre of the ring was more theoretical than actual. The various fronts had a total circumference of more than five thousand miles and each of them seemed vital. When, after months of feverish effort, the spring offensive in the Urals was broken, Trotsky, believing that Kolchak had substantial reserves in Siberia, favoured a lull on the eastern front. This would enable him to switch troops south to dislocate Denikin's plans for a summer offensive: and also, with luck, to force a way through the Polish cordon in east Galicia which had so far frustrated the hope of making military contact with the beleaguered Soviet Republic in Hungary.

The political commissars on the eastern front, backed by Stalin and Zinoviev, demanded a pursuit of Kolchak. Trotsky's decision was overruled, and when the pursuit revealed that Kolchak *had* no reserves, he came under heavy critical fire. Hastening to the Ukraine, he found that Left communist commissars had given a free hand to local partisan groups in an attempt to turn the war into a genuine 'people's campaign'. The Red Army, weak in numbers, was, he found, demoralized by neglect, conflicting orders, and slovenly provisioning. Local partisans were better fed, clothed and equipped. They were even holding their own political assemblies. Furious, Trotsky demanded reinforcements, supplies, and the dismissal of 'fancy' commissars. His demands were ignored. Denikin, having begun his break-out in May 1919, drove swiftly on, capturing Kharkov, Tsaritsyn and Ekaterinoslav and heading for Odessa and Kiev.

In July Trotsky arrived in Moscow, his temper and reputation in shreds. He was forced to admit 'error' on the eastern front, and blamed for disrupting the southern front by his arrogant interference with local commanders. S. Kamenev, a Stalin-Zinoviev nominee, ousted Vatzetis, Trotsky's choice, as Commander-in-Chief of the Red Army. Trotsky's henchmen were removed from the Revolutionary War Council and replaced by protégés of Stalin. Trotsky countered by resigning from the Politburo, the Commissariat of War and the Revolutionary War Council. Lenin, however, not only refused the resignation, but gave Trotsky a sheet of paper on which was written: 'Comrades: knowing the harsh character of Comrade Trotsky's orders, I am so convinced, so absolutely convinced, of their rightness, expediency and necessity for the success of our cause that I endorse them without reservation.' With this blank cheque in his pocket, Trotsky plunged into a bitter wrangle with Kamenev over the strategy of the campaign. Kamenev planned to strike in the Don Valley Cossack area. Trotsky wanted to concentrate on the central sector, with Kharkov and Donetz as the main objectives. In this heavily industrialized region the Red Army would have the backing of most of the population and the use of a network of roads and railways. In the Don Valley the population was solidly hostile and railways almost non-existent. After fierce argument, Kamenev's plan was authorized. Trotsky travelled sulkily to the front, flashing reproachful mesages to Lenin. On August 11th he wired the Politburo that the Red Army in the Ukraine was starving, that at least half the soldiers had no boots, no underwear, no tunics.

While the Politburo bickered, Kiev, the cradle of Russian civilization, trembled anew for its fate. During the five months after November 1918 the city had been occupied in succession by the German puppet Skoropadsky, the Ukrainian nationalist leader Petlyura, and the White Volunteer Army. Refugees from Moscow and Petrograd and marauding troops jostled each other in the streets and fought for accommodation. Army rifles, burgled chandeliers, furs, jewellery, ikons and crucifixes, a barbaric wealth of loot and salvaged heirlooms, were sold in the market-place and the shops. The chaos was so appalling that when in February 1919 the Red Army marched in, even the bourgeois rejoiced. ('I'm against the ideas of these Bolsheviks,' said a refugee lawyer from Moscow, 'but at least they've *got* ideas.') In the next six months Kiev's riotous progressivism had made Moscow and Petrograd seem almost timid. Ilya Ehrenburg, who was in the thick of it, remembered that time as one of continuous intellectual experiment and *joie de vivre*. He himself was put in charge of a Section of Aesthetic Education for Mofective Children. 'Mofective' was short for 'morally defective'. The section, mostly composed of psychiatrists and Froebel-trained teachers (but with a heavy sprinkling of poets, painters and musicians), decided to analyse the effects of vivid colours on nervous children, debated the pros and cons of choral declamation as an influence on the collective consciousness, and argued over the use of eurhythmics in the rehabilitation of juvenile prostitutes. An Applied Art Section staged exhibitions of folk art, started embroidery and poetry workshops, encouraged peasant talent, and commissioned painters to decorate the main streets with Ukrainian traditional designs. Writers and artists formed their own union and were given offices in a former bourgeois mansion. Ehrenburg taught versification to beginners and did not lack for pupils.

Even in August, when the Red front broke and rumours of frightful pogroms reached the city, the activity of the entranced progressives did not abate. They accelerated old projects and began new ones, discussed publication dates for the next volumes of Chekhov's collected works, and worried about the scale, style and position of a monument to the revolution.

Ehrenburg, in time snatched from his official duties, wrote a poem celebrating the rich confusion of those days of hunger, suspense and ardent idealism:

> Nineteen-nineteen. However did they manage, poor dears!
> The children of the new age will read of the battles,
> Learn the names of the leaders and orators,
> The numbers of the dead and the dates.
> They will never know how sweet the roses smelt on the field
>   of battle,
> How blackbirds sang amid the voices of the guns,
> How beautiful life was at that time.

KILL THE JEWS, SAVE RUSSIA was the slogan, and virtually the sole idea, of many of Denikin's officers, and the only one which they troubled to impress upon their troops.

At Fastov, near Kiev, Jew-hunting Cossacks joked about their pastime – 'We have leave', they said, 'to have a party for three days.' Two thousand Jews were massacred, hundreds more beaten up and mutilated. On the third day the Cossacks set fire to two hundred

Jewish houses. Nearly a thousand families were left homeless. In Kiev itself skin-saving citizens thrust portraits of Marx and Lenin under the floorboards and put up the pictures of the Martyr Tsar which they had preserved for just such an emergency. If they were Jews they were wasting their time. The Whites — ragged, lice-ridden wretches maddened with vodka and blasé with slaughter — made no exceptions. It was Fastov all over again. Men, women and children screamed the whole night long, so that it seemed to Ehrenburg that 'the houses themselves were screaming, the streets, the whole town'. This, wrote a White journalist who saw the pogrom, was a time for repentance. 'Will the Jews', he asked, 'beat their breasts, cover their heads with ashes, and repent before the whole world because the sons of Israel took such an active part in the Bolshevik madness?'

New posters appeared, idealized portraits of Denikin and Kolchak, a picture of a gigantic horse trampling a Jew. Refugees — among them Ehrenburg — hid in goods trucks and in ships' holds, dreading the cry of 'Any Yids in there?'

Marooned in the Crimean coastal village of Koktebel, Ehrenburg organized a children's playground and a modelling class. When the weather was warm he dressed in a pair of pyjamas — his best clothes. After all, he reasoned, as he skipped about with the children, was there any limit to the vicissitudes one might have to endure in such historic times? Veresayev, a doctor and fellow-refugee, made his rounds on a bicycle dressed in a nightshirt, and was paid in eggs and lard. He, Ehrenburg and other scarecrow intellectuals argued incessantly about the 'meaning' of the distant revolution. Veresayev's melancholy, Chekhovian view of life was affronted by the dogmatic arrogance of Bolshevism. Frightened by the endless suffering and the oversimplification of complex human emotions, Ehrenburg wondered if he was afraid because the revolution was forcing him, like the whole of Russia, to enter the dark tunnel to a brilliant age. He was not sure. He could only suppose, and hope, that it might be so.

Trotsky, always at his best in a crisis, was in no doubt at all. Young people, he said, addressing a Communist Youth Rally, would defend the revolution with greater zest if they grasped the exciting implications of this moment in history. It was not enough to see the war simply in terms of a battle between Soviet democracy and degenerate plutocracy. They should have some vision of mankind's slow, stumbling ascent from the 'dark animal realm' to ever higher peaks of civilization, with socialism as the great goal and motive force. He pictured primitive man as gripped by superstition, creating for himself little gods and princes and tsars. Later, man had replaced many gods by one God and many tsars by one Tsar. But he had not stopped, could not stop, there. 'He has renounced tsars and gods and has made an attempt to become the free master of his own life. These hundreds of thousands of years of man's development would be a mockery if we were not to attain ... a new society in which all human relations will be based on co-operation and man will be man's brother and not his enemy.' In the blast-furnace of history his traditional lethargy was being smelted out of the Russian character. 'Tongues of flame scorch us but steel us ... Happy is he who in its heart and mind feels the electrical current of our great epoch!'

While Trotsky laboured to electrify the communist élite with something of his own crackling energy and sense of destiny, Mikhail Kalinin, the Soviet President, himself a peasant by origin, laboured to penetrate the cynical apathy of the peasants. Kalinin visited hundreds of villages – answering questions, redressing grievances as far as he was able, always turning the current of discontent into the channel of hatred for the privileged classes. 'Formerly the so-called elect of the Lord were in the seats of government,' he would say. 'Now Kalinin is at the head of the government. The grey, uncouth muzhik with his dirty feet has climbed upon the throne of the elect. The aristos will not pardon us for this. Of course we make mistakes, because we are learning how to govern. But we cannot put a wise man from the priveleged classes at the top, because he will betray us. Perhaps Kalinin is stupid, but the mass of workers and peasants pushed him to the fore ...'

As Yudenich's army (equipped with British tanks, planes, rifles, ammunition and medical stores) neared Petrograd and Denikin's reached Orel, 250 miles south of Moscow, posters, leaflets and agitators combined to portray the horrors of a White victory. A reign of terror and hunger for the workers; for soldiers the whip, sadistic barrack discipline, saluting and 'Your Honour-ing'; for Jews, pogroms; for children, a return to ignorance and squalor; for anyone with intelligence, a regime of cretinous obscurantism; the triumph of foreign capitalists – since the debts of the Tsar would be 'honoured' at the expense of the people; a new revolution, a new civil war. Times were bad, but they would get better once the White locusts had been destroyed. Day after day cartoons showed White generals and pot-bellied, top-hatted, cigar-smoking capitalists smashing workers and peasants with their fists, trampling on their bound bodies, hanging them on gibbets. In mid-October a Party Week launched a drive for new members, relaxing the normally stringent conditions of entry. This test of proletarian loyalty had an encouraging response: Moscow alone yielded nearly fifteen thousand recruits.

Yet there was gloom among the Bolshevik leaders: doubts as to whether the people would respond to yet another alarmist flogging. Lenin was convinced that Yudenich's offensive was too formidable to be resisted. At a grim meeting of the Politburo on October 15th he proposed the abandonment of Petrograd and the concentration of all available resources around Moscow. He even foresaw that Moscow might fall, and the Soviet government and its 'revolution' move eastwards—a possibility which had never been far from his mind since October 1917. Trotsky would have nothing to do with such defeatism. He had not the underground mentality. He had always fought in the limelight. If the revolution was to go down, he said, it must go down fighting. Petrograd, 'the stone cradle of the revolution', must not be abandoned.

Trotsky proposed that reinforcements should be switched to Petrograd from the White Sea and Polish fronts. He volunteered to take personal charge of the defence of the city, while Stalin dealt with Denikin. Reluctantly, Lenin allowed Trotsky to go to Petrograd, though still withholding final authorization of his plan. The next day, on his train, Trotsky dictated communiqués of aggressive confidence. He sneered at Churchill's project for an anti-Bolshevik crusade of fourteen nations. They were nothing more, he said, than so many 'geographic notions'. The Whites would be more interested in fourteen British and French divisions, but the French and British workers had seen to it that this was impossible. Even if Yudenich took Petrograd his troops would lose the battle of the streets. The White Guards would be lost in that labyrinth of stone, where 'every house will be a threat, a deadly danger ... We can surround some streets with barbed wire, leave others open and transform them into booby-traps. All that is needed is that a few thousand people shall be firmly resolved not to surrender ... ' Two or three days of such street fighting would change the invaders into a terrified flock of cowards.

In Petrograd some trembled with fear, some with joy, at the approach of Trotsky and his seasoned trouble- and traitor-shooters. Zinoviev, the nominal ruler of the city, was in a state of abject funk, capable of little more than despairing telephone calls to Lenin. Five months earlier Stalin's ruthless competence had been sufficient to beat back the Whites. Now it seemed that nothing less than a miracle was needed. The starving Red soldiers on the Estonian front, riddled with lice and typhus, entering their sixth year of war (and their third for a revolution which they had made to get peace), were deserting *en masse*. In the forests of Pskov the Greens (so called from the woods in which they took refuge) numbered several tens of thousands. The army had been further demoralized by desertion and treachery among high-ranking officers. White troops were entrenched on the outskirts of Petrograd. Bolshevik officials were certain that the game was up. The wives and children of known leaders had already been evacuated. The leaders themselves were arranging new identities, growing or shaving beards. The first heavy snow had fallen. The Smolny Institute, headquarters of the Petrograd Soviet, had been sandbagged and ringed with guns. But military and engineering experts considered resistance futile.

After more than a year of almost continuous crisis, Trotsky and his technicians had reached a point where the impossible was done immediately and miracles took only a little longer. This was their biggest assignment, and it was carried out with split-second efficiency. Cars sped from the train, carrying sanitary detachments, engineering specialists, street-fighting and artillery experts. In their black leather uniforms they looked like creatures from another planet. Suspect army officers were shot or demoted. Sewer pipes were used to build barricades. Streets were cleared and mined, houses stuffed with snipers, guns moved to positions of advantage. Posters informed the citizens that it was 'impossible for a little army of 15,000 ex-officers to master a working-class capital of 700,000 inhabitants'. At a session of the Petrograd Soviet Trotsky whipped up the will-to-resist: 'In these dark, cold, hungry, anxious days,' he said, his metallic voice vibrating with emotion, 'Petrograd presents to us again the grand picture of rallying self-confidence and heroism. This city which has suffered so much, which has burned with so fierce an inward flame, which has faced so many dangers, this city which has never spared itself, this beautiful Red Petrograd, will remain what it has always been—the torch of the revolution!'

Amid roars of acclamation it was resolved to fight to the death. The whole audience burst into song. Victor Serge, a Red trooper and a member of the Defence Committee, reflected that the psalms sung by Cromwell's Roundheads before going into battle must have sounded like this.

Word came that the Politburo had authorized Trotsky to fight within the city. But Lenin still wanted preparations to be made to evacuate official documents, dynamite power stations, and scuttle the Baltic fleet—in case of defeat. Trotsky reported that such measures would not be necessary. The situation was under control. Provisions and reinforcements from the Polish front began to arrive. Swarthy Bashkirian cavalry passed through the streets, chanting guttural songs to the accompaniment of a shrill, eerie whistling.

The sudden appearance of British tanks spread consternation. Trotsky himself, on horseback, rallied retreaters and beat them back into line. He spread a rumour that the tanks were just a bluff—they looked impressive but were made of wood. He also detailed a group of workers to knock together, at high speed, a few wooden mock-tanks, carefully controlled glimpses of which, though they never got near the firing-line, helped to raise morale. Every able-bodied worker was enrolled in an emergency Red Guard. Women's battalions were formed. Within a week of Trotsky's arrival, the Whites were being pressed back, and on October 21st were routed at a battle on the Poltovo Heights, ten miles south of Petrograd. The semicircle of besiegers broke and fled towards the Estonian frontier. 'Red fighters!' Trotsky proclaimed in an Army Order of October 24th, 'on all fronts you are meeting with the hostile artifices of the English. It is from English guns that the counter-revolutionary troops fire at you ... The women and children of Archangel and Astrakhan are murdered and mutilated by English airmen and English high explosives. English ships shell our coasts ... But even now, at the moment of the most bitter fight against England's hireling Yudenich, I call upon you: never forget that this is not the only England that exists. Apart from the England of profits, bribery and blood-thirstiness, there exists the England of labour, of spiritual power, of great ideals. It is the England of the Stock Exchange, the vile and honourless England, that fights against us. Toiling England, its people, is with us.'

Trotsky, the miracle-worker, himself passionately longed for a miracle—the revival of a strong, militant and victorious international

Socialism which alone could make his interminable caulking of the leaks in the battered Soviet hulk more than a fearful, if superbly executed chore.

Stalin tackled the defence of Moscow with no misgivings or *arrières pensées*. He had never believed in the European revolution. To him, collaboration with socialists outside Russia, with their dismal record of pretentious talk and fragile action, was a kind of treachery, an intellectual blind alley. Better to concentrate on propaganda in Persia, India and China, where Soviet Russia would appear as the dispenser of civilization. 'The West,' he wrote, 'with its imperialist cannibals, has become the centre of darkness and slavery. The task is to destroy that centre, to the joy of the toilers of all countries.' But before that task could be performed, the counter-revolution – in all its forms and aftermaths – had to be destroyed.

The breaking of Denikin was surprisingly easy. After the long advance from the Ukraine the Whites were exhausted, demoralized and aimless (what did the capture of Moscow mean to them but the prospect of another 'party'?). An army of perhaps 200,000 men straggled over several hundred miles. Its supply lines were stretched to breaking-point. The advance guard had occupied Orel on October 14th. Six days later it evacuated the town and began a gruelling retreat, harried by the newly formed Red cavalry which, led by Budyenny, gained a crushing victory near Voronezh. This was particularly gratifying to Stalin. For though Trotsky had given the famous order ('Proletarians to horse!'), the demand for a regular Soviet cavalry had come from Stalin, Budyenny, and the rest of what Trotsky had contemptuously called 'the N.C.O.s' Opposition.' When, on the second anniversary of the revolution – which happened to be his fortieth birthday – Trotsky returned to Moscow to be acclaimed as the architect of victory, he was aware that, in their serial duel, Stalin had gained another advantage. Trotsky (and Petrograd) were awarded the Order of the Red Banner. But so was Stalin. Furthermore, while Budyenny was allowed to harry the retreating Whites to his heart's content, Trotsky had been forbidden to pursue Yudenich's army into Estonia. This, decided Lenin, would 'antagonize English liberals' and 'play Churchill's game'.

But Trotsky's mind was already leaping ahead to meet other challenges. In December, with the northern front all but liquidated, Kolchak smashed, negotiations proceeding between Estonia and

Soviet Russia for peace, and Denikin's final defeat only a matter of time, Trotsky drafted a report on the course of the civil war which was in effect an obituary on the counter-revolution. A hundred and fifty thousand Orenburg Cossacks, led by their Ataman, marched across central Asia, driven on over thousands of miles by fear of Bolshevik vengeance and a fierce love of independence. A hundred and twenty thousand perished. Months later the rest stumbled across the frontier of Chinese Turkestan. The Ural Cossacks, similarly motivated, struck southwards over the deserts towards Persia. 'Every night halt', reported their leader, General Akulinin, 'is a cemetery.' Terrible and spectacular was the Whiteslide.

General Anton Denikin, like Kolchak a man of complete if somewhat obtuse integrity, was perhaps the most pitiable victim of the White-slide. His father, born a serf, had worked hard to gain a commission in the army. He himself had become a general through merit and application, not influence. He believed in the soldierly ideals of duty, honour and patriotism with a fervour which was useful but laughable to the cynical riff-raff which used him. He failed to control the chronic drunkenness and violence which demoralized his army and made a mock of his laboriously composed 'liberal' proclamations. General Mai-Mayevsky, the military governor of Kharkov, was often blind drunk for days at a time. Corruption and speculation were orgiastic. Grain and sugar, army stores, manufactured goods, mostly brought at huge expense and trouble in British vessels (after acid wrangles between Churchill and the Shipping Controller) to the Black Sea port of Novorossisk, were caught up in a maelstrom of profiteering. 'About the middle of 1919,' reported J. E. Hodgson, a British officer who served in south Russia, 'the British sent out complete equipment for a 200-bed hospital at Ekaterinodar. Not a single bed ever reached its destination. Beds, blankets, sheets, mattresses and pillows vanished as if by magic. They found their way to the houses of staff officers and members of the Kuban government ... Britain sent Denikin enough soldiers' clothing to equip an army twice the size of our own peace establishment. He never claimed to have more than 300,000 men at his disposal; yet neither at the Tsaritsyn nor at the Don front did I ever see as many as twenty-five per cent of the fighting men in British kit ...'

In December 1919, five months after the post had first been mooted by the Cabinet, H. J. Mackinder, Member of Parliament for a Glasgow constituency and Reader in Geography at the University of London, arrived in the Ukraine to act as British High Commissioner in South Russia. Shaken by the chaos into which he was plunged, Mackinder, a reluctant missioner from the start, resigned almost immediately, and returned to London to compose a cagey but encouraging report for the Cabinet. Denikin, he mildly suggested, had not made the best use of the material he had received from Britain. Russia had been 'bled white of brain-power'. There was an almost complete lack of administrative capacity. This was true of the Bolsheviks too, 'but they have enlisted the help of the Jews.' The British Military Mission had not, in his opinion, exercised the moderating influence which might have been expected of it. Altogether, he could not recommend more than a modest continuance of support to Denikin. But he advocated firm support to 'the full range of anti-Bolshevist states from Finland to the Caucasus', and reported that Pilsudski, in a specially granted interview, had expressed confidence that the Polish army would soon advance to Moscow and topple the Soviet regime. Denikin was a bad risk: but all was not lost—and France was committed to bear the brunt of a Polish campaign. This was just the kind of talk that the Cabinet, and especially Lloyd George, Austen Chamberlain and Sir Joseph Maclay (the Shipping Controller), wanted to hear. It was not long before Mackinder was knighted.

Lloyd George negotiated the Whiteslide with an effortless political slalom, speeding impressively towards a pre-arranged finishing-line on which fluttered the legend: THE MAN WHO ALWAYS DENIED THAT THIS WAR COULD BE WON. In a Guildhall speech on November 8th he applauded his own prescience. 'I dared', he said, 'to predict—it was not a popular prediction, but my business is to give honest advice to the nation' (cheers)—'I dared to predict that Bolshevism could not be suppressed by the sword. Other methods must finally be resorted to for restoring peace and good government in that distressed land ... Civilization cannot afford a distracted and desolate Russia.' On November 13th, in the Commons, Lloyd George openly condemned the blockade, and described Russia as 'one of the great resources for the supply of food and raw material'. Four days later, during yet another debate on Russia (the eighth since the House had begun its session in February), he put on one of his most astonishing displays of mental agility. He re-repudiated

Bullitt ('I never knew there was such a man as Bullitt in existence until President Wilson said to me, "There is a young fellow who has come back from Russia. I should be glad if you would see him.") He claimed that intervention had been both a duty and a very considerable success ('France, Japan, America — Britain has contributed more than all those powers put together, and I boast of it because I consider it an obligation of honour on our part'). But Britain could not afford to 'undertake the responsibility of financing civil war in Russia indefinitely'. His masterpiece of table-turning came when he spoke of the Whiteslide as being not a disaster but a positive blessing. Denikin, Kolchak and Yudenich had made no secret of their desire for a completely restored Russian Empire. Did not this recall the warning of Lord Beaconsfield, 'who regarded a great, gigantic, colossal, growing Russia, rolling onwards like a glacier towards Persia, and the borders of Afghanistan and India, as the greatest menace the British Empire could be confronted with?' Looked at from this point of view, were not the Bolsheviks, so eager to promise self-determination to the constituent parts of the former Romanov Empire, the lesser evil?

For sheer virtuosity, Lloyd George's taming of a virulently anti-Bolshevik Commons by the invocation of a White Menace from the wreckage of the Whiteslide matched Trotsky's revivalist triumph in Petrograd. He created such an atmosphere of complete, if belated, realism, that there was hardly a ripple of surprise or protest when Sir Robert Cecil jeered at Churchill: 'I could not help when I heard him last week having a picture of my right hon. friend riding at the head of Cossacks making a triumphal entry into Moscow. That was the kind of tone he took'; or when Lieutenant-Colonel C. E. Malone, who had just returned from a visit to Soviet Russia, remarked: 'We have heard a great deal about shaking hands with murderers, but if that argument had been used in November 1918 we would never have concluded peace with Germany ... Who has been supplying marauding bandits and partisan leaders with arms, munitions, tanks, aeroplanes — aye, and even men? Who has been stimulating anarchy and civil war? I would like to know what that is if it is not shaking hands with murderers. I call it *cuddling* with murderers. In Russia the first people to assure you of the impossibility of Bolshevism would be the Bolshevists themselves. Every day they are modifying their agrarian and industrial policy ... Believe me, as surely as President Poincaré drove through the streets of London last week, it will not

be many years before the President of the Russian Soviet Republic
will be entertained in London, probably at Buckingham Palace.'

On November 20th, recognizing that the Whiteslide was by way
of burying a multitude of sins and truculences, Chicherin put out
diplomatic feelers. Relations with Russia, he reasoned, were quite
possible in spite of profound political differences. 'We feel strongly',
he said in a broadcast message, 'the need for economic help from
more fully developed countries such as Great Britain ... I therefore
welcome the declaration of the British Premier as the first step towards a sane policy corresponding to the interests of both countries.'

A PITIABLE EXHIBITION, headlined *The Times*, horrified by the
tone of the Commons debate. There had been one or two redeeming
speeches, such as the one in which Lieutenant-Colonel Guinness
described the Soviet government as 'a carnivorous organization',
and added: 'You can no more expect Bolshevism to live within its
own boundaries than you can expect a man-eating tiger to live in a
stall and feed on carrots.' Unlike Lloyd George, he did not see the
Federal Soviet Republic as a weakened version of the Tsarist
Empire. What, he asked, would happen if Germany managed to
'control' Russia, and drew China into her 'system' as well? What
chance would the democratic nations have to 'curb the ambitions of
a Russo-German-Chinese block established astride the Urals, with
the advantage of interior lines, a colossal reserve of manpower, and
far greater unity of control than anything which could be put up
against them by the League of Nations?' *The Times*, too, brandished
this triple Bolshevik bogy, and during the last two months of 1919
produced its most frenzied selection of Abyss and atrocity tales.
Refugee noblewomen of British birth, former governesses in
aristocratic Russian families, expelled clergymen, army officers – all
contributed to this anthology of class spite and classic prurience.

According to some accounts, the British military authorities in
south Russia did their best to keep up a steady flow of the right kind
of material. Margaret Barber, the daughter of an Anglican clergyman, protested vigorously at the treatment she received. A Red
Cross nurse who had served in various parts of Russia since the end
of 1916, she was a woman of strong character who had been much
impressed by the *camaraderie* of the revolution ('one easily adopted
the custom of calling everyone, man or woman, high or low,
tovarich'), the sharing of hardship and food, the lack of constriction

and cant. She had disliked the atmosphere of peevish resentment in the English Governesses' Home in Moscow and had no patience with the upper-class Russians who assumed that because she was English she would be in favour of a restoration of the good old times ('I usually told them that they had brought it upon themselves by doing so little to better the condition of the masses'). When, in October 1919, Miss Barber travelled from Astrakhan to Taganrog to arrange the return of some Armenian refugees to the Caucasus, she was disgusted by the vicious anti-Bolshevik talk and excessive eating and drinking of the Russian and British officers. She told them sharply that she had nothing to complain of except a shortage of food. She was then, she claimed, virtually imprisoned in the British Hospital, put in a special ward, and frequently cross-examined about her 'experiences' among the Reds. She noticed that other British women – often ex-governesses – were hurried back to England because they had 'experiences' to offer.

The Misses May and Eileen Healy alleged that there had been eight torture houses in Kiev. Crosses had been cut on priests' backs. One torturer, a Jewess, had played with her victims, putting them against a wall and spattering bullets around them. Eight thousand people had been murdered in six months (another correspondent put the number at 27,000). In the garden of one torture house they had seen 127 naked and mutilated corpses (did they count them?). The Bolshevik leaders, they said, were mostly Jewish or Latvian. Drunken orgies were frequent, and even the brutalized guards took cocaine and morphia to dull the ache of what remained of their consciences. Miss Josephine Inigo Jones told of the Red Terror in Kharkov. In prison there she had seen women raped by soldiers, 'a large pot in which was a boiled man', and floors 'literally strewn with fingernails and human gloves'.

But the acknowledged masterpieces of Northcliffe's campaign came from a clergyman and an officer of the British Military Mission in south Russia. Their accounts of Bolshevik bestiality were reprinted as pamphlets, and sold briskly. The Rev. R. Courtier-Foster, former British chaplain at Odessa, told how Bolsheviks bayoneted the wounded, tore men and women apart with winches, and scalded them to death. 'Week by week,' he wrote, 'the newspapers published articles for and against the nationalization of women. In south Russia the proposal was not legalized, but in Odessa bands of Reds seized women and girls and carried them off to the port, the timber yards and the Alexandrovsky Park for their own purposes. Women used in this way were found in the mornings either dead or mad or dying. Those found alive were shot. One of the most awful of my own personal experiences was hearing at night from my bedroom windows the frantic screams of women being raped to death in the park opposite.' Decently dressed men and women had been stripped of their clothes — and boots — and sent home naked through the frost and snow. He had, he claimed, seen soldiers spitting on the Ikon of the Thorn-Crowned Face of Christ. Acts of indecency had been committed 'in broad daylight in parks and public gardens'. Clergy were tortured or murdered by hundreds; churches desecrated and turned into cinemas or drinking saloons; the Blessed Sacrament seized and insulted. 'Lenin and Trotsky', concluded the Rev. Courtier-Foster, 'may well chuckle from within the recesses of the polluted Christian Church of the Kremlin as they make overtures to a duped world. Is Christianity a living force in western Europe? The Red Tyrants of Moscow think it can be flicked aside like an old glove.'

The officer's diatribe was in the form of a letter to his wife. The only sacred building spared by Jewish communists in towns captured by the Reds, he wrote, was the synagogue. Christian churches were often used as torture halls, where men and women were crucified. He enclosed a selection of atrocity photographs showing crucifixions, women with their breasts cut off, with their bodies slit open, and (in one case) with unborn twins half dragged out of the womb. According to him Red Soldiers were 'authorized to seize any girl they fancied ... Those who struggled were killed. The rest, when used, were mutilated and thrown into the rivers which flow through Ekaterinodar.' He hoped that his wife would show the photographs (the subjects of which, as critics pointed out, could easily have been supplied by White-Cossack torturers) to all her friends and acquaintances. 'People at home, apathetic fools that they are, do not deserve to be spared. They must be woken up ... I pray I shall rouse you and all our friends to a white heat of enthusiasm for this crusade, and of holy hatred for the Bolsheviks.'

Stories of the atrocious Vengeance of the Abyss might keep class hatred alive, but they could not prolong intervention. Under the headline BOLSHEVIST IN ROYAL UNDERCLOTHING, *The Times* featured the abominable case of a certain Posrednicky, formerly a sailor in the Russian navy, who at the time of his arrest by the Polish police, was wearing an undershirt which had belonged to the late Tsar: a fine pale-blue garment with the monogram N. A. (Nikolai Alexandrovich) surmounted by a crown embroidered in red. Posrednicky stated that he had been in Ekaterinburg at the time of the murder of the Imperial Family, and that a quantity of Royal underclothing had been seized and hawked round for sale. Could insolence and lèse-majesté go further? But there was no end to Bolshevik insolence. On January 1st, 1920, Moscow Radio sent out a buoyant New Year's greeting. 1919 had been a year of victory for the Russian working classes, it said. Under the mighty blows of the Red Army the horde of Tsarist generals had reeled back. 'With Red standards and a shout of victory we shall break into the New Year. In 1920 the civil war will be ended. There will be Soviets in Berlin, Washington, Paris and London.'

Major-General Sir Frederick Maurice, military correspondent of the *Daily News*, warned that Kolchak and Denikin were finished, that 'the Road to India is open to the Reds', and that by trying to bar the West to Soviet Russia the Allies were 'tending to drive her in the very direction where she can do us most damage'. On January 14th the Supreme Council gave audience to two representatives of the Paris office of the Russian Co-operative Movement. They claimed that the movement (which in fact was under strict government control) had 25 million members and no politics, and that there was in south Russia a surplus of ten million tons of wheat for export. Seeing in the fiction of a deal with the 'non-Bolshevik' co-operatives a useful way of saving ideological face, the Supreme Council announced two days later that the Allies had decided, 'in view of the sore need of the Russian people', to grant facilities to the Russian Co-operative organization to import manufactured goods in exchange for grain, flax and other agricultural produce. It stressed that this was a humanitarian gesture and implied no change in the attitude of the Allied governments towards the Soviet regime.

But the fact remained that a corner of the blockade had been lifted, the imperialists forced to change their tune, and the claim of the Russian Communist Party to world leadership of revolutionary socialism strengthened beyond challenge.

The victory of the Russian revolution, like the victory of all revolutions, had been a Pyrrhic one. The process of dislocation begun by the world war had by the end of 1919 robbed the towns of northern and central Russia of more than a third of their population. Starvation and disease had turned the country into a vast charnel-house, a perpetual shuffle of death. Thousands of fugitives from the advance of Yudenich's army on Petrograd in October had fled to the forests near Lake Peipus and perished of typhus. *Pravda* reported that when the tattered uniforms of Red Army soldiers were, at lengthy intervals, disinfected, a pile of lice that looked like grey sand covered the floor to a depth of two inches. Limbs were amputated without anaesthetics, wounds bandaged with newspaper. Gangrene, typhus and cholera killed more men than the enemy.

Worst of all, in a society hovering so near to barbarism, was the death of so many of the most generous-minded, self-reckless revolutionaries. Vladimir Mazin, Serge's comrade, could not bear to sit in an office churning out revolutionary propaganda. He insisted on joining the Red Army, was made a political commissar, but seized a rifle and was killed in action. 'He who sends men to their death', he wrote to his wife, 'must see that he himself gets killed.' There were not a few like Mazin in Soviet Russia in 1919. They were not Party men, these honorary Bolsheviks. They suffered in the knowledge that they were fighting, not for a perfect revolution, but for the lesser of two evils. They had, often, the suicidal streak of utopians sickened by the world's slow stain. They were eager, like the more fanatical young Bolsheviks, to fight to the death against the accursed life.

This brain-and-ideals drain seemed to some observers the saddest thing that happened in the civil war. 'In three years', lamented Albert Rhys Williams, an American journalist who had been with John Reed in the first stages of the Bolshevik revolution, 'half the young communists of Russia were slaughtered. It was an incalculable loss, for these were men who could withstand the corruption of office and the poison of power.'

V

THE GREAT OUTSIDERS

---

1. *Nestor Makhno*

By the end of 1919 Lenin could claim that only the discipline and drive of the Communist Party had made possible the successful defence of the revolution. Already, at a time when the party was full of brilliant individuals and guided by a man who did his utmost to give their talents wide scope, the dogma of infallibility was hovering. Soviet Russia had been saved by the party. Communists should live only for it, since they had no effective existence apart from it, since only through it could they serve the revolution. 'The big public event', noted Beatrice Webb in her diary in February 1920, 'is the victory of Soviet Russia over all her enemies and the transformation of the Bolshevist government into a bureaucratic administration exercising far-reaching coercive power over the life and liberty of the individual citizen ... It is clear that Bolshevism is government from above with a vengeance.'

This transformation might gratify the Webbs, but to libertarian revolutionaries it was an intolerable blasphemy and betrayal. The crushing of the L.S.R.-Anarchist revolt of summer 1918 had checked the 'revolutionary' counter-revolution. But from the bubbling ferment of the Ukraine came a formidable challenger of Soviet authoritarianism – Nestor Makhno, one of the most resourceful guerilla leaders known to history. Makhno continued to plague the Soviet government until the late summer of 1921. But the peak of his extraordinary career was reached in the autumn of 1919.

All over Europe and Russia the Great War, planned in the cities, had torn the peasants from the land. The post-war socialist revolutions treated the peasants as so many pawns in the complicated game of city intellectuals. Gorky regarded them as a drag on the wheels of progress. Lenin humoured them like idiot children. Trotsky, in the

New Communist Manifesto, wrote impatiently of 'the peasant who still cannot see beyond the spire of his village church'. Rosa Luxemburg was dimly aware that they had somehow to be fitted in the Socialist Commonwealth. The Hungarian communists, in their tearing impatience with these dumb, reactionary oxen, reached for their guns—as did all the city folk sooner or later, whether they were White or Red. It was humiliating to have to depend on such obstructive creatures for food—and soldiers; maddening that one could not fight wars or make plans without them; infuriating to feel, somewhere at the back of one's superior mind, that wheedled, threatened, shot, flogged, even roasted on sheets of red-hot iron, they yet regarded it all as so much passing peevishness, only to be expected of people whose values had been debased in sinful human ant-heaps, people who were not peasants. The madness would cease. The madmen would return to their prisons of stone and concrete. The peasants and the land would remain. They alone were indispensable, immutable.

They had dreams too. Dreams of a time before towns and money and greedy landowners existed, when they were left alone to manage their own lives and everything was clear and slow and simple. Behind the resistance of the 'Greens' in Russia, the sullen hostility of the peasants of Austria and Hungary and Bavaria, there was something of this longing. It flared openly and passionately in Andalusia. But in the Ukraine it was worked out on the most massive and militant scale and in Nestor Makhno it found its most resourceful interpreter. The Ukraine, almost as large as France, and one of the world's richest agricultural areas, had struggled for centuries against invasion—by Turks, Poles, Germans, Tsarist Russia. With their strong tradition of the *volnitza* (free life) the Ukrainians saw the Russians as a race of slaves, and the Russian and Jewish population of the towns as alien intruders.

Ukrainian nationalist propaganda was far more effective than Denikin's in seducing local Red Army recruits. 'Join us and clear the Ukraine of all these Trotskys, Rakovskys, and other speculators of the revolution,' ran a typical appeal. 'Re-establish the genuine rule of the Soviets. Help your brothers, who rebelled with rakes and pitchforks, and fight for land and liberty, for the genuine power of the workers. Down with the age-long bloodsuckers and enemies of the people ... Long live the Ukrainian Independent Soviet Republic!' Ataman Grigoriev, a partisan chief who fought with the Red Army for a time, deserted when ordered to invade Rumania in aid of the Hungarian revolution. His troops seized Elizavetgrad and Grigoriev issued a manifesto summoning the peasants to march on Kiev and Kharkov to overthrow the government of 'the adventurer Rakovsky' (Rakovsky, a Rumanian Jew, was the Bolshevik Governor of the Ukraine). Partisan pogroms could be as ferocious as those of Denikin's Cossacks. Trying to win over Tkachenko, a Red Army commander, Grigoriev wrote: 'Why do you stand up for the hook-nosed commissars? Let's take Odessa again and loot it so thoroughly that the place will be pulled to pieces.'

The constant ebb and flow of Whites, Reds, nationalists and freebooting partisans destroyed all respect for authority in the Ukraine. The only man capable of commanding widespread respect, and even affection, in this shambles was Makhno. His peasant hatred for the towns, his Ukrainian hatred for the Russian invaders, was lifted out of the rut of mere revenge by a genuine if fitful anarchist faith. Born in 1889 of a peasant family at Gulyai-Polye in south Ukraine, he had worked from the age of seven as cowherd, farm labourer and blacksmith. In 1905, when sixteen, he had been caught up in the wave of anarchism which swept the Ukraine. Instinctively distrusting 'pure' anarchism (with its subtle pacifism and excuses for inaction), he became an anarcho-communist. Two years later, during a peasant revolt, he was sentenced to life imprisonment for his part in the murder of a Tsarist police officer. In the Butyrky Prison, Moscow, he was often put in irons and in damp, cold punishment cells for chronic insubordination. He contracted tuberculosis. He also got the only education he ever had—from Peter Arshinov, a fervent and articulate anarchist carpenter.

Freed, with other political prisoners, in March 1917, Makhno hurried back to Gulyai-Polye to get the revolution rolling. He was elected chairman of the local Committee for the Defence of the Revolution, which allocated land, cattle and agricultural equipment to groups of ten peasant families. 'In every one of these communes,' wrote Makhno later, 'there were a few anarchist peasants, but most members were not anarchist. Yet they behaved with that anarchist solidarity of which only those are capable whose natural simplicity has not been corrupted by the political poison of the cities. For the cities always give out a stench of lying and betrayal.' Makhno and his colleagues had no set plans. They hoped that somehow the communes would grow and form the nucleus of an independent co-operative republic. In the midst of all this highly practical yet idyllically tinged activity the Bolshevik revolution passed almost unnoticed. It merely signified that the politicians of Petrograd and Moscow, after interminable talk, were trying to do what Gulyai-Polye had done already. Another government had come into being, which, like all governments, would come to the villages demanding food and soldiers. 'After we threw out the fool Nicky Romanov,' said the peasants, 'another fool took his place, but he had to go too. Who will now play the fool at our expense? The Lord Lenin?' Some, resigned to their fate, said: 'We cannot do without some fool. The towns have no other purpose than this.'

Makhno hated this fatalism. He set himself to rouse the peasants to fight any government which tried to play the fool at their expense. No one could have been better equipped for the task. Shortish and squat, bearlike in gait and strength, with a face expressive of cunning as well as bonhomie, Makhno was no ascetic taskmaster. He was the most riotous carouser of the whole countryside, and never missed an excuse for a giant binge and some random fornication. 'Batko (Little Father) got drunk again today' was a frequent entry in his long-suffering wife's diary. 'Talked very much. Wandered drunk along the street playing an accordeon and exchanging curses with everyone. Fell asleep after dancing and more talking.' But his revelries never impaired his energy, which, despite tuberculosis, was phenomenal. After an hour or two of sleep he was ready for the fields.

The Austro-German occupation of the Ukraine soon menaced his little enclave of peasant communalism. In spring 1918 he went to central Russia to see Bolshevism in action and get in touch with anarchist groups. He found anarchists disorganized and planless and heard Trotsky condemning them as a lot of gangsters. To Makhno, Moscow was 'the capital of the Paper Revolution', noisy with resolutions and slogans and nauseous with political fraud and double-talk. Prince Kropotkin, whom he asked for advice about how to lead an anarcho-communist revolution, stroked his long white beard and vaguely remarked that selflessness and integrity were important. Lenin was genial but patronizing. The anarchists were politically negligible, he said. The defence of the revolution required ruthless organization and an efficient army. In a chaotic area like the Ukraine anarchist partisans might for a time be useful—but only as 'speeders of the victory of communism'. From Lenin Makhno, though tongue-tied and awkward in the presence of the great man, got his advice—ruthless organization and an efficient army; and a clear warning that nonconformist allies would be tolerated only so long as the Red Army was too weak to do without them. Thus briefed—and provided, at Lenin's order, with a false identity and passport—Makhno slipped through the German lines and returned to Gulyai-Polye.

In the Ukraine, under the regime of Skoropadsky, restoration of estates to their former owners was in full swing. Gathering about him a band of peasant fighters, Makhno ambushed and slaughtered German patrols and stripped them of weapons, ammunition and uniforms. He used the uniforms to entice more patrols to death at point-blank range, and to gain entry to the landlords' mansions, where, at the height of convivial hospitality, his alcohol-proof warriors massacred the enemies of the people. As the news of his exploits spread, hundreds of recruits—peasants, factory hands, White and Red deserters, Russians, Jews and Greeks: all the weird revolutionary flotsam of the area—joined him. By September 1918 the Makhnovite Army was powerful enough to defeat a German division. Makhno, the idol of the peasants, could count on their support—on fresh horses, provisions, intelligence of enemy plans, complete secrecy about his own—despite savage reprisals. He worked out a technique of dispersing his army at moments of crisis. They would merge into the villages until the danger was over, then reassemble, arming themselves from stores that had been buried in remote spots, and reappear when they were least expected. In December 1918 a mixed force of Makhno partisans and Red Army troops captured Ekaterinoslav. Makhno, as was his invariable custom, released all prisoners and blew up the prison. He also paid off an old score by shooting the judge who, eleven years earlier, had sent him to jail. By January 1919 the Bolsheviks were glad to reach an agreement with the Makhnovites for common action against Denikin's forces ('the gold epaulettes' as Makhno contemptuously called them). For the next six months, Makhno's kingdom east of the Dnieper was completely controlled by his Revolutionary Insurgent Army. Once again, behind this shield of force (in itself a contradiction of anarchist principle—as was the use of conscription, which he justified on the ground that 'forced' men would not be shot by the Whites) he fostered his society of free peasant communes.

Consignments of grain were sent, as a fraternal gesture, to the

workers of Petrograd and Moscow. But the Ukrainian Soviet
government at Kharkov was ignored. The Makhnovites set up their
own regional Soviet of Workers, Peasants and Insurgents. V. M.
Eichenbaum (Voline), Peter Arshinov, and other leaders of the
Nabat (Tocsin) Confederation of Ukrainian Anarchist Organizations,
attached themselves to Makhno's headquarters and tried to play some
rôle in propaganda and policy-making. In April 1919 a Regional
Congress at Gulyai-Polye gathered delegates from seventy-two
districts representing more than two million people. Among other
things, it resolved to abolish police forces and law courts ('true
justice cannot be administratively organized, but must come as a
living, free, creative act of the community').

Makhno, until now referred to in *Pravda* as a 'champion of the
toiling masses', was cursed as the leader of a 'kulak' rebellion. A
telegram from Dybenko, the local Red Army chief, denounced the
congress as counter-revolutionary and outlawed its organizers.
Makhno's Revolutionary Military Council boldly retorted: 'Whose
interests should the revolution defend? Those of the party or those
of the people who set the revolution in motion with their blood?
If you and your like continue, "Comrade" Dybenko, to pursue this
kind of policy, if you believe it right, then carry your dirty little
business to its conclusion. Proclaim counter-revolutionary all those
who first raised the standard of revolt and social revolution in the
Ukraine, who acted without waiting for your permission ... Proclaim
illegal any congress called without your approval. But know that
the truth will in the end conquer force.'

The Makhnovite news-sheet, *The Road to Freedom*, edited by
Voline and Arshinov, offered further provocation. Trotsky was
dismissed as 'a man of limited qualities but immeasurable pride and
malevolence, a competent orator and polemicist who has become,
thanks to the miscarriage of the revolution, the "infallible" military
dictator of an immense area.' During the crisis of Grigoriev's
defection Trotsky, swallowing his pride, appealed to Makhno's
'revolutionary honour'. Makhno answered that the insurgent army
remained unchangeably faithful to the revolution of the peasants
and workers, 'but not to tools of violence like your commissars and
Chekas.' In May two Cheka agents were sent to murder Makhno.
Both were captured and shot. Trotsky was so maddened by this
insolent peasant challenge that he cut off supplies of arms and
ammunition in the hope that the Whites would 'eliminate this centre

of ideological opposition'. He damned the Makhnovite movement as petty-bourgeois counter-revolution, and sneered at the 'fantasy' of free workers' communes. 'It would', he reported to Moscow, 'be better to yield the whole Ukraine to Denikin, a straightforward counter-revolutionary who could easily be compromised later by means of class propaganda, while the Makhnovite devilry stirs the masses to their depths and rouses them against us.' His fury reached a climax when the Makhnovites invited the rank-and-file of the Red Army to send representatives to a congress of peasants, workers and insurgents in mid-June. The congress was forbidden, and Trotsky ordered that all delegates should be arrested immediately and brought before a revolutionary military tribunal.

He also demanded that, in view of the seriousness of Denikin's offensive, Makhno should surrender his command. Makhno bluffed. He allowed his men to merge with the Red Army, but instructed them to desert whenever he summoned them. He then rode off with a picked force of cavalry, crossed the Dnieper, recruited more partisans, wiped out Red and White garrisons impartially, and incited the peasants to form communes. Grigoriev, whom he regarded as a squalid adventurer with no feeling for 'the revolution', suggested that they should form an alliance. Makhno invited Grigoriev and his bodyguard to a banquet, got them drunk, shot them, and took over Grigoriev's army. In August he ordered his units with the Red Army to return. They came, bringing with them a large number of deserter-recruits and a welcome haul of weapons and ammunition. Makhno now had an army of some 20,000 men — four infantry brigades, one cavalry brigade, an artillery detachment, and a regiment equipped with 500 machine-guns. He launched an all-out attack on the Whites, thin on the ground and vulnerable due to the absence of most of Denikin's forces in the north.

After capturing several towns, the insurgents were defeated before Odessa. There followed a long retreat in sweltering autumn heat. The entire population of many villages, fleeing from the Whites, made it a veritable folk migration. Thousands of cattle enveloped Makhno's 'kingdom on wheels' (his infantry, as well as the villagers, travelled in peasant carts) in clouds of dust, through which, on the black Anarchist flags, gleamed slogans embroidered in silver — LIBERTY OR DEATH, THE LAND TO THE PEASANTS, THE FACTORIES TO THE WORKERS. At the end of September, having drawn the White army hundreds of miles westwards in exhausting pursuit punctuated by fierce rearguard actions, Makhno suddenly counter-attacked. Using a favourite trick, he left part of his army in front of the enemy as a decoy, then flung his fast-moving cavalry and infantry (in carts mounted with machine-guns) into a double outflanking movement which ended in a devastating onslaught from the rear. In a four-week recoil offensive, the Makhnovites swept south towards their commander's native steppes, taking, in quick succession, Berdiansk, Alexandrovsk, Nikopol, Mariupol, and, late in October, Ekaterinoslav, Denikin's former headquarters and the largest town of south central Ukraine.

In their wake they left a rubble of dynamited prisons and police stations. They tore down telegraph poles and wrecked railway stations — symbols to them of the hated tyranny of the towns. They shot landlords, rich peasants (kulaks) and priests, and gave away their lands. They issued paper money on which was printed the information that no one would be prosecuted for forging it. Morale, in those last three months of 1919, was sky-high. As a result of their victories, the Makhnovites had added fifty field guns, four armoured trains, four armoured cars, 1,000 machine-guns, 3,000 cavalry, and perhaps 15,000 infantry to their original strength. They now mustered a force more than equal to the average Soviet army on the southern front. They were convinced that they would soon finish off the Whites, shatter the Reds, and surge westward to plant free communes all over Europe.

With such a noble prospect opening, Voline and the other camp-following anarchist intellectuals hoped that Makhno would make an effort to reform his way of life. They were sadly disappointed. Makhno's personal courage and popularity were unlimited. When ill (he nearly died of typhus), or, as several times happened, severely wounded, he insisted on being carried in a cart with the vanguard of his army until he was well enough to ride a horse. He fought and worked until he dropped — and a few hours later shook his sleeping officers awake. He lived like a peasant and was always accessible to the peasants, ready to talk or drink with them or help with the harvest flailing. He despised anti-semitism, and personally shot a soldier found chalking DOWN WITH THE JEWS on a wall. He even made a Jew the head of his private Cheka (an anarchist army was bad enough: but oh, Kropotkin! an anarchist Cheka!). No former Tsarist officers were allowed to hold posts of command, nor anyone of bourgeois background. Looting was strictly forbidden, and many insurgents were shot for disobeying this veto. A system of anarchist commissars, elected by the rank and file, was instituted. Officers were mostly elected, and nominated officers with whom the men were dissatisfied were transferred to other commands. Drunkenness and gambling were officially taboo.

But Makhno himself and his military clique ignored the resolutions of the Revolutionary Military Council. They did, in fact, as they pleased. 'Under the influence of drink,' complained Voline, 'Makhno became irresponsible ... personal caprice, often supported by violence, replaced his sense of revolutionary duty; the despotism, the absurd pranks, the dictatorial antics, of a warrior chief ... replaced the calm reflection, perspicacity, personal dignity and self-control ... which a man in his position should never have abandoned ... Another failing of Makhno and many of his close associates was their attitude towards women. Especially when intoxicated, they could not refrain from behaviour that was improper —disgusting would often be the correct adjective—amounting almost to orgies in which certain women were obliged to participate.'

The Makhnovite movement was too much a welter of improvisation, too busy enclosing its transient jewels of peasant libertarianism in a setting of partisan bayonets, to show if it could have achieved any lasting social revolution. Makhno set little store by formal education, probably regarding it as sufficient if his communards were gradually permeated by a handful of convinced anarchists with the few ideas that were necessary—a distrust of all politicians and all attempts at government from the towns, a belief in their own ability and right to manage their own lives, a determination to die rather than yield that right. Voline and Arshinov submitted plans for schools free of state or church influence, to be owned by the peasants and run on libertarian lines. But Makhno barely tolerated his theoreticians. They were useful for drafting proclamations and arranging meetings and rubbing up a townee kind of gloss which seemed to impress some people. But he had no more real respect for them than had Stalin for Bolshevik sophists like Radek and Bukharin, or Kolchak and Denikin for Menshevik and Social Revolutionary hair-splitters. True, Arshinov had given him some good ideas, but they would have *remained* ideas if it had not been for him and his fighters. These intellectuals completely lacked the common touch, though most of them were of working-class origin. If that was

what book-learning did for a man, of what use was it? At the fourth
Makhnovite Congress in June, some villagers had raised difficulties.
Settling everything by fraternal discussion might be fine in theory,
but what of human nature? If a bridge or a road between two
villages needed mending, who was going to do it? How would the
matter be settled? Makhno would have knocked a few heads
together and helped to do the job himself. Voline loftily and
incomprehensibly declared that for anarchists there was 'no such
thing as determined possibility or determined impossibility'.

Much as Makhno and his followers would have liked to blow up
not only prisons and police stations but whole towns, they had to
admit that these blots on the landscape had come to stay. The
socialists had to depend on the peasants for food and cannon-fodder.
The Makhnovites had to depend on the towns and their factories for
the sophisticated weapons with which they defended their primitive
ideals. Some kind of bargain had to be struck. But how? The first
necessity was to impress on the townspeople that *this* army was
different: that it did not loot, or massacre Jews, or intend to set up
a military dictatorship. The threat of the firing squad was used to
put the far from saintly partisans on their best behaviour. The
intellectuals were set to work composing a proclamation that was
plastered on the walls of each captured city. 'Workers! Your city is
for the present occupied by the Revolutionary Insurgent (Makhnovite) Army. This does not serve any political party. On the contrary,
it seeks to free the region of all political power ... It strives to protect
the freedom of action of the workers against all exploitation and
domination. Workers and peasants, understand straight away that
the Makhnovites can only help by giving opinions or advice ... They
cannot, and in any case will not, govern or prescribe for you in any
way.'

Social Revolutionaries, L.S.R.s, Mensheviks and Bolsheviks were
allowed freedom of speech and publication: but Bolshevik agitators
were told to 'go and take up some honest trade rather than seek to
tyrannize over the workers.' At a regional congress held in Alexandrovsk in October an attempt was made to create free organizations
of industrial workers. It was not a success. The workers were
frightened by what amounted to an order to be anarchistically free –
at a time when they knew that the town would probably be recaptured
first by Whites, then by Reds, in a matter of weeks. They were
mainly concerned with their wages, which had not been paid for

months. Makhno lost all patience with these helpless weaklings, always expecting someone to pay them or think for them. 'Organize yourselves properly and decide what your wages should be,' he told them. Angered by heckling from S.R.s, L.S.R.s, Mensheviks and Bolsheviks, he roared that they were 'nothing but bourgeois mongrels' and deserved a dictatorship.

Makhno was as baffled by the cities as the Bolsheviks by the villages. Alexandrovsk and Ekaterinoslav were evacuated without reluctance when, in December 1919, the retreating Whites and pursuing Reds came south again. The Bolsheviks thanked the Makhnovites for their 'heroism' in conquering the southern Ukraine for the revolution, but ordered them to the Polish front. Makhno refused, and was again outlawed. The peasant anarchists prepared to face the undivided wrath of authoritarian socialism, the full weight of the revenge of the cities of the north. They met the challenge with great courage and resourcefulness. But Makhno's time of glory was over: the time when he had put into practice, crudely, fleetingly but effectively, what Social Revolutionary, Kropotkinist and Tolstoyan intellectuals preached – and had created, wherever he could carve out a space, those peasant communes which they had seen as the ideal basis for a healthy socialistic society. While the anarchists of Moscow could do no more than refuse to collaborate with Bolshevism in any way (or issue vague proclamations about the whole earth belonging to all the peoples), Makhno had forged an anarchist army and an anarchist republic. He was the Caliban of peasant actuality which pure anarchists could not bear to contemplate or stop trying to make respectable.

2. *Il Comandante*

In Italy violence was in the air. But the great storm awaited by the Third International did not break. The Socialists for the most part contented themselves with revolutionary phrase-making and preparations for a prolonged siege of bourgeois democracy. Fascism, still a negligible force, flopped in the November elections. Mussolini and Marinetti were jailed for causing armed disturbances. The Socialists gained the largest number of seats, but were run close by the newly formed Catholic Popular Party, which easily outbid them for peasant support. Since the Socialists had committed themselves to a policy of non-collaboration with bourgeois parties, the result was to leave the old liberal gang of Francesco Nitti and Giovanni Giolitti in possession.

The prospect of such stagnation appalled Marinetti. 'Put the artists in power!' he wrote in a manifesto composed in prison. 'They will solve the problem of well-being in the only way in which it can be solved—spiritually. They will magnify a hundredfold the capacity to dream. Thanks to them the time will come when life will no longer be a drudgery of bread and work, nor a drudgery of philistine leisure, but a conscious, daring work of art. Every man will live his best possible romance.'

The one person capable of making a revolution in Italy was in fact, an artist. Gabriele d'Annunzio, ageing boudoir buccaneer, theatrical war hero, and arch-anti-philistine, combined a charismatic gift of leadership with a contempt for party politicians and a talent for invective as powerful as Marinetti's and a good deal more personal. The so-called statesmen of the Entente reminded him, he wrote, of waxwork imitations of humanity. 'Fighters,' cried d'Annunzio, 'we have fought; workers, we have worked; citizens, we have suffered and resisted—only to find ourselves today covered with this heap of filth which cannot even serve as manure for the nation's cabbage.'

If there was one mood which most Italians, of whatever political orientation, shared in 1919, it was a mood of frustrated nationalism,

The Paris Peace Conference had agreed to the restoration of the 'lost lands' of Trentino (containing some 250,000 Germans) and Trieste. But, with Woodrow Wilson prominent, it had refused to 'honour' the clauses of the 1915 Secret Treaty of London which had promised Italy large sections of the Dalmatian coast, excluding the port of Fiume, as a reward for her military alliance. At the end of the war the Dalmatian coast, as far north as Fiume, had been occupied by the Yugoslavs. Fiume itself had been taken over by an Inter-Allied Commission of French, British, American and Italian troops, pending the decision of the Big Four. Wilson, however, had made no secret of his belief that both Dalmatia and Fiume should be Yugoslav, and had addressed an Appeal to the Italian people, urging them to show their nobility by foregoing the ill-gotten gains which their corrupt leaders were demanding. This move had the effect of inflaming public opinion, already worked upon by d'Annunzio, against the American Tartuffe. He was burned in effigy in the streets, ranted at and consigned to perdition by dozens of nationalist and fascist orators and journalists. 'The greatest humiliation,' said Ardengo Soffici, a fascist writer, 'after the vogue of German ware among us, is that of seeing Europe today at the mercy of the Anglo-Saxon race. To see Italy and France, the ancient lords of the earth, eternal emanators of the sunlight of civilization, begetters of ideas, social patterns and civil customs—of all that is great and glorious in the world, hanging on the lips of big nobodies and of savages barely civilized, of the Welsh attorney and the Presbyterian Wilson! No! For my racial pride this is worse than the toad which Chamfort had to swallow every morning!'

Until the end of the war Fiume had acted as the port for Budapest. Italian settlers, amounting to nearly half the total population, had not begun to go there until the 1890s, as minor officials in the Habsburg bureaucracy. While they formed a majority in the old town, the industrial suburbs were almost wholly Yugoslav (Croat). Since there was no other good or adequately equipped port on the Dalmatian coast, Fiume was obviously vital to the economy of the new Yugoslav state. Such arguments, however, did not count with d'Annunzio. As early as 1915, swooping over Dalmatia in an aeroplane, he had dropped this message on the coastal town of Zara: 'Oh believe in the joy of your second spring, when the Corinthian acanthus will flower again and twine around your Latin columns!' To him it was unthinkable that ignorant Slavs should rule a country which owed such architectural beauty and historic interest as it possessed to the empire-builders of Ancient Rome. Ethnographic and economic statistics were so much impertinent nonsense beside Italy's spiritual right to her former domain.

It was, he considered, his duty to create a focus for heroic values. He, who had always lived beyond his financial, physical and spiritual income, would teach all Italians to do the same. Like Nestor Makhno, d'Annunzio dreamed of recreating a golden pre-capitalist age; like Makhno, though at a more sophisticated, Byronic level, he united the libertine and the libertarian in his own person; like Makhno, he set out on his greatest adventure in the autumn of 1919. Peasants figured somewhat mistily in the poet's vision. His ideal was a city state which would combine the virtues of classical Athens and Rome and Renaissance Florence. There beauty would be truth, truth beauty; a new civilization, a world centre for a rebel 'proletariat of creators', would be brought into being; and the beards of the 'three old idiots, Lloyd George, Clemenceau and Wilson' (none of them had beards, but what of that?) would be hilariously pulled. D'Annunzio's golden age, like Makhno's, was mythical. But then he had always believed that man did not live by facts alone.

For some months d'Annunzio had been in touch with rebellious army officers. In September he moved to Venice, which was to be the assembly point for his expedition. Having, partly on the strength of his wartime exploits, partly in the hope of keeping him quiet, been offered the post of General Director of Civil Aeronautics, he gave out that he was preparing for an epoch-making flight to Tokyo. At dawn on September 10th, wearing the uniform of a lieutenant-colonel of the Novara Lancers and a pair of dark glasses (he had damaged his right eye in 1916 when thrown against a machine-gun during a bumpy landing) he set out in a car filled with flowers at the head of a convoy of three hundred volunteers. They were joined on the way to Trieste by other contingents, notably four hundred Sardinian grenadiers. At 11 o'clock on the morning of September 12th, General Pittaluga, the Italian Military Governor of Fiume, was informed that an expeditionary force of about a thousand men had entered the city. Hurrying to the spot, he apologetically explained to d'Annunzio that as an Allied official it was his duty, and that of the machine-gunners he had brought along, to resist such usurpation. D'Annunzio whipped open his greatcoat, revealing a tunic loaded with gold, silver and bronze medals, and an Officer's Grand Cross of the Savoy Military Order, and said: 'Fire first on these!' General Pittaluga burst into tears and embraced the usurper. 'I cannot', he sobbed, 'be the cause of spilling Italian blood.' The machine-gunners, too, wept with emotion, and joined the liberators. In a delirium of hurled blossoms, cries of '*Viva Fiume Italiana!*', and carnival cheers, d'Annunzio entered into his kingdom, the very apotheosis of his life-style. In the governor's palace the General and the Rebel drank to *Fiume Italiana* in goblets of vermouth. From a balcony, President Grossich proclaimed that 'by the inflexible will of the people' the city had been delivered to 'Gabriele d'Annunzio, that hero of heroes, that great Soldier-Poet.'

Nearly all the Italian soldiers in Fiume went over to d'Annunzio. His own legionaries stood guard at crossroads and in front of banks and public buildings. The crews of Italian naval ships in the harbour locked their officers up until they agreed to make common cause with the 'true' Italians. French, British and American troops, under orders to avoid 'incidents', stayed in their barracks. On September 14th, given full military honours by the legionaries, they marched out of Fiume, and d'Annunzio occupied the former Allied headquarters. Many among the crowd in the piazza fell on their knees as he kissed the Italian tricolour and told them: 'In this mad and vile world today, Fiume is the symbol of Liberty.'

The Italian revolution had begun.

Il Commandante, as he called himself, was an old if indomitable fifty-six. It was not only that he had lost an eye. Nearly forty years of being a rebel, of sustaining the role of Gabriele d'Annunzio (even the name was an invention), had taken a heavy toll. Capponcina, the mansion near Florence where he lived during his stormy affair with Eleonora Duse, had resembled a cross between a bizarre chapel and a barbarian chief's loot-strewn fortress. The walls were painted in various shades of gold, the windows glowed with fifteenth-century stained glass. Rare psalters and works of devotion stood side by side with recherché pornography, all exquisitely bound and gilt. Fine tapestries and rich velvets, altar tables, religious statues and paintings, skulls and mummified feet, heady scents (often concocted by d'Annunzio himself), made the place a mad, rambling shrine of dogged decadence. Twenty servants, thirty borzois, a stable of thoroughbred horses, and hundreds of pigeon-doves had completed the setting. To keep in physical shape d'Annunzio fenced and did dumb-bell exercises each day in his private gymnasium. But by 1919 the slim, olive-skinned youth with the profusion of curly chestnut-coloured hair had become a paunchy roué with bad teeth, one artificial and one watery and protuberant eye, and a blotchy complexion. He was also completely bald as the result of a duel with a journalist who had described him as 'an elegant provincial, dissolute by design'. The physician in attendance, seeing blood pouring from a cut on d'Annunzio's head, had poured a whole bottle of ferrous perchlorate over the wound, destroying the capillary bulbs.

Nothing, though, could destroy his sense of destiny. He had studied in minute detail the life of Cola di Rienzo, his favourite historical character and the inspiration of his attempt to force Italy to be great. Born in 1313 the son of a Roman innkeeper and a washer-woman, Cola di Rienzo had, by virtue of his brilliant gifts as an orator, been appointed an apostolic notary by the Pope. Appalled by the state of Rome—its churches and classical buildings crumbling from neglect, government made impossible by endless vendettas between nobles and their private armies—Cola, himself a great collector of antiquities, had become obsessed by the desire to resurrect its ancient glory. For a short time, by sheer force of personality and flamboyant mystique, he had succeeded in establishing a kind of dictatorship. He had designed his own banner, devised gorgeous pageants, clothed his followers in splendid uniforms, written many magniloquent proclamations, given himself ever more sonorous and high-flown titles, inaugurated a new calendar starting with Year One of the Restoration of the Roman Republic, and believed that he was a second Christ. He had created the illusion of living in an age of wonder in which time and enemies could be defied by heraldry, pageantry and heroic eloquence.

Gabriele d'Annunzio set out to repeat Cola di Rienzo's magic. His legionaries wore black shirts with a skull-and-crossbones emblem, carried daggers in their belts, and saluted Roman-style with extended right arms. Volunteers who came to Fiume would find Il Comandante on his knees, his head bowed in prayer, to receive and conse-crate them. A Fiuman national anthem was composed. The words ITALIA O LA MORTE were traced in vast letters in a square, filled with citizens, and photographed from the air. The photograph was sent to Paris as living proof of the popular will of the city. D'Annunzio shut himself up for eighteen hours at a stretch in his study in the governor's palace. Clad in a monkish gown ('I have just seen him in his poet's uniform,' reported one awestruck youth), he composed appeals, manifestoes and speeches which were translated into several languages and broadcast by his own private International.

Fiume began to resemble Marinetti's theatre of futurism, with d'Annunzio as chief impresario and leading actor. Almost daily crowds, who had been taught to give the Roman salute and to chant in unison 'Eia! Eia! Alala!' (a cry which, according to d'Annunzio, had been used by Achilles to spur the horses of his chariot), filled the piazza in front of the palace, waiting for him to appear on the balcony. From there, in what he considered a democratic dialogue between governor and governed, he hurled taunts at the rest of the world, and especially at Wilson and Nitti. 'On one side the man from across the Atlantic, with his hard jaw, florid face and flat feet: on the other the man of Lucca, continually doing violence to his fatness and shortness of breath by bending down to lick the said flat feet.' The greed and hypocrisy of Britain, that nation of shopkeepers, was another target. 'That voracious empire,' he ranted, 'which has seized Persia, Mesopotamia, Arabia and most of Africa ... which is eyeing Constantinople, gradually swallowing up China, daily buying more islands in the Pacific.' Was the Free State of Fiume to join those other lands – Ireland, Egypt and India – 'spiritually murdered' by Britain? It had been suggested that the League of Nations should take over Fiume, but what was it but another instrument of British perfidy? D'Annunzio proposed to found a League of Oppressed Nations, and had, he said, written to Sir Eric Drummond, the newly appointed General Secretary of the League, to tell him that Fiume was the symbol of a sacred crusade against Britain.

Foreign press reactions to d'Annunzio's coup ranged from the solemn to the flippant. The Allies, lectured *The Times*, could not tolerate it without openly abdicating their authority. A 'triumph of lawlessness in the Adriatic' would be followed by 'reckless and criminal adventures from the Baltic to the Black Sea'. The London *Nation* blamed President Wilson for his choice of Fiume, with its 45,000 inhabitants, for a showdown after 'permitting wrongs that affected many millions at other corners of the map to pass without protest'. But the absurd choice had been made, and if the Supreme Council failed to make its will respected in Fiume, it would transfer its authority to the League of Nations 'in a condition so maimed that the experiment of international government will resemble an attempt by a rider with a paralysed hand to pretend that he is guiding his horse'.

The New York *Nation* applauded d'Annunzio's impertinence. 'Into a sordid and unhappy world he brings joyous colour, adventure, romance, a readiness for self-immolation and a typically Italian appreciation of what he is doing. In his own estimation he is Cyrano de Bergerac and the Three Musketeers rolled into one. He may not be a hero to his valet, but he is to himself. If he does not become a movie hero we shall miss our guess.'

On October 12th d'Annunzio celebrated the thirtieth day of the Holy Entry into Fiume with pageantry, fireworks and speeches, and three days later launched his thousandth manifesto. He had not yet inaugurated a new calendar, like Cola de Rienzo, but he would have nothing to do with prosaic measurements of time. When an associate remarked, 'We have now been in Fiume for two months,' d'Annunzio corrected him — 'Not so, my friend! We have been in Fiume for sixty days of passion and sixty nights of anguish!'

By then he was perfecting plans for a raid on Zara, the capital of Dalmatia, which also had a large Italian population, and was under temporary Italian trusteeship. On November 14th he left Fiume in a destroyer, followed by Vice-Admiral Millo with three other destroyers and a thousand legionaries. Shouting through a megaphone 'I, Gabriele d'Annunzio, Comandante of Fiume, am going to Zara!' he had no difficulty in slipping his task-force past the idle curiosity of the blockading fleet, and presented Admiral Millo to an ecstatic crowd as the first Governor of Italian Dalmatia. Firing off nothing more lethal than a terse proclamation ('Fellow citizens! D'Annunzio is here. No need for words. Go on weeping for joy. Dalmatia is joined for ever to Italy!'), and leaving behind about five hundred legionaries, he swept back to base — to discuss plans for further raids on Spalato, Cattaro and Antivari.

His *chef de cabinet*, Major Domenico Giurati, was dispatched to Rome where, in an exchange of notes, he rejected Nitti's proposal to occupy Fiume with regular troops on the 'solemn understanding' that the government would 'not accept any solution of the problem which would separate the commune of Fiume from the territory of Italy'. Giurati had been instructed to demand 'annexation pure and simple', not only of Fiume but of Zara and other centres under temporary Italian or Allied occupation. Giurati carried out his instructions, but he, Millo, and several other senior officers, alarmed by d'Annunzio's whirlwind methods, resigned. Encouraged by their action the Fiuman National Council voted in favour of an official occupation. D'Annunzio riposted by ordering a plebiscite, in the course of which the ballot boxes were seized by *arditi*. Fiume did not know how to liberate itself from its Liberator, who claimed to act by divine inspiration, dreamed of 'living for ever the life of a rebel', and talked of bringing his sword to the aid of rebels in Ireland, Egypt, India and Arabia. His sentiments and actions, said *The Times*, were incomprehensible to any sane person. 'His psychology is all in this reflection, made the other day to a friend: "It would be sad if this marvellous Middle Age should end."'

Most alarming of all, indications were multiplying that d'Annunzio, despite his medievalism, was far from being an ultra-conservative; signs that he was not only a mountebank, but a Red mountebank. In 1904, during a short appearance in the Italian Parliament, he had protested against the boredom of Giolitti's government by taking his seat among the socialist deputies, who at least, he said, had a semblance of life. As ruler of Fiume he proposed to open relations with the Bolsheviks, and was in touch with militant socialists and anarchists. Captain Giuletti, Secretary of the Federation of Marine Labour, re-routed more than one ship (loaded with stores and armaments for Denikin) from Novorossisk to Fiume, and connived with d'Annunzio's pirate fleet in the capture of several merchant vessels with useful food cargoes. He also put d'Annunzio in contact with Nicola Bombacci (then a left-wing Marxist who favoured armed rebellion) and Errico Malatesta, an active anarchist since the 1870s, who had just returned to Italy after a long exile. Malatesta considered that the time was as ripe as it ever would be for revolution, and that Fiume might be as good a starting point as any. He, Giuletti, Bombacci and d'Annunzio discussed a march on Rome to be followed by the dissolution of Parliament, the abolition of the Papacy, and the proclamation of a republic with d'Annunzio as President.

As Il Comandante's conservative supporters peeled off, Fiume fizzed with flamboyant radicalism. Idealistic young men formed themselves into libertarian groups which met each evening in their favourite cafés. One of the largest—the Union of Free Spirits Tending Towards Perfection Under the Sign of the Yogi—took as its themes the abolition of money, the ideal fraternal army, the embellishment of life, and free love. Legionaries planned to invite the Red Army to join them in an invasion of Europe that would destroy 'the bourgeois-industrial blight' and replace it with 'the spiritual civilization of Fiume'.

D'Annunzio's personal secretary and political adviser, Alceste de Ambris, was a former anarcho-syndicalist. The two collaborated on a constitution which envisaged compulsory physical training of the young, generous old-age pensions, a magnificently progressive educational system, aesthetic instruction in depth, and unstinting unemployment relief. There were to be six categories of workers and employers, reminiscent of the medieval guilds of Florence, embracing all aspects of commercial life. A College of Ediles was to 'preside over the Beauty of the City' in art, architecture and pageantry. Choirs, orchestras and public fanfares were to be organized at the expense of the state. D'Annunzio refused to recognize ownership as 'the absolute dominion of the person over the thing'. Only 'constant producers of the common wealth, constant creators of the common power' were to be accepted as citizens of the republic. Though the Army of Liberation would keep an orthodox system of grades, there was to be an Army Council consisting of representatives of all ranks with equal voting and debating rights.

D'Annunzio had emerged as the last hope of libertarian revolt, as (in Lenin's words) 'the only real revolutionary in Italy'. He had mesmerized a whole population, and had put himself, in his late and physically ruinous middle age, at the head of a rebellion of 'flaming youth'. It was a fantastic achievement: and it began to look as though, beneath his magic barrage of bombast, Fiume would continue to lead a charmed existence, and that he himself would die in his bed rather than on the barricades. 'Fiumanism', said the *Testa di Ferro*, the legionaries' weekly news-sheet, 'is no longer just a name. It is a precise and palpitating fact. At last we have a great and clear mission in the world. We are the advance guard of all nations on their march to the future. We are the island of wonder which will carry its incandescence to continents stifled in the darkness of brutal commerce. We are a handful of illuminated beings who sow throughout the world seeds of beautiful revolt, a revolt which is purely Italian and will germinate into the most violent and magnificent blossoms ... Republic? Monarchy? Names are of no interest to us. All institutions are worm-eaten and must be utterly renewed.

All the ancient faiths are discredited, all the old formulae are smashed. We shall put our faith in and obey no man but our sole and superb leader, Gabriele d'Annunzio, who has given to Fiume the political constitution which will be best suited to the City of the Holocaust.'

Gliding like a comet above the sad wreckage of Marxist revolution in Europe, went d'Annunzio's favourite dictum: 'Every insurrection is an attempt at creation.'

VI

LAST RECKONINGS

---

1. *The Strange Calvary of Woodrow Wilson*

Italian workers in the United States clubbed together to send money
—and a gold-hilted sword—to the bourgeois-baiter in Fiume. Few
of them indulged in any nonconformist attitudes on their own
account, for in America any hint of insurrection was viewed as an act
of criminal sedition.

Early in June 1919 a series of mysterious explosions, attributed to
anarchists, occurred almost simultaneously in eight places. One of the
targets was the home of Attorney-General A. Mitchell Palmer in
Washington, D.C. Palmer—'the Fighting Quaker', as he liked to be
called—was quick to propose more stringent anti-radical laws, and
easily persuaded Congress to finance an all-out Red hunt to be
organized by a special Anti-Radical Division set up in the Federal
Bureau of Investigation under the direction of J. Edgar Hoover.
Palmer was not without zealous rivals. On June 12th a committee
to investigate 'the scope, tendencies and ramifications of seditious
activities in New York', chaired by State Senator Clayton R. Lusk,
had started work. Within a few weeks, strong-arm raids had been
carried out on the Soviet Russian Bureau in the World Tower
Building and the Rand Socialist School. The Lusk Committee
claimed that there was ample evidence of rampant Bolshevism among
the workers, that more than fifty radical publications were read
by at least 500,000 potential revolutionaries in New York City
alone, and that preparations for a Bolshevik revolution were well
advanced.

The threat of a nation-wide general strike, set for July 4th, to
force the release of Thomas Mooney (a construction worker
imprisoned for life in 1916 for his alleged part in a San Francisco
bombing which had killed nine people), was presented as the third
instalment of the Seattle-Winnipeg sequence. In New York 11,000

policemen and detectives kept a 24-hour watch on federal, state and county buildings: also on the Stock Exchange and the homes of prominent citizens. Hundreds of special deputies were sworn. Two companies of regular army troops were drafted into Chicago, where the entire police force, reinforced by a thousand volunteers, was on duty. Federal agents were stationed thickly all over the Pacific North-west to thwart a rumoured I.W.W. 'rising'. In California the authorities jailed hundreds of known or suspected Reds.

The fact that there was nothing more explosive than Independence Day fireworks did not cool the fever of the Red-hunters. Only a massive show of strength, they claimed, had forced the Reds to postpone their attempt. But the danger was still there. The Nineteenth Amendment, granting votes to women, was attacked in the Senate as part of the cancer of Bolshevism that was spreading over the land. The American Legion got busy with drumhead courts-martial on local 'radicals', who were clubbed, kicked, punched and otherwise brutally run out of town. Its favourite slogan, LEAVE THE REDS TO THE LEGION, and the knowledge of what it meant in physical pain and commercial ruin, frightened many people into cancelling subscriptions to black-listed journals and clearing their bookshelves of obnoxious literature. Karl Marx was joined by Henry Thoreau, Benjamin Tucker, Ralph Waldo Emerson, and even Walt Whitman in a furtive burning or burying of dangerous evidence.

On August 26th, 49-year-old Mrs Fannie Sellins, an organizer for the United Mineworkers, tried to intervene when some drunken deputy sheriffs opened fire on a picket line of striking miners employed by the Allegheny Steel Company at West Natrona. She was clubbed to the ground and shot. A deputy crushed in her skull with a cudgel. The corpse was dragged by the heels and flung into the back of a truck, together with the body of a dead miner. No attempt was made to prosecute the murderers. The business community was solidly behind the steel companies. Customers assured their suppliers that if it came to a showdown, they would gladly wait a year or more for delivery. The important thing was that no concessions should be made to the unions.

At about the same time as Mrs Sellins was being murdered in West Natrona, James H. Maurer, Chairman of the Old Age Pension Commission of the State of Pennsylvania, who had been officially authorized to travel to Europe to study pension systems, was being hauled off his ship just before sailing time by federal agents. The Department of Justice had turned up a letter in which Maurer had mentioned that he was glad to have the chance to study 'Bolshevism' at first hand.

Maurer was an out-and-out conservative: but state and federal authorities were by now as oblivious to sober facts as d'Annunzio or Zinoviev. The American labour movement was crippled by feuds between moderates and militants, and even the militants were split. In Chicago at the beginning of September about 70,000 of the Socialist Party's 100,000 members peeled off to form separate communist parties. The Communist Labour Party, led by John Reed, Benjamin Gitlow and William B. Lloyd (a millionaire's son), represented the American-born element. It captured only 10,000 of the rebels. At a separate convention the rest—almost all members of the Russian, Latvian, Estonian, Lithuanian, Polish, Ukrainian, Hungarian and Yugoslav federations—formed the American Communist Party under the leadership of Louis Fraina and Charles Ruthenberg. They regarded the Communist Labour Party as a collection of bourgeois *déclassés* who had exaggerated ideas of their own importance. The rump of the Socialist Party, headed by Morris Hillquit (that object of Trotsky's scorn) and Victor Berger, proclaimed: 'We are the party. The others are only a lot of anarchists.'

The Chicago squabble provided ample evidence of weakness and self-stultification. But politicians and journalists seized on the fact that John Reed's supporters had met in the I.W.W. hall, and that Fraina's faction had named the hall in which it met the Smolny Institute. They quoted a 'blasphemous' communiqué in which Debs referred to Jesus Christ as 'the great Divine Tramp who never had a dime, but who understood and loved the common folk'. They featured a speech in which Reed had attacked the notion that a socialist majority in Congress or State legislatures would have any real effect on the balance of power. 'If you had a socialist President,' he argued, 'the Supreme Court would still come to the defence of Capital. If you had a socialist Supreme Court, J. P. Morgan would organize a White Guard and the interests of capital would still be protected. So it will always be. The struggle is between economic forces and cannot be settled on the political field.' Wasn't this clear evidence that the Reds were thinking in terms of civil war and a bloody attack on existing institutions? The A.F.L. might plead innocence, but its real function was to act as a respectable front for the Bolsheviks of industry.

When, on September 19th, the Boston police force, after months of fruitless negotiation with Police Commissioner Edwin Curtis, struck in support of its demand to affiliate to the A.F.L. (as police in other cities had done), the furore was tremendous. Bolshevism, squealed the Boston *Herald*, was attempting to rock the very cradle of American democracy. Minor riots and looting in the unpoliced city were described as worse than anything in Petrograd in 1917. Five thousand State Guards joined a volunteer force of Legionnaires, businessmen and Harvard students to 'save the situation'. Three rioters were shot, and Calvin Coolidge, the deservedly obscure Governor of Massachusetts, acquired sudden fame with his 'tough' telegram to Gompers — 'There is no right to strike against the public safety by anybody, anywhere, any time.' He and Curtis were praised for quelling a Soviet revolution. LENIN AND TROTSKY ARE ON THEIR WAY, warned the *Wall Street Journal*. 'Bolshevism in the United States is no longer a spectre,' croaked the *Philadelphia Public Ledger*. 'Boston in chaos reveals its sinister substance.' When Harold Laski, then teaching history at Harvard, and celebrated for his (as yet) non-Marxist radicalism, accused Curtis of deliberately provoking the strike, he was violently criticized. What right had an Englishman — a Jew at that — to interfere? 'Ours is an American city, not a polyglot boarding house,' said the Boston *Evening Transcript*. 'Is Mr Laski an instructor in American or Soviet government? The parents of the sons entrusted to his care are entitled to know. The followers, from Maine to California, of Straight Americanism, will, we think, insist upon knowing.' Hauled before the Committee of the Board of Overseers of the University, the delinquent tutor was asked: 'Mr Laski, do you believe in bloody revolution?' 'Mr Wigglesworth,' was his reply, 'do I *look* as if I did?'

At Cleveland the United Mineworkers' Convention, defying John L. Lewis and the official leadership, demanded a six-hour day, a five-day week, wage increases of up to a hundred per cent, and the nationalization of the mining industry. It also talked in terms of an alliance with the transport unions, notably the Railway Brotherhoods — which had prepared a plan for public ownership of the railroads. Since the name of the lawyer who had drafted it was Plumb, the project was inevitably described as 'Plumb Bolshevistic ... a plan which might well have been formulated by Lenin', and 'a bold, naked attempt to sovietize the railroads of this country'.

Emma Goldman and Alexander Berkman, the Russian-born anarchists, released from two years' hard labour, were immediately hauled before the Immigration Bureau to show cause why they should not be deported. 'Every human being', said Emma Goldman in a written statement, 'is entitled to hold any opinion without becoming liable to prosecution' (her own opinions had led her to attack the state, oppose the war, and champion birth control and the rights of homosexuals). 'The object of deportation and the anti-anarchist law is to stifle the voice of the people ... to exile those who do not fit into the scheme of things which our industrial lords are so anxious to perpetuate ... With all the intensity of my being I protest against the conspiracy of imperialist capitalism against the life and liberty of the American people.'

There had been a time when President Wilson had believed that politics and big business could be, and should be, separated; when he, or at least his liberal-minded investigators, had said that in the battle between management and labour, labour often had justice on its side. He may have seen the enormous report compiled by his Industrial Relations Commission. He may have glanced at the impassioned testimony of Bill Haywood. 'There is a class struggle in society ... this struggle will go on in spite of anything that this commission can do or anything that you may recommend to Congress. I dream that there will be a new society some time, in which there will be no political government, no states, and Congress will not be composed of preachers and lawyers as it is now ... but of experts in the different branches of industry, who will consider the welfare of all the people and discuss how the machine can be made the slave of the people instead of a part of the people being made the slaves of machinery and of the owners of machinery.' But, being a lawyer and a preacher, Wilson thought in terms of more commissions, of conferences at which mutual adjustments would be made, more Wilsonian sermons preached, and the Morgans and Haywoods of this world so imbued with the spirit of rational brotherliness that they would be indistinguishable from each other save by such accidents as their clothes and their bank accounts.

Soon after his return to Washington early in July, he called for an industrial peace conference at which both 'sides' would state their case. But he made no attempt to moderate the actions of Mitchell Palmer or to release Eugene Debs or any of the political prisoners who crowded the jails of America. He was tired, and had no time for such details. He had to undo the evil work of Senator Cabot Lodge, re-establish his hold over the affections of the people, and lead them by the hand to peaks of idealism from which their petty strifes would be seen in all their ugliness and for ever abandoned. There had been a time—for instance at Turin in January 1919 ('a country', he had said, 'is owned and dominated by the capital that is invested in it')—when Wilson had shown a fleeting grasp of economic reality. But moral mountaineering, a rhetorical rising above it all, was now, more than ever, the only solution he had to offer. Hundred per cent Wilsonianism strove with hundred per cent Americanism—of which it was little more than a diluted and sublimated version. On July 10th in the Senate, with the great bound volume of the Peace Treaty before him, Wilson solemnly urged immediate ratification. The treaty's most vital contribution to the future of mankind was the League of Nations. The world looked to America to provide moral leadership. 'The stage is set, the destiny disclosed. It has come about by no plan of our own conceiving, but by the hand of God who led us into this way. We cannot turn back. We can only go forward, with lifted eyes and freshened vision. It was of this we dreamed at our birth. America shall in truth show the way. The light streams upon the path ahead, and nowhere else.'

The path was densely packed with obstacles. Lodge's propaganda machine had seen to that. Wilson's League, he charged, would impair American sovereignty, surrender the Monroe Doctrine, entangle America in European and Asiatic intrigues, put American 'boys' at the mercy of a foreign institution which might at any time summon them to fight for obscure and even downright repugnant causes—such as the quelling of the Irish nationalists for the benefit of the British government. Lodge, the new Chairman of the Senate's Foreign Affairs Committee, had played on the resentments of every large (white) racial minority: not only Irish-Americans (who considered that Wilson should have put in a strong plea for Irish self-determination), but German-Americans (angered by his failure to modify the terms of the treaty), and Italian-Americans furious at his obstinacy over Fiume. Wilson's 'bartering' of the Fourteen Points had effectively alienated his liberal support, as had his failure to denounce the frightening erosion of civil liberties. Wilson could hardly have escaped a glimmering awareness that he was the most unpopular man in America – and withal not above suspicion as a 'parlour Red'.

This did not deter him. Did not Satan concentrate his heaviest fire upon the elect? Was not Senator Lodge obviously an instrument of Satan? Must not his defeat be given priority over all else? In late August, sapped by humid heat, suffering from daily tension headaches, and evidently on the verge of complete collapse, Wilson decided to make his bid for the Soul of America.

When the Presidential train left Washington on the night of September 3rd it was the beginning of a railroad odyssey comparable in spiritual passion and geographical scope with Trotsky's forays around the battlefields of the Russian civil war. But Wilson's train was armed only with a determination to be loved, to be justified, to force a whole nation to share in a personal drama of redemption. In the next twenty-two days the President covered eight thousand miles, delivered forty-two set speeches, took part in automobile parades in city after broiling city (waving his top hat, fixedly smiling, clutching the side of the vehicle to stay on his feet), attended banquets and receptions, and sacrificed the privacy he craved to allow local politicians and journalists to travel with him from one stop to the next.

Columbus, Indianapolis, Omaha ... Gruelled by a dogged display of cracker-barrel affability that was foreign to his whole nature, Wilson spent the long nights composing and polishing his speeches. He pulled out every rhetorical stop in a series of decision-forcing either/or's. Either the League, headed and vitalized by America, or new and terrible wars. ('Ah, my fellow citizens, do not forget the aching hearts ... do not forget the forlorn homes from which those boys went and to which they will never return.') Either the League, or an armaments race and the Prussianization of American democracy. ('If we must stand apart ... we must have a great standing army. ... You can't handle an armed nation by vote ... You have got to have a concentrated, militaristic government.') Opposition to the treaty was the result of downright ignorance or private malice. ('The facts are marching, and God is marching with them. It is welcome or surrender. It is acceptance of great world conditions and great world duties, or scuttle now and come back later.')

On September 23rd, in Salt Lake City, he faced fifteen thousand people crammed into the Mormon Tabernacle, an apt venue for a sermon of pure fantasy. In an atmosphere so fetid that Mrs Wilson nearly fainted, he spoke for an hour and a half. His clothes were soaked with sweat. Even at the hotel, after stripping and taking a shower, the sweating continued. Edith begged him to rest for a few days, but he refused. At Denver, Colorado, on the morning of September 25th, his headaches were more blinding than ever, his limbs so fluttering with nervous tremors that he could barely control them. In the afternoon, more dead than alive, he travelled a hundred miles south to Pueblo. A captive audience of fifty thousand in the fairground there was too tempting to miss. The pain in his head seemed to be splitting his skull. He stumbled up the steps to the platform to deliver what proved to be the last public address of his life. He was not trying, he said, to justify himself, but to vindicate great principles. His speech became slurred, and he wept with pain and emotion as he ended: 'Now that the mists of this great question have cleared away ... we have accepted the truth and it is going to lead us, and through us the world, out into pastures of quietness and peace such as the world never dreamed of before.'

Many of the crowd wept. So did the reporters. So did Mrs Wilson. The President was helped, half-sobbing, to the train. Seldom, even in 1919, that year of terrible and tender demagogy, had an orator so moved an audience. People sensed that they were listening to the last words from the Cross upon which Wilson had spread himself, daring his enemies to knock in the nails. They mourned the death of a President and of his haunting but impossible illusion. That night, as the train moved towards Wichita, Kansas, Wilson's physical agony became unbearable. Admiral Grayson, his personal physician, could not alleviate it. At 4 a.m. his personal secretary, Joseph Tumulty, found the President huddled in a chair, the left side of his face partly collapsed, tears of bewilderment on his cheeks. He had felt this coming on yesterday, he managed to say. He did not know what to do. But somehow he must complete his speaking schedule. If he did not, Lodge would call him a quitter, his whole western pilgrimage would be called a failure, the treaty and the League would be lost. At 5 a.m. he fell asleep at last, but awoke two hours later, shaved, and put on fresh clothes. Only after his wife, Grayson and Tumulty had implored him to rest and regain his strength did he agree to cancel the rest of his programme.

Grayson issued a bulletin stating that the President was suffering from nervous exhaustion and would need to rest for a considerable time. The blinds in the train were drawn, the track before it cleared. On October 2nd, in the White House, his left side was paralysed by a stroke. Cerebral thrombosis was complicated by inflammation of the prostate gland. Grayson's vague bulletins gave no real information. Cabinet Ministers were refused admission to the sick-room. Wild rumours flew about Washington. Wilson was dead. He had gone mad and was confined in a straitjacket. The press, uncertain of its ground, called an impatient, semi-funereal truce.

Tremulous, white-bearded, pillow-propped, concealing his paralysed left arm under the coverlet, the President proved even less accommodating about the treaty than he had been in August. Lodge must compromise, he certainly would not (had he not earned, by his agony and bloody sweat, the luxury of total obstinacy?). Lodge was not bothered. But people, starving people, in Europe were. 'Mainly owing to political conditions in the United States,' reported the London *Spectator*, 'the Supreme Economic Council has been almost inactive since July, waiting, without definite authority or powers, to hand over its work to the Economic Department of the League of Nations Secretariat. Economic dislocation has grown steadily worse throughout Central Europe; disease and famine are almost unchecked, no serious attempt has been made to cope with the appalling evils underlying the depreciation of European currencies.'

Wilson's railroad Calvary had been, in its way, magnificent: but it had certainly not exorcized war or the threat of Bolshevism. 'People talk of the world on the morrow of the Great War,' said Winston Churchill in an after-dinner speech at the Ritz Hotel late in November, 'as if somehow or other we have been transformed into a higher sphere ... Yet never was there a time when people were more disposed to turn to courses of violence or show such scant respect for law and customs and tradition.' Europe had been almost completely balkanized, so far as it had not been Bolshevized. He could see no reason 'to advise young gentlemen to neglect as obsolete the study of the profession of arms'.

2. *Judge Gary's Triumph*

On September 27th, as Wilson's train sped back to Washington, the *Nation* printed a savage attack. 'Now comes our world-beating presidential prestidigitator, snatching a few brief moments from the great international shell game by which he seeks to preserve unbroken the heart of the world. He addresses to us a homily on the virtues of work, exhorts us to redouble our exertions and in no case to lay down our tools until he shall have time to draw from his hat his celebrated programmeless industrial conference, guaranteed to blossom under our eyes into a new heaven and a new earth. Samuel Gompers, trusty Man Friday to the Presidential Crusoe, seconds his master right nobly, and all the old labour leaders join the big and little chief in sitting on the lid. All in vain. A veritable epidemic of strikes rages.'

Wilson was beyond recall or criticism. But America was not short of 'Christian' crusaders (it had, after all, begun as a sequence of grimly competitive puritan theocracies). The Christian Hired Man and the Fighting Quaker were ready to take over.

In mid-June, frightened that the officially, if tepidly, backed steel drive would turn into another rank-and-file revolt (and so plunge the A.F.L., by association, deeper in the Red), Gompers asked Judge Gary for a conference. He did not even get a reply, and a ballot among the members of the twenty-six unions concerned showed an overwhelming majority in favour of strike action. On August 26th Gompers again requested Gary to meet the National Committee, but was told that 'the officers of the Corporation respectfully decline to discuss with you, as representatives of a labour union, any matters relating to employees.' The President appealed to both sides for moderation, and announced his intention of calling an industrial conference 'to discuss fundamental means of bettering the whole relationship of capital and labour.' The National Committee voted for strike action to start on September 22nd, unless Gary and his colleagues were willing to come to terms. They were not. Henry Clay Frick, who twenty-seven years earlier had proved his toughness by surviving bullet and knife wounds inflicted by a would-be assassin, wrote to John D. Rockefeller Jr: 'I am utterly opposed to collective bargaining and representation and ready to close every mill.' Bloated with five years of colossal wartime profits, the steel trusts could easily have afforded a complete shut-down.

Despite frantic efforts, the strike did not achieve this. Two hundred strike announcements were broadcast in a dozen different languages: 'IRON AND STEEL WORKERS! A historic decision confronts us. If we will but stand together like men our demands will soon be granted. But if we falter and fail, we will sink back into a miserable, helpless serfdom. Now is the time to insist on our rights as human beings.' The committee raised 400,000 dollars. This kept the strikers and their families from starving for the next $3\frac{1}{2}$ months; but it was not enough to compete with the steel trusts and the patriotic organizations in the propaganda war. W. Z. Foster's pamphlet, *Syndicalism*, written eight years earlier while he was still a Wobbly, was reprinted in huge quantities and circulated to newspapers and politicians all over the country. 'The wages system must be abolished,' he had written. 'The thieves at present in control must be stripped of their booty and industry so reorganized that every individual shall have free access to the social means of production. ... The syndicalist considers the State as a meddling capitalist institution ... He is a radical opponent of "law and order", since he knows that for his unions to be "legal" in their tactics would be for them to become impotent ... He knows he is engaged in a life and death struggle ... with him the end justifies the means.'

Foster could protest as much as he liked that he had 'reformed', that the strike was official, that it had been forced by employer obstinacy. But though he had left the I.W.W. he had put on record his determination to 'revolutionize' the existing unions. The fact that he was the driving force of the committee was sufficient to damn the strike as the climax of the Red Menace. The fact that he was organizing it with the blessing of Gompers proved, not that he was innocent, but that the A.F.L. was his accomplice. 'It is to this exotic beast of prey', concluded the New York *Sun*, 'that Judge Gary refuses to extend the olive branch!'

Comforted by the knowledge of inexhaustible financial reserves, the approval of the captains of every industry, a cable from J. P. Morgan ('Heartiest congratulations on your stand for the open shop ... I believe American principles of liberty deeply involved and must win if we stand firm'), and a ready-made labour-smearing case, Judge Gary rested complacently in his Long Island mansion on September 22nd, when an estimated 250,000 workers (about half the total labour force in the steel industry) walked out of the mills. This was the biggest strike in the history of America. But to Gary it was the biggest gift to reaction (or in his phraseology, 'enlightened management') which could conceivably have been made. When the strike had been broken—and he did not for a moment doubt that it would be—unionism would be crippled and the way of the Corporations made straight.

Nearly seventy per cent of the steelworkers were immigrants, so it was easy to picture the strike as 'foreign'. A remark made by the superintendent of the Homestead Mill—'This is a Slovak strike'—was widely quoted. 'The foreign element', charged the New York *Times*, 'is steeped in the doctrines of the class war—ignorant and easily rushed.' Some verses in the Corporation-sponsored *Gary Works Circle* put the point with professional polish:

> Said Dan McGann to a foreign man who worked at the self-
> same bench,
> 'Let me tell you this', and for emphasis he flourished a
> monkey-wrench,
> 'Don't talk to me of this bourgeoisie, don't open your mouth
> to speak
> Of your Socialists and Anarchists, don't mention the Bolshevik.
> For I've had enough of this foreign stuff, I'm sick as a man can be
> Of the speech of hate, and I'm telling you straight that this is
> the land for me.'

At the end of the strike's first week the committee estimated that 375,000 men were out. The Steel Trust press, notably in Pittsburgh, countered with headlines such as CONDITIONS ALMOST NORMAL IN ALL STEEL PLANTS—though at the same time running full-page appeals to GO BACK TO WORK AND STAND BY AMERICA. National newspapers added a final (and effective) touch of the absurd by printing stories that 'vacationing' steelworkers, brimming with wages, were expected to start an insolent spending spree in New York hotels. Bolshevist, syndicalist, anarchist, un-American—and pleasure-bent: the steel strikers had it coming to them from every angle.

Judge Gary did not rely on lead soldiers for victory. They were used to build an impression of impending violence which would justify 'precautions' on a massive scale. And they were massive. Steel plants were surrounded by armed guards and droves of special deputies, those hated and trigger-happy class warriors. In western Pennsylvania, where the companies obliged by completely taking over 'law enforcement', it was estimated that in the twenty miles between Pittsburgh and Clairton there were 25,000 men under arms and that in some areas there was a deputy sheriff for every striker. Picket lines were broken up, free speech was a crime — for which in Farrell four strikers were killed and eleven wounded. In small mill towns bludgeon-swinging 'Black Cossacks' rode their horses on to the sidewalks and even into stores and company houses.

At least six hundred *agents provocateurs* did their best to spread rumours, undermine morale and incite to violence. It seldom came but it was easily manufactured. One press story told of a ferocious gun battle between the Black Cossacks and an 'Army' of Wobblies and 'Bolsheviks' in Sharon, Pennsylvania — where three blocks were reported to be filled with an 'arsenal' of weapons. On the strength of this, many strikers were arrested and earmarked for deportation. More than 30,000 Negro strike-breakers were drafted into the mills. Protest riots against negro scabs on October 14th gave an excuse for General Leonard Wood (angling for nomination as Republican presidential candidate) to march federal troops into East Chicago and Gary, Indiana, though eleven companies of State Militia already had the 'situation' well in hand.

On October 6th, as General Wood was proclaiming martial law in Gary, President Wilson's National Industrial Conference opened in the Pan-American Building in Washington, D.C. Disobeying doctor's orders, the Martyr President had dictated a message stiff with rhetorical queries, which was read out to the delegates. 'At a time when the nations of the world are endeavouring to find a way of avoiding war, are we to confess that there is no method to be found for carrying on industry except in the spirit of, and with the very method of, war? Must suspicion and hatred and force rule us in civil life? Are our industrial leaders and our industrial workers to live together without faith in each other, constantly struggling for advantage over each other, doing naught but what is compelled? My friends, this would be an intolerable outlook ... an invitation to national disaster. From such a possibility my mind turns away, for my confidence is abiding that in this land we have learned how to accept the general judgment upon matters that affect the public weal.' Judge Gary and John D. Rockefeller Jr appeared as representatives of management. This alone was enough to ensure deadlock. For though there were representatives of labour and the public, decisions had to be accepted by all three sections, and even then were not binding. Gary had successfully argued against including the steel strike on the agenda of the conference (too controversial), which confined itself to a generalized inquiry into ways and means of ending 'industrial strife' and 'resuming the natural course of industrial and economic development'. On October 21st, after two weeks of uneasy sparring, the conference collapsed when Gompers's carefully worded resolution acknowledging 'the right of wage-earners to bargain collectively in respect to wages, hours of labour, and relations and conditions of employment' was treated like a Communist Manifesto. Gompers's inevitable walk-out was described by the *Wall Street Journal* as further evidence that organized labour had 'succumbed to the I.W.W.s and Russian Bolsheviks'. The tardy decision of the A.F.L.'s Executive Council, hitherto lukewarm, to give the fullest financial and moral support to the steel strikers, was similarly interpreted. Even if the steel mills were working at low pressure, and dozens of unskilled negro scabs were being injured or killed at the furnaces, the machinery of guilt by association and innuendo was functioning like a dream.

The coal strike, though approved by the United Mine Workers' Union (U.M.W.) whose president, John L. Lewis, was even more bitterly anti-Red than Gompers, received the full Gary treatment. Scheduled to start on November 1st, 1919, in support of demands for a standard nation-wide contract, a sixty per cent wage increase, a six-hour day and a five-day week, it had been, alleged the coal magnates, ordered and financed by Lenin and Trotsky. The New York *Tribune* insisted that the miners, 'red-soaked in the doctrines of Bolshevism', were clamouring for a strike as 'a means of syndicaliz-ing the coal mines ... and even starting a general revolution in America'. On October 30th Attorney-General Palmer, 'shocked' by this trial of strength between a 'minority' and the 'will of the people', secured a federal court injunction forbidding the U.M.W. leaders to take any part in the strike. John L. Lewis and his fellow officials technically obeyed the injunction. But on November 1st nearly 400,000 miners struck work. The fact that they did so was adduced as further evidence of Red control of the unions. A second injunction ordered the U.M.W. leaders to call off the strike by November 11th. Lewis complied – 'We are Americans,' he said, 'we cannot fight the government.' Many miners, nevertheless, stayed out for another month. Coal stocks dwindled, factories and schools closed, railway services were cut. On December 3rd a federal court cited Lewis and eighty-three other U.M.W. officials for violating the second injunction. President Wilson authorized the Fuel Administration to offer a flat fourteen per cent wage increase and a promise of arbitration on the other demands. On December 10th this offer was accepted. The coal crisis was over.

The steel strike went on – by a unanimous but anxiously debated decision reached by the committee on November 24th. In a desperate attempt to find mediation, the organizers turned to the Interchurch World Movement, which represented thirty Protestant Churches. Its report, highly sympathetic to the strikers, was promptly rejected by Gary. In December just over 100,000 men were still out. The steel belt press hammered away with the now familiar story that they were 'ignorant foreigners unable to understand the truth, and blessed only with the belief that in some magical way they are to be put in possession of the mills'. The *Open Shop Review* and the National Security League monotonously reiterated that the strike was an attempt by 'Bolshevists and Anarchists' to destroy the government. The Senate Committee made public its conclusion that the strike had been organized by 'a considerable element of I.W.W.s, anarchists, revolutionists and Russian Soviets,' who had exploited the crisis 'as a means of elevating themselves to power'.

Still the American public felt cheated. The bomb scares of May and June had been too anonymous. The general strike at Seattle, the Boston police strike, even the steel and coal strikes, had not eased a dull ache of unrelieved desire. Not all the fabrications of the press, the National Security League, the American Defence Society, the National Civic Federation and the American Legion could conceal the fact that the contest had been one-sided. Strikers had occasionally rioted. They had been killed and wounded and arrested. But they had not really hit back. The bloody Bolshevik revolution had pulled its punches. It had, indeed, behaved like a giant sissy. Excited to a pitch of sexo-ideological delirium, Respectable America groaned for its rightful, its promised orgasm. Lenin and Trotsky could not provide it. They were too far away, too much part of the whole titillatory technique. At last, on November 11th, 1919, the I.W.W., that trusty, home-grown terror of the board rooms and residential districts, known and hated by every Babbitt in the land, obliged.

It happened, the great release, in Centralia in the timber state of Washington, where the I.W.W. still waged war on the 'slave camps' of the lumber trusts, where memories of the Everett Massacre and the Seattle 'Soviet' were still raw. But there was another side to the hatred of the Wobblies for the dollar-mad business community with its smart lawyers and pimping entrepreneurs: and of the lumber bosses for the hobo-anarchs of the I.W.W. The Wobblies were much closer to Henry Thoreau and Jack London than to Karl Marx. They fought, instinctively, for the 'true' America of the homestead and the loner against the 'false' America of the hiring financier and the hired lawyer and politician; for the human voice against the Voice of the Party (whatever its label); for the individual against the Chambers of Commerce; for a mythical West against a cash-register East; and for the odd-ball against the respectable. The Wobblies were, in the deepest and most apolitical sense, subversive; living affronts to a chain-store civilization and reach-me-down values; spiritual successors to the Red Indians as number one public enemy and conscience-botherer. That was why the suburbs raged so exceedingly against them. That was why they had to be exterminated.

The logging town of Centralia was one of the last strongholds of I.W.W. militancy. The local bosses had in 1918 created a Legion of Loyal Loggers to check its influence. In 1919, with wartime controls loosening and immense wartime profits in the bank (the price of timber had risen from sixteen to as much as 120 dollars per thousand feet), they decided to have a showdown with the 'Reds'. The American Legion was primed, even paid, to start the job. In March a squad of Legionnaires, watched by Chamber of Commerce patriots, stormed the I.W.W. hall in Centralia, laid about them with gas pipes and rubber hoses, burned all the books and pamphlets, and auctioned off the fittings for the Red Cross. A new hall was hired. Amazingly, provocatively, I.W.W. membership increased. The next big 'raid' was openly planned for Armistice Day, and the Wobblies were ready for it. It was cold and damp, with mist rolling in from

Puget Sound and dripping from the spruce trees. The parade was led
by members of the local Elks Lodge, followed by a brass band, Boy
Scouts, and a large detachment of armed Legionnaires. When the
Legionnaires swung off towards the new I.W.W. hall, Wesley
Everest, an ex-Army sharpshooter who had put on his own uniform
for the occasion, shouted: 'I fought for democracy in France, and
I'm going to fight for it here. First man that comes in here, why he's
going to get it.' The patriots took no notice. Three were killed (one
of them a wealthy member of the Centralia Protective League) as the
Wobblies opened fire. Everest emptied his rifle magazine into the
crowd and ran for the hills, armed with a revolver. He killed one
pursuer (the nephew of a local lumber baron) before he was
overpowered. His teeth were smashed in with the butt of a shotgun.
A rope was tied round his neck and hitched to a bough. But the
crowd changed its mind and took him to jail.

That night Centralia was plunged into darkness as the power
supply was cut. A lynch mob broke into the jail, took Everest out of
his cell, beat him unconscious, dragged him to a waiting limousine
packed with Chamber of Commerce avengers, and pitched him on to
the floor. On the way to the bridge over the Chekalis River, the
vengeance of the Babbitts began. Bending over the hobo in army
uniform, a Brother Elk tore open his trousers and (perfectly inter-
preting the will of millions of concupiscent nonentities) cut off his
penis and testicles with a razor. Everest screamed and begged them
to shoot him. They hanged him from the bridge in a glare of head-
lights, first half-strangling him on a short rope, then giving him a
full, neck-breaking drop. Not until then did they get out their guns
for a little target practice. The 'second American revolution' had
acquired its most famous martyr. But Respectable America had
acquired four martyrs, a glow of orgasmic well-being, and a sense of
renewed dedication. Its new enemy was its old enemy, after all. It
knew whom it had to hate most.

The 'massacre' had been caused, said the Mayor of Centralia, by 'the
laxness of the Federal Government in dealing with seditionists,
Socialists, slackers, and the riff-raff of the human race.' There was
wild applause in Congress at the statements of Senator Poindexter
and Representative Johnson, both of Washington. How much
longer, asked the former, would the government wait before
crushing 'this miserable human vermin which seeks to destroy

civilization?' Johnson demanded all-out war on 'these damnable curs and traitors'. The shots which killed the heroes of Centralia had, he said, 'been aimed at the heart of this nation'. On November 15th, in a violent police raid on I.W.W. headquarters in New York authorized by the Lusk Committee, Wobblies were bludgeoned and hurled into the street, the premises completely wrecked. Along the west coast hundreds of Wobblies and 'radicals' were jailed. In Kansas City twenty-seven were given sentences totalling 123 years on vague charges of 'conspiracy against the government'. The Pittsburgh *Post* was not satisfied: it urged the use of firing squads for radicals. The *United Presbyterian*, consistent in bloodthirstiness, considered that every Bolshevik should be 'forced to change his course or swing at the end of a rope'. Criminal anarchy laws blossomed profusely in an Indian summer of national hysteria. The I.W.W. had put life—and death—into the Red Scare.

Mild Victor Berger, leader of the rump of the American Socialist Party, and about as wild a revolutionary as Karl Kautsky or Ramsay MacDonald, was denied admission to Congress although duly elected for a second time in December 1919 for the Fifth Wisconsin District. First elected in November 1918 he had been permanently barred five months later by a Special House Committee on the ground that his socialist pacifism was 'off the same cloth as Russian Bolshevism'. At the second attempt, those who voted for him were described as 'deluded, unthinking fools opposed to American institutions'. Early in 1920, five socialist members of the New York Legislature were evicted and their party declared an illegal organization. As a result of the 'investigations' of the Lusk Committee, many New York schoolteachers were dismissed, or allowed to keep their jobs only if they dropped their subscriptions to the *Nation*, the *New Republic* and the *Dial*, or at least kept their opinions and their reading to themselves. The New York Public Library was arraigned for possessing a copy of Benjamin Tucker's translation of Bakunin's *God and the State*. The *New York Times* estimated that there were at least five million 'parlour Reds' in America, notably school or university teachers and clergymen, with another fifteen million 'under their influence'. Charlie Chaplin, trial lawyer Clarence Darrow, veteran social worker Jane Addams, economist Thorstein Veblen, and even President Wilson (by the end of December beginning to hobble about the White House with the aid of a stick) were mentioned as prominent parlour Reds, or Pinks. The Centralia shootings were used by Republicans to boost their chances in the 1920 Presidential election by wholesale allegations of Wilsonian laxity. It was stated that some fifty per cent of government officials were 'infected'. The American Civil Liberties Union was described as 'a Bolshevik front', as was the Russian Famine Fund Committee, the National Council for the Reduction of Armaments, and the National League of Women Voters. When Calvin Coolidge was elected for a second term, by a huge majority, as Governor of Massachusetts, it was widely hailed as 'A DEFEAT OF THE SOVIETS — Massachusetts — God bless her — again and amen!'

On December 21st, 249 deportees (the first of thousands, promised the Fighting Quaker, who also had his eye on the Presidential nomination) sailed from New York on the *Buford* — an ancient and barely seaworthy vessel that had been used as a troop transport in the Spanish-American war — en route for Soviet Russia via Finland. Pictured as resourceful desperadoes to the last man, they were heavily guarded by 250 soldiers. Yet four-fifths of them were simple, bewildered working men who had been seized and often savagely beaten up in a series of raids on the headquarters of the Union of Russian Workers; forty-three were described as Anarchists; seven were public charges, petty criminals or social misfits. Twelve of them left behind families, who tried to break through the Ellis Island gates — a pathetic but forlorn attempt misrepresented by the headline, REDS STORM GATES TO FREE PALS.

The only notable and articulate passengers on the 'Red Ark' were Emma Goldman and Alexander Berkman, involuntarily but jubilantly returning to their native land after thirty years of much-penalized libertarian agitation in the United States. They had their doubts about the methods of the Soviet government, but saw the Russian revolution, with all its mistakes and sufferings, as essentially a movement of liberation. In *Deportation: Its Meaning and Menace*, a highly emotional pamphlet composed in the Ellis Island jail, they sent a last message to their kind of Americans. It was no use, they said, blaming President Wilson or hoping for any Saviour. They must make their own freedom. It would be a stern fight. The aim of hundred per cent Americanism was 'to root out the last vestige, the very memory of traditional American freedom'. Not only foreigners, but natives and naturalized citizens, were to be 'mentally fumigated, made politically reliable and ideologically Kosher', by eliminating social critics and industrial rebels, by denaturalization and banishment, by exile to the Isle of Guam or to Alaska ('the future Siberia of the United States'). 'Join your efforts, lovers of humanity. Do not uphold the hand that strangles life. Align yourselves with the Dreamers of the Better Day ... The idealists, the seekers of a slaveless world, speak for your heart. Give them a hearing.'

The pamphlet ended with a few shrewd quotations from prominent Americans which in 1919 would have meant prosecution for criminal anarchy and sedition. Abraham Lincoln would have been jailed, so would Thomas Jefferson. So, especially, would William Lloyd Garrison ('when I look at these crowded thousands and see them trample on their consciences and the rights of their fellow men at the bidding of a piece of parchment, then I say my curse be on the Constitution of the United States') and Ralph Waldo Emerson ('every actual State is corrupt. Good men must not obey the laws too well'). With these parting shots, Goldman and Berkman, those ageing but irrepressible anarcho-progressives, on-and-off lovers and faithful comrades, set out on the long journey to Soviet Russia. Their pamphlet did not receive wide circulation. The Postmaster-General saw to that. The press pictured them as cursing the country that had tolerated them for too long, but fondling 'thousands of good American dollars' (their admirers, mostly working-class people, had subscribed to a farewell fund). Some prominence was given to Emma's remark – 'I do not consider it a punishment to be sent to Soviet Russia. I consider it an honour to be chosen as the first political agitator to be deported from the United States' – but the main stress was on the need for more, larger, Red Arks. 'The ultra-red faction', sneered the New York *Tribune*, 'is feeling a trifle ultramarine.'

On January 8th, 1920, the coal strike was at last called off. The National Committee's proud message – 'All steelworkers are now at liberty to return to work pending preparations for the next big organization drive' – was a brave attempt to mask total defeat. The mighty effort had not wrung a single concession. Twenty strikers had been killed, unknown hundreds badly injured – unknown because they dared not go to company-town doctors for fear of being put on a black-list. The second American revolution had fizzled. So had its offshoot in Canada, where the leaders of the Winnipeg

'Soviet' were brought to trial before an array of prosecuting lawyers who had been active on the strike-breaking Citizens' Committee, a carefully screened jury, and a judge who declared that most workers were overpaid, and that Canada was 'the people's country'. Seven of the eight accused were convicted of sedition and jailed. In Kitchener, Ontario, a socialist alderman was frogmarched to the headquarters of the Great War Veterans, made to kiss the Union Jack, and publicly ducked in a pond.

All over North America 'the new virility ... pink with health' (in the words of Mr Edward Price Bell, a well-known journalist) was flexing its muscles — with the men (and women) of the American Legion, that compendium of soggy nostalgia and small-town prejudice, showing the way. 'The Legion', announced its first commandant, Colonel Franklin d'Olier of Philadelphia, 'will combat Bolshevism and incendiary radicalism all the way ... We shall have a National Americanism Committee ... We shall drive home the great democratic principle that the interests of all the people are above those of any special interest or any class or section.' Mr Price Bell pointed out that the Legionnaires were not idle dreamers or 'intellectual superannuates'. They were soldiers, sailors and marines and their mothers, sisters, wives and daughters — in a word, America's Best. They might be of English, Welsh, Scottish, Irish, Dutch, German, Scandinavian or Italian stock — but their 'spiritual core' was American. 'There is not the ghost of a hyphen among them. Their spirit is the spirit that conquered the far-spreading American wilderness and built a mighty civilization there. If they show themselves illiberal, lawless, intolerant, in places, it is illiberalism and lawlessness and intolerance answering to their like ... these are but the bubbles and foam on a tremendous tide bearing towards a beautiful shore.'

On January 2nd, 1920, anti-radical raids in twenty-three States netted more than four thousand suspects, often without the formality of a warrant. They were held incommunicado and denied the right to legal counsel. Eight hundred were forced to march in chains to the dockside at Boston for shipping to Deer Island, where conditions were such that two died of pneumonia, one went mad, and one committed suicide. In Detroit, another eight hundred were kept for six days in a dark, windowless corridor in a derelict public building. When some were transferred to another building, photographs were taken of them and published in the papers as examples of the kind of filthy, degenerate terrorists who were out to take over America.

Seven hundred people were released (without apology) after third-degree interrogations. They included a New Jersey man who had been arrested in the street 'because he looked like a radical', and thirty-nine citizens of Lynn, Massachusetts, seized while discussing the establishment of a co-operative bakery. Drawings of a phonograph invention found in a socialist club in New Brunswick were sent to demolition experts because they were thought to show 'the internal mechanism of various types of bomb'. Undeflected by such absurdities, Palmer sweepingly charged that the 'alien element' dominated 'domestic radicalism' and was directly controlled by Lenin and Trotsky. 'Each and every adherent of this movement', he claimed in a would-be spine-chilling peroration, 'is a potential murderer or thief ... Out of the sly and crafty eyes of many of them leap cupidity, cruelty, insanity and crime; from their lopsided faces, sloping brows and misshapen features may be recognized the unmistakable criminal type.'

The triumph of Gary and Gary's God was complete. In the spring of 1920, at a large meeting held in New York under the auspices of the Interchurch World Movement (possibly keen to redeem itself from accusations of Bolshevism after its steel strike report), it was proposed to raise seventy million dollars to 'expand and standardize Christianity ... to compel people to see the Programme of Christ'. After four pretty young women dressed as angels had blown 'The Lost Chord' on cavalry trumpets, John D. Rockefeller Jr rose to speak. Force, he said, had been tried, and had failed to solve the problems of industry. 'So now we are hearing leaders in the business world say that the Golden Rule must be introduced as the only real solution. We are coming to realize that after all the solution is to be nothing new, but the restoration in our hearts and lives of the spirit of the simple Carpenter of Nazareth.' Judge Gary, now as always, insisted that 'if we are sincere and fair in our treatment of others, we may hope for similar treatment from them.'

His victory over the Red Mirage had re-sanctified big business and sponged away the mud of such powerful muckrakers as Lincoln Steffens. It also seemed to prove that Morgan, Gary, Rockefeller and Wall Street were God's chosen instruments, and that if you couldn't beat them you might as well try to join them.

3. *A Man for All Classes*

In Britain workers' control had become the shibboleth of the squabbling sectaries of the extreme Left, now effectively isolated from the main stream of the Labour movement. Robert Smillie and the miners had become – as Lloyd George may have foreseen – a bore. Other workers were jealous of the incessant publicity given to their grievances and to Smillie's antiquated oratory. After all, Britain was something more than a lot of coal mines with some trees and grass growing on top.

The increased numerical strength and cohesion of the unions did not indicate a massing for revolution, only a determination to safeguard wages and if possible to share in the proceeds of an industrial boom which seemed likely to last for a long time. The new interest of the Labour movement in foreign affairs – condemnation of British policy in India, Ireland and Egypt, and of intervention in Russia – was a sign that it was trying to become, under the tuition of the Webbs, less insular. It was grooming itself for the day when it would provide a government. Ramsay MacDonald no longer spoke of soviets (as he had early in 1919, peeved by his defeat in the general election). Rather did he, and other I.L.P. leaders, join the Webbs in denouncing the 'dictatorship' of Lloyd George and crying up Labour's mission to 'revitalize' the House of Commons.

All this, however, was not obvious to the militants of the British bourgeoisie, as represented by the 370 diehard M.P.s who continued to be the most troublesome rank-and-file rebels in the land. To them the Coal Commission, the National Industrial Conference, and the Profiteering Act were part of a social revolution which, albeit gradually, was breaking the ramparts of their world. Everywhere they saw signs of 'Bolshevik' infiltration. The *Saturday Review* voiced their feelings under the headline BOLSHEVISM AT OXFORD. 'At a moment when the social structure is threatened with a more dangerous upheaval than ever before in history,' it commented, 'the appointment of Mr R. H. Tawney to a lectureship at Balliol College is not merely an academic but a national outrage.' Many undergraduates, influenced by the prevailing contempt for tradition, needed no encouragement to pose as revolutionists. It would be a crying scandal if Oxford were to 'sink into an annexe of the Fabian Society, ruled by the presumptuous pedants of the Adelphi'.

The *Saturday Review* spoke for them, too, when it pictured the Conservative and Unionist Party as drowsing under the spell of the Welsh Wizard, and lashed out at the domination of *nouveaux riches*. 'The Tory Party', it said, 'has become the party of the profiteer, who merely wishes to keep what he has got. The Manchester capitalist of the last century, unable to conquer, has absorbed Toryism.' Their natural leader was Winston Churchill, equally keen on a trial of strength, just as horrified by the sapping of tradition. But he was too nonconformist, too hopelessly Churchillian, to fit into the strait-jacket of their simple loyalties. Sir Eric and Sir Auckland Geddes, those hard-bitten Scottish industrialists, Ministers respectively of Transport and of Reconstruction, were also known to favour a showdown. But they were *nouveau riche* types. Yet a showdown, a muted British Centralia, had become a psychological necessity. Realizing this, Lloyd George decided to let the True Blues off the leash. Since March the railwaymen had been pressing for increased and standardized wages. In September, after a long delaying action, Sir Eric Geddes made an offer which would have left the lower grades even worse off than before the war. The offer was presented as final.

Predictably, the railwaymen were not alone in seeing this as the first instalment of a general attack on wages. Their decision to strike at midnight on September 26th if negotiations were not reopened was soon followed by a strong hint from the Transport Workers' Federation that it might follow suit. Six hundred thousand railwaymen 'holding the community to ransom', with the prospect of a transport strike which would complete a virtual blockade of the public! The sheer statistics of the threat made for panic animosity and a disinclination to examine the justice of the railwaymen's case.

On September 27th Lloyd George sent a 'policy' telegram to the Chairman of the County Council at Caernarvon regretting that he would be unable to fulfil a speaking engagement 'due to the sudden outbreak of a strike on the railways'. He could, he said, recall no strike entered into so lightly, with so little justification, and with such entire disregard of the public interest. The state was running the railways at a loss mainly due to the 'enormous' increase in the wages of railway workers since the beginning of the war. The Geddes offer was a generous one, and the government had reason to believe that the strike had been engineered by 'a small but active body of men who have wrought tirelessly and insidiously to exploit the labour organizations of this country for subversive ends. I am convinced', he ended, 'that the vast majority of the trade unionists of the land are opposed to this anarchist conspiracy.'

This oblique way of setting the cat among the pigeons received saturation publicity, and Lloyd George sat back to enjoy the flutter and to preside over the folding of the wings. Beatrice Webb was in a dither of excitement. Here was a strike which had been forced upon the workers. There was no tincture of the nonsense of workers' control about it. The Fabians of the Labour Research Department, led by Sidney Webb and R. H. Tawney, were able to put their talents as publicists unreservedly at the service of the 'men'. Rumour was rife. The government was said to be preparing drastic measures – for confiscating the railwaymen's funds, starving their families, running the railways with troops. The trade unions were said to be planning soviets to take over the government of the country.

Emergency rationing of power, fuel and food was decreed. Field-Marshal Sir Douglas Haig, Commander-in-Chief of Home Forces, and Major-General Fielding, Commanding the London District, attended a Cabinet meeting. Upper and middle class enthusiasts joined army and navy 'volunteers' in public service. Lord Drogheda, Lord Portarlington, Sir Frederick Tichborne, the Hon. Edward Knollys, and almost the entire able-bodied membership of the Guards Club reported at Paddington Station for duty as porters or clerks. Lady Drogheda and a squad of eager noblewomen drove cars for the Ministry of Food. Hyde Park was turned into a milk (and, according to the *Daily Herald*, machine-gun) depot. J. H. Thomas, P.C., M.P., General Secretary of the National Union of Railwaymen (N.U.R.) was described by the *Pall Mall Gazette* as 'the man who has deliberately preferred violence to reason, and like the Kaiser himself rushed on the crisis of his bid for power'. The government, insisted *The Times*, dare not make any more concessions. It must stand firm. 'Like the war with Germany, this must be fought to a finish.' For this was more than a matter of wages. The railway-men, in leaping at the throat of the nation, were motivated by 'greed, ambition and lust for power'. The 'civil war', said the *Saturday Review* (which hailed the 'counter-revolution' under the headline

GREAT GEDDES!) was 'a sordid squabble over wages, blown up to white heat by a handful of British Bolshevists'.

In America the railwaymen's revolt, coinciding as it did with the steel strike and the threat of a coal strike, was given panic coverage — which in turn was prominently featured in the Northcliffe press. 'Is Great Britain a nation,' asked the *New York Times*, 'or is it the preserve of railwaymen, miners and transport workers?' The whole world (said the New York *World*) was hoping that 'forces for agreement are at work beneath the surface of events which seem gloomy almost beyond precedent'. Sane trade unionism, urged the *Philadelphia Public Ledger*, could not allow 'madmen and enemies of democracy to get hold of the levers of power and run a noble ship on the shoals of disaster'. The *World*, commenting on the London printers' bid to force newspaper proprietors to state the strikers' case, warned: 'We all know from whom the lesson was learned. One of the first ukases of the Soviet autocrats of Russia called for the suppression of all newspapers except their own. Bela Kun adopted the same policy ... and the Red Spartacists of Bavaria turned as naturally to the shackling of the press as to the slaughter of hostages.' Lord Northcliffe's reply, that 'rather than be dictated to by anyone I will stop publication of my newspapers', could not fail to be widely applauded. 'Better a press silent by the will of its owners than a press enslaved by a class.'

Such was the tension worked up by the professional flesh-creepers of Fleet Street that the Rev. Dick Sheppard, in a much-publicized plea, begged Lloyd George to 'summon the nation to prayer for the guidance of God in the present industrial strife'. *The Times* publicly chastised the Stewards of the Jockey Club for not cancelling the October meeting at Newmarket. Lords Penrhyn, Durham and Lonsdale had evidently 'failed to realize the duty laid upon them by their great position ... to set an example to the thousands who look up to them'. To hold a meeting at the headquarters of horse racing while the country was girding itself to defeat a plot to subvert the authority of Parliament! To incite citizens to the waste of invaluable petrol! This was indeed 'a lamentable example of how not to play the game'. The Stewards acknowledged their error. The last three days of the meeting were cancelled.

In the afternoon of October 1st, at 10 Downing Street, Lloyd

George received a deputation from the Transport Workers' Federation, including Ernest Bevin, the dockers' leader, and accompanied by J. R. Clynes and Arthur Henderson, the Secretary of the Labour Party. All emphasized that the strike would spread unless the government resumed negotiations with the railwaymen. Bevin reported that members of his union throughout South Wales and the Midlands were pressing him to call them out. He, Clynes and Henderson begged the Prime Minister to make some gesture that would enable them to check a mounting resentment that threatened to get out of control. Lloyd George refused to recant his charge of anarchism, but expressed his willingness to see the executive of the N.U.R. – if they understood that negotiations could not be reopened until the men had gone back to work. That night the deputation returned with the N.U.R. leaders. The two deputations, after prolonged huddles in the Cabinet Room, took it in turns to plead with a stern yet paternal Lloyd George, who managed to convey the impression that he, like them, was awaiting what J. H. Thomas, in a voice husky with emotion, referred to as 'a ray of hope'.

On October 5th the strike ended. Wages were to be pegged at war-level, starting at a minimum of 51 shillings, for a year, the men were to receive the arrears of pay which Geddes had threatened to withhold for 'breach of contract', and negotiations were to be continued. J. H. Thomas, addressing a mass meeting at the Royal Albert Hall, remarked, to thunderous cheers: 'I have been attacked because I am the first Privy Councillor who has led a railway strike' (cries of 'Good luck to you, lad!'). 'I have mistaken the meaning of this honour if it carries an obligation to desert the people who have placed me in the position I now occupy.' He and his colleagues, he added, were 'unanimously of the opinion that it was due to the Prime Minister's efforts and not to some of his Ministers that a settlement has been reached'. Lloyd George himself, in another Guildhall speech on October 7th, did not hesitate to highlight his own merit. The volunteer transport organization which had done so much to mitigate the hardships caused by the strike had owed its existence, he explained, to his foresight. The lessons of the strike were simple. 'The first is that you cannot hold up the community. The second is equally important. The community must make it clear to all classes ... that it means to deal justly and fairly with their claims. A man's property, whatever form it takes, whether land or buildings or labour – if the community needs it, it must pay a fair price for it. We must make it clear that the nation means to be a just master, a fair master, a generous master – but always a master in its own house.'

Two days later, at 10 Downing Street, Lloyd George wound up revolutionary proceedings for 1919. Robert Smillie and the Executive of the Miners' Federation, accompanied by a large deputation from the Trades Union Congress Parliamentary Committee, arrived on his doorstep with what seemed a well-founded sense of grievance. Why, they asked, had the government refused to act on the findings of the Sankey Commission and nationalize the mining industry? There was, said Smillie, no question of syndicalism. They all realized that the government and the coalowners would have an equal say with the miners. But ... But he and the rest of the deputation, when they could slide a word in edgeways, were overwhelmed by a devastating flow of well-informed loquacity. Such an experiment, said Lloyd George, had not been tried any-where, except for five years in Germany, in the Saar Valley, where conditions were 'very peculiar'. He could not accept that 'public service' was necessarily an incentive to harder work: certainly he had not noticed that this was the case in the postal services. Resistance to the installation of new machinery did not always come from mean-minded capitalists – Mr Herbert Hoover had told him that when he tried to introduce machinery in a Welsh mine, the men themselves had prevented him. Nationalization was a slippery word, capable of many different interpretations. As for the quaint idea that the government was bound to accept every recommendation made by a Royal Commission and so abdicate its right of independent judgment – why that would make a farce of parliamentary democracy. Then came his most powerful, flattering thrust. 'Most of you gentlemen belong to a party different from the one I belong to. You are looking forward to the prospect of assuming the responsibility of government yourselves. I should be very surprised if, when you come to form a government, you adopt such an attitude towards the report of a Royal Commission into any subject you may care to appoint.' He did not wish to 'say anything which would create bitterness', but the deputation must realize that the case for nationalization had been weakened by the railway strike – settled, fortunately, without bloodshed (murmurs of 'Hear, hear!'), but occurring in an industry where 'at least some of the elements of nationalization already existed'.

The government had therefore decided to abide by its proposals to nationalize the coal deposits and 'make a donation towards a fund for improving the conditions of life of the miner in the villages in which he dwells and from which he carries on his perilous trade.' It also intended to 'give the miner an effective voice by means of pit committees', and (if the unification scheme was adopted) by means of representation on District Boards. Silenced, scarcely contriving a thin scatter of questions, and feeling, like the railway leaders, that they had only got as much as this because of the Prime Minister's magic power over his reactionary colleagues, the deputation withdrew. 'We are very much obliged to you', said Smillie, 'for having met us.'

VII

WHERE DID IT ALL GO?

---

1. *The Romantic Amateurs*

In November 1918 the Western world had been in a utopian ferment such as it had not known since the French Revolution and the liberal surge of 1848. One by one the cavalier Spartacists, the anarcho-bohemians of Munich and Fiume, the ardent Marxists of Budapest, the syndicalists of North America and Catalonia, the peasant anarchists of Andalusia and the Ukraine, had made their challenge. One by one they had been overwhelmed or forced to retreat by the big battalions of conservatism. The Russian revolution had been adored and feared because it had seemed the mightiest explosion of militant utopianism. While crushing their own impossibilists in the name of reason, the Bolsheviks had called upon the impossibilists of Europe to fight the battles of a revolution which was completely changing its character.

Everywhere, by the end of 1919, the dreamers of a slaveless world, with their belief in the buried genius of the masses, had been cuffed into hiding, jailed, deported, shot, discredited, disillusioned. Yet it was they who had set the Red Mirage quivering in the heavens. Thrust fantastically and often unwillingly to power, they had made unbearable demands on human nature. They had asked the masses to make, and to go on making, their own decisions, to gird themselves for a serial Golgotha, to live in a constant state of tension and exaltation. Vibrantly impatient yet deeply compassionate; hating injustice yet shrinking from force; sickened by the violence done to their intellectual integrity in the gutter scrimmages of politics; conditioned by a bourgeois sense of decency even while they lashed the bourgeoisie — Rosa Luxemburg, Kurt Eisner, Ernst Toller, Balabanova, had suffered death by a thousand cuts of conscience before they were thrust from the stage.

In Hungary, where the old order had been most seriously mauled, it took its most comprehensive revenge. Fifteen thousand 'subversive' books were withdrawn from the Budapest Central Library and burned. Terrorist gangs continued to operate unchecked. By January 1920 ten thousand 'traitors' had been shot, twenty thousand driven into forced labour camps where many perished of hunger or typhus. The more prominent Bolsheviks were publicly executed, and tickets for the performance sent to the Allied Missions. 'The Anti-Semitic League of Hungary', proclaimed posters, 'desires to solve the Jewish question without compromise—by a thorough disinfection. We demand that the government immediately carry into effect the object of our League—namely, a Hungary without Jews.'

In March 1920 Admiral Horthy was made Regent with dictatorial powers. Count Albert Apponyi went to Paris to sign the Treaty of Trianon. Hungary lost two-thirds of her territory to Rumania, Czechoslovakia, Yugoslavia and Poland. Her population dwindled from 21 millions to 8 millions. The anti-Bolshevism of the Admiral and the Counts had availed no more than the westernizing liberalism of Károlyi to prevent Hungary from becoming the chopping-block of Europe. The restored aristos ate, drank and made merry as best they could, leaving an assortment of charitable organizations to feed the multitudes in their cellars, shanty-towns and cattle-trucks. Italian, French and English capitalists scrambled to 'reconstruct' Hungary so that she would be able to pay the enormous reparations demanded by the Treaty of Trianon. Italo-Hungarian, Anglo-Hungarian and Franco-Hungarian banks took over the country's finances. A British syndicate acquired an oil-prospecting monopoly. The Crown of Hungary was hawked, unsuccessfully, to the highest bidder. Many Hungarians, not all of them proletarians, began to remember the four-month Soviet regime of 1919 as a golden era of national unity and integrity.

The beer halls of Munich, for six weird months the scene of the rival Councils of Eisner, Toller, Mühsam, Leviné and Levien, now resounded to the even more fantastic oratory of Adolf Hitler. In November 1919, when Ludendorff and Hindenburg presented themselves for 'trial' as war criminals, the Freikorps provided a guard of honour for the two hero-victims of Jewish stab-in-the-back socialism. In *The Economic Consequences of the Peace* John Maynard Keynes diagnosed that Europe's revolutionary élan had died of sheer physical exhaustion, leaving a dangerous vacuum of power and ideas. 'There may be ahead of us', he wrote, 'a long, silent process of semi-starvation and of a gradual, steady lowering of the standards of life and comfort ... We are at the dead season of our fortunes ... Our power of caring beyond the immediate questions of our own material well-being is temporarily eclipsed ... Never in the lifetime of men now living has the universal element in the soul of man burned so dimly.'

Through the dust which rose above the wreckage of the failed utopianism of Wilson and the romantic revolutionaries of Europe, Soviet Russia began to look like the last hope of intellectual salvation. The Bolshevik realm had been battered, maligned, blockaded and invaded. But it was still *there*, its leaders were still trying to achieve that 'vast, clumsy, creaking turn of the helm' for which militant progressives, tired of the fixed course of parliamentary democracy, yearned. Communists in America, Britain, Holland, Italy, France and Scandinavia appealed to Moscow for advice. How could they be most effective? What should be their priorities? Should they take any part in the parliamentary rigmarole or not? In September 1919 Zinoviev issued a long circular letter, the first of a long sequence of increasingly sharp lessons prepared by the Russian 'professionals' for the floundering dilettantes of social revolution. The main requirement for any group, whatever its label, which meant business was that it should aim at 'a dictatorship of the proletariat in the form of Soviet power'. That was the long-term objective. In the short term, it was the duty of all practical communists to stop bickering and form a united party, which while concentrating on the formation of militant cells in the trade unions, should not neglect to 'infiltrate' and 'exploit' bourgeois parliaments.

Five months earlier Zinoviev had predicted that all Europe would go communist, that the irresistible forces of the international revolution would bear down on the last bastion of capitalism in the United States. Then there had been a vision, however fanciful, of independent contingents co-operating on equal terms in a great army of liberation. Future congresses of the Third International would be held in Vienna, Berlin, Paris, and London. Now he was spelling out the Russian ABC of revolution to a scatter of half-contrite, half-resentful beginners.

These fledgling communists were not likely, even if they were dimly aware of his existence, to encourage Nestor Makhno in his fight to keep alive what he regarded as the true spirit of revolution, or to see his anarcho-communist peasant movement as a serious alternative to Bolshevism. After all, one *was* living in the twentieth century. The Workers' Republic had, in its struggle to survive, to haul itself up to a Western level of industrial efficiency. For Tolstoy or Tolstoyans to form toy agricultural communes and preach the simple life was understandable. But for a whole nation of peasants to contract out of the march of progress and try to contaminate the towns with their archaic poison — this was an impertinence not to be forgiven.

Yet Makhno persisted in his impertinence. Trotsky made a determined effort to undermine his popularity with the peasants by abandoning the previous policy of collectivization. The Cheka ruthlessly liquidated Makhnovites or Makhnovite sympathizers in the villages. Makhno's security police retaliated in kind. The Reds shot all prisoners. The Makhnovites shot all officers — unless the ordinary soldiers interceded for them. The Cheka made a second attempt to assassinate Makhno. It seemed to Baron Peter Wrangel, who had succeeded Denikin as the White Commander-in-Chief, that Makhno must surely at last be willing to join forces against the common enemy.

Makhno not only refused, but patched up a truce with the Reds for joint action against Wrangel. He did so partly out of implacable hatred for the Landlord's Army, partly in order to bargain for the release of Makhnovites and 'pure' anarchists captured or arrested by the Bolsheviks. He also demanded that in areas occupied by his people, the peasants and workers should be free to build their own 'associations' — which might later, if they so decided, be federated with Soviet Russia. Hard-pressed by a Polish invasion and facing a strong Wrangel offensive, the Reds granted these demands and concluded an alliance (Bela Kun, back in Moscow, was one of the signatories). In Petrograd and Moscow the anarchists made ready for celebration congresses. But in mid-November, after the Whites had been driven from the Crimea, the Bolsheviks repudiated the agreement. Anarchists in Petrograd and Moscow were arrested *en masse* and their leaders shot. The Red Army gave its undivided attention to the elimination of Makhno. In his last desperate resistance, he was wounded six times. At the end of August 1921, with 250 of his closest comrades, he crossed the Dniester into Rumania. Ahead of him lay a miserable ordeal in the prisons of Rumania and Poland, and years of exile in Paris, where he lived on until 1935, tuberculous, alcoholic, a bitter and lonely peasant who hated the city. Only the anarchists of Spain remembered his glory and kept him from starvation.

What the Freikorps had done to the cavaliers of Spartacus and the dreamers of Munich, the Red Army did to Makhno's bucolic buccaneers. East or west, Noske or Trotsky, the eternal High Command knew and exterminated its deadliest foe, the spirit of anarchic liberty. Yet the tough resistance of the Makhnovites in the south and the Greens in the north helped to force the concessions to the peasantry that were part of the New Economic Policy launched in 1921. The Bolsheviks' repudiation of the treaty with Makhno was a direct cause of the Kronstadt Rebellion of the same year, in which anarchists were again prominent. Makhno's prison tutor, Peter Arshinov, forgetting the wild, unedifying ways of Batko, claimed that he had left an imperishable legacy to all who had ears and courage to hear it. 'Makhnovism', he wrote, 'is universal and immortal. Wherever the labouring masses do not let themselves be subjugated ... they will always create their own popular social movements, act according to their own understanding. This is the essence of Makhnovism — "Proletarians of the whole world, look into the depths of your own beings, seek out the truth, and realize it yourselves".' The Russian civil war was full of heroic episodes: but none more so than the saga of Makhno and his rebels. It is a natural for a film epic — but one which Soviet studios are unlikely to make.

All through 1920, while Makhno was locked in a murderous and unreported grapple with the know-alls of city socialism, while police and syndicalist *pistoleros* shot it out in the streets of Barcelona (where more than two hundred people were killed in sixteen months), d'Annunzio was grabbing headlines in his private mouth-war with sordid philistinism. In the plutocratic press he was assassinated and calumniated as often as Lenin and Trotsky. FRESH ATTEMPT ON LIFE OF CRAZY POET, or CHORUS GIRLS AND CHAMPAGNE were typical recurrent headlines. According to one English Sunday newspaper 'the snake-like glitter of d'Annunzio's eye' proved that he was a cocaine addict, and his eighteen-hour poetic 'fasts' were dedicated to sex orgies. In his own estimation, however, he remained the leader of a spiritual crusade. 'We may all perish in the ruins of Fiume,' he said in one of his balcony speeches, 'but from the ruins the spirit will rise. From the indomitable Irish Sinn Fein to the red flag which in Egypt unites the Crescent and the Cross, every uprising of the spirit will be rekindled from our sparks.'

In the autumn of 1920, Sir Osbert Sitwell, visiting the City of the Holocaust as correspondent of the *Nation*, sensed that behind the 'pervading braggadocio' and the flowing black cravats of the *arditi* 'flickered an unmistakable enthusiasm'. D'Annunzio's realm offered, at the least, an alternative to the 'inexorable Scylla and Charybdis of modern life, Slum-Bolshevism or Democratic Bungalow-Rash'. As Sitwell entered the Regent's office a Portuguese journalist, bowing low as he walked backwards from the Presence, was assuring d'Annunzio that his country regarded him as 'the Christ of the Latin world'. The walls were covered with banners and medieval religious images. A huge fifteenth-century bell took up much of the floor space. On the desk lay a pomegranate, d'Annunzio's personal symbol. Eagerly he asked, 'What new poets are there in England?' He was, he confessed, tired of being cut off from his library. The company of soldiers and peasants was beginning to pall.

When, on December 23rd, Premier Giolitti (calculating that there would be no newspapers for three days) sent the Italian fleet to Fiume with instructions to bombard the place if the Regent would not surrender, d'Annunzio was perhaps not so heart-broken as he pretended to be. He, too, was bored. He had made his gesture, bearded the three old idiots, defied the Supreme Council, the League of Nations, and the Italian and Yugoslav governments for fifteen months, without sacrificing the life of a single legionary. It was time to ring down the curtain on 1919's most decorative and diverting tableau of revolt. To the League of Nations it was the end of 'an awkward incident'. To Italians it was an occasion for national mourning. On December 27th, when the news broke, shops and theatres all over the country closed in protest.

At the Vittoriale, his magnificent home on the shores of Lake Garda, attended by a few of the faithful, d'Annunzio kept alive the memory of Fiume by a self-devised cult ritual performed in a circle of marble statues by the light of the moon. He dreamed vaguely of leading a national revolution supported by all the forces of progress (among which he did not include Mussolini's fascists), but confined his militancy to spoof-sensational interviews – describing, for instance, how in hot weather he combined culture with hygiene by sitting naked beneath a fountain reading an edition of Dante printed on rubber pages; or alleging that he had eaten roast baby and found it delicious.

Disgusted by the Russian revolutionaries' evident eagerness to come to terms with the Obscene Waxworks of the West, he reserved his most macabre jape for a Bolshevik victim. When, during the Genoa Conference of 1922, Grigori Chicherin, the immensely erudite and hypochondriac Commissar for Foreign Affairs, visited the Vittoriale, he was invited to dine in the Franciscan refectory. Two legionaries carried in an exquisitely damascened scimitar, laid it upon the table, and withdrew, locking the door behind them. D'Annunzio, glaring at his guest and fondling the blade, suddenly announced: 'My dear friend, for certain reasons I have resolved to cut your head off.' After an interval in which Chicherin's normally pale face went quite livid with apprehension, d'Annunzio frowned peevishly, dropped the scimitar, and said: 'What a pity! I am not in form tonight. I'm afraid I'll have to postpone the matter to another day.'

It was the kind of practical joke that Makhno might have appreciated. It was also a parable of, and a fitting epitaph for, the bourgeois-paling threats and irresolute performance of the romantic revolutionaries of 1919.

2. The Professionals

The romantic revolutionaries suffered, like the Jews, from a double stigma. The Jews were maligned as the evil geniuses of Bolshevism and the main pillars of capitalism. The romantic rebels, tormented as they were by humanitarian qualms (and blamed by hotheads for their squeamishness), were grotesquely pictured as callous, blood-thirsty fiends. Yet the German Spartacists and the Red Army of Munich probably killed fewer class enemies between them than the anarcho-syndicalist *pistoleros* of Barcelona. Rosa Luxemburg and Ernst Toller, Max Levien and Eugen Leviné, put themselves at the head of a workers' revolt out of loyalty rather than conviction. One had to strike a blow against arrogant injustice, to 'make a little try' (as D. H. Lawrence put it) 'that the Risen Christ should be risen'.

By the middle of 1919 Lenin regarded the ethical revolutionaries of Europe as a liability. They had not even been willing to act on the logic of their scruples and restrain their followers from adolescent insurrections that misled the Bolsheviks and added to the general confusion. The double image which they had helped to create — of insensate cruelty and administrative futility, a mixture of the charnel-house and the madhouse — had strengthened the hand of reaction. They richly deserved the double drubbing which they got from infuriated bourgeois and exasperated Bolsheviks — from those, in fact, who had a practical, *professional* approach to power.

The rage of Lenin was not entirely just. He had, certainly, sent sober advice to Berlin, Munich and Budapest, and sometimes it had been ignored. But the pattern of the Bolshevik experiment was still so obscure, even to Lenin, that he could not reasonably expect hasty messages from one chaos to another to be received as the voice of authority. He would have been the first to complain if the romantics had not made their loyal if amateurish efforts to ease (and emulate) the agony and the daring of Russia.

But in Russia the masses — peasants and industrial workers — had set the revolution in motion. They had proposed, the Bolsheviks

disposed. In the West even the factory workers had to be proposed to, and for the most part (remembering the claptrap of the
Second International) resisted any advances from bourgeois socialist
intellectuals. Frustrated by this class barrier, harassed by frantic
appeals for action from Moscow, damned as Bolshevik terrorists by
Berlin, Paris, London, Washington, Rome and even Vienna,
exploited by the Red Mirage-mongers of Comintern and the Supreme
Council, theirs was an impossible situation. When it was all over,
Lenin poured scorn on them in a malicious pamphlet entitled *The
Infantile Disease of Leftism*. Better, they had thought, a good failure
than a bad success. Better, Lenin insisted, an impure success than a
noble failure. Impurities might, in time, be removed. A noble
failure could never be adjusted.

The professionals swept the board in 1919. Under the slogan 'Sus
aux Bolchévistes' Clemenceau's Bloc National gained a crushing
victory in the French elections of November. The socialists, split on
the issue of whether or not to join the Third International and form
a separate Communist Party, were routed. For the first time since
1871 the French Chamber was openly Rightist.

In the United States, Morganism, the epitome of no-quarter big
business, had emerged victorious. The great confidence trick which
ended a decade later in the Great Crash had been expertly set up.
Organized labour was routed. Steelworkers streamed out of Foster's
union. In the steel mills a twelve-hour day was the rule until 1923.
A.F.L. membership, despite the frenzied anti-Red tirades of Samuel
Gompers and John L. Lewis, declined steadily. In 1920 the combined
membership of the two communist parties, soon to be merged,
dropped from 70,000 to 16,000. The National Association of
Manufacturers established an Open Shop Department and published
an *Open Shop Bulletin* and an *Open Shop Encyclopaedia*. In the press,
from the pulpit, in pay packets, in leaflets distributed in schools,
from hoardings, and by patriotic speakers (often garbed as Uncle
Sam), Americans were relentlessly reminded that all unionists were
enemies of the American System and the American way of life, and
the dupes, if not the conscious tools, of Bolshevism.

Wilson's New Freedoms, like Wilson himself, had vanished without
trace. Abroad, the memory of him and his fourteen-pointed
hypocrisy was execrated. Herbert Hoover had supplanted him as the

saviour of Europe. Hungary had been the scene of his most characteristic achievement: there he had withheld the services of his organization from both Bela Kun and the Archduke Joseph, only to feed a
particularly loathsome type of 'republican' fascism into existence.
From the Baltic to the Adriatic, from the Black Sea to the North Sea,
Hoover's empire stretched and his lieutenants ruled. He had
accomplished one of the most astounding logistic feats known to
history. Fifteen million tons of food had been shipped across the
Atlantic for 'the salvation and stabilization of Europe'. He rendered a
two-billion-dollar account for his operations on the Supreme
Economic Council ('if there were six fewer ciphers on these figures,'
he said, 'I might be worried'), and a supplementary 100-million-
dollar account for emergency relief. By the autumn of 1919 his work
of organization was completed. His efficiency was regarded with
awe. In Estonia, Belgium, France, Poland and Italy streets were
named after him—Hooverstrasse, Via Hoover, Rue Hoover. King
Leopold bestowed upon him the title of Citizen and Friend of
Belgium. Lille struck a medal in his honour. Warsaw put up a
monument to him.

At the end of 1919 Hoover was the darling of the frightened
capitalists and aristocrats of Europe. All his brilliant professionalism
went to defend the indefensible, and to make certain the rise of
National Socialism—a travesty of the people's revolutions of 1919,
but at least a travesty and not a blank denial. Hoover's global
defence of the American bourgeois revolution of the eighteenth
century was, like the Great War itself, a giant technological prodigy
with the brain of a midge, a period piece in contemporary costume.

In Germany proletarian fury and disillusion coincided with a
growing desire among the more reckless nationalists of the Right to
smash the farcical 'democratic' Weimar façade now that it had served
its dual purpose of placating the Peace Conference and stifling the
social revolution. Extremists of Right and Left itched to lance the
boil of bourgeois democracy. In January 1920 a huge K.P.D.-
organized crowd of workers, noisy but unarmed, demonstrated
outside the Reichstag in Berlin. Amid howls of 'All power to the
Workers' Councils!' the police opened fire with machine-guns,
killing forty-two demonstrators. On March 13th General von
Lüttwitz and a few thousand Freikorps troops, recently returned
from the Baltic and resisting demobilization, staged a coup. The

government fled first to Dresden, then Stuttgart. Dr Wolfgang Kapp, a founder of the rabidly extremist Fatherland Party, was proclaimed Chancellor. Noske could not raise any troops to quell *this* revolt. Yet four days later, after a nation-wide general strike, the Kapp *putsch* collapsed. In the Ruhr the workers rose *en masse*. In Chemnitz Majority Socialists and communists joined forces in a 'Council' government led by a communist. In Leipzig and Hamburg, socialist rebels took over without firing a shot.

It seemed as though socialists had at last united, as if the German revolution had been given a second chance. Karl Legien, the veteran trade-union leader, called on Majority and Independent Socialists and communists to sink their differences and form a coalition government. Immediately the old bitternesses revived. The Independents and the communists rejected Legien's approach. Pausing only to sack the hated Gustav Noske, Ebert formed another coalition — with the Catholic Centre — and sent the newly reorganized Reichswehr in to smash the Red Ruhr.

The Weimar Republic, loathed by liberals, radicals and reactionaries alike, was allowed to continue its shadowy existence until the Reichswehr had gathered sufficient strength, the Allies had lost all semblance of military supremacy and cohesion, and the generals were ready to unloose a revolution led, democratically, by ex-Corporal Adolf Hitler. Already in 1920 General von Seeckt, the architect of the new Reichswehr, was thinking in terms of an alliance with Soviet Russia. When it came to undoing the Treaty of Versailles, restoring German supremacy, and putting Poles and Czechs in their place, ideology did not matter. The professionals of the German High Command, disciplining themselves to patience, bided their time and picked their moment.

Observing the fate of the do-or-die rebels of Germany and Hungary, the Austrian Social Democrats could permit themselves a certain complacency. Deprived of its imperial setting, forbidden to unite with Germany, treated with hostility by the peasants, harassed by Bela Kun's agitators and the ultimatums of Allied Military Missions, starving, despondent, and simmering with sub-revolutionary resentment, it had seemed that Vienna would never survive, least of all under socialist rule. Yet from this harsh genesis grew the most sustained and dedicatedly professional experiment in municipal socialism yet seen. Within their city state, the Austrian Social

Democrats, combining belief in evolutionary methods with fervent Marxist zeal, worked miracles of steady reformism which amounted, in aggregate, to a social revolution. The brisk battle with the communists for the allegiance of the workers had in itself been an education in democracy. Otto Bauer rated it as one of the most remarkable episodes of 1919. 'In the American Declaration of Independence,' he wrote, 'democracy was defined as a system of government conducted with the assent of the governed. Never and nowhere has democracy in this sense been more completely realized than in this first phase of the Austrian revolution.' The government, lacking all means of coercing the people, had not been able to rule at all 'except by laboriously procuring, daily and even hourly, the assent of the governed'. These methods had been imposed by weakness: but their triumph, he submitted, was 'the measure of the human greatness of the revolution'. The workers took part in local government, sat on school committees, grew their own food on the 60,000 allotments that encircled Vienna, set up their own co-operative building enterprises, and helped to create a health service which, like the housing schemes and the educational system, became the envy of Europe.

Where else, argued Bauer, after all the turmoil of 1919, had there emerged any comparable example of the development of the worker from 'a mindless tool in the hands of the employer ... nothing more than an exhausted animal in his leisure hours' into 'a versatile, cultivated personality who, capable of regulating his life and his labour, will no longer tolerate a master because he needs none?' Progress towards full socialism was, after all, 'nothing but this evolution of the labouring animal into a personality'. But, peculiar alike in its advantages and disadvantages, Vienna remained a lonely, precarious enclave of democracy in depth, submerged at last in the tide of Nazi revolution.

While the Austrian Social Democrats laboured to create an oasis of welfare socialism in a wilderness of bleak reaction, Lloyd George, the supreme professional politician of his time, had, in the teeth of almost universal distrust and hostility, established a personal dominion that had virtually transformed Great Britain into his private kingdom. The *Daily Herald* accused him of dictatorial ambitions, the *New Statesman* of fostering a pernicious atmosphere of political irresponsibility, the *Nation* of deliberately wrecking

Liberalism, the *Spectator* of being a political vampire who had sucked the life-blood out of Conservatism and Liberalism and was about to do the same to the Labour Party. Beatrice Webb referred to him as 'a man of low moral and intellectual values'. Progressives blamed him for not being more progressive; the new intelligentsia for being a pompous old windbag; Tories for not being more Tory; big business for being so socialist; the labour movement for not being more socialist.

But he did not expect friendship or affection. He wanted scope and time to satisfy his compulsion to play politics, his talent for juggling with opposites and removing Britain's miniature mountains. He got what he wanted. Still no one could think of an alternative to him. He was The Man Who Had Won the War, and was respected by the industrialists and trade-union leaders who had helped him to streamline the war effort. He was The Man Who Had Quelled the Rumblings of Revolution, with the help of the same combination. To each party and each pressure group — even the Clyde Workers' Committee — this twentieth-century Cromwell had, like a broad-minded and infinitely experienced father, given hints of sympathy and understanding. He usually began by placating the jingo majority in the Commons, confident that if public opinion did not reach a height of indignation sufficient to justify his intervention, he could always screw it up the mark. He appeared, with brilliant timing, at the ripe moments as the leader of a liberal rescue operation, the enemy of 'unsound' extremists of every kind.

To Lloyd George, the foe of stagnancy *and* of fundamental revolution, there was safety in numbers. He was a maestro of permissiveness; a virtuoso of deadlock; the ringmaster of a democratic circus in which, at the flick of his whip, the tame lions of labour and management alternately roared and returned to their perches; the slick editor of an anthology of protest; the defender and extender of the therapeutic babel of Speakers' Corner, whose mock pugnacity a handful of policemen is sufficient to deter from violence. He defeated social revolution by diffusion, and encouraged Britons to amuse themselves with a Chinese box of minority-mindedness, a basket of hobby-horses.

In 1919, while creating scope for himself, Lloyd George, almost as a by-product, created Britain as it still is, the classic land of delegations, demonstrations and protest letters; of lost but lively hopes; of minorities receding into an infinite distance, mutually hostile but collectively proud of being a living proof of the superiority of the tolerant British way of life—too happily and constantly in 'revolt' to have the time or the inclination to make a revolution.

The Bolsheviks had not captured a Ship of State, they had boarded a derelict. During 1919 famine, disease, cold, infant mortality, battle, and Red and White firing squads had claimed over four million lives. Five millions more died in 1920. It was estimated that in the Urals and the Don Valley, conquered and reconquered by armies riddled with typhus, the population had been reduced by over thirty per cent. The living standard of the workers had plummeted to less than a third, industrial output to less than a sixth, of pre-war level. Inflation was colossal. Nearly half the industrial work force had deserted the towns. Peasant revolts were continual. Cultivated land had shrunk to sixty per cent of the pre-war area. The harvest yield was down to less than fifty per cent. The British Labour delegation which toured Soviet Russia in May and June 1920 reported that the towns were getting barely half the food they needed. Every effort was being made to give children priority: but even so children got less than two-thirds of what they required. Milk was unobtainable save at a prohibitive price. Fats, green vegetables and albuminous foods were in dangerously short supply. Lack of drugs, linen and blankets in the hospitals, and above all of disinfectants and soap, had made the control of typhus almost impossible. Half the doctors engaged in the fight against typhus had themselves perished. 'We are appalled', said the delegation's report, 'at the condition of virtual famine in which the whole urban population—manual and intellectual workers alike—are living.'

The delegation was shocked to find that the Third International, world headquarters of revolutionary socialism, was still 'an entirely *ad hoc* body' with 'no formal constitution or rules' and a complete lack of orderly office procedure. Sylvia Pankhurst, in Moscow for the Second Congress of Comintern in July 1920, noticed a huge, fly-swarming refuse tip outside a 'model' maternity hospital. H. G. Wells, visiting Petrograd and Moscow four months later, recorded an impression of 'vast, irreparable breakdown and emergency government'. In Petrograd every wooden house had been demolished for fuel. Shops, houses and people were desperately shabby, streets rutted and weed-grown. Few citizens had a change of clothes.

World-renowned scientists, including Pavlov, were half-starved and wore mufflers to conceal their collarless shirts.

When Ilya Ehrenburg returned to Moscow in 1920 after his tribulations in the Crimea, Meyerhold put him in charge of all children's theatres. Though now a high-ranking Soviet cultural official, Ehrenburg possessed no trousers and was forced to wear his long, threadbare Parisian overcoat everywhere (he was refused admission to one theatre because he could not take it off). In public kitchens the third-grade rations consisted of a bowl of thin skilly and another of watery stewed apples. Bread was damp and clay-like. Boys and girls of 14 worked in the short-handed factories. Bands of children carried on illicit street trading. Wells, like Gorky, was haunted by a fear that only a little more suffering would push the country over the brink of barbarism. European Russia would die. Asiatic Russia would take over. 'The simple, ancient rhythm of the horseman plundering the peasant and the peasant waylaying the horseman will creep back across the plains ... The cities will become clusters of ruins in the waste. The roads and railroads will rot and rust. The river traffic will decay ...'

At the end of 1919 Trotsky advocated the conversion of 'un-employed' units of the Red Army into labour battalions. In the Urals the Third Army (immobilized since there was no transport for it) was set to timber-felling and farming. Soldiers of the Armies of the Caucasus and the Ukraine were drafted into the mines. 'Display untiring energy in your work, as if you were in battle,' exhorted Trotsky. 'We must become conscious, self-sacrificing builders of the socialist economy. Bread for the starving! Fuel for the freezing! This is now the slogan of our team.' Defending his ideas at the Ninth Party Congress in March 1920, Trotsky reasoned that though labour compulsion was unthinkable under 'full socialism' it would 'reach the highest degree of intensity' during the transition period. Soviet Russia must strip down for an indefinite age of war communism. 'The working masses', he argued, 'cannot be allowed to stray about. They must be ordered about like soldiers ... Deserters ought to be formed into punitive battalions or put into labour camps.' A system of 'socialist emulation' should be introduced, with bonuses for efficient workers. Trade-union 'prejudices' should be ignored, and the trade unions act as government agencies in the struggle for economic survival.

'The most temerarious and the least experienced governing body in the world', wrote H. G. Wells of the Bolsheviks. 'In some directions its incompetence is amazing. In most its ignorance is profound. Of the diabolical cunning of "capitalism" and of the subtleties of reaction it is ridiculously superstitious.' Its naivety reminded Wells of 'those now-forgotten suffragettes who used to promise us an earthly paradise as soon as we escaped from the tyranny of man-made laws'. From their battered and barely mobile chassis, a pitiful wreck to all observers who had not the eyes of faith, these professional catastro-phists beckoned like excited inventors seated in a prototype of infinite potentiality. To them the lesson of 1919 was not that the assault on capitalism had failed because capitalism was too tough, but that the rest of the world had lacked communist parties on the Russian model and that the revolutionaries of the West had been misled by the false Red Mirages of libertarianism and workers' control. In Russia it was the party, only a few hundred thousand strong but rigidly disciplined, that had beaten off every foe within and without. Once drive home this lesson on an international scale and ultimate success was sure. The masses had not been given the right kind of leadership. Soviet Russia alone could provide it.

Every sign of labour revolt in the West was interpreted by a Bolshevik calendar. The Kapp *putsch* in Germany was, according to Lenin, the equivalent of Kornilov's unsuccessful rebellion of September 1917. It showed that the German workers only needed a little prodding to push on to the 'October' stage. Since there were no Germans suitable for the job, a Bolshevik technician or two should be enough to stimulate the necessary action. Lenin's *The Infantile Disease of Leftism*, the textbook for the Second Congress of Comintern held in Moscow in July and August 1920, attacked, on the basis of Russian experience, anti-parliamentarian 'purist' groups in Britain, Germany, France, Italy and the United States. To stand on principle was to invite failure. 'The whole history of Bolshevism, both before and after the October revolution, is full of cases of manoeuvring, of conciliation, of compromises with other parties, including bourgeois parties.' It was utopian to imagine that a new society could be created by 'specially virtuous people bred in hot-houses' or that the workers could function as a kind of collective saviour. Practical communists knew that socialism must be painfully shaped from 'the mass of human material twisted by centuries of slavery, serfdom, capitalism, petty nationalist economies, and the war of all against all'.

Comintern must become 'a single communist party with branches in different countries' and not just a 'letter-box' like the Second International. When members of the British delegation (amongst them William Gallacher and Sylvia Pankhurst) pleaded for some latitude, Lenin demanded implicit and unquestioning obedience. Heretics would simply be excommunicated. The Russian communists would rather carry on the struggle alone than in the company of amateurs. The Hungarian 'failure', it was explained, had been largely due to a misguided union of communists and Social Democrats. A list of Twenty-One Conditions for Admission to the Communist International made the position clear. Though required to make alliances of convenience with bourgeois socialist parties, revolutionists were ordered to form distinct communist parties under the centralized control of Comintern. These must be ready to take 'illegal' as well as 'legal' action, including active propaganda in the armed forces as well as the trade unions; to remove all 'reformists' from responsible positions and to expel all those whom Comintern might designate as open or secret enemies of the cause; to ridicule and undermine the Amsterdam International of 'Free' Trade Unions and the League of Nations' International Labour Organization. It was to be split, split and split, until one reached the rock-bottom of the elect on which the World Federation of Soviet Republics would be founded.

After prolonged emotional and ideological bombardment, most of the visiting amateurs were convinced. The Conditions were almost unanimously approved. After the final session of the congress, Lenin was hoisted on the shoulders of John Reed and two other American delegates. Infuriated, he kicked out and raised some nasty bumps on the romantic revolutionaries' heads. So one job had been completed. But there were others just as urgent. The victory of Moscow had to be followed up with all possible speed. Zinoviev was sent to Halle, near Leipzig, where the German Independent Socialists were meeting to vote on affiliation to Comintern. In a speech of gigantic length (it went on for four hours) he maintained that the German socialists' view that world revolution was no longer imminent was not only untrue (what of sit-in strikes in Italy, the 'soviets' in England, signs of revolt in Austria and the Balkans?) but motivated by sheer cowardice. To those who accused him (correctly) of fantasy-mongering and a reckless desire to gamble with the lives of the workers, he shouted back (also correctly) that a craven fear of real revolution 'ran like a thread' through their whole policy. They were afraid – of dislocation, of hunger, of 'what we have in Russia'. Zinoviev returned to Moscow in triumph. The conference had voted to join Comintern. In December 1920 the K.P.D. and the majority of the U.S.P.D. met in Berlin to found a United German Communist Party with a membership of 350,000 and the prospect of becoming a real power in the land.

Only three months later Bela Kun, now doing 'ruthless' penance for his dealings with Social Democracy, played a considerable part in cutting the membership of the new German Communist Party by more than half. When some copper miners in Mansfeld seized their mines and some chemical factory workers near Halle seized their factories, Kun urged the communists to lead a general rising. But despite isolated outbreaks, a few acts of arson and dynamiting, and the deliberate incitement of unemployed workers to terrorize 'black-legs', the attempt was a miserable failure. This Kapp *putsch* in reverse undid the results of Zinoviev's marathon oratory and was a gift to reformist socialism. *But* the right of the Russian communists to demand and get push-button responses and sacrifices from the laggards of Europe had been established. No cost, no disciplinary humiliation, would henceforth be too great for Comintern's branch membership, whose task was to expiate the sins of the failed revolutionaries of 1919 by slavish obedience. At the same time, Lenin, determined to enforce discipline in his own team, was busy smashing the Workers' Opposition, the last kick of Infantile Leftism in Soviet Russia. 'All these reflections about freedom of speech and criticism,' he sneered during the tenth party congress. 'Comrades, do not let us talk only about words, but about their content ... It is a great deal better to discuss with rifles than with the theses of the opposition. We need no opposition! Either on this side or on that.' The Workers' Opposition was branded as a 'syndicalist and anarchist deviation incompatible with membership of the Russian Communist Party'. The Central Committee was instructed to achieve 'the complete abolition of all fractionalism.'

The spirit of the idealist rebels of 1919 had been, like the corpse of John Reed (who died of typhus and was given a hero's grave in the wall of the Kremlin), definitively buried.

In 1919 the Third International had been — as Zinoviev remarked — 'just a propaganda machine'. Now it was an Inquisition. Outside Russia only Bolshevik envoys or nominees were allowed to make mistakes (experiments). Inside Russia the Central Committee, the Politburo and the Orgburo defined what a mistake was. Lenin still queued up at the barber's and occupied a small servant's room in the Kremlin. But he had one great privilege. He was the only person allowed publicly to admit that the Soviet government had been wrong.

To such a monologic pass had the fine deviationist babel of 1919 been brought. Hundred per cent Marx-Leninism squared up to hundred per cent Americanism. Conformity confronted conformity.

Such was the triumph of professional realism.

3. *The Frozen Fountain*

C. E. Montague, on the western front, had seen a vision of millions of men harrowed up, waiting for some great spiritual husbandman. They had lost faith in politicians, natural rulers, bloodthirsty civilians, and newspapers. 'Imagine', he reflected later, 'the spiritual revival there might have been if some man of apostolic genius had had the ploughing and sowing of the broken soil:

> The frozen fountain would have leapt,
> The buds gone on to blow,
> The warm south wind would have awaked
> To melt the snow.'

The war and the Russian revolution had emptied minds of a great clutter of cant and shaken people to their depths. From the Abyss, material and spiritual, welled up a longing for a new birth. The democracy of the trenches, the immensity of mortality, must, it was felt, have an apocalyptic outcome. The common people had done colossal penance for the sins of their rulers. They would inherit and cleanse the earth. A reign of peace and justice would begin. In comradeship (that key and lovely word) the City of Humanity would be built. Tricky politicians and parasitic lawyers, those emblems of the rottenness of the old dispensation, would be no more. A spirit of service would replace the spirit of greed in commerce and industry.

Nothing had alarmed progressives more than the prospect that the 'noble' masses would really take matters into their own hands and dump *all* their bourgeois bosses off their backs in a sustained orgy of direct action. Luxemburg, Eisner, Toller—all, despite sincere protestations of humility, believed it to be their historic mission to teach the masses how best to fulfil *their* historic mission. Their real fault, in the eyes of the Webbs and other prudent reformers, was that they had set a bad example of impatience and sentimental romanticism. If only they had been content to write constructive articles and reports and influence the right people and be *sensible* and face facts, they might have been useful infiltrators and not dead or discredited rebels.

But if Europe was a blank of reaction, Soviet Russia had come through and was extolling the virtues of long-term planning and state socialism. Experience – and Lenin – had mellowed the Bolsheviks. Soviet Russia, with all its inevitable faults, was clearly the main surviving centre of dynamic, rational progressivism. The idiocies of the Peace Conference and the adolescence of the Spartacists had been offset by the emergence of a regime of systematic socialism which already controlled the destinies of 150 million people and might well prove to be the most, perhaps the only, significant development of 1919.

When the Soviet Union had passed through its emergency phase, the long process of liberalization would surely begin. As early as October 1919 the London *Nation* was already detecting signs of it. What was so wicked about trying to haul the peasants out of the Middle Ages and make efficient farmers of them? Why perpetuate the old lies about Bolsheviks, when there was already 'a cloud of witnesses ... to an exalted public spirit ... stretched to the utmost limits of man's capacity to suffer for an idea?' Lenin, the arch-fiend, ruling Russia on 'one scanty meal a day and 1,800 dollars a year – say a tenth of the price of Mr Churchill's motor car'; Bolshevik 'murderers' covering Soviet Russia with new universities, polytechnics and schools; an illiterate people which 'frequents only the drama of humanism and intellectualism ... and has banished sentimental trash to make room for the classics and for manuals of social and political thought'.

In 1920 the cloud of witnesses grew larger. Often, though not un-critical, they were inclined to suppress or qualify criticism of an ex-periment which had been forced to struggle against such odds and whose general tendency was acceptable. George Lansbury, an ardent Christian and socialist, was the first and most emotional. In his view the Bolsheviks, though atheist, were straining every nerve to put Christ's teachings about social justice into practice. No other nation had made or was willing to make such an effort as Soviet Russia to 'create healthy minds in healthy bodies'. The report of the British Labour Delegation, though firmly rejecting the Soviet form of government as unsuitable for Britain, stressed that most of the accounts of it in the capitalist press 'proved to be perversions of the facts'. A tremendous attempt was being made to abolish social in-equalities and to inculcate 'the idea of the duty of all citizens to take part in reconstructive work for the State'. H. G. Wells, the Labour Delegation and Sylvia Pankhurst were impressed by the Bolsheviks' educational drive—even if, as Wells remarked, it was basically an attempt to remedy a universal lurch towards slum conditions, with the government playing the role of 'a gigantic Dr Barnardo'. Sylvia Pankhurst contrasted education in the Workers' Republic, education for an ideal, with 'the superficial, spurious Empire-worship and snobbery of elementary schools in Britain' and 'the selfish, mercenary cult of "getting on" taught by parents anxious for the welfare of their children in a cruel, competitive world'. She also heartily agreed with the woman in Petrograd who, at a march past of Red Army troops, clad in a weird assortment of old clothes and captured French and British uniforms, turned to her and said: 'It is cruel to force the young men of Russia to fight for progress against the whole world.'

Civil war, blockade, famine, plague, and the growing concentration on 'practical' politics, had not yet stifled the feeling that the revolution would be incomplete if it did not achieve a radical change in values. Anatol Lunacharsky, the Commissar of Education (as bristling with academic brilliance and degrees as Rosa Luxemburg herself), was a paragon of *avant-garde* patronage. Lenin, often against his will, allowed Lunacharsky's catholic kingdom to remain as a liberal showpiece. Its range extended from mass-literacy drives and mass publication of the classics of world literature to the protection and encouragement of experimentalism in the arts. He backed Bogdanov's Proletcult (with its contempt for tradition and its dogged resolve to foster a 'proletarian' style), Meyerhold's 'bio-mechanical' theatre, Eisenstein's pioneering films, and a State Jewish Theatre. Somehow, in 1919, Lunacharsky managed to find time to write a play about Oliver Cromwell and the first volume of a projected chronicle of the Bolshevik experiment, in which he referred to himself as 'the poet of the revolution ... to me it was a stage, inevitably tragic, in the world-wide development of the human spirit towards the Universal Soul, the greatest and most decisive act in the process of God-building, the most striking and definite deed in the realization of the programme which Nietzsche had so felicitously formulated when he said "there is no sense in the world but we ought to give sense to it".' It was Lunacharsky who, for the benefit of the culture-conscious French communists, came up with the slogan, 'Those who are against the bourgeoisie are with us.'

Alexandra Kollontai, Lenin's wife Krupskaya and Lenin's reputed mistress Inessa Armand (head of the Communist Party's Women's Department) were convinced that the collective ideal could only be realized through the emancipation of women and real comradeship between the sexes. To achieve this, the capitalist concept of the 'home' had to be demolished. Individual housekeeping was doomed. Crèches, day nurseries, kindergartens, children's infirmaries and colonies, free schooling and free school meals would enable women to take their full part in the great work of socialist reconstruction. The crisis conditions of war communism, argued Kollontai, had given a terrific impetus to communalization. In Petrograd in 1919 almost ninety per cent of the whole population (and in Soviet Russia as a whole some 12 million town-dwellers) had been fed communally. Housing shortages had forced the development of communal quarters and hostels. Here was a revolution indeed. 'The kitchen which enslaved women even more than motherhood,' exulted the ultra-feminist Kollontai, 'ceases to be the prerequisite of family life.' The days when women 'stooped over a stove to win a husband's approval' were numbered. It was a definite gain that the family household unit was disappearing. 'Of course there are women who cling obstinately to the past. These mistresses-in-law manage even now, in community centres, to turn their lives into an idolatry of the frying-pan. But they have no future, since they are of no use to the Working Collective. The Workers' Republic treats women primarily as participants in its productive efforts. The mother's function is held to be a highly important but complementary obligation, not only towards the private family but to society. To remove the care of motherhood but leave untouched the joyous smile which is born of a woman's contact with her child—such is the Soviet government's principle in solving the motherhood problem.'

Kollontai's hopeful conclusions were drawn from a crazy turmoil of improvisation in which there was little opportunity for cool thinking or long views. In the towns, tens of thousands of children were brought to reception centres for de-lousing and separated from their desperately poor or incompetent parents. The child victims of war communism were ideal material for Bolshevik indoctrination, and were expected to act as shock troops in the campaign against adult ignorance and counter-revolutionary tendencies. The fact that in overcrowded, inadequately supervised co-educational hostels girl pupils frequently became pregnant was hailed by some doctrinaire extremists as a triumph of emancipation. ('What the bourgeois mind is pleased to call immorality is making satisfactory progress in our schools. Numbers of young girls of fifteen and under are already pregnant.') One – hostile – observer claimed to have been present in a Petrograd hospital in 1920 when a worker's wife burst into a crowded clinic sobbing that her son of fourteen had had sexual intercourse with his sister of twelve after attending a course of 'anti-bourgeois' lectures at the local Young Communist Club. Furthermore he had given his sister V.D. 'You ought to be ashamed of yourself!' scolded the communist nurse. 'Why worry? Both of them just followed their natural instincts. No need to make such a fuss. It's just a disease like any other. Your children will be cured – and they must tell their friends where to come when they get ill.'

Some young Bolsheviks maintained that the sex act was simply the satisfaction of a bodily need and should be treated in a spirit of scientific curiosity. The chaos of war communism made for promiscuity; and this too was seen as revolutionary progress. But it led to the dumping of many 'free-love babies' on the steps of foundling hospitals. In November 1920 abortion was legalized. 'Because', the decree stated, 'the moral survivals of the past and the difficult economic conditions of the present still compel many women to resort to this operation, the People's Commissariats of Health and Justice, anxious to protect the health of the women, and considering that methods of repression have failed, have decided to permit such operations to be performed freely and without charge in Soviet hospitals.'

Kollontai, though criticizing sexual irresponsibility, defended, in a remarkable trilogy of novels, what she called 'the rights of the winged Eros'. The sexual urge, she reasoned, could not be confined. Pleasure as well as procreation had its 'sovereign rights' and knew no ideological bounds. In *Free Love* the heroine, theoretically emancipated, suffers cruelly from jealousy about her lover's affairs – and especially his infatuation with a dressy bourgeoise – but finally acknowledges and repents the selfishness of her attitude. In *The Love of Three Generations* a communist mother is shocked to find that her daughter Zhenia has been sleeping with her stepfather Andrey, that she is pregnant, and does not know (or care) by whom. Zhenia is irritated by her mother's concern. 'If I were to sell myself, or if they had all raped me, I would understand. But I did it voluntarily. As long as we like each other we stay together. No one is the loser –

unless one considers that because of the abortion I'll have to stop work for a couple of weeks. After all, Mother, you can't expect to keep Andrey to yourself. That would be a nasty proprietary attitude. It's your bourgeois upbringing coming out.'

Inessa Armand, whose attitude to sexual emancipation closely resembled Kollontai's, had in 1915 written to Lenin that 'even a fleeting passion and liaison' was 'purer' than 'the kisses without love of shallow and philistine spouses'. To which he answered that this was mere sentimental bourgeois libertinism. The real contrast was that between a sham bourgeois marriage and 'a proletarian civil marriage with love'. By 1921 Kollontai-Armand romanticism and the experimental lechery of the Bolshevik 'underground' were being sternly condemned by Lenin. The end of war communism and the crushing of the Kronstadt Rebellion spelt *finis* to the libertarians of lust. They too, it was announced, were objective counter-revolutionaries.

Bourgeois conventions were re-enthroned as proletarian morality. But the moral and physical energy with which they had been challenged, and the fact that the Bolsheviks had 'banned' illegitimacy, cut away the mumbo-jumbo from marriage and divorce, and legalized abortion gave the Workers' Republic a special prestige among radical progressives.

The Red Mirage was still there, though bitterly deplored by those who had been most cruelly deceived by it.

Balabanova had gone to the social democratic haven of Vienna. There she lived in a tiny furnished room, wrote poems, renewed contacts with the friends in Austria and Italy who had been so maligned by Lenin, and asked herself, and her like-minded visitors, why socialism, already surrounded by enemies, should now be faced with the deadliest enemy of all—Bolshevism. For it seemed to her that Bolshevism meant the suppression of socialism.

In Berlin, where they had fled at the end of 1921, Emma Goldman and Alexander Berkman wrote bitterly about their experiences. 'On January 1st, 1920,' remembered Berkman, 'when we touched the soil of Russia, a feeling of solemnity, of awe, almost overwhelmed me ... I had a strong desire to kneel down and kiss the ground consecrated by the lifeblood of generations of suffering and martyrdom, to embrace humanity, to lay my heart at its feet, to give my life a thousand times to the service of the social revolution.' Emma

Goldman had been no less moved. 'Soviet Russia,' she had written, 'sacred ground, magic people. You have come to symbolize humanity's hope, you alone are destined to redeem mankind. I have come to serve you, beloved *matushka*.'

Their offers of service had been rejected. They had been assigned to tour the provinces collecting exhibits for the Museum of the Revolution in Petrograd, shunted away from the centre of things. They had met Spiridonova (a kindred spirit), haggard and indignant, on the run disguised as a peasant woman, and had seen Kropotkin under virtual house-arrest. They had been thrilled by the Kronstadt Rebellion and agonized by its bloody suppression. They had seen Mollie Steimer, an anarchist who like themselves had been deported from the United States, jailed and re-deported. After nearly two years of enforced silence, they set themselves to explode the myth of Soviet Russia as 'the modern Socialist Lourdes to which the blind and the lame, the deaf and the dumb are flocking for miraculous cures'. Outside a few show schools, they wrote, the much-vaunted Soviet educational system barely existed. The tawdry-palatial Rest Centres, full of futurist murals and huge idealized statues (where, as H. G. Wells had reported, the main object seemed to be to teach uncouth workers not to spit on ex-patrician parquet), were boastful propaganda pieces. Prostitution still flourished, and girls were procured for visiting delegates – what else could one expect of Bolshevik cynicism? Lenin might be willing to admit mistakes. But he never ceased to issue orders which it was death to disobey. Imperialist intervention had not weakened the Bolsheviks: it had helped them to destroy the people's revolution. Worst of all, a 'legion of literary prostitutes' and misguided socialists, mesmerized by the 'success' of the Bolsheviks, were strenuously denying the very existence of things which Lenin tried to justify as inevitable. They even accepted the lie that the thousands of rebels who had been massacred in Kronstadt were 'agents of Entente imperialism'.

The growing cult of Bolshevism, as well as the uncritical damnation of *all* revolutionaries as Bolsheviks, had made truth more than ever a native of the rocks. 'Never', protested Emma Goldman, 'was I more convinced of the logic and justice of Anarchism. I mean to expose the fallacy of the Bolsheviks as the holy symbol of the social revolution, not because I have lost faith in revolution or made my peace with Government, but rather because the experience of Russia, more than any theories, has demonstrated that *all* government, whatever its forms or pretences, is a dead weight that paralyses the free spirit and activities of the masses.'

Bertrand Russell, who accompanied the British Labour Delegation, had, unlike Arthur Ransome, been plunged into deep depression by his six weeks in Soviet Russia. There was no question of studying the Soviet system. It was already dead. He felt that everything he valued in life was being crushed in the interests of 'a glib and narrow philosophy'. Only by calling to mind the horrors of Tsarism could he begin to make allowances for the horrors of Bolshevism. The awful standardization, the merely distributive justice, were, he supposed, inevitable. They left 'no room for envy, except of the fortunate victims of injustice in other countries'. He was appalled by the arrogance of this smug little clique of efficiency experts and their promises, when the body of the new society (complete with electrification, mechanized agriculture and near-Western industrial output) had been constructed, to inject the requisite amount of soul. 'The men of my dreams,' he lamented, 'erect, fearless and generous, will they ever exist on earth? Or will men go on fighting, killing and torturing to the end of time, till the earth grows cold and the dying sun can no longer quicken their futile frenzy?'

All through 1919 the writers of Europe had wrestled with the problem of 'commitment'. How could Marinetti's 'proletariat of the spirit' assume its rightful rôle of redemptive leadership?

Clarté, a group founded by three middle-class French intellectuals — Henri Barbusse, Raymond Lefebvre and Paul Vaillant-Couturier — was motivated by a horror of imperialist war and petty nationalist thinking. With Barbusse's anti-war novels, *Under Fire* and *Light*, as a basis, it tried to launch an 'International of the Mind'. In October 1919 appeared the first number of its journal, *Clarté*, whose editorial committee included Anatole France, Georges Duhamel, Charles Gide, Vicente Blasco Ibañez, Jules Romains, E. D. Morel, Upton Sinclair, H. G. Wells, Israel Zangwill and Stefan Zweig. Intent on keeping its message at a high level of sweet reason and internationalist goodwill, it failed to do much more than preach to an elite of the converted. It did not satisfy the militants in the great schism of the French Socialist Party. 'Truth', Barbusse had written, 'is only revolutionary by reason of error's disorder. Revolution is order.' If that was so, why didn't *Clarté* come out openly on the side of those

great order-mongers, the Bolsheviks? Even the aged Anatole
France, in an address to school teachers, had remarked: 'I wish with
all my heart that a delegation of teachers of all nations might soon
join the Workers' International in order to prepare in common a
universal form of healthy education.' It was not long before Barbusse
was writing about 'revolutionary social geometry' and being
criticized by Romain Rolland for butchering life ('that surging
source of subconscious energies, primitive forces, and cosmic
radiance') with such trite Marxist formulae.

But it was Germany that produced the most hectic, complex
intellectual fever-chart of the period. Expressionism, that peculiarly
German literary phenomenon, pushed its obsessive analysis of the
conflict between the generations, of the artist as the outcast foe of
society (and potential saviour of the equally despised but inarticulate
masses) to fantastic extremes of ecstasy and despair. The Expres-
sionists distrusted political action, preferring to rely upon what
Franz Werfel called 'the irresistible dynamite of insight'. Leonhard
Frank coined the typical Expressionist slogan – 'a wave of love will
open the hearts of men'. Ernst Toller emphasized the primacy of
spiritual values as against the base materialism of Marx and Mammon.

The hero of Toller's play, *The Transfiguration*, makes his most
vehement attack on an arid, unloving Bolshevist agitator who incites
the people to bloody revenge. The socialist revolution, he insists,
must be all-redemptive, all-compassionate. In *Not the Murderer*
Werfel showed a youth in violent revolt against his father. But just
when he is on the point of murdering the 'tyrant' he sees him
suddenly as a lonely old man, frightened and helpless. Pity, and a
realization of shared humanity, overwhelms him. He realizes that
there can be no clean break with the past, in which everything is
rooted, out of which everything grows. Dietrich, the hero of Fritz
von Unruh's *Plaza*, at the moment of achieving revolutionary power,
rejects it as the source of all corruption and urges his followers to 'act
out the revolution of love' individually, without leaders, without
enemies. When the Army of the Revolution marches out to battle
with the Army of Reaction, he sees it as a matter of indifference who
wins. Either way there will be violence, pointless suffering, 'a
ghostly battle of dead fantasies'.

Georg Kaiser's *Gas I*, written in 1918, epitomized the predicament
of the artist-saviour. The Son, rebelling against his billionaire
father's values, decides to share with the workers the profits of the

gigantic gasworks which supply the whole world with power. This has the effect of making the workers slave even more frantically. When a terrible explosion kills thousands of his demented 'partners', the Son preaches an anti-industrial sermon. He will close the gasworks and pay for everyone to move into the countryside, where they can work out their redemption in communes of fraternal simplicity. This suggestion brings a storm of abuse from industrialists and workers. The men follow the Engineer (a fanatical believer in the scientific-industrial process) back to the shattered factory, prepared to 'live from explosion to explosion' rather than endure the spiritual strain of the revolution of love. By 1920, in *Gas II*, Kaiser was offering a vision of utter pessimism. The unholy partnership of militarism and industrialism has produced constant, total war. This time the Engineer defeats the Son's redemptive appeal by revealing the invention of a poison gas which will ensure 'victory' to their 'side'. Refusing to accept this new triumph of evil, the Son blows up the gasworks, destroying himself and his misguided fellow creatures. The quiet of the grave settles upon a world whose only real salvation is complete annihilation.

Max Brod, in his novel *The Great Risk*, published late in 1919, also imagined a berserk machine age reaching its logical culmination in the interminable 'activism' of war. The 'new men' live in a burrow beneath a forgotten battlefield. Their community, called Liberia, consists of rootless, neurotic intellectuals in total recoil from their attempt to elbow a redeeming way among the masses. Traditional art, with its tensions of good and evil, has been replaced by an utterly stylized, abstract drama, in which recumbent, gestureless actors recite anti-activist liturgies. The audience looks down at the 'horizontal theatre' as into a tomb. Activist deviations are punished by death. The Liberian dictator is ready to dynamite the burrow if his kingdom of impotence is seriously threatened by any disruptive semblance of life.

The Expressionist saviours were soon in full flight from their terrifying insights. Franz Werfel (who put the blame on God for creating a universe which He ruled with 'police powers of terror and grace') saw them as sick men to whom the idea of revolution was a psychological drug. 'The crooks of politics', he remarked, 'are saints compared with them'.

By the end of 1919 the proletarians of Europe had reached much the same conclusion, but they extended it to include most Socialist intellectuals. Tired of being died for, rhapsodized over, and encouraged to tread painful Golgotha-paths of self-knowledge, they were ready to follow some brawny Engineer from explosion to explosion. Mussolini, a *bona fide* Man of the People, prepared to inaugurate a regime of brute, incessant activism. The legend of Cain and Abel, he said, was the reality, international brotherhood 'a fable to which men listen during the bivouac or the truce'. The answer to the farce of parliamentary democracy was to have One Representative, one inescapable and charismatic face. The great enemy was stagnation (a very real enemy too in the era of Harding, Coolidge, Stanley Baldwin, Ramsay MacDonald and the Weimar Republic). The task was to gather together the loose revolutionary ends, the flapping psychic flexes, of 1919 and plug them into a common source of energy.

The Allies could hardly have been expected to assist the Marxist rebels of Germany, Bavaria and Hungary to seize or keep power. They were too obsessed by a standardized Red Mirage which did not then exist save in Bolshevik or anti-Bolshevik propaganda. One can only speculate as to whether Spartacism or Hungary's brand of communist social democracy might, if they had survived, have inspired the growth of a series of idiosyncratic communist regimes in Europe; or regret that America was not, as Zinoviev and Bukharin predicted she would be, forced to come to terms with socialism by a continental federation of Soviet republics. In 1919 H. G. Alsberg, correspondent of the New York *Nation*, commented: 'If the Entente hopes to see a form of bourgeois socialism develop, then it should see that Hungary is not allowed to starve.' Twenty-six years later, when the Red Army, equipped by Britain and America, set up a Stalinist empire in Eastern Europe, the Allies — and the satellite People's Democracies — paid a heavy price for the Paris Peace Conference's dismal, if understandable, failure of imagination.

It did much to create the infantile either/or in the shadow of which we still live. When in 1946 Count Michael Károlyi returned to Budapest and tried once more to serve the people, he reasoned that the Bolshevik regime in Soviet Russia had survived (when the dictatorships of Mussolini, Horthy and Hitler had crumbled) not simply because of Stalin's ruthlessness but because, through all its murderous windings, it had retained some moral impetus and justification.

Victor Serge, who died in penniless exile in Mexico in 1947, never ceased to believe this. He looked back to the chaotic, comradely times of 1919 in Petrograd as a golden age: but he also looked forward to a socialist renaissance in Russia. Because of the moral vacuum that had succeeded the maelstrom of 1919, Stalinism was for the moment — but only for the moment — the only practical choice. 'Although', wrote Károlyi in later years, 'I was aware that Stalinism was not socialism, I believed that it was the first step towards it. One had to choose. Unable to protest against what was happening in Hungary, I refused to play the enemy's game. So I fell between two stools — the only place I could honourably take.'

The clean sweep longed for and fought for in 1919 did not take place, except fumblingly in the ersatz Fascist and Nazi people's revolutions. The old routine of pseudo-representative democracy, of parliaments stuffed with lawyers profiting from a double brief, continued. It still continues. Even after a second world war Europe was dominated by such heraldic survivals as Churchill, Adenauer, de Gaulle and Franco. A muddled, subconscious groping for workers' control is still kept within 'constitutional' bounds, still represented as a communist-inspired interruption of 'normality'. Politicians are no more popular than they were in 1919. But a huge back-turning movement — the revolution of the snigger, encouraged by the mass-produced irony and quasi-satire of television and press — has brought the Western world dangerously close to the anti-activism of Max Brod's Liberia, or the attractive pseudo-activism of the Dadaists, who in 1919 issued *their* manifesto — against ideologies, against earnestness, against leadership. Why, they asked, all this self-important bother about 'an epoch which is neither better, nor worse, nor more reactionary nor more revolutionary than other epochs'? Dada offered the possibility of a new kind of International 'tied to no frontier, religion or profession. You can join the Dada Club without any obligation. In it each one is President — a politician, a businessman could be a Dadaist.' It offered, too, the prospect of perpetual, whimsical, dude revolution. 'Dada wants to keep the pot boiling, to prevent sedimentation. Dada lives dangerously, says Yes to a life which progresses by contradictions ... Against the anaemic abstractions of Expressionism! Against all literary theories of betterment! Long live Dadaist happenings in the world! To be against this manifesto is to be a Dadaist!'

The evidence seems strong that the revolutionary urge has got stuck in a reflex, gleefully commercialized, rejection of bourgeois values whose main objective, if it has one, is the achievement of group marriage (perhaps not a bad idea: the concept of the family is due for an overhaul) and the vindication of the rights of transvestites and foot fetishists; that verbal obscenity and a non-stop celebration of the sex act will remain the fashionable 'humanist' methods of challenging the machine age and the machine mind; that a second-hand drop-out ethos will continue to spread until its very universality provokes a reaction from the 'underground'; that all save a few old-fashioned activists (cherished for their quaintness) will echo the sentiments of the German Expressionist poet Gottfried Benn, who, disgusted by the brawl of commitment, wrote: 'Of course I hear the great questions of our time: the individual or the community, dedication to the social unit or sublimation, how far one is permitted to cut oneself off, to withdraw, to live one's own aristocracy. But I have no other answer than that which existence teaches me. Every-thing is permitted that leads to experience.'

Yet this kind of disgust easily shades into a longing for violence. Benn hated the dullness of the Weimar Republic. He wrote of the need for 'immanent spiritual strength, substance from the darkness of the irrational'. And so he welcomed Hitler. Such is the danger of the frozen fountain. George Orwell longed to see it flow again with that ardent faith in human brotherhood and perfectibility which powered the romantic revolutionaries of 1919. He (like d'Annunzio) longed to rout the statistic- and machine-worshipping professionals, what-ever their political label. The student revolts, the cult of Fidel Castro, and even more of Che Guevara (who combined something of Makhno's guerrilla brilliance with much of Toller's humanitarian tenderness) indicates that this longing is now shared by hundreds of thousands, perhaps millions, of people who want to see the crass Democratic/Communist either/or smashed to smithereens by the kind of men — 'erect, fearless and generous' — of whom Bertrand Russell dreamed in the utopian wreckage of Soviet Russia.

A formidable pressure of radical, romantic impatience is gathering in the West. It could be that it will force the fountain to flow with a beautiful vengeance.

Bibliography

I. BOOKS

Adamic, Louis, *Dynamite: The Story of Class Violence in America* (London, Jonathan Cape, 1931). Adamic observes that there was a great deal more violence after the crushing of the I.W.W. than before: 'Labour racketeering, as it has developed in the United States, is a natural and even necessary product of powerful and chaotic social and economic forces that have been operating in this country uncontrolled since the beginning of the industrial revolution in the 1840s — gangsterism was a central factor in the American class struggle, first on the capitalist side and then on the side of labour.'

Agar, Herbert, *The Saving Remnant: An Account of Jewish Survival since 1941* (London, Rupert Hart-Davis, 1960).

Allen, F. L., *Only Yesterday* (New York, Bantam Books, 1959). A social documentary of America in the 1920s, with a brief account of the Red Scare of 1919 and the last stand of Woodrow Wilson.

Allen, F. L., *The Lords of Creation: The Story of the Great Age of American Finance* (London, Hamish Hamilton, 1935). The lives, times and apotheosis of Andrew Carnegie, J. P. Morgan, John D. Rockefeller, Henry Clay Frick etc. told with wry but uncensorious detachment.

Angell, Norman, *The Great Illusion: A Study of the Relation of Military Power to National Advantage* (London, Heinemann, 1909). A smug classic on the futility of war — and a classic illustration of the futility of mere rationalism.

Anon, *Woman Under Fire: Six Months in the Red Army* (London, Hutchinson, 1929). A Russian noblewoman's diary of her awful experiences under the Bolsheviks. Full of lecherous, sadistic commissars and fierce nostalgia for prelapsarian Russia.

Anstey, Frank, *Red Europe* (Glasgow, Socialist Labour Press, 1921: first published in Melbourne, 1919). The impressions of an Australian politician-journalist in Europe, 1918–19. Full of contemporary press quotes, good (if pugnaciously pro-Red) on the impact of the Bolshevik revolution, Allied intervention in Russia, and the British and French army and navy mutinies of 1919. It also contains some seldom-seen Soviet Russian posters, both educational and anti-capitalist, of the period. The book crackles with excitement, indignation, and a naive but engaging utopianism.

Ashmead-Bartlett, Ellis, *The Tragedy of Central Europe* (London, Thornton Butterworth, 1923). The adventures of an English newspaper correspondent who was prepared not only to damn the Reds in print but actively to help their enemies.

Babel, Isaac, *Collected Stories* (London, Penguin Books, 1961). For the superb, highly wrought, short stories describing the attempts of a Russian-Jewish intellectual to come to terms with the tough and sometimes squalid realities of the Red Army during the Polish campaign of 1920.

Babel, Isaac, *Marya* (London, Penguin Books, 1966). One of three Soviet plays in one volume, this is a moving account of the seedy flotsam of the revolution—black marketeers and starving or petty-criminal patricians—in Moscow in early 1920.

Balabanov, Angelica, *Impressions of Lenin* (University of Michigan Press, Ann Arbor, 1964). The serio-comic experiences of the Mary Pickford of the Second International in Soviet Russia, 1919–21. The clash between communism and Social Democracy, between revolutionary idealism and revolutionary realism, in miniature—and, partly because it is so concentrated, much more revealing than most, if not all, full-scale books on the subject.

Barbusse, Henri, *Under Fire* (London, Everyman's Library, 1926). First published in France in 1917—where it won the Goncourt Prize—this harrowing indictment of war's waste ends with a moving description of a group of French soldiers talking about the fraternal society of the future on a rain-lashed, hell-churned 'capitalist' battlefield. Ignoring the rest of the book, Lenin remarked: 'You see, even the soldiers turn towards communism.'

Barbusse, Henri, *Light* (London, J. M. Dent, 1933). Overlong, and an uneasy mixture of realism and rhetoric (both of which, taken separately, are good, and sometimes magnificent), this was the key-book of the French left-wing literary revolt of 1919. Barbusse himself, after a long and agonized fluttering on its fringes, finally joined the Communist Party.

Barzini, Luigi, *The Italians* (London, Hamish Hamilton, 1964). Brilliantly illuminating on Mussolini, Gabriele d'Annunzio — and on their hero, the 13th-century 'dictator', Cola di Rienzo.

Bauer, Otto, *The Austrian Revolution* (London, Leonard Parsons, 1925). Sometimes brilliant—especially in its analysis of World War I as the last and greatest of the bourgeois revolutions—yet always slightly smug; the epitome of Austrian Social Democracy.

Bell, Tom, *Pioneering Days* (London, Lawrence & Wishart, 1941). The memoirs of a Clydeside militant who, like most of his fellow-rebels, later became a communist.

Bennett, Geoffrey, *Cowan's War: The Story of British Naval Operations in the Baltic, 1918–20* (London, Collins, 1964).

Berkman, Alexander, *Now and After: The ABC of Communist Anarchism* (New York, Vanguard Press and Jewish Anarchist Federation, 1929).

Blücher, Evelyn, Princess: *An English Wife in Berlin* (London, Constable, 1920). Graphic but often unintentionally side-splitting anecdotes of the plight of German High Society during the revolution.

Borkenau, Franz, *The Communist International* (London, Faber & Faber, 1938). Still perhaps the best account of Lenin's concept of revolution, his war on Social Democracy, and his rôle as a 'modernizer' – as well as of the genesis and changing rôle of Comintern. It contains, too, a wide but trenchant survey of Left socialist groups in Britain, Europe and Scandinavia during and just after World War I.

Brailsford, H. N., *Across the Blockade* (London, Allen & Unwin, 1919). The superb dispatches of the great English radical journalist in collected form. Unforgettable impressions of life under the Allied blockade in Germany, Austria, Poland and Soviet Hungary – and some blistering comments on the Treaty of Versailles.

Braunthal, Julius, *In Search of the Millennium* (London, Gollancz, 1945). A moving account of the tribulations of the scrupulously democratic revolution in Vienna, by the man who, as Deputy War Minister, helped to create the hilariously (and sometimes paralysingly) democratic Austrian Reichswehr. With a passionately partisan introduction by H. N. Brailsford.

Brenan, Gerald, *The Spanish Labyrinth: An Account of the Social and Political Background of the Spanish Civil War* (Cambridge University Press paperback, 1964). First published in 1943 and still the best source for an understanding of Spanish anarchism and anarcho-syndicalism.

Brody, David, *Labour in Crisis: The Steel Strike of 1919* (New York, J. B. Lippincott Company, 1965). A scholarly but readable thesis on the strike that turned into a battle for the 'soul' of America.

Brogan, D. W., *The Development of Modern France* (London, Hamish Hamilton, 1940). Some excellent pages on Clemenceau and the Paris Peace Conference, and on Clemenceau's peasant mentality.

Broad, Lewis, *Winston Churchill: The Years of Preparation* (London, Hutchinson, 1943).

Brown, Percy, *Germany in Dissolution* (London, Andrew Melrose, 1920). A forgotten but perceptive account of the late 1918 revolutionary fling, by an English prisoner of war interned at Rühleben. Brown describes how, with puzzled punctilio, the guards in his camp sent two delegates to Berlin to 'find out how to form a soldiers' council', and remarks: 'The revolution expressed itself in moods which electrified the air. Nothing could have withstood that mood if it had expressed itself in violence. When Berlin paused for two days, on the 9th and 10th of November 1918, its citizens enjoyed their first and last real experience of liberty.'

Bullitt, William, and Freud, Sigmund, *Thomas Woodrow Wilson: a Psychological Study* (Weidenfeld & Nicolson, 1967).

Bullock, Alan, *Hitler: A Study in Tyranny* (London, Pelican Books, 1967). A massive biography with a tiny glimpse of Hitler in the bohemian chaos of 'Soviet' Munich in 1919.

Burns, Emile, *Karl Liebknecht* (London, Martin Lawrence, 1934).

Camus, Albert, *The Rebel* (London, Hamish Hamilton, 1953). A philosophical essay on the meaning of, and the difference between, rebellion and revolution. Like Bertrand Russell, Camus deplores the fact that the Russians treated Marx's pseudo-scientific formulae with reverence long after they had been laughed away by the Western intelligentsia – and so started a new chain-reaction of crude 'superstition'.

Carr, E. H., *The Bolshevik Revolution, 1917–23* (London, Pelican Books, 1960). Three long volumes of relentless, tight-reined scholarship. Wide in scope, rich in quotations, footnotes and appendices.

Caute, David, *Communism and the French Intellectuals, 1914–60* (London, André Deutsch, 1964). For a look at Barbusse and the *Clarté* group in 1918–19.

Chabod, Federico, *A History of Italian Fascism* (London, Weidenfeld & Nicolson, 1963). Valuable for its account of the horror of Liberal Italian politicians, including Orlando and Sonnino, at the too-complete collapse of the Habsburg Empire.

Chamberlin, William Henry, *The Russian Revolution, 1917–21* (London, Macmillan, 1935). Still probably the best and most exciting account of the *social* revolution, and very good on intervention and civil war.

Chesterton, G. K., *The End of the Armistice* (London, Sheed & Ward, 1940). For some interesting reflections on racism – nationalism gone mad – by a man who had come pretty close to fostering it in his First World War writings about the Huns.

Childe, Vere Gordon, *How Labour Governs: A Study of Workers' Representation in Australia* (London Publishing Company, 1923). Contains a stirring and sympathetic account of the I.W.W. in Australia.

Churchill, Winston, *The World Crisis: The Aftermath* (London, Thornton Butterworth, 1929).

Churchill, Winston, *Great Contemporaries* (London, Fontana Books, 1959). For orotund glimpses of Foch, Clemenceau, Balfour, Boris Savinkov and Curzon – and the celebrated demolition job on Trotsky (alias Bronstein).

Cohn, Norman, *Warrant for Genocide: The Myth of the Jewish World Con-*

spiracy and the Protocols of the Elders of Zion (London, Eyre & Spottis-woode, 1967).

Cole, G. D. H., *A History of Socialist Thought*, Vol. IV, Parts I and II — *Communism and Social Democracy, 1914-31* (London, Macmillan, 1965). Invaluable, exhaustive, but surprisingly dull for long stretches. Franz Borkenau's *The Communist International* (see above) is a good corrective or antidote.

Cole, G. D. H., and Postgate, Raymond, *The Common People, 1746-1946* (London, Methuen, University Paperbacks, 1961). An attempt by two passionate Social Democrats, Cole with a guild socialist background, Postgate with a near-Bolshevik one (at least in 1919) to look at British history from the underdog's point of view.

Comfort, Richard A., *Revolutionary Hamburg: Labour Politics in the Early Weimar Republic* (Stanford University Press, 1966). The story, in tepid thesis terminology, of how the workers of Hamburg, for five years (1918-23), revolted unsuccessfully against militarism and 'collabora-tionist' trade unionism in a vain groping for workers' control.

Degras, Jane (editor), *The Communist International, 1919-1943* (Oxford University Press, 1956). Issued under the auspices of the Royal Institute of International Affairs, this gives not only a wide selection from key documents but also useful background information.

Dell, Floyd, *Were You Ever a Child?* (New York, Alfred Knopf, 1919). A good example of flailing anti-Victorian progressivism.

Deutscher, Isaac, *Stalin: A Political Biography* (Oxford University Press, 1949).

Deutscher, Isaac, *The Prophet Armed: Trotsky, 1879-1921* (Oxford University Press, 1954).

Dillon, E. J., *The Peace Conference* (London, Hutchinson, 1919). A classic on-the-spot account, by the correspondent of the *Philadelphia Public Ledger*: full of picturesque details and insights, hypercritical of the Big Four, and in general conveying the impression that the world would have been a far better place if well-informed foreign correspondents had been in charge of the proceedings in Paris.

Dos Passos, John, *1919* (London, Constable, 1932). A fascinating novel-biography of the year in newsreel technique. With famous impression-istic mini-sketches of John Reed, Wesley Everest, Bill Haywood, Woodrow Wilson ('on April 19th sharper Clemenceau and sharper Lloyd George got him into the cosy little threecard game they called the Council of Four ... from the day he landed in Hoboken he had his back to the wall of the White House, talking to save his faith in words ... in the League of Nations ... in himself and in his father's God. He strained every nerve of his body and brain, every agency of his government

(anybody who disagreed was a crook or a red: no pardon for Debs) ...
In Seattle the Wobblies whose leaders were in jail ... whose leaders had
been lynched, who'd been shot down like dogs ... lined four blocks as
Wilson passed, stood silent with their arms folded staring at the great
liberal as he was hurried past in his car, haggard with fatigue, one side of
his face twitching') and J. P. Morgan Jr ('wars and panics on the stock
exchange, machinegunfire and arson, bankruptcies, war loans, starvation, lice, cholera and typhus: good growing weather for the House of
Morgan'). Worth reading for its montages of contemporary press quotes
alone.

Dos Passos, John, *Mr Wilson's War* (London, Hamish Hamilton, 1963).
A long, quasi-rehabilitation. Seemingly an act of extended literary
penance for the author's roughish handling of Wilson in his novel *1919*
(see above). The general effect is of Dos Passos's newsreel technique run
in slow and uncut motion by a careless projectionist. But there are good
things – especially Wilson at the Peace Conference and his relations with
his second wife and with Colonel House.

Dukes, Sir Paul, *Red Dusk and the Morrow: Adventures and Investigations in
Red Russia* (London, Williams & Norgate, 1922). An account of Secret
Service work in Soviet Russia in 1918–19 which reads like a John
Buchan or 'Sapper' thriller.

Duranty, Walter, *I Write As I Please* (London, Hamish Hamilton, 1935).
The chapter on 'Lenin and Others' contains vivid impressions of
Alexandra Kollontai and Sergei Yesenin. There is also a glimpse of
Kollantai and Isadora Duncan talking together in the latter's dressing-
room in Moscow in 1923 ('Isadora sent me out for a bottle of vodka and
then she and Kollontai' – the first woman ever to be appointed an
ambassador – 'sat and talked about life and love and men and what they
thought of them'). Alas, Duranty did not get down a report of the
conversation – 'delivered at high tension by two past mistresses in the
Art of which they spoke'. The vodka paralysed his memory.

Ehrenburg, Ilya, *Men, Years, Life*, vols. 1 & 2 (London, MacGibbon &
Kee, 1961).

Ellis, Havelock, *On Life and Sex* (New York, Signet Books, 1962).

Filene, Peter, *Americans and the Soviet Experiment, 1917–33* (Harvard
University Press, 1967). An excellent, uncluttered thesis with many
quotes from the press and politicians. One of the most recherché
quotes is from William Bullitt's novel, *It's Not Done*, published in 1926 –
'We want to show them that treaties are sacred and debts and religion.
They've all become atheists and I'm for blockading them and starving
them and killing them till they return to their senses and become decent
Christians again.' In 1933 Bullitt became the first American Ambassador
to Soviet Russia.

ZZZ

Fischer, Louis, *Men and Politics* (London, Jonathan Cape, 1941). Fischer maintains that 'there was no German revolution. The lower strata did not rise up and smash the upper crust. Royalty, nobility and plutocracy, momentarily frightened, took refuge and waited ... those from the depths were denied the satisfaction of having fought on the barricades, stormed palaces, and shot traitors ... If it was a revolution it was a typically German revolution. Nobody stepped on the grass.' This is really jaundiced hindsight. I hope my text makes it clear that there was a great deal of stepping on the grass in 1918–19 in Germany, and that the German revolution, though it failed, certainly did exist.

Fischer, Louis, *The Soviets in World Affairs* (London, Jonathan Cape, 1930). For dramatic and curious details of intervention and civil war, the minutiae of Soviet diplomacy, the activities of Savinkov, Sazonov and other Russian émigrés at the Paris Peace Conference – and their contacts with Churchill at the War Office in London.

Fisher, H. A. L., *A History of Europe* (London, Edward Arnold, 1938). The masterpiece of the English Liberal historian and statesman – who in 1919 in Cabinet meetings pleaded for humanity and commercial commonsense in Britain's dealings with Soviet Russia. Elegant, fluent and pontifical, it sometimes descends from noble generalizations and a kind of laissez-faire compassion for the ignorant, suffering human race to malicious asides (Trotsky is described as 'a brilliant Jew who had graduated in petty crime') and tart, unexpected details (of Wilson: 'Over the Poles and their Corridor, as over the Czechs and the Slovaks, he cast his peculiar benediction, perhaps desiring to right the errors of history, but perhaps also recalling how useful was the Polish vote at home, and how numerous and weighty were the Czechs in the city of Chicago').

Fleming, Peter, *The Fate of Admiral Kolchak* (London, Rupert Hart-Davis, 1963).

Footman, David, *Civil War in Russia* (London, Faber & Faber, 1961). A comprehensive coverage. Especially good on Kolchak and Nestor Makhno, it also contains a useful month-by-month table of the main events of the civil war.

Foster, William Zebulon, *The Great Steel Strike* (New York, B. W. Huebsch, 1920). A passionate account by the ex-Wobbly who organized the strike – and later became a leading American communist.

Frölich, Paul, *Rosa Luxemburg* (London, Gollancz, 1940). The most readable biography of this extraordinary woman, written by a man who was a close associate of hers in 1918–19, a member of the Central Committee of the German Communist Party from 1919–24, and a communist delegate in the Reichstag for most of the 1920s. Contains such memorable Luxemburg quotes as the following on the consequences of World War I: 'It is our hope, our flesh and blood, which is falling in swathes like corn under the sickle ... the advance guard of the world proletariat, the workers of Great Britain, France, Germany and Russia are being slaughtered *en masse* ... That is a greater crime by far than the brutish sack of Louvain and the destruction of Rheims Cathedral. It is a deadly blow against the power which holds the whole future of humanity, the only power which can save the values of the past and carry them over into a new and better society ... Profits are rising as working-men fall. And with each one sinks a fighter for the future, a soldier of the Revolution ... The madness will cease only when the workers of Germany and France, Great Britain and Russia extend to each other the hand of friendship and drown the bestial chorus of imperialist hyenas with the thunderous cry of "Workers of the World, Unite!" '

Fry, E. C., *Tom Barker and the I.W.W.* (Australian Society for the Study of Labour History, Canberra, 1965). The swashbuckling story of the English-born leader of the movement for workers' control in Australia during 1914–18.

Gallacher, William, *Revolt on the Clyde* (London, Lawrence & Wishart, 1936). A splendidly pugnacious autobiography, from which Gallacher's account of Lloyd George ('that pompous little peacock') with the Clyde Workers' Committee stays in the memory. During a tense meeting, Lloyd George passed round a box of cigars. The militant workers refused them self-righteously and took out their pipes. Whereupon 'Lloyd George, always ready to take a trick, stuck his hand in his pocket, pulled out a pipe, and said, "That's right, boys. Why should we be formal? If we are going to talk, let's be comfortable. And what's more comforting than a good pipe?" ' The book also contains a rousing version of the George Square 'massacre' of January 31st, 1919, during which Gallacher punched the Chief Constable of Glasgow on the jaw— about the nearest the British revolutionaries came to doing violence to their class enemies, except for a dastardly assault or two on gentleman porters during the rail strike.

George, Alexander and Juliette, *Woodrow Wilson and Colonel House: A Personality Study* (New York, Dover Publications, 1965). A deeply researched but rather muscle-bound attempt to probe the psychological background and interplay of this curious relationship. Less flamboyant, but more reliable, than the Freud-Bullitt psycho-biography.

George, David Lloyd, *Through Terror to Triumph* (London, Hodder & Stoughton, 1915). War speeches that for all their rhetoric have real power and some flashingly brilliant phrases. Churchill's 1940 morale-boosters suffer by comparison.

George, David Lloyd, *War Memoirs*. 6 vols. (Nicholson & Watson, London, 1933–6).

George, Frances Lloyd, *The Years That Are Past* (London, Hutchinson,

1967). Interesting anecdotes about Lloyd George at the Peace Conference and his clashes of opinion with Winston Churchill over intervention in Russia – by the great politician's personal secretary, long-time mistress, and second wife.

Germanetto, Giovanni, *Memoirs of a Barber* (London, Martin Lawrence, 1931). Reminiscences of the Italy of 1918–19 by a Socialist barber who later became a prominent communist.

Ginger, Ray, *The Bending Cross: a Biography of Eugene Victor Debs* (Rutgers University Press, 1949). A competent book about an unforgettable character. In 1918 Debs advocated a Labour Defence Fund 'sufficient to provide each member with the latest high-power rifle, the same as used by Corporation gunmen, and 500 rounds of ammunition ... You should have no more compunction in killing them than if they were so many mad dogs or rattlesnakes ... When the law becomes the bulwark of crime and repression, then an appeal to force is not only morally justified but a patriotic duty.' Just before he was sentenced to ten years' penal servitude, Debs, in a moving peroration, told the judge: 'Your Honour, years ago I recognized my kinship with all living things, and made up my mind that I was not one whit better than the meanest of the earth. I said then and I say now that while there is a lower class, I am in it; while there is a criminal element, I am of it; while there is a soul in prison, I am not free. I never more clearly comprehended than now the great struggle between the powers of greed and the rising hosts of freedom. The people are awaking. In due course they will come into their own.'

Goldman, Emma, *Living My Life* (London, Duckworth, 1932).

Goldring, Douglas, *The Nineteen Twenties* (London, Nicholson & Watson, 1945). Catches the mood of Bolshevik-worship and hatred of 'dirty' politicians among some middle-class rebels. (Richard Aldington told the author: 'I'm still a pretty good shot with a rifle. If any of these damned politicians try to start another war, I'll take a pot at him, if it's the last thing I do!' Alas, he didn't.)

Goldsmith, Margaret, *Seven Women Against the World* (London, Methuen, 1935). Includes excellent potted biographies of Emma Goldman and Rosa Luxemburg.

Gordon, Harold J., *The Reichswehr and the German Republic, 1919–26* (Princeton University Press, 1957). An analysis of the relations between the Majority Socialists, the Freikorps and the High Command.

Gorky, Maxim, *Days With Lenin* (London, Martin Lawrence, 1932). A work of piety, but also a work of art – and better on Lenin than most formal biographies.

Graves, Robert, *Goodbye to All That* (London, Jonathan Cape, 1929). First-hand observations of the army mutinies of 1919 and the mood of trench cynicism (and underlying idealism). Amusing details about the 'revolution' at Oxford University—for instance, ex-officer undergraduates forming a 'soviet' at St John's College to force improvements in the catering system.

Graves, Robert, and Hodge, Alan, *The Long Week-End: A Social History of Great Britain, 1918–39* (London, Faber & Faber, 1940).

Graubard, S. R., *British Labour and the Russian Revolution, 1917–24* (Harvard University Press, 1956). Detailed coverage of the socialist press, socialist conferences and resolutions, parliamentary debates, etc.

Gray, Camilla, *The Great Experiment: Russian Art, 1863–1922* (London, Thames & Hudson, 1962). Outstandingly good in words and illustrations on the cultural ferment in Soviet Russia, 1917–21.

Gunther, John, *Inside Asia* (London, Hamish Hamilton, 1939). For an account of Gandhi's break with the British in 1919 and the beginnings of the civil disobedience campaign.

Hansard, *Parliamentary Debates, 1919*.

Hardy, George, *Those Stormy Years* (London, Lawrence & Wishart, 1956). The memoirs of a Yorkshireman who went to America, joined the I.W.W., was a defendant in the great I.W.W. trial in Chicago in 1918, and later became a communist.

Hausmann, Raoul, *Courrier Dada* (Paris, Éditions La Terrain Vague, 1958).

Haywood, William Dudley, *Bill Haywood's Book* (New York, International Publishers, 1923). The memoirs of the I.W.W. hero, written or ghosted in Moscow, where Haywood died, alcoholic and disillusioned, in 1928.

Hicks, Granville, *John Reed: The Making of a Revolutionary* (New York, The Macmillan Company, 1936). A satisfying if sometimes over-idealized biography of the playboy-intellectual who founded the first American Communist Party, died of typhus in Moscow in 1920, and was buried in the Kremlin Wall—a few days after telling two thousand Asiatic delegates to a Bolshevik Conference at Baku: 'No, comrades, Uncle Sam never gives anything free of charge. He comes with a sack of hay in one hand and a whip in the other, and whoever believes his promises will pay in blood. Don't trust American capitalists.'

Hoare, Sir Samuel, *The Fourth Seal* (London, Heinemann, 1930). An account by the arch-appeaser of the 1930s of his time as Chief of British Military Intelligence in Russia. Useful impressions of Captain Cromie and Admiral Kolchak ('very British in type' according to Hoare).

Hobsbawm, E. J., *Primitive Rebels: Studies in Archaic Forms of Social Movement in the 19th and 20th Centuries* (Manchester University Press, 1959). For an interesting appendix on Nestor Makhno.

Hughes, Philip, *Pope Pius XI* (London, Sheed & Ward, 1938). Helpful background to the Polish chaos as well as an account of the counter-revolutionary activities of the future Pope when he was Vicar Apostolic to Poland in 1918–19.

Irwin, Will, *Herbert Hoover: A Reminiscent Biography* (London, Elkin Mathews and Marrot, 1929.)

Kaas, Baron Albert, and De Lazorovics, Feodor, *Bolshevism in Hungary: The Bela Kun Period* (London, Grant Richards, 1931). A near-classic of reactionary platitude and mythology. The book contains extremely useful appendices with translations of decrees and proclamations issued by the Kun government, and also some verbatim reports of Soviet debates.

Károlyi, Count Michael, *Faith Without Illusion* (London, Jonathan Cape, 1956). The memoirs of the renegade patrician who headed the liberal-socialist revolution of late 1918 in Hungary, only to be humiliated by the Allies and edged out by the Bolsheviks—a fate not uncommon among European liberals of the period. A. J. P. Taylor, in his introduction, justly says that the early chapters 'rank with the writings of Sir Osbert Sitwell as a picture of how the European aristocracy lived in the days before the Fall'—of which the later chapters give a vivid impression.

Keynes, J. M., *The Economic Consequences of the Peace* (London, Macmillan, 1919). A persuasive, epigrammatic account of the Paris Peace Conference which ridicules Wilson, blackguards Clemenceau, but shows a certain grudging admiration for Lloyd George. Full of Bloomsbury Group superiority, of which it is a classic statement.

King, Beatrice, *Changing Man: The Educational System of the U.S.S.R.* (London, Gollancz, 1936). A well-written, well-documented, pro-Bolshevik survey of the educational revolution from its beginnings in 1917.

Koestler, Arthur, *Darkness At Noon* (London, Jonathan Cape, 1940). For a subtly but sensationally dramatized view of the predicament of the Bolshevik Old Guard in the Stalinist purges of the 1930s: the dangers of 'pure reason run amuck'—and ironically playing into the hands of robot, 'neanderthal' killer-bureaucrats.

Kollontai, Alexandra, *Free Love* (London, J. M. Dent & Sons, 1932).

Kornbluhk, Joyce L., *Rebel Voices: an I.W.W. Anthology* (University of Michigan Press, Ann Arbor, 1964).

Landau, Rom, *Paderewski* (London, Nicholson & Watson, 1934). Vivaciously yet atrociously written, but the main facts are there.

Landau, Rom, *Pilsudski, Hero of Poland* (London, Jarrolds, 1930). The same comment applies.

Lansbury, George, *My Life* (London, Constable, 1931).

Lawrence, D. H., *Selected Letters* (London, Penguin Books, 1961). Lawrence instinctively distrusted the shibboleths of the progressives and revolutionaries of the post-war decade. These letters offer some searing glimpses of his pet aversions.

Leighton, Isabel (editor), *The Aspirin Age, 1919–41* (London, Penguin Books, 1964). For useful local colour on the Peace Conference in a chapter—'The Forgotten Men of Versailles'—by Harry Hanson, then Paris correspondent of the New York *Globe*.

Levin, Dan, *Stormy Petrel: The Life and Works of Maxim Gorky* (London, Frederick Muller, 1967).

Lindsay, Jack (editor), *Russian Poetry 1917–55* (London, Bodley Head, 1955).

London, Jack, *The People of the Abyss* (London, Isbister & Co., 1903).

London, Jack, *Essays of Revolt* (New York, Vanguard Press, 1926).

Luce, Robert L. (editor), *Fifty Years of the New Republic* (London, Allen & Unwin, 1965).

Lunacharsky, Anatol, *Revolutionary Silhouettes* (London, Allen Lane, The Penguin Press, 1967). Lunacharsky's impressions of Lenin, Trotsky, Zinoviev and other Bolshevik leaders—with Stalin a notable absentee. First published in 1919, they are here prefaced by Isaac Deutscher.

Macartney, C. A., *The Social Revolution in Austria* (Cambridge University Press, 1926).

Mann, Tom, *Memoirs* (London, Labour Publishing Company, 1923).

Martin, Kingsley, *Harold Laski: A Biographical Memoir* (London, Gollancz, 1953). For details of the tribulations of Laski during Boston's Great Red Scare.

Marty, André, *The Epic of the Black Sea* (London, Modern Books, 1940). A partisan account of the mutiny of the French Fleet in the Black Sea in 1919, written by one of its ringleaders, who later became a communist.

Marwick, Arthur, *The Deluge: British Society and the First World War* (London, Bodley Head, 1965).

Marx, Karl, *Selected Works* (London, Lawrence & Wishart, 1942). In two volumes, prepared by the Marx-Engels-Lenin Institute in Moscow.

Masters, D. C., *The Winnipeg General Strike: A Study in Western Labour Radicalism* (University of Toronto Press, 1950).

Mayer, Arno J., *The Politics and Diplomacy of Peacemaking: Containment and Counter-Revolution at Versailles* (London, Weidenfeld & Nicolson, 1968).

Mencken, H. L., *The Vintage Mencken* (New York, Vintage Books, 1955).

Middlemas, Robert Keith, *The Clydesiders* (London, Hutchinson, 1965). For a workmanlike analysis of the relations between the Marxist militants of the Clyde and the airy-fairy humanitarians of the I.L.P., and a detailed account of the background, organization and collapse of the Glasgow 'revolution' of January 1919.

Mitchell, Allan, *Revolution in Bavaria, 1918–19: The Eisner Regime and the Soviet Republic* (Princeton University Press, 1965).

Mitchell, David, *Women on the Warpath: The Story of the Women of the First World War* (London, Jonathan Cape, 1966). For the development of Sylvia Pankhurst from suffragette to freelance communist.

Mitchell, David, *The Fighting Pankhursts* (London, Jonathan Cape, 1967). More details on Sylvia Pankhurst, the most colourful British 'Bolshevist' of 1919, and her ideological battles with Lenin and her violently Conservative mother, Emmeline.

Montague, C. E., *Disenchantment* (London, Chatto & Windus, 1922). A key book for the disillusionment—by the war itself and by the post-war settlement—of the ardent Rupert Brooke-type liberal volunteers of 1914.

Montessori, Maria, *Secrets of Childhood* (London, Longmans, Green, 1936).

Morel, E. D., *Truth and the War* (London, National Labour Press, 1916). The masterpiece of the great radical crusader whose diatribes against the British government's responsibility for the war became so violent that German socialists, trying to bring home the guilt of *their* government, begged him to desist.

Murray, Robert K., *Red Scare: A Study in National Hysteria* (University of Minnesota Press, Minneapolis, 1955).

Myers, Gustavus, *A History of the Great American Fortunes* (New York, Random House, 1936). First published in 1909 and a 'must' in I.W.W. halls, this relentless indictment of the motives and methods of big business was brought up to date by the author and still makes lively—and required—reading.

Nearing, Scott, *Education in Soviet Russia* (New York, International Publishers, 1926).

Nettl, J. P., *Rosa Luxemburg* (Oxford University Press, 1966). An authoritative but overlong biography of the most learned, passionate and noble Marxist of them all.

Nevinson, H. W., *Last Changes, Last Chances* (London, Nisbet, 1928).

Nicolson, Harold, *Peacemaking 1919* (London, Constable, 1933). A classically urbane account of the Peace Conference, with excerpts from the young scholar-diplomat's diaries.

Nicolson, Harold, *Some People* (London, Constable, 1927). Semi-fictionalized period pieces, including a memorable glimpse of Lord Curzon at work and a satirical story about a know-all foreign correspondent at the Peace Conference—given his come-uppance by Lloyd George.

Obolensky, Dmitri (editor), *The Penguin Book of Russian Verse* (London, Penguin Books, 1967).

Ortega y Gasset, José, *The Revolt of the Masses* (London, Unwin Books, 1963). First published in 1923, this long essay deplores the tendency of an age of mass democracy to degenerate into a mindless welfare orgy, with 'the people' opening their big mouths ever wider to be crammed with demoralizing goodies. It refers to the Bolshevik experiment as 'the great commonplace of revolutions' but sadly accepts the fact that the increase in the sheer *number* of people in the world (despite war, plague, classocide and genocide) makes some form of collectivism inevitable.

Orwell, George, *The Road to Wigan Pier* (London, Gollancz, 1937) and *The Lion and the Unicorn: the Genius of British Socialism* (London, Secker & Warburg, 1941). In the former, Orwell lamented that socialism, which in 1919, when he was a schoolboy at Eton, had made such a wide and generous appeal, now 'smelt of machine-worship and the stupid cult of Russia' (just the kind of thing that Ernst Toller, for instance, had said in 1919). In the latter, written at the time of Dunkirk, Orwell argued that if it could be made clear that defeating Hitler meant wiping out class privilege, the indispensable middle class of technical and professional experts might be won for the social revolution. Like Bukharin in 1919, he imagined a last stand of reaction in some semi-colonial country—probably India. He forecast that the war would 'bankrupt the majority of public schools if it continues for another year or so', and advocated a stern egalitarianism ('the lady in the Rolls Royce is more damaging to morale than a fleet of Goering's bombers'). Once more the opportunity passed, and in *Animal Farm* Orwell repeated the conclusions of the romantic rebels of 1919—that all revolutions corrupt and absolute revolutions corrupt absolutely. In *1984* he repeated his conviction that 'successful' revolution was the bane of mankind, and 'unsuccessful' rebellion, even by a few scattered groups or individuals (that 'archipelago of goodwill' of which Barbusse had written in 1919) the salt and hope of the earth.

Parkes, James, *Antisemitism* (London, Vallentine, Mitchell, 1963).

Paul, Eden and Cedar, *Creative Revolution* (London, Allen & Unwin, 1920). English left-wing socialist intellectuals yearning after Bolshevik 'activism' and decrying the 'outworn farce' of parliamentary democracy.

Pearsall Smith, Logan, *Trivia* (London, Constable, 1918).

Philips Price, Morgan, *My Reminiscences of the Russian Revolution* (London, Allen & Unwin, 1921).

Plivier, Theodore, *The Kaiser Goes, the Generals Remain* (London, Faber & Faber, 1933). A documentary novel of the German revolutionary spree of October and November 1918: particularly good on the rebel sailors of Kiel and the hectic demagogy of Karl Liebknecht.

Pollitt, Harry, *Serving My Time* (London, Lawrence & Wishart, 1940).

Popoff, George, *City of the Red Plague: Soviet Rule in a Baltic Town* (London, Allen & Unwin, 1932). An understandably biased but vivid account of the Bolshevik occupation of Riga: written by a Riga-born journalist who returned to his native town as a refugee from Red Petrograd — only to find the long arm of the revolution catching up with him again.

Postgate, Raymond, *The Bolshevik Theory* (London, Grant Richards, 1920). A lively attempt to explain Bolshevik 'democracy' to the English — with excerpts from Soviet decrees, Comintern manifestoes, and the *New Communist Manifesto* of 1919.

Pribicevic, Branko, *The Shop Stewards' Movement and Workers' Control in Britain* (Oxford, Basil Blackwell, 1959). An exhaustive thesis by a Yugoslav student, with an interesting foreward by G. D. H. Cole.

Ransome, Arthur, *Six Weeks in Soviet Russia* (London, Allen & Unwin, 1919).

Reed, John, *Ten Days That Shook the World* (London, Penguin Books, 1967). Reed's account of the first days of the Bolshevik revolution, published in 1919. Much over-rated — Reed was not the great journalist his admirers have cracked him up to be — but necessary for an understanding of Reed's 'people'-worship and romantic revolutionism.

Reinhold, Dr Peter, *The Economic, Financial and Political State of Germany Since the War* (Yale University Press, 1928).

Renshaw, Patrick, *The Wobblies: The Story of Syndicalism in the United States* (London, Eyre & Spottiswoode, 1967). The most recent, but surprisingly dull, book on the Wobblies. Its most useful service is to sketch the astonishingly wide spread of the Wobbly version of workers' control.

Rhodes, Anthony, *The Poet as Superman: A Life of Gabriele d'Annunzio* (London, Weidenfeld & Nicolson, 1959). For a fairly full account of d'Annunzio as the 'Dictator' of Fiume.

Ribemont-Dessaignes, G., *Déjà Jadis, ou Du Mouvement Dada à L'Espace Abstrait* (Paris, René Juillard, 1958).

Rogers, Will, *The Cowboy Philosopher at the Peace Conference* (New York, Harper, 1919). Shrewd and sometimes very funny. The celebrated American comedian claimed, 'You can't tell Peace from War without this book.'

Rossi, A. (pseudonym), *The Rise of Italian Fascism* (London, Methuen, 1938). Describes the links between Gabriele d'Annunzio, militant Socialist rebels, and Errico Malatesta, the veteran Italian anarchist.

Russell, Bertrand, *Roads to Freedom: Socialism, Anarchism, Syndicalism* (London, Allen & Unwin, 1918). Russell recommends guild socialism as the best road.

Russell, Bertrand, *The Practice and Theory of Bolshevism* (London, Allen & Unwin, 1920). The book Russell wrote after his six-week visit to Soviet Russia in 1920.

Russell, Bertrand, *Autobiography*, vols. I and II (London, Allen & Unwin, 1967 and 1968). For Russell's early development of the theory and practice of free love, and extracts from diaries and letters written during his Russian trip of 1920.

Sayers, Michael, and Kahn, Albert, *The Great Conspiracy Against Russia* (London, Collet's Holdings Ltd., 1946). A comprehensive, pro-Soviet survey of Allied intervention in 1917–21.

Shapovalenko, S. G. (editor), *Polytechnical Education in the U.S.S.R.* (Paris, UNESCO, 1963). Polytechnical theory and practice since 1917.

Schlesinger, Rudolf (editor), *The Family in the U.S.S.R.* (London, Routledge & Kegan Paul, 1949). A very useful compendium. Contains Engels on the origins of the family; Lenin's correspondence with Inessa Armand on sexual emancipation; the 1918 Soviet marriage law; the 1920 decree on the legalization of abortion; and excerpts from the writings of Alexandra Kollontai on the emancipation of women, the 'new morality', and the coming triumph of collectivism – also a clip from her novel, *The Love of Three Generations*.

Schneider, Herbert W., *Making The Fascist State* (Oxford University Press, 1928). A first-class, heavily-documented coverage. Appendices give numerous quotations from the writings and speeches of Mussolini, Marinetti and other Fascist-Futurists, from c. 1910–1920.

Sender, Toni, *Autobiography of a German Rebel* (London, Routledge, 1940). The sad experiences of an idealistic Independent Socialist in 1918–19. Herbert Morrison, who wrote a preface, described the book as 'the best study of post-war Germany from a socialist point of view that I have read'.

Serge, Victor (pseudonym), *Memoirs of a Revolutionary* (Oxford University Press, 1963). The Russia of 1919 as seen by an honorary (and tenuous) Bolshevik with a violently utopian anarchist background. Witty, exciting and often deeply moving.

Seton-Watson, H., *The Pattern of Communist Revolution: A Historical Analysis* (London, Methuen, 1960).

Shaw, George Bernard, *What I Really Wrote About the War* (London, Constable, 1931). A sparkling collection, including *Commonsense and the War* (1914), various reflections on the Russian revolution, *Peace*

Conference Hints (1919) and many newspaper and magazine articles of the period.

Shub, David, *Lenin* (London, Pelican Books, 1966). Anti-Bolshevik yet full of a grudging admiration for Lenin. Has a useful, if loaded, selection from Lenin's writings.

Silone, Ignazio, *Fontamara* (London, Methuen, 1934). For an ex-communist novelist's look at the beginnings of fascism and communism in post-war Italy.

Silone, Ignazio, his essay on why he left the party in *The God That Failed: Six Studies in Communism* (London, Hamish Hamilton, 1950). For the story of how an English communist's 'honesty' made the Kremlin rock with laughter.

Sitwell, Sir Osbert, *Noble Essences* (London, Macmillan, 1950). For some details about Ronald Firbank in 1919 and an entertaining account of the author's interview with d'Annunzio in 1920.

Smillie, Robert, *My Life for Labour* (London, Mills & Boon, 1924). Remarkable mainly for a typically 'lofty' — but perceptive — foreword by Ramsay MacDonald, which goes far to explain why he was so loathed by Marxists and indeed all militant socialists in Britain. 'Smillie's ideal', he writes, 'is to lead in the righting of wrongs. The poverty of his kith and kin draws him to them as the distress of a damsel commands knightly service. Robert Smillie will to the end be a chivalrous knight of the common folk. His opposition is based, as was Keir Hardie's, not on hatred but on visions, not upon pockets but on conscience, and is always tempered by charity ... Economic interests are mighty things, but they can never bring peace in a rational and moral society. The rebellions which they stir are market-place brawls, the oppositions which they create destroy but do not fulfil. For steady evolutionary progress and social creation something more is required ... that something Smillie got from the tales and ditties of his grandmother ...'

Sokel, Walter H., *The Writer in Extremis: Expressionism in 20th Century German Literature* (Stanford University Press, 1959). A brilliant survey of a remarkable and neglected phenomenon.

Steffens, Lincoln, *Autobiography* (New York, Harcourt Brace, 1931). Wonderful, highly idiosyncratic reporting on the Bolsheviks in 1917 and 1919 — and also on the Paris Peace Conference and what, in Steffens's opinion, made President Wilson tick.

Steinberg, Isaac, *Maria Spiridonova, Revolutionary Terrorist* (London, Methuen, 1935).

Steinberg, Isaac, *In the Workshop of the Revolution* (London, Gollancz, 1955). A long, angry, anti-Bolshevik I-told-you-so by the Social Revolutionary who was Commissar for Justice in the first Soviet government — until he himself was clapped into jail by the Bolsheviks.

Steiner, Rudolf, *In the Changed Conditions of Our Times* (London, Steiner Publishing Company, 1941). Six lectures given at the Goetheanum, Dornach, Switzerland—world headquarters of Anthroposophy—in November/December 1918. 'The programme of Wilson speaks of the human being in general, but this abstract humanity does not exist. What exists is always the single, individual human being. In this individual human being we can become interested ... only through our full humanity, not through mere thinking. When we Wilsonize or Bolshevize, sketching an abstract picture of humanity, we extinguish what we should develop in the relationship of man to man.'

Stewart, Bob, *Breaking the Fetters* (London, Lawrence & Wishart, 1967). The memoirs of a militant Scot who progressed from temperance reform to communism.

Stuart, John (editor), *The Education of John Reed* (New York, International Publishers, 1955). Selected writings.

Swinson, Arthur, *North-West Frontier: People & Events, 1839–1947* (London, Hutchinson, 1967). For an account of the tribulations of the British Raj during the Indian riots of 1919 and the Third Afghan War—though there is more information on the latter in the third volume of E. H. Carr's *The Bolshevik Revolution* (see p. 350).

Taylor, A. J. P., *The Troublemakers: Dissent Over Foreign Policy, 1792–1939* (London, Hamish Hamilton, 1956). For background on E. D. Morel, H. N. Brailsford, Bertrand Russell, Ramsay MacDonald and other stars of Britain's radical pressure group: shows how their account of the origins of World War I and the iniquities of the Peace Conference became virtually the official version.

Taylor, A. J. P., *The Habsburg Monarchy, 1815–1918* (London, Macmillan, 1941).

Taylor, A. J. P., *The Course of German History* (London, Hamish Hamilton, 1945). For the chapters on the German revolution, in which Taylor shows a tenderness, unusual in such a political realist, for Eisner and the more wildly utopian Independent Socialists.

Taylor, A. J. P., *The First World War: An Illustrated History* (London, Hamish Hamilton, 1963).

Taylor, A. J. P., *The Origins of the Second World War* (London, Hamish Hamilton, 1961). Excellent on the anti-Versailles roots of appeasement and for a brief, cool résumé of the Paris Peace Conference.

Taylor, A. J. P., *The Rise and Fall of Lloyd George* (Cambridge University Press, 1961). Probably the most coruscating, and certainly the most concise, study of the politician whom Lenin most admired.

Thorez, Maurice, *Son of the People* (London, Lawrence & Wishart, 1938). The autobiography of the French communist leader, with a few graphic if simple-minded comments on the 'feebleness' of French socialists in 1919.

Toller, Ernst, *I Was A German* (London, Bodley Head, 1934). The moving, if sometimes near-hysterical, autobiography of the idealistic playwright who got caught up in the hilarious maelstrom of revolution in Munich. In his introduction Toller, who committed suicide in 1939, writes: 'Not only my own youth is portrayed here, but the youth of a whole generation ... it followed many different paths, believed in false prophets, but always tried to hear the voice of reason and of truth.'

Tolstoy, Count Leo, *The Slavery of Our Times* (Free Age Press, Maldon, Essex, England, 1900). On non-violent opposition to the State, and the virtues of the simple, or at least simplified, life.

Tressell, Robert, *The Ragged-Trousered Philanthropists* (London, Panther Books, 1967). First published in 1914, this is a long, lovable novel about the obstinate unsocialism of the British working classes.

Trotsky, Leon, *The Essential Trotsky* (London, Unwin Books, 1963).

Tuchman, Barbara, *The Proud Tower: A Portrait of the World Before the War, 1890–1914* (London, Hamish Hamilton, 1966). A vivid, detailed impression of the first mutterings of mass democracy and the rearguard actions of the ancien régimes.

Turner, Ian, *Industrial Labour and Politics: The Dynamics of the Labour Movement in Eastern Australia, 1900–1921* (Australian National University and Cambridge University Press, 1965). For details of the I.W.W. and the One Big Union movement in Australia, 1914–21.

Voline (V. M. Eichenbaum), *The Unknown Revolution* (London, Freedom Press, 1955). A 'pure' anarchist's half-hero-worshipping, half-horrified account of his experiences with Nestor Makhno.

Webb, Beatrice, *Beatrice Webb's Diaries, 1912–1924* (London, Longmans, Green, 1952). Edited by Margaret Cole, these not only provide indispensable anecdotal and general background, but prove that the Webbs were just as firmly convinced as Lenin of the right and duty of an intellectual aristocracy to dragoon the masses for their own good.

Weir, L. MacNeill, M.P., *The Tragedy of Ramsay MacDonald* (London, Secker & Warburg, 1938).

Wells, H. G., *Russia in the Shadows* (London, Hodder & Stoughton, 1920). An account of his visit to Moscow and Petrograd in 1920.

Wells, H. G. *The Outline of History* (London, Cassell, 1951). For the chapter on the post-war settlement and the inter-war period. Wells sees Woodrow Wilson as a classic illustration of the Henry James theme of the 'innocent' American baffled by the evil subtleties of Europe.

Willcocks, Mary Patricia, *Towards New Horizons* (London, Bodley Head,

1919). The *Saturday Review*, in an apopleptic notice headed 'Bolshevism in Petticoats', described this as 'mischievous and inflammatory nonsense ... discipline in the army is sneered at ... English people recommended to settle the land question with the same speed as the Russian peasants ... Sexual promiscuity is described as "simplicity of outlook" or "free alliances" ... and the marriage law denounced as "the creation of an artificial class that has lost its grip on reality" ... We trust that the aims of this silly Bolshevist shrew will always remain on the horizons: and that if she ever reaches the skyline it will be with gyves upon her wrists and in the company of a male guard.' The same journal, at about the same time, commented on the proposal to admit women lawyers to practice: 'The vision of the family solicitrix ought to inspire the most stickit comic dramatist ... Throughout the long generations the Benchers have always been faithful to their unique trust, and now that they are confronted for the first time with the problem of epicenity, they will, no doubt, deal faithfully with it.'

Williams, Albert Rhys, *Through the Russian Revolution* (New York, Boni & Liveright, 1921).

Winter, Ella, *Red Virtue: Human Relationships in the New Russia* (London, Gollancz, 1933). Good stories of how the communist drive for equality between the sexes met with violent opposition in the villages.

Winwar, Frances, *Wings of Fire: A Biography of Gabriele d'Annunzio* (London, Alvin Redman, 1957).

Woodcock, George, and Avakumovic, Ivan, *The Anarchist Prince: A Biographical Study of Peter Kropotkin* (London, T. V. Boardman, 1950).

Woodcock, George, *Anarchism: A History of Libertarian Ideas and Movements* (London, Pelican Books, 1963). For Nestor Makhno, anarcho-syndicalism in Spain, and some comments on Gustav Landauer and Erich Mühsam.

Woolf, Leonard, *Downhill All the Way* (London, Hogarth Press, 1967). Volume IV of his autobiography, covering the years 1919–39. Woolf tells the story of how in 1919, when he was editing the *International Review* (a monthly financed by the Quaker Rowntrees), he was approached by Theodore Rothstein, a Jewish communist, with the offer of a collection of recent Lenin speeches for publication. After a stealthy hand-over of documents under the clock of the Law Courts in the Strand, Woolf was 'raided' by the police, who seized the speeches and vetoed their publication. Woolf's fury at this stupidity was matched — even over-matched — by his distaste for Rothstein, whom he describes as an otherwise cultured and civilized person who 'inside the magic circle [of his Bolshevist faith] was a cross between a schoolman and a dancing dervish ... a civilized savage who would expound at great length in that dreadful jargon of meaningless abstractions which has become the language of communism and the excuse for torturing or killing hundreds of thousands of human beings.'

Woolf, Virginia, *A Writer's Notebook* (London, Hogarth Press, 1953).

Wyndham Lewis, Percy, *Blasting and Bombardiering* (London, Calder & Boyars, 1967).

Zetkin, Klara, *Reminiscences of Lenin* (London, Modern Books, 1929). For a very interesting report of a conversation with Lenin in 1921 on 'revolutionary morality'.

2. PAMPHLETS, LEAFLETS AND REPORTS

I found most of these in the London Library's extensive collection. Others were made available to me by Mr James Klugmann in his own library, and the rest in the British Museum Reading Room. It is interesting to note that fourteen items were published by the Workers' Socialist Federation or the People's Russian Information Bureau, both of which were under the wing of Sylvia Pankhurst, who brought to her freelance communism (she was expelled from the Communist Party of Great Britain a few months after it was formed) all the tireless and spectacular fervour which she had earlier given to the suffragette movement. Any student of the period must come deeply into her debt, because apart from her copious pamphlet production, her weekly newspaper, *The Workers' Dreadnought*, provides by far the liveliest and widest coverage of left-wing 'happenings' in the United Kingdom as well as of the Bolshevik revolution — seen (at this stage), through starry eyes.

Anon, *The Story of Bolshevism: A Warning to British Women* (London, National Publications, 1919). Possibly written by Sylvia's rabidly anti-Bolshevik elder sister, Christabel Pankhurst.

Barber, Margaret, *A British Nurse in Soviet Russia* (London, A. C. Fifield, 1920).

Berkman, Alexander, *The Russian Tragedy* (Der Syndikalist, Berlin, 1922).

Berkman, Alexander, and Goldman, Emma, *Deportation: Its Meaning and Menace — A Last Message to the People of America* (New York, M. E. Fitzgerald, 1919).

Birukov, Paul, *The New Russia* (Glasgow, I.L.P., 1919). A Tolstoyan condemns Allied intervention, denies that Lenin was a German agent, and ridicules the story of the nationalization of women in Soviet Russia.

British Labour Delegation to Soviet Russia, Report of (London, 1920). The signatories of this report were: Ben Turner (Labour Party, Chairman of of the delegation); Margaret Bondfield, A. A. Purcell, and H. Skinner (Trades Union Congress); Ethel Snowden, Tom Shaw and Robert Williams (Labour Party); Charles Roden Buxton and Dr Leslie Haden

Guest (Joint Secretaries). The report was endorsed by R. C. Wallhead and Clifford Allen on behalf of the Independent Labour Party (I.L.P.).

Bukharin, Nicolai, *Soviets or Parliament* (London, Workers' Socialist Federation, 1918).

Bullitt Mission to Soviet Russia, Report of. (I read this in slightly abbreviated form in the New York *Nation*, International Relations Section, Section II, October 4th, 1919.)

Comintern, *The Shame of Being A Scab, Say, What Are You?* and *The Work of the Soviets* (Petrograd, 1919). Three sparkling anti-capitalist leaflets from the brilliant and fervently idealistic team of the infant Third International.

Crooks, Rt. Hon. Will, P.C., M.P., *The British Workman Defends His Home* (London, Whitehall Press, 1918). A classic statement of the 'patriotic' Labour war-line.

D'Annunzio, Gabriele, *Italy or Death* (Fiume, 1919).

Finnish Communist Party, *An Open Letter to Comrade Lenin* (London, People's Russian Information Bureau, 1918).

Gallacher, William, and Campbell, J. R., *Direct Action* (Glasgow, Scottish Workers' Committee, 1919).

Goldman, Emma, *The Crushing of the Russian Revolution* (London, Freedom Press, 1922). A reprint of her articles in the New York *World*.

Gorky, Maxim, *On the Bolsheviki* (London, People's Russian Information Bureau, 1918).

Grosz, Georg, *L'Art et La Société Bourgeoise* (Paris, Dossiers Partisans, 1967). How the Hogarth of the Weimar Republic turned from pictorial savaging of the bourgeoisie to 'constructive' communism.

Hunt, Alice Riggs, *Facts About Communist Hungary* (London, Workers' Socialist Federation, 1919). The impressions of an American woman journalist in Bolshevik Budapest.

Kemp, Rear-Admiral, and Young, Douglas, *British Consul Replies to Anti-Bolshevik Slanders* (London, People's Russian Information Bureau, 1919). Reprint of correspondence between Rear-Admiral Kemp, Senior Naval Officer in North Russia in 1918, and Douglas Young, former British Consul at Archangel, which appeared in *The Times*.

King, Joseph, *Russia and her Allies: An Account of British Policy Towards Russia and of the Military Intervention of the Allies against the Soviet Government, with an enquiry as to whether the Russian Revolution is likely to be overthrown by the Militarist-Financial forces now ranged against it* (Glasgow, Reformers' Bookstall, 1919). A substantial, closely-argued, pamphlet — a reminder that 1919 was probably the last golden year of pamphleteering in Britain.

Kollontai, Alexandra, *Communism and the Family* (London, Workers' Socialist Federation, 1920).

Kollontai, Alexandra, *The Workers' Opposition* (London, printed privately by E. Morse, 1962). A translation of the pamphlet circulated among delegates to the Russian Communist Party Congress in March 1921 at the time of the Kronstadt Rebellion. In it Kollontai, the general's daughter who, with A. Schlyapnikov, headed the Workers' Opposition, vehemently opposed the semi-capitalist programme of Lenin's New Economic Policy. She warned that if the initiative of the workers continued to be thwarted, the revolution itself would die. 'The creation of communism can and will be the work of the toiling masses themselves ... If there is comradeship in our Party, it only exists among the rank-and-file ... the sooner the Party leaders follow the road marked out by the revolutionary workers, the sooner shall we step over the line beyond which humanity, having freed itself from objective economic laws, and profiting by the rich scientific treasure of the workers' collective, will begin to create the human history of the communist epoch.'

Kun, Bela, *Revolutionary Essays* (British Socialist Party, 1919). A selection of articles which appeared in *Pravda* during 1918.

Marchand, René, *Allied Agents in Soviet Russia* (London, People's Russian Information Bureau, 1919).

Nearing, Scott, *A Nation Divided or Plutocracy versus Democracy* (Chicago, Socialist Party of the United States, 1920). The pamphlet insists that plutocrats are also revolutionaries: 'If Edison, Steinmetz, Ford, Taylor, Rockefeller and Hill had served a year in prison for every revolutionary twist they gave to the productive mechanism, they would have spent their entire lives behind bars. The last few years have witnessed a paroxysm of revolutionary change in every phase of commerce and industry ... There must be a similarly bold revolution in human relationships. Job ownership—the Joker in the Plutocratic Pack of Trump Cards—must go, also plutocratic control of the press and politics.'

Newbold, J. T. Walton, *Bankers, Bondholders and Bolsheviks* (Glasgow, I.L.P., 1919).

Newbold, J. T. Walton, *Capitalism and the Counter-Revolution* (London, Workers' Socialist Federation, 1919).

Pandemic of Influenza, 1918–19, Report on (London, His Majesty's Stationary Office, 1920—compiled by the Ministry of Health).

Pankhurst, Sylvia, *Housing and the Workers' Revolution* (London, Workers' Socialist Federation, 1919). A Kollontai-like vision of the new collectivism.

Paul, Eden and Cedar, *Independent Working Class Education* (London, Workers' Socialist Federation, 1918).

Philips Price, Morgan, *The Origin and Growth of the Russian Soviets* (London, People's Russian Information Bureau, 1919). Substantial, authoritative, and charged with emotion.

Ransome, Arthur, *The Truth About Soviet Russia* (London, Workers' Socialist Federation, 1919).

Roebuck, C. M., *The Nationalization of Women: The Natural History of a Lie* (Glasgow, British Socialist Party, 1919). Traces the origin and growth of the legend of Red Lust in great detail.

Schmitt, C. H., *The Hungarian Revolution: An Eye-Witness's Account of the First Five Days, October 31st to November 5th, 1918* (London, Workers' Socialist Federation, 1919).

Seymour Cocks, F., *Russia and the Allies* (London, People's Russian Information Bureau, 1919). A reprint of articles in the *Herald*.

Trotsky, L., *A Paradise In This World* (London, British Socialist Party, 1918). A fiery utopian speech of April 1918. Interesting, too, for a careful statement of the Bolshevik attitude to anarchists.

Zangwill, Israel, *Hands Off Russia* (London, Workers' Socialist Federation, 1919). Probably the most devastating demolition of the interventionist case.

3. NEWSPAPERS AND PERIODICALS

Apart from those indicated in the text, I have consulted the following periodicals (the first five English, the other three American): *The Common Cause* (National Union of Women's Suffrage Societies), *The Economic Journal*, *The Masses* (vaguely syndicalist—editor, W. F. Watson), *The Spur* (anarchist—editor, Guy Aldred), *The Century Magazine*, *The Dial*, *The North American Review*.

The New Europe (U.K.) and—especially—the International Relations Section of the New York *Nation* provide an invaluable selection of decrees, manifestoes and speeches from Soviet Russia and Hungary (both Bolshevik and opposition), Spartacus/K.P.D. in Germany, the Eisner and Soviet regimes in Munich, the Fascist/Futurists in Italy, and Socialist groups in Poland and Czechoslovakia. The Library of the Royal Institute of International Affairs made available a collection of press cuttings covering the period from November 1918 to the end of 1920 which gave me a journalistic bird's-eye view of the whole turmoil. The *New Europe* and the *Nation* also contain many excerpts from the European and Russian press which are useful in themselves and as pointers to further research.

Overland (quarterly, Melbourne) of May 1966 has an entertaining article by Wobbly Tom Barker entitled 'How I Did My Time at Albury and was Deported to Chile.'

The Journal of Contemporary History (quarterly, London) of April 1967 devoted to the theme of 'Literature and Society' contains useful essays on writers in the early Weimar Republic, Henri Barbusse and the *Clarté* group, Romain Rolland, George Orwell's patriotism, and D. H. Lawrence's ragings against industrial regimentation.

The article from which I quote at the end of Chapter 4, Section 4 (*Lenin's Greatest Ally*) appeared in the *Sunday Times Magazine* in April 1967. Entitled 'Inside the Soul of Chairman Cherkasov', it was written by George Feifer and was the first in a series on Soviet Russia fifty years after the Bolshevik revolution.

I should perhaps explain that the *Daily Herald*, launched in 1912, became a weekly during the war (as the *Herald*) but resumed daily publication on April 1st, 1919.

4. WAR CABINET AND OTHER PAPERS IN THE PUBLIC RECORD OFFICE, LONDON

(*Note:* It seemed worth giving a detailed summary of these, which not only show Churchill at his fighting anti-Bolshevik best, but offer some insights into the mentality and methods of a government forced to come to grips with the revolt of the masses even if not with a shooting revolution.)

WC 514, January 8th, 1919: Meeting on Co-ordination of Demobilization, attended by three generals, including General Sir William Robertson, C-in-C Home Forces, who is instructed to 'meet the delegates of the soldiers assembled in Horse Guards' Parade and to inform them that officers will be sent at once to Park Royal to investigate their alleged grievances'.

WC 515, January 10th, 1919: Discussion on the military situation in Russia. Field-Marshal Sir Henry Wilson, Chief of the Imperial General Staff, points out that as a result of demobilization 'unrest' and the fact that it is 'notorious that the prospect of being sent to Russia is immensely unpopular' it is impossible to relieve British troops in north Russia and Siberia. He also pleads for stricter press and radio censorship, and is supported in this by Winston Churchill. Churchill suggests that 'it might be advisable to let Germany know that if she is prepared to organize her eastern front against Bolshevism, the Allied governments will raise no objection ... it is a matter for serious consideration whether we should not now decide to bolster up the Central Powers, if necessary, in order to stem the tide of Bolshevism'.

WC 522, January 30th, 1919: Urgent discussion of 'the labour situation' in Glasgow. Bonar Law thinks it vital for the War Cabinet to be 'satisfied that there is a sufficient force in Glasgow to prevent disorder ... It is certain that if the movement in Glasgow grows it will spread all over the country.' General Sir William Robertson reports on the troops available in Scotland.

WC 523, January 31st, 1919: Further discussion of the Glasgow/Belfast situation. The Rt Hon. R. Munro, K.C., M.P., Secretary for Scotland, says it is clear that this is 'a Bolshevist rising and not a strike'. The Deputy Chief of the Imperial General Staff reports that six tanks and 100 motor lorries are on their way north.

WC 527, February 4th, 1919: Lord Curzon suggests a permanent Committee of Industrial Unrest. Churchill complains that trade-union officials cannot control the rank-and-file ('the curse of Trade Unionism is that there is not enough of it—with a powerful Union either peace or war can be made'.) The Cabinet decides to appeal to the Royal Automobile Club and to private owners to supply motor volunteers in case of emergency and to 'place their cars at the disposal of the working classes for the purpose of conveying them to and from their work'.

WC 531, February 12th, 1919: (Lloyd George presiding). Long discussion on the Situation in Russia. Churchill maintains that the vacillation of the Allies is disheartening Generals Denikin and Krasnov. 'If we are going to withdraw our troops it should be done at once. If we are going to intervene we should send larger forces. I believe that we ought to intervene ... If the Allies will not help Russia, Japan and Germany will certainly do so, and in a few years' time we shall see the German Republic united with the Bolsheviks in Russia and the Japanese in the Far East—forming one of the most powerful combinations the world has ever seen.' Lloyd George says that he understands that 'to do any good' at least 150,000 men would be needed, apart from massive supplies of war material to the Whites. Lord Curzon favours a 'bolstering' policy, with British and possibly Scandinavian volunteers.

GT 6978, February 1919: Conditions in Germany: Report by V.77, including Munich, Berlin, Cassel, Frankfurt, Mannheim, Heidelberg, Karlsruhe, Baden-Baden and Offenburg. The report states that the strength of the Spartacists, especially with Germany still under stringent Allied blockade, is that 'they have nothing to lose and everything to gain by a continuance of anarchy'. Many of their leaders, he says, are 'idealists from the "modern" intellectual and artistic classes and are much more dangerous than the adventurers. They combine a fanatical belief in their ideals with considerable learning and eloquence, and surround their political dogmas with a halo of "modernistic" art and letters which makes a special appeal to the intellectual snobbism characteristic of the German mentality. Such people are Erich Mühsam, Franz Pfempfert, Karl Hirsch, Johannes Becher etc. ... Karl Radek (Sobelsohn is his real name) is probably a mixture of the two, and combines strong instincts and habits of criminality with an almost religious belief in Bolshevism as a doctrine, and a conviction that Lenin and his followers have a mission to the world.'

CAB/23/76: Memorandum on Allied Effort to Support Loyal Russian Governments up to February 18th, 1919. This estimates that to date a total of 202,400 troops 'has been dispatched to various portions of the former Russian Empire' (British and Indian 44,600; French 13,600; American 13,700; Italian 3,000; Japanese 80,000; Serbian 2,500; Czechoslovak 42,000; Greek 3,000).

CAB/23/76, February 21st, 1919: Confidential Memorandum on the Prinkipo Proposal, prepared by the Political Intelligence Department of the Foreign Office. This is simply the text of Zinoviev's speech to the Petrograd Soviet on January 27th, 1919. ('The French bourgeoisie are warlike because the workers' revolution is especially near to them. The water is mounting to their throats and they are prepared to play *va banque* ... The English bourgeoisie is spreading all kinds of gossip ... the Bolshevik party has split. Lenin, forsooth, has been arrested more than once by us. At the head of one part of our party stands Lenin, and at the head of the opposition party are supposed to stand Trotsky, Zinoviev, Peters and Radek. Lies such as these show that their position is not a healthy one. The position of these gentlemen must be very bad if they relate such Arabian fairy tales to their readers.')

WC 542, March 6th, 1919: Cabinet considers complaints from Sir Joseph Maclay, Shipping Controller, about the vast tonnage being used to take war material to Denikin in south Russia. Churchill argues that since plans have already been made to withdraw British troops from that area and to compensate Denikin with war material and a military mission, it is important to fulfil the agreement: this will enable Great Britain 'to retain the power to control him if he does not fall in with our wishes' — otherwise he might well interfere with the Georgian Menshevik Republic and other independent states in the Caucasus. Curzon agrees that it is necessary to keep a check on Denikin.

WC 550, March 24th, 1919: Cabinet discusses a report from General Greenly, Chief of the Military Mission in Rumania, and a supporting memorandum from Lord Curzon (Acting Secretary of State for Foreign Affairs) urging substantial support 'to enable Rumania to defend her frontiers and to resist internal Bolshevism' — to the tune of a credit for £500,000 for the purchase of railway material, another for over £400,000 to buy military stores and animals, and the use of shipping to transfer material and stores. Austen Chamberlain (Chancellor of the Exchequer) does not see why the burden cannot be shared among the Allies. Curzon pleads that the danger in Rumania is acute, and that 'she is the sole outpost remaining to us in the East of Europe'. Churchill submits that there is no time for delay—or for waiting upon a decision from the Paris Peace Conference: 'The Bolshevik armies are pressing right on to the Rumanian frontier. Hungary, whom we thought we had crushed, has, according to the latest reports, once more assumed a hostile attitude towards the Allied Powers, this time in Bolshevik guise.'

The Railways: In view of the government's pretence, at the time of the strike in September/October 1919, that the railwaymen had suddenly 'declared war' on 'the community', it is interesting to note that throughout March the Cabinet frequently discussed the 'railway situation' and that on March 20th the Industrial Unrest Committee proposed that in the event of a railway strike all existing systems of insurance benefit should be suspended.

FO 800/250/PRO, April/May 1919: Private Papers of the Rt Hon. Cecil Harmsworth, Under-Secretary of State for Foreign Affairs, concerning the Blockade.

WC 560, April 29th, 1919: Churchill stresses that his military advisers have for some time favoured a relaxation of the blockade—'as there would be less chance, if this were done, of Germany relapsing into complete anarchy ... if Germany were allowed to do a certain amount of trading, the threat to reimpose the blockade would have greater effect than if it had never been raised.' Curzon favours retaining full blockade 'until it is known whether or not the Germans will sign the Preliminary Peace Terms'. Churchill expresses the hope that Bonar Law, during his visit to Paris, will draw Lloyd George's attention to a War Office memorandum advocating recognition of Kolchak's government (Kolchak's armies were then enjoying a brief success on the Urals front, and advancing westwards towards Moscow). Recognition, thought Churchill, would 'greatly facilitate future operations': but it would be advisable first to 'obtain a declaration from Kolchak regarding his democratic policy on land questions etc.'

GT 7322 CAB 24/PRO, May 1919: Memorandum on the Soviet Governments in Munich and their Suppression, prepared by the Political Intelligence Department, Foreign Office. ' ... A student appropriately named Toller (madman) emerged as the leader of the Independent Socialists and a commander of the Red Guard ... All the leaders in Munich seem to have been pure adventurers like Gustav Landauer, Erich Mühsam and Dr Franz Lipp ... Dr Lipp has been repeatedly interned in lunatic asylums. An Argentinian, Silvio Gezell, was Finance

Minister, and a Czech Minister of Communications (in the first Soviet government) ... This was a caricature even of Sovietism ... its chief activity was plastering the buildings of Munich with proclamations of decrees issued by the Central Council. The press was commandeered and compelled by way of propaganda to publish futurist woodcuts — a Munich speciality ... (but) the second Soviet government was Sovietism, Communism and Bolshevism in deadly earnest, as the bourgeois of Munich soon realized to their cost ... '

WC 563, May 6th, 1919: Churchill urges the Cabinet to approve a plan to transport 1,200 Russian officers to England for training (and to Archangel, Murmansk, Novorossisk or Vladivostock after training), also to feed, outfit, and provide them with spending money during their stay in the United Kingdom. He reports that Kolchak's 'purely Russian army' is 'really rolling forward', that Kolchak himself proposes to go to Archangel 'very soon', and that 'plans are being made to hand over to him the whole of our obligations in Northern Russia'.

WC 573, May 29th, 1919: Austen Chamberlain and Sir Albert Stanley (President of the Board of Trade) strongly object to War Office demands for more locomotives and rolling stock to be sent to General Denikin, since 'the transport situation in Great Britain gives cause for profound anxiety' and 'the burden of fighting the Bolshevists in Russia is now being borne by Great Britain alone and the situation is becoming intolerable'.

GT 7386 CAB 24/PRO, May 31st, 1919: The Communist Revolution in Hungary. A Special Report prepared by the Home Office Directorate of Intelligence. In this report Károlyi is described as 'a vain and rather stupid man who was regarded as being so pro-Entente that at one time he was suspected of being an Entente agent. He came to power with promises he could not perform' (unlike Lloyd George of course). The report stresses that '25 out of 32 Communist office holders are Jews'. Bela Kun, 'though so prominent in the newspapers, is perhaps the least important member of the government. He is described as a clever self-advertiser ... The more serious Ministers apologize for him, saying that he is an illiterate man and deserves great credit for having done as well as he has with no equipment but that of a third-rate orator ... They are nervous when he goes to see Foreign Ministers by himself. He likes it but they dread it, for he gets into difficulties when he tries to explain Communist doctrines.' Georg Lukacs, the son of a wealthy banker, a distinguished art critic and formerly Professor of Philosophy at Heidelberg University, is described in the report as 'the author of the ambitious education scheme, under which children are removed from their parents and educated in confiscated palaces until they are 24. He tried to compel nine or ten thousand bank clerks, out of employment, to act as schoolmasters' (in fact Lukacs offered employment as teachers to out-of-work lawyers). 'He is an amiable dreamer.' Josef Pogany, for a time War Commissar, then Deputy Commissar for Foreign Affairs, was, says the report, openly accused by the Red Army of being a sham Bolshevik in the pay of the German General Staff. Julius Helvesi, formerly an engineer in an electric-light factory and now Commissar for Social Production, is pictured as being 'in an advanced state of consumption ... His idea is that qualified engineers are the salt of the earth, the real kings of creation, and that the revolution is to rest upon their shoulders. These men are now strutting about the factories ... bursting with self-importance.' Josef Saxe, Commissar for Press Propaganda, had spent ten years in London as correspondent for the German socialist paper *Vorwärts*. 'He had', says the report, 'an extraordinary belief in his own powers ... On his return to Budapest he described himself as being in a quandary because he did not wish to tie himself up in Hungary when there was a chance of his being offered an important post in the British Cabinet on the outbreak of revolution, which he believed to be imminent ... after some consideration he decided to take office in order to gain experience. He hopes before long to come to London.' Kun's secretary and personal assistant, Alpari, is reported to be the real brain of the Hungarian revolution.

WC 584, June 24th, 1919: Cabinet reproves Home Secretary Edward Shortt for detaining four foreign delegates to the Southport Labour Party Conference.

WC 591, July 10th, 1919: Bonar Law directs that the type of motor car at the disposal of Ministers and junior officials shall be changed — 'the expensive type of car should be sold and a single inexpensive type substituted ... I have been informed that few abuses are causing greater discontent than the fact that junior officials are seen passing through London in powerful cars, the upkeep of which is maintained out of the public purse.' (Note: the *Daily Herald* in particular had been running a campaign — with photographs — on this point.)

WC 592, July 14th, 1919: During a discussion of British commitments in Russia, Austen Chamberlain grumbles about 'pouring money in this way into the Russian sieve,' and H. A. L. Fisher, President of the Board of Education, suggests that 'the Bolshevist government is losing some of its more objectionable features'. Lord Curzon undertakes to prepare a memorandum on the internal situation in Russia for the consideration of the War Cabinet.

WC 599, July 25th, 1919: Yet another discussion of the military situation in Russia. Churchill states that 'it is quite conceivable that the anti-Bolshevist movement may collapse within the next few months.'

WC 601, July 29th, 1919: Lengthy discussion of British policy in Russia. Lloyd George insists that it was never intended to interfere in Russia's internal affairs or to conduct an anti-Bolshevist campaign, but merely (i) to reactivate the eastern front against the Germans, (ii) to assist our 'friends', and (iii) to defend the right of self-determination in the Baltic States, the Ukraine, Georgia etc., against Bolshevik designs. Churchill stresses the success of intervention in containing the Red Army.

WC 612, August 12th, 1919: Lloyd George tears Lord Curzon's memorandum to pieces, since in his view it implies that intervention has been in the nature of an anti-Bolshevist campaign. Churchill repeats his praise for the 'negative' achievements of intervention (see above). He and Curzon agree that a Political Representative should be sent to south Russia to keep an eye on Denikin.

WC 627, October 2nd, 1919: Cabinet memorandum reporting Lloyd George's dealings with a delegation from the Transport Workers' Federation the previous afternoon (during the Rail Strike).

GT 8322 CAB/24/90, October 11th, 1919: Special Report on Russia, circulated by the Home Secretary. ' ... The Bolshevik Government still continues in power, but its sphere of influence is gradually decreasing and there are not wanting signs that its end is within measurable distance ... '

CAB/24/90, October 15th, 1919: Churchill's even more jubilant memorandum to the War Cabinet on the Situation in Russia. 'At the present time the military situation, taken as a whole, is such that it would be prudent to count upon the collapse and destruction of the Bolshevik power and its replacement by some form of government based upon the forces of Kolchak and Denikin ... I do not believe that it will be open to us to choose between a "strong Russia" or a "weak Russia". There is going to be a United Russia.'

FO/800/251/PRO, October/November/December, 1919: Private Papers of Sir H. J. Mackinder, M.P., Relating to his Mission to south Russia (including Mackinder's correspondence with Lord Curzon and his report on his brief tenure of office as British High Commissioner in South Russia).

CAB/23/18, January, 1920: Memorandum to the War Cabinet of an Allied Conference held in London on the subject, mainly, of Allied interests and policy in the Caucasus. This states that the Shell Company is 'anxious to obtain the permission of the British Government to take steps to bring oil from Baku and Grosny to this country'. The company 'owned all the oil-providing wells in these districts. A very large quantity of oil is available which is naturally the property of the Shell Company ... It was agreed that subject to further inquiry by the

Secretary of State for Foreign Affairs into the political aspects of this
question, Sir Hamar Greenwood should authorize the Shell Company
to take steps to obtain the oil in south Russia and Trans-Caucasia'.
The Conference also agreed not to enter into further agreements for
aid to 'anti-Bolshevist elements in Russia', which should nevertheless
be free to purchase war material in Allied countries. Each Power
should 'have discretion to leave on the spot all political or other missions which may either be attached to anti-Bolshevist elements or the
dispatch of which may already have been decided upon; and to leave
Bolshevist Russia, as it were, within a ring fence'. The Conference
considered that a strong Poland was 'in the interests of the Entente
Powers' and left for further consideration 'the question of the form and
extent of the assistance to be given to her for the defence of her territories'. Field-Marshal Sir Henry Wilson noted in his diary: 'It is
amazing to see the Frock' (politician's) 'mind. In St James's Palace is
sitting the League of Nations, their principal business being the limitations of armaments. In Downing Street is sitting the Allied Conference of Lloyd George, Millerand, Nitti and a Japanese, who are
feverishly arming Finland, the Baltic States, Poland, Rumania, Georgia,
Azerbaijan, Armenia, Persia, etc.'

*Home Office Reports on Revolutionary Organizations in the United Kingdom
and Morale Abroad*

I have made use of a series of these pulse-taking documents (CAB/24/74,
CAB/23/76, CAB 24/79, GT 7305/CAB/24/PRO, and CAB 23/80). I
liked the explanation offered for the forty-hour-week demand by a
report of January 1919 (CAB 24/74) — 'probably the men got 47 hours
too easily without having to fight for it'; and a revelation of official
error in the report for March 19th (CAB/23/76) — 'through an unfor-
tunate mistake on the part of an officer of the Ministry of Labour
an invitation to attend the Prime Minister's Industrial Conference was
sent to the Police Union, and a Metropolitan Police Constable named
Marston was included among the fifteen Labour representatives chosen
to meet the employers. Marston is one of those who hold that the Police
should side with the men in any labour disturbance, and the invitation
is regarded as a recognition of the Police Union by the Government ...
an impression which the efforts of the Home Secretary in the House
of Commons have not dispelled.'

Index

ADAMSON, WILLIAM, 122
Addams, Jane, 302
Adenauer, Konrad, 94
Adler, Friedrich, 58, 159. 160
Adler, Victor, 58
Afghanistan, 186–7
A.F.L. (American Federation of Labour), 26, 27, 32–4, 130, 132, 133–4, 287–8, 294, 295, 323
Alfonso XIII of Spain, 16
All-Russian Congress of Internationalist Prisoners-of-War, 43
Allen, Herbert, 23
Alsberg, H. G., 120–21, 344
Amalgamated Society of Engineers, 125, 128
Amanullah, King of Afghanistan, 186
Ambris, Alceste de, 282
America, 14–15, 17, 20, 22, 26–30, 32–4, 71, 75, 78–9, 80–81, 98–9, 133–5, 138, 145–6, 160, 189, 203–6, 209–10, 285–306, 323, 344; Federal Food Board, 92; strikes, 130–32, 285–6, 294–9, 304–5; expeditionary force in Russia, 165–6, 177–8, 232, 235, 236, 240; Communist Labour Party, 287; Communist Party, 287, 323; Centralia massacre, 300–302; Federation of Labour, see A.F.L.
American Legion, 203–4, 286, 299, 300, 305
American National Civic Federation (N.C.F.), 134, 299
American National Security League (N.S.L.), 134, 299
American Socialist Party (A.S.P.), 122, 203, 205, 287, 302
Amet, Vice-Admiral, 176–7
Amsterdam International of 'Free' Trade Unions, 331
Andrassy, Count Julius, 118
Apponyi, Count Albert, 316
Arco-Valley, Count Anton, 115
Armand, Inessa, 337, 339
Arshinov, Peter, 268, 271, 319
Asquith, Margot, 83
Auer, Erhard, 113, 114, 115
Australia, 135
Austria, 56–8, 92–3, 94, 96, 102–3, 192–3, 211, 215, 218, 224, 325–6; Social Democrats, 57–8, 102, 192–3, 325–6; Volkswehr, 192, 193

Avalov-Bermondt, Colonel, 201

BAKAYEV, IVAN, 155
Bakunin, Michael, 37
Balabanova, Angelica, 154, 161, 162, 163–4, 339
Balfour, A. J., 17–18, 23, 64, 140, 141, 214
Ballin, Albert, 46
Baltic States, 18, 35, 87–91, 108, 178, 200–202, 212, 213, 236–7
Barber, Margaret, 258–9
Barbusse, Henri, 341–2
Barkatullah, Professor, 187
Barth, Emil, 54
Bauer, Otto, 326
Bavaria, 45, 47–8, 112–17, 121, 178–81, 190–92, 316; People's Party, 113, 114
Belgium, 15; Relief Commission, 80–81
Bell, Edward Price, 305
Benes Eduard, 141, 145
Benn, Gottfried, 346
Berger, Victor, 287, 302
Berkman, Alexander, 289, 303–4, 339–40
Berne Conference, 159
Bernstein, Eduard, 159
Bevin, Ernest, 311
Black Sea, 176, 215
Bloc National, 323
Blok, Alexander, 66, 85
Blücher, Princess, 53
Boehm, General Vilmos, 119, 197
Bolsheviks, Bolshevism, passim
Bombacci, Nicola, 281
Brailsford, H. N., 94–5, 96, 97, 119–20
Branting, Hjalmar, 159
Braunthal, Julius, 58, 193
Brest-Litovsk, Treaty of, 18, 22, 35, 38, 41, 176
British Labour Party, 122, 185, 194, 216, 234; delegation to Russia, 328, 331, 335–6, 341
Brod, Max, 343, 345
Brunswick, Ernst August, Duke of, 46
Bryusov, Valeri, 156
Budyenny, S. M., 254
Bukharin, Nicolai, 41, 153, 160, 186, 187
Bulgarian Revolutionary Social Democrats, 219
Bullitt, William, 173–5, 183, 211–12, 257
Burleson, Albert S., 204
Byedny, Demyan, 158

CAMPBELL, LIEUTENANT A., 168
Canada, 30–31, 132–3, 206–9; Social Democrats, 206
Carnock, Lord, 58, 172
Catalan Workers' Republic, 32
Cecil, Lord Robert, 98
Chagall, Marc, 156
Chaliapin, Feodor, 152
Chamberlain, Sir Austen, 98, 185, 242, 256
Chaplin, Charlie, 302
Cheka (Extraordinary Commission) political police, 39–40, 153, 318
Chelmsford, Lord, 186, 187
Cherkassov, Timofei Petrovich, 245
Chicherin, G. V., 43, 153, 159, 160, 232, 258, 321
Churchill, Winston, 13–14, 22, 25, 83, 168, 257, 308; and strikes, 123, 124, 125, 128; anti-Bolshevik crusade, 147–148, 213, 233–4, 236–7, 243, 251, 293; support of White armies, 147–8, 212–213, 233–4, 242; compared with Trotsky, 233
Clarté, 341
Clemenceau, Georges, 79, 80, 112, 173, 214; and armistice, 14, 24, on Wilson's Fourteen Points, 15; and economic encirclement of Bolsheviks, 24–5, 95, 148; and Peace Conference, 83, 141, 145, 146, 147, 217; and blockade of Germany, 98; attempted murder, 139; his Bloc National, 323
Clyde Workers' Committee, 126, 327
Clynes, J. R., 311
C.N.T. (Confederation of Labour, Spain), 32, 135–6
Coal Commission, 193–4
Comintern, 162–5, 215, 220–21, 226, 231, 328, 330–32; Executive Committee (E.C.C.I.), 162, 165, 215
Confédération Générale du Travail (C.G.T.), 26
Connolly, James, 31
Cook, A. J., 31
Coolidge, Calvin, 288, 303
Cornwall, Lieut.-Colonel J. H., 168
Cottin, Emile, 139
Courtier-Foster, Rev. R., 259–60
Creel, George, 148
Crimea, 21, 38, 249
Cromie, Captain, 20
Crowe, Sir Eyre, 144
Croy, Duke and Duchess of, 53
Curtis, Edwin, 288
Curzon, Lord, 16, 187, 216, 234–5, 242
Czechoslovak Legion, 21–2, 23, 41, 42, 178, 240, 242
Czechoslovakia, 178, 192, 200, 220–21, 236, 316

DADAISTS, 345
Dalmatia, 103, 104, 146, 275, 280
D'Annunzio, Gabriele, 73, 77, 103, 104, 194–5, 274–83, 319–21
Darrow, Clarence, 302
Debs, Eugene, 26–7, 30, 79, 290
Denikin, General Anton, 39, 175, 176, 178, 183, 184, 213, 232–8, 246, 250, 251, 254–6, 269, 318
Deutsch, Julius, 58
Dittmann, Wilhelm, 54
Dmowski, Roman, 63, 64, 95, 101
Dohnanyi, Ernö, 230
D'Olier, Colonel Franklin, 305
Duncan, James, 131
Dupont, Coleman, 134
Dyer, Brig.-General Rex, 186
Dzherzhinsky, Felix, 40, 50, 54, 101

EASTMAN, MAX, 84
Eberlein, Hugo, 161–2
Ebert, Fritz, 49, 50, 52, 53, 55, 107, 108, 109, 325
E.C.C.I. (Comintern Executive Committee), 162, 165, 215
Egelhofer, Rudy, 180–81, 190
Ehrenburg, Ilya, 159–60, 247–9, 329
Eichhorn, Emil, 107, 109
Eichhorn, General, 38
Eisner, Kurt, 47–8, 112–16, 159, 167
Erdelyi, Mor, 199
Esterhazy, Prince, 59
Estonia, 213, 232, 252, 254
Eugénie, Empress, 140
Everest, Wesley, 301
Expressionism, 342–3, 346

FASCISTS, 104–5, 274
Federation of Foreign Groups of the Russian Communist Party, 42–3
Feisal, Emir, 140
'Feodorova', 74–5, 76
Fielding, Major-General, 309
Finland, 41, 43, 213, 232, 237
Firbank, Ronald, 77
Fisher, H. A. L., 234
Fiume, 104, 146, 275–7, 279–83, 319–20
Foch, Marshal, 24, 55, 138
Foster, William Zebulon, 33, 130, 135, 295
Fourteen Points, Wilson's, 15, 19, 44, 62, 64, 147, 290
Fraina, Louis, 287
France, 14, 15, 18, 21, 23, 26, 31, 68, 79, 97, 138–49, 175, 189, 194, 215–16, 235, 323, 341–2; expeditionary force in Russia, 175–8, 232, 236, 251; Bloc National, 323; Socialist Party, 323, 341
Franchet d'Esperey, General, 24, 62, 165, 176–7, 199, 219

Frank, Leonhard, 342
Franz Josef, Emperor, 56, 57
Frederick Augustus III of Saxony, 53
Free Association of Anarchists, 75
Free Love, Bureau of, 74-5, 76
Freikorps, 108-9, 110, 111, 167, 168, 169, 170, 181, 190, 218, 316, 319, 324
French Socialist Party, 323, 341
French Union of Economic Interests, 218
Frick, Henry Clay, 294-5
Fried, Yolan, 199
Futurism, 71-2

GALLACHER, WILLIAM, 126, 127, 129, 331
Gandhi, Mahatma, 186, 187
Garbai, Alexander, 118, 173
Gary, Judge Elbert H., 33-4, 134, 135, 208, 294, 296-8, 306
Geddes, Sir Auckland, 99, 308
Geddes, Sir Eric, 185, 235, 237, 308
Germany, 22, 24-5, 31, 35, 38, 44, 45-56, 87, 92-3, 94, 97, 98-100, 105-17, 139, 165, 167-71, 189, 190-92, 211, 215, 218, 316, 324-5, 330, 331-2, 342-3; Majority Socialists, 48-9, 53-4, 105, 111, 112, 168, 325; Social Democratic Party (S.P.D.), 49, 50, 52, 55-6, 114, 116, 215; Revolutionary Shop Stewards' Organization, 49, 54, 107-8; Independent Socialist Party (U.S.P.D.), 49-50, 54, 56, 105, 107-8, 114, 116, 117, 168, 191, 215, 325, 331-2; Workers' and Soldiers' Councils, 53-4, 111, 112, 113, 168, 170, 180; Communist Party (K.P.D.), 106-9, 111-12, 114, 116, 167, 215, 324, 352
Gezell, Silvio, 179
Gitlow, Benjamin, 287
Giuletti, Captain, 281
Giurati, Major Domenico, 280-81
Godfrey, A. K., 207, 208
Goldman, Emma, 71, 289, 303-4, 339-41
Golovin, General, 212, 213
Goltz, General Rüdiger von, 87, 88, 201-2, 212, 238
Gompers, Samuel, 27, 33, 122, 130, 132, 294, 295, 323
Gorky, Maxim, 39, 67, 154, 224, 329
Graves, General William S., 240, 243
Grayson, Admiral, 292-3
Great Britain, 13-14, 17-18, 20-21, 23, 31-2, 66, 68-70, 77-8, 146, 160, 182-5, 189, 193-4, 216-17, 255-60, 307-13, 326-8, 344; army mutinies, 123-4; strike movement, 124-30, 159, 308-12; expeditionary force in Russia, 165-6, 175, 212, 213, 232, 234, 236, 245, 251, 253
Greek Socialist Workers' Party, 220
'Green Guard', 238, 252, 319

Grigoriev, Ataman, 264-5, 268, 269
Grimm, Robert, 66
Gröner, Wilhelm, 49, 55
Guest, Dr Leslie Haden, 229
Guinness, Lieut.-Colonel Walter, 182, 258

HAASE, HUGO, 49, 54, 105, 191
Haig, Sir Douglas, 309
Haller, General, 62
Hamburger, Eugen, 119
Hammond, J. L., 218
'Hands Off Russia' campaign, 184-5, 216
Hanson, Ole, 131-2, 204, 205
Hardwick, Thomas W., 204
Harmsworth, Cecil B., 98-9
Haubrich, Josef, 119
Haywood, Bill, 26, 27, 29, 30, 76, 289
Healy, May and Eileen, 259
Heaps, Abraham, 133, 208, 209
Heinrich of Prussia, Prince, 53
Helvesi, Julius, 119
Henderson, Arthur, 311
Hillquit, Morris, 122, 287
Hinchley-Cooke, Captain W. E., 168
Hitler, Adolf, 316, 325, 346
Hoare, Sir Samuel, 20, 220
Hodgson, J. E., 255
Hoffmann, Johannes, 116, 179, 181
Holland, 66
Holmes, Oliver W., 204
Hoover, Robert, 80-81, 92, 97-8, 99-100, 211, 226, 233, 312, 323-4
Hoover, J. Edgar, 285
Horthy, Admiral Nicholas, 18, 229-30, 316
House, Colonel Edward, 15, 78, 83, 84, 85, 143, 171
Howe, Frederick C., 204
Hungary, 15, 58-62, 117-21, 165, 171-3, 189, 195-200, 213, 219-31, 264, 316, 324, 331, 344; Social Democrats, 60, 61-2, 117-18, 219, 223, 224, 226, 230-231, 331
Hunt, Alice Riggs, 198, 199
Huszar, Karl, 230, 231

INDIA, 185-7
Industrial Workers of the World, see I.W.W.
Interchurch World Movement, 299, 306
International Labour Organization, 331
Italy, 15, 72-3, 103-5, 135, 146, 189, 194-195, 215, 274-83, 319-21; Social Democrats, 72, 104, 194; Socialist Party, 194-5, 215, 274
Ivanov-Rinov, General, 240
Ivens, William, 133, 207, 208, 209
I.W.W. (Industrial Workers of the World, also Wobblies), 26-34, 75, 76, 129, 130-32, 134, 203, 286, 295, 300-302

JANCZIK, FRANZ, 228
Japan, 15, 23, 235, 236, 240
Jebb, Eglantyne, 97
Jogiches, Leo, 50, 51, 101
Johns, R. J., 132, 133, 209
Jones, John, 182
Jones, Mother, 26–7, 135
Josef, Archduke, 60, 226–7, 324

KAISER, GEORG, 342–3
Kalinin, Mikhail, 250
Kamenev, L. B., 40, 44, 163
Kamenev, S., 247
Kapp, Dr Wolfgang, 325, 330
Karl, Emperor of Austria-Hungary, 57, 60–61, 226
Károlyi, Count Alexander, 59
Károlyi, Count Julius, 199
Károlyi, Count Michael, 59–62, 118, 121, 198, 344, 345
Kautsky, Karl, 49, 159, 160
Keppel, General, 242
Kerensky, Alexander, 20
Kerr, Philip, 173
Keynes, Geoffrey, 99
Keynes, John Maynard, 14, 211, 212, 316–17
Khaki Election (1918), 77–8, 138
Kiel mutiny, 18, 45–6, 49, 180
Kirkwood, David, 127, 129
Kolchak, Admiral, 39, 175, 183, 184, 212–213, 232–7, 238–45, 246, 254
Knox, General, 240
Kollontai, Alexandra, 70, 337, 338–9
K.P.D. (German Communist Party), 106–9, 111–12, 114, 116, 167, 215, 324, 332
Krestinsky, N., 153
Kropotkin, Prince, 36, 39, 266, 340
Krupskaya, Nadezhda, 70, 337
Kuhnt, Stoker First Class, 170
Kun, Bela, 43, 60, 62, 117–21, 172–3, 195, 198, 199, 219, 220, 221, 222, 225–6, 228, 318, 324, 332
Kunfi, Sigismund, 118, 119, 173, 198, 221, 226

LABRIOLA, ANTONIO, 154
Landauer, Gustav, 113, 116, 117, 178, 190
Landis, Judge K. M., 204
Landsberg, Otto, 53
Lansbury George, 17, 335
Lansdowne, fifth Marquess of, 18
Laski, Harold, 288
Latvia, 87–91, 200–202, 212, 213
Law, Bonar, 126–7, 194, 226
Lawrence, T. E., 140
League of Nations, 78, 84, 97, 145–7, 184, 185, 211, 214, 218, 290–91, 320, 331
Leeper, Allen, 171

Lefebvre, Raymond, 341
Left Social Revolutionary Party (L.S.R.), 37–8, 39, 41
Legien, Karl, 325
Lenin, V. I., 20, 21, 22, 36, 38, 70, 78, 152, 154, 165, 174, 175, 178, 179, 186, 251, 333; aim to turn war into international civil war, 18–19, 66; defended by Stalin, 39, 40; and Trotsky, 40–41, 247; seeks American workers' support, 43; offers help to defeated Germany, 44; and Baltic States, 87; and Spartacus, 112; and Hungary, 121, 195, 196, 220, 223; favours Social Realism in art, 158; and first congress of Third International, 161, 163–4; and Comintern, 189–90, 331; attitude to peasants, 224; and Makhno, 266; scorn for European revolutionaries, 322–3, 330–32; his *Infantile Leftism*, 323, 330–31
Lettow-Vorbeck, General von, 170
Levi, Paul, 116, 161
Levien, Count, 201
Levien, Max, 114, 116, 178, 180–81, 322
Leviné, Eugen, 114, 116, 117, 178, 180–181, 190, 322
Lewis, John L., 288, 298–9, 323
Lewis, Percy Wyndham, 77
Libertad, Albert, 155
Liebknecht, Karl, 49–50, 51, 52–3, 54, 55, 79, 105–10, 111
Lindner, Alois, 115
Lipp, Dr Franz, 179
Lippmann, Walter, 84, 85
Lithuania, 50, 88, 91, 92, 213
Little, Frank, 29
Litvinov, Maxim, 150
Lloyd, William B., 287
Lloyd George, David, 13–14, 24, 80, 84, 99, 146, 148, 173, 175; and Khaki Election, 77–8, 138; at Peace Conference, 78, 83, 141, 171, 183, 217; and industrial unrest, 129, 307–13; urges realistic treatment of Germany, 171; on Bolshevik danger, 171; on intervention, 182–4, 234–5, 237, 242, 256–8; and 'Whiteslide', 256–8; his personal dominion, 326–8
Lodge, Cabot, 290–91, 292, 293
London, Jack, 16
Long, Walter, 185
Lou Tseng-Tsiang, 142
Lowther, Colonel Claude, 182
L.S.R. (Left Social Revolutionaries), 37–8, 39, 41
Ludwig III of Bavaria, 48
Lukacs, Georg, 119, 120, 226
Lunacharsky, Anatol, 336
Lusk Committee, 285, 302
Lüttwitz, General von, 108, 109, 324

Luxemburg, Rosa, 49, 50-52, 54-5, 101, 105-7, 109-10, 180, 213-14, 264, 322
Luzhenovsky, General, 37
Lvov, Prince, 20, 147

MacDonald, Ramsay, 159, 307
McKay, Charles, 126
Mackensen, General von, 220
Mackinder, H. J., 255-6
Maclay, Sir John, 256
Maclean, John, 216, 224
Macy, Everit, 134
Maisky, Ivan, 240
Makhno, Nestor, 263-73, 276, 317-19
Malatesta, Enrico, 281
Malevich, Kasimir, 157, 158
Malone, Lieut.-Colonel C. E., 257
Mandel, Georges, 79
Mandelstam, Osip, 76
Mann, Tom, 31
Marchand, René, 68
Marchlevsky, Julian, 50, 101
Marinetti, Filipo, 72, 274, 341
Martens, Ludwig, 203
Maurer, James H., 286-7
Maurice, Major-General Sir Frederick, 261
Max of Baden, Prince, 44, 49
Mayakovsky, Vladimir, 71-2, 156, 157
Mazin, Vladimir, 155, 164, 262
Mencken, H. L., 13, 33
Mensheviks, 36, 38, 39, 40, 239, 240, 242
Michaelis, Georg, 111
Middle East, 185
Miller, General, 232, 241
Milyukov, P. N., 20
Miners' Federation, 31, 97, 194, 312
Mirbach, Count, 38
Model, Edgar, 90, 200
Monet, Claude, 14, 79
Money, Sir Leo Chiozza, 129
Montague, C. E., 334
Montessori, Dr Maria, 70-71
Mooney, Thomas, 285
Morel, E. D., 82, 97
Morgan, J. P., 26, 33, 134, 204, 295
Mühsam, Erich, 113-14, 117, 178, 179, 191
Müller, Richard, 49, 54, 108, 168
Munro, R., 127
Mussolini, Benito, 72-3, 104-5, 194-5, 274, 344

National Committee for Organizing Iron and Steel Workers, 33
National Industrial Conference, 129, 193
National Socialism, 324
National Union of Railwaymen (N.U.R.), 31, 309, 311
Nechayev, Sergei, 37
Neuring, Herr, 170

Nevinson, Henry, 93-4
New Freedoms, Wilson's, 84, 323
Newbold, J. T. Walton, 184-5
Nicolson, Harold, 142, 144, 171-3, 182, 212
Nitti, Francesco, 274, 279, 280
Northcliffe, Lord, 141, 310
Norway, 31
Noske, Gustav, 49, 50, 52, 108, 111, 116, 168, 169, 170, 190, 193, 325

One Big Union (O.B.U.), 27, 28, 31, 132-3, 135, 206
Orlando, Vittorio, 103, 140, 146
Orwell, George, 223, 346
Oven, General von, 181, 190
Overman, Lee S., 204

Paderewski, Jan, 63-5, 95, 141
Page-Croft, Brig.-General, 182, 194
Palmer, A. Mitchell, 204, 285, 290, 298, 306
Pankhurst, Christabel, 75
Pankhurst, Sylvia, 71, 125, 216, 217, 328, 331, 336
Paris Agreement (1917), 21
Pascal, Pierre, 68
Peace Conference, 65, 66, 78-9, 82-4, 138-49, 217-18, 275, 335, 344
Peace Day, 216-17
Peidl, Julius, 226, 231
Pettit, Captain W., 173-5
Pflügk-Harting, Captain-Lieutenant von, 213
Pieck, Wilhelm, 54, 109, 110
Pilsudski, Josef, 62, 63, 64, 178
Pittaluga, General, 276-7
Platten, Fritz, 66, 161, 162
Plumer, General, 99
Pogany, Josef, 172, 226
Poincaré, Raymond, 82
Poland, 50, 62-5, 92, 94-6, 101-2, 178, 232, 236, 237, 256, 316; National Committee, 62, 63; Social Democrats, 107
Polish Legion, 63
Pollitt, Harry, 130
Portarlington, Lord, 309
Preobrazhensky, 41
Price, Morgan Philips, 67
Pritchard, William, 133, 207, 208, 209
Proshyan, Prosh, 39
Protocols of the Elders of Zion, 74, 75
Pyatakov, G., 41

Queen, John, 133, 209

Radek, Karl, 41, 56, 101, 106, 107, 162
Rakosi, Matyas, 119, 216
Ramsay, David, 128, 129

Ransome, Arthur, 68, 150, 151, 153, 159, 165
Reclus, Elisée, 154
Red Army, 21–2, 36, 41–2, 43, 44, 87–91, 106, 134, 139, 151, 175, 176, 193, 200, 201–2, 213, 215, 220, 233, 236, 241, 243, 244–8, 252–5, 259–61, 264–5, 267, 269, 318–19, 329, 344; Hungarian, 119, 193, 197, 200, 219, 222; German, 180, 181
Reed, John, 29–30, 84–5, 148, 262, 287, 331, 332
Rees, Brig.-General H. C., 168
Reinstein, Boris, 160
Robertson, General Sir William, 127
Robins, Major Raymond, 68
Rockefeller, John D., 26, 134
Rockefeller, John D., jr, 204, 295, 298, 306
Rodchenko, Alexander, 157
Röder, Baron and Baroness, 53
Rolland, Romain, 82, 144, 342
Rommel, Captain Erwin, 170
Roosevelt, Theodore, 29
Rumania, 15, 93, 177, 197, 200, 220, 222, 225, 227, 232, 236, 316
Russell, Bertrand, 19, 67, 71, 341, 346
Russell, Bob, 133, 206
Russia, passim
Ruthenburg, Charles, 287
Rykov, A., 153

Sadoul, Jacques, 68, 160
Sankey Commission, 129, 194
Sapieha, Prince, 64
Saratov Decree, 75
Savinkov, Boris, 37, 147, 242
Sazonov, Serge, 147
Scheidemann, Philip, 49, 50, 52, 53, 107, 109, 116
Second International, 26, 43, 154, 160, 189
Seeckt, General von, 325
Segre, General, 58
Seidel, Herr, 168
Sellins, Mrs Fannie, 286
Serge, Victor, 154–6, 157, 159, 164, 165, 253, 345
Shatov, Bill, 155
Shaw, G. Bernard, 21, 80, 144
Sheppard, Rev. Dick, 310
Shinwell, Emanuel, 126, 127, 129
Shortt, Edward, 182
Siberia, 232, 234, 235, 239–41, 246
Sinzheimer, Dr Hugo, 47
Sisson, Edgar, 22
Sitwell, Sir Osbert, 320
Smillie, Robert, 97, 129, 194, 307, 312–13
Smith, Logan Pearsall, 77, 218
Smuts, General Jan, 121, 171, 172–3, 211
Snowden, Mrs Philip, 230

Social Revolutionaries (S.R.), 37–9, 85, 240, 242
Soffici, Ardengo, 275
Sonnino, Baron, 103
Sorel, Georges, 26
Souchon, Admiral, 46
South Africa, 31
South America, 31
Spain, 31–2, 135–6, 319; General Union of Labour (U.G.T.), 32; Confederation of Labour (C.N.T.), 32, 135–6
Spartacus group, 49–52, 54–5, 56, 105–12, 114, 139, 165, 167, 168–71, 180, 215, 322, 335
S.P.D. (German Social Democratic Party), 49, 50, 52, 55–6, 114, 116, 215
Spiridonova, Maria, 37–8, 76, 85, 154, 340
S.R. (Social Revolutionaries), 37–9, 85, 240, 242
Stalin, Josef, 39–40, 41, 160, 246, 251, 252, 254
Steffens, Lincoln, 173, 211
Steimer, Mollie, 340
Steinhardt, Hubert, 162
Stopes, Dr Marie, 71
Stromfeld, Colonel Aurel, 197
Stutchka, Peter, 88–9, 201, 202
Sunday, Billy, 205
Supreme Economic Council, 81, 98, 99, 200, 293, 324
Switzerland, 66–7; Social Democrats, 66
Szamuelly, Tibor, 60, 62, 117, 119, 196–7, 198, 223–6

Tatlin, Vladimir, 156, 158–9
Tawney, R. H., 129, 307, 309
Third International, 112, 158, 189, 216, 219, 317, 328, 333; founding of, 159–66
Thomas, J. H., 122, 309, 311
Tichborne, Sir Frederick, 309
Tisza, Count Istvan, 59, 61
Toller, Ernst, 113, 117, 178–81, 190–92, 322, 342
Tranmael, Martin, 31
Transport Workers' Federation, 31, 32, 308, 311
Trianon, Treaty of, 316
Triple Alliance (of unions), 31, 97, 128, 194, 213, 234
Troelstra, Pieter, 66
Trotsky, Leo, 18, 20, 21, 39, 44, 107, 160, 245; and Red Army, 22, 41–2, 246–7, 329; and Lenin, 40–41, 247; on America, 122; and first congress of Third International, 161, 162, 166; compared with Churchill, 233; and civil war, 246–7, 249–50, 251–5; defence of Petrograd, 251–4; attitude to peasants, 263, 268–9; and Makhnovites, 268–9; and labour compulsion, 329

UKRAINE, 21, 38, 39, 43, 44, 165, 175, 177, 247–9, 254, 256, 264–73
Ungen-Sternberg, Baron Roman von, 73, 243
Union of Democratic Control, 82
Union of Revolutionary Internationalists of Bavaria (V.R.I.), 114
United German Communist Party, 332
United Mineworkers' Convention, 288
United Mine Workers' Union (U.M.W.), 298–9
United States Food Administration (U.S.F.A.), 81, 97–100, 102
Uritsky, 38, 41
U.S.P.D. (German Independent Socialist Party), 49–50, 54, 56, 105, 107–8, 114, 116, 117, 168, 191, 215, 325, 331–2

VAILLANT-COUTURIER, PAUL, 341
Varga, Eugen, 119, 221, 226
Vatzetis, Colonel, 41
Veblen, Thorstein, 302
Versailles Treaty, 210–12, 214, 218, 325
Villard, Oswald Garrison, 93
Vix, Colonel, 61, 118
Vogel, Lieutenant, 213
Voline (V. M. Eichenbaum), 268, 270, 271
Vorovsky, V., 150

WALTER, BRUNO, 48
Watson, W. F., 124–5, 129–30
Webb, Beatrice, 16, 19, 45, 122, 263, 309, 327
Webb, Sidney, 16, 78, 129, 309
Wedgwood, Colonel Josiah, 222, 236
Weimar Republic, 112, 117, 168, 324–5
Wells, H. G., 328–9, 330, 336, 340
Wels, Otto, 55
Werfel, Franz, 342, 343

White Russians, 38–9, 85, 147, 181, 183, 238, 242–5, 246, 247, 249, 250–51, 253, 254–8, 268–70, 273, 318
Wilhelm II, Kaiser, 49, 53
Willcocks, Mary Patricia, 69, 71
Williams, Albert Rhys, 262
Williams, Robert, 32
Wilson, Sir Henry, 24, 138, 171
Wilson, Woodrow, 14–15, 24, 63, 80, 98, 113, 140, 169, 194, 289–91, 302–3; his Fourteen Points, 15, 19, 147, 290; and Poland 63, 95; and Peace Conference, 66–7, 78–9, 81–4, 138, 141, 143–9, 173, 217; and Italy and Fiume, 73, 175, 275, 279, 290; and League of Nations, 84, 145–7, 290; his New Freedoms, 84, 323; contrast with Lenin, 175; attacks on, 289–91, 294; and industry, 289–90, 297–8, 299; railroad odyssey, 291–3; illness, 292–3, 294
Wilton, Robert, 75
Wobblies, see I.W.W.
Wood, General Leonard, 297
Woolf, Leonard, 15
Woolf, Virginia, 15, 216–17
Wrangel, Baron Peter, 318

YARDLEY, MAJOR HERBERT O., 140
Yesenin, Sergei, 157–8
Young, George, 169
Yudenich, General Nikolai, 175, 212–13, 232–8, 250–51, 253, 254
Yugoslavia, 103, 192, 222, 236, 275, 316

ZANGWILL, ISRAEL, 184
Zinoviev, Grigori, 40, 42, 151, 158, 160, 162, 164–5, 169, 187, 189, 193, 214, 231, 246, 252, 317, 331–2